Managing the Global
Supply Chain

To Phil, who lost his battle to cancer in April 2007. We owe him a lot for his entusiasm and constructive contributions to this edition.

Tage Skjøtt-Larsen, Philip B. Schary,
Juliana H. Mikkola & Herbert Kotzab

Managing the Global Supply Chain

3rd Edition

Copenhagen Business School Press • Liber

Managing the Global Supply Chain, Third Edition

© Copenhagen Business School Press, 2007
Printed in Denmark by Narayana Press, Gylling
Cover design by Busto | Graphic Design
Third edition, second impression 2008

ISBN 978-91-47-08793-8 (Sweden)
ISBN 978-87-630-0171-7 (Rest of the world)

Distribution:

Sweden
Liber AB, Baltzarsgatan 4
SE-205 10 Malmö, Sweden
Tel + 46 40 25 86 00, fax +46 40 97 05 50
www.liber.se
Kundtjänst tel +46 8 690 93 30, fax +46 8 690 9301

Rest of Scandinavia
DBK, Mimersvej 4
DK-4600 Køge, Denmark
Tel +45 3269 7788
Fax +45 3269 7789

North America
International Specialized Book Services
920 NE 58th Ave., Suite 300
Portland, OR 97213, USA
Tel +1 800 944 6190
Fax +1 503 280 8832
E-mail: orders@isbs.com

Rest of the World
Marston Book Services, P.O. Box 269
Abingdon, Oxfordshire, OX14 4YN, UK
Tel +44 (0) 1235 465500, fax +44 (0) 1235 465555
E-mail Direct Customers: direct.order@marston.co.uk
E-mail Booksellers: trade.order@marston.co.uk

Overview of Contents

Contents

Preface

Much has changed within the theory and practice of supply chain management since the second edition of the book, published in 2001. One of the most profound changes has been the massive outsourcing of production and services to low-cost countries in the Far East, Eastern Europe, and South America. The supply chain has become truly global, coupled with its positive and negative consequences. On the positive side, the supply of products and services from all over the world has become more efficient. In the West, we take it for granted that we can buy fresh vegetables, fashion clothes, and sophisticated consumer electronics from everywhere. The flipside of the coin is the increased vulnerability of the global supply chain to disruptions caused by natural disasters, wars, strikes, or terrorist attacks. The more global, leaner, and specialized the supply chain is, the higher the exposure to unexpected and unpredictable disturbances. Managing the global supply chain is therefore becoming a necessary competence for survival in the competitive marketplace.

The third edition has been rewritten to take into consideration additional themes that have become relevant in managing the global supply chain. Themes that we have kept include: the triad of activity, process and organization and the importance of inter-organizational relationships. Some of the operating practices present in these themes are still in vogue. However, certain themes that were not strongly evident before have come into prominence, and are hence included in this edition: the consumer-driven supply chain, global sourcing, the importance of innovation management and new product development, supply chain sustainability, and the need for performance measurement and management in the supply chain.

The tremendous increase of interest in supply chain management, both in corporate strategy and academic curricula, has made this topic stimulating, and a burden at the same time. It is exciting because managing the supply chain can become a new way of doing business, possibly replacing the older orientation. The burden is that there is so much more to include in general discussions, especially when recognizing that every supply chain is unique and each industry's approach to respective tasks is different. Our hope is that this edition can inspire and stimulate discussions, even though it might make the job of encompassing the field even more challenging.

Supply chain management, as an emerging discipline, is constantly searching for theories and constructs that can explain and guide the underlying development process. We have found that it is necessary to apply complementary theories to explain inter-organizational relationships and management decisions in a supply chain. In this book we draw insights from institutional economics, strategic management, and socio-economic theories.

While Professor Philip B. Schary and Professor Tage Skjøtt-Larsen, wrote the two first editions, this edition has been co-authored by Associate Professor Juliana H. Mikkola and Professor Herbert Kotzab, both from Copenhagen Business School.

We would like to acknowledge the contribution of our colleagues, Assistant Professor Kim Sundtoft Hald, who wrote Chapter 11 on Performance Measurement and Management, which is his area of expertise. We would also like to thank Aseem Kinra, PhD.-student, who gave constructive comments to Chapter 14, Hitesh Gadhia, M.Sc.-student, who did a great job in proof-reading the book, and Martin Starcke, M.Sc.-student, who helped us with drawings and references.

Tage Skjøtt-Larsen
Philip B. Schary
Juliana H. Mikkola
Herbert Kotzab

1. Introduction to the Supply Chain

»Serious supply chain management is thinking about an
end-to-end process, which transcends individual departments
– and even companies«.

Michael Hammer, quoted in Quinn (2001).

No organization, whether business, government or non-profit, can stand-alone. It depends on connections to other organizations in a network relationship. The supply chain is a concept of closely coordinated, cooperative networks, competing with other networks (Christopher 2005). The focus is on managing processes that engage other firms as partners in managed relationships to perform the activities necessary to fulfill the process. It is propelled by the realization that no organization can be good at all things, and by the expanding reach and ease of access to information and communication technology. This perspective is necessary not only for growth, but survival in the struggle for global markets. No firm alone can accomplish the complete process of meeting the demands of the market in the face of intense competition, rapidly changing technologies, and evolving customer requirements.

This book is about the management of the *global supply chain*, the process of supply, production, and distribution that makes other strategic objectives possible. The underlying concept of the supply chain is simple, a linear sequence of operations organized around the flow of materials from source of supply to their final distribution as finished products to ultimate users. Traditionally it includes sources of material resources, and the organization of processors, distributors, and users. It also involves supporting enterprises to provide transport, communications, and other specialized functions. Together, they become a single coordinated entity that transcends organizational boundaries.

The notion of the supply chain is not new. It is possible to trace the historic commodity chains that supplied the Roman Empire two thousand years ago. They were organized essentially as a series of individual enterprises, connected through independent buying and selling transactions, bound by the geography of resources and the available technologies. As resource use changed, or as local supply was consumed, the chains shifted in response to the market, guided by prices. These commodity chains however, were limited by the available technology and organizational development. Management lacked the capability to coordinate operations. The only alternative to the market was *vertical integration*, the direct ownership of supplier or customer organizations. Formal management structures appeared in place of independence, authority to plan and control was derived through management hierarchy.

The world now faces global competition, focusing on rapid response to customer needs at low cost, accompanied by market access and rapid deployment of technology. A significant shift is taking place from mass production with standardized products and services, towards customized production of both products and services. Change requires new ways to manage the supply process. The development of new information and telecommunication technologies combined with efficient, fast and relatively cheap global transportation systems opens new possibilities. This enables enterprises to reach beyond their own organizational and geographical boundaries to coordinate operations and management through the entire supply chain, without the investment and problems of direct ownership. They also require cooperation between organizations on an unprecedented scale.

Introduction to Supply Chain Management

The concept of the supply chain underscores the importance of operations as a counterpoint to strategy. The underlying framework is the *value chain* of Michael Porter (1985). Porter described a series of primary activities that add value to the output of the firm: inbound logistics, operations, outbound logistics, marketing & sales, and services. The primary activities are supported by external purchased inputs, technology, and human resources. They also require management, including strategic direction and planning, operational planning, finance, accounting, and quality management. Differences among value chains become sources of competitive advantage. The value chain is illustrated in figure 1.1.

Figure 1.1. The Value Chain

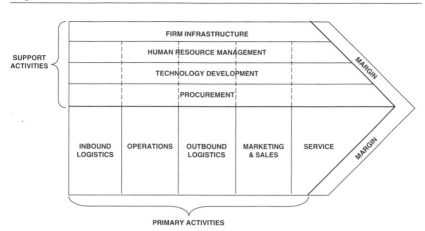

Source: Porter (1985:37)

A firm's value chain is embedded in a larger stream of activities that Porter (1985:34) calls a *value system.* The value system consists of the interrelationships between various value chains. For instance, the supplier has a value chain, creating and delivering input to the customer's value chain that again produces and delivers input to its customers. The value system can be a simple sequence of upstream and downstream value chains or it can be a complex network of interrelated value chains. Our focus is on design and operation of the supply chain as a management process. We must recognize the scope of the entire chain, extending beyond organizational boundaries. Finally, the imperative is to manage it as an integral unit for the benefit of its members and the leading organization.

The Supply Chain

The supply chain emerged because it provides potential solutions to the problems of duplication and responsiveness. The concept of the supply chain itself is not new. It has embraced a concept of direct, extended coordination of operations across the entire supply process, replacing both the market and hierarchy as the means to manage the flow process.

The supply chain encompasses all organizations and activities associated with the flow and transformation of goods from raw materials, through to the end user, as well as the associated information and monetary flows (Handfield & Nichols 2002:8). Mentzer (2001) defines a supply chain as *a set of three or more companies directly linked by one or more of the upstream and downstream flows of products, services, finances, and information from a source to a customer*. He distinguishes between a *basic supply chain,* consisting of a focal company, an immediate supplier, and an immediate customer, an *extended supply chain,* which includes the immediate supplier's suppliers, and the immediate customer's customers, and an *ultimate supply chain* that involves all companies from the initial supplier to the ultimate customer.

Cooper et al. (1997) define the scope of the supply chain as »dirt to dirt.« This definition encompasses both the source of raw material to final consumption and the return operations, which reuse, remanufacture, or recycle materials and products.

Supply Chain Management (SCM)

The concept of supply chain management is relatively new, and there is still a lack of a generally accepted definition. One frequently quoted definition is given by Cooper et al. (1998): *Supply chain management is the integration of business processes from end user through original suppliers that provides products, services and information that add value for customers and other stakeholders*. It emphasizes integration of business processes. *Integration* means coordination across functional lines and legal corporate boundaries. This coordination may be organizational, e.g. inter-organizational teams and interfaces at various management levels, system-related, e.g. integrated information and communications systems, and Internet connections, or planning-related such as exchanges of order data, inventory status, sales forecasts, production plans, and sales and marketing campaigns. *Business processes* become directly related to the production of products, services, and information. Examples of business processes in a supply chain are: Order Fulfillment, Customer Service, Procurement-to-pay, Time-to-market, and Returns.

The influential US-based Council of Supply Chain Management Professionals (CSCMP) has recently adopted another definition:

SCM encompasses the planning and management of all activities involved in sourcing and procurement, conversion, and all Logistics Management activities. Importantly, it also includes coordination and collaboration with channel partners, which can be suppliers, intermediaries, third-party service providers, and customers. This definition states a difference in scope between supply chain management and logistics, it acknowledges that logistics is one of the core functions contained within supply chain management (Mentzer 2001:20). Logistics deals with the physical and controlling connections between organizations. Supply chains establish the overall tasks and organizations over the entire set of activities involved in the product and service flow beginning to end product delivered to a final customer. The supply chain encompasses and becomes the environment for logistics activities.

Bechtel & Jayaram (1997: 19) define five different supply chain management schools of thought:

- *Functional chain awareness*, where a chain of functional activities provides a basis for materials flow.
- *Linkage/logistics* emphasizes the linkages between functional areas and with a focus on logistics and transportation.
- *Information*, emphasizes information flow in both directions among chain members.
- *Integration* of processes across the supply chain towards an objective of customer satisfaction.
- A *future perspective* describing a demand-driven seamless comprehensive pipeline emphasizing relations as well as transactions.

In this book, we adopt the vision of the future perspective with a focus on inter-organizational relations and processes between the participants in the supply chain.

The Customer Orientation

These definitions assume that the supply chain anticipates customer demand and customers receive products from off the shelf. The direction of physical flow in Porter's value chain is clearly pointed toward the customer. This is a *push* orientation, product and materials move toward the final market, driven by forecast demand. A more recent view, one that we adopt here, is that customers initiate supply chain decisions, configuring products and initiating orders that *pull* products through the chain. The supply chain originates with the customer, and decisions flow backward through the supply, even influencing the choice of supply chain members. In some cases, the flow becomes a hybrid.

A similar approach is the *Value Stream* which starts with the customer, specifies the final product and volume, determines activities and then jointly defines the role of partners and their contribution to value (Hines 1996a). The reality is that we can only anticipate customer demand to a limited extent, limiting the ability to push. The rest becomes a pull environment, emphasizing the ability to react quickly to customer orders.

Multiple Management Perspectives

The supply chain is open to different interpretations, depending on the management perspective. Logistics, manufacturing and corporate strategy offer differing views on what constitutes the supply chain. *Logistics* orients the supply chain towards connecting the firm to its immediate customers and suppliers. Each firm makes independent decisions. The tools of logistics are transportation, inventory, and information. Logistics stresses *functional (activity) integration* such as balancing production capacity against holding finished product inventory within each firm or *trade-offs* between fast, but expensive airfreight versus slower, but cheaper sea transport and high safety stocks. It does not ordinarily deal with the operating decisions of other firms. In practice, this concept has been stretched by the need to achieve broader goals.

The major contribution of logistics has been the idea of *product flow*. Materials and other resources enter organizations. They are transformed through production and then are distributed to users. This process crosses functional boundaries, areas of specialized operations. It also influenced and in turn is influenced by other functional areas as shown in figure 1.2.

Figure 1.2. Product Flow in Logistics

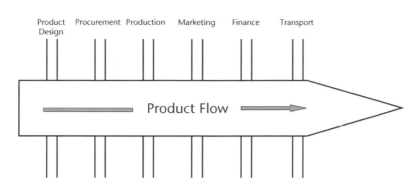

Logistics interacts with every area of the firm. It raises the question of how to cross the barriers that separate these functional areas from each other. This has been difficult because the historic evolution of business has encouraged the development of these separate *functional silos* as cost centers without formal consideration of other areas within the firm.

Manufacturing interprets the supply chain as an extended factory, with successive suppliers feeding a final stage of production, followed by distribution. It is less concerned with links to other areas than production, but more with internal production processes. There is little direct involvement with distribution or transport except by implication.

The strongest argument is that it provides a focus. Transforming material into delivered products is the core of supply operations. Supply chain decisions about where manufacturing takes place and how it is linked to other stages enlarges the scope of operating decisions beyond the conventional view of the factory. Manufacturing affects both material supply and distribution. In turn, production decisions are shaped by requirements of other areas of operation.

The *Corporate strategy* discussion often refers to the supply chain in general but in unclear imprecise terms and ultimately focuses on production. Furthermore, it deals with supply in terms of aggregate rather than specific product flows. The contribution of the chain is usually considered to support other areas such as marketing and production, rather than to play a central role of coordination. However, recent discussion recognizes that the management of processes is an important source of competitive advantage. The ability of organizations to establish working inter-organizational systems is not easily emulated.

Each view has merit. However, we seek a comprehensive view that recognizes these perspectives as part of a common system. The logistics perspective comes closest to this holistic view. However it has the limits of organizational boundaries. Figure 1.3 illustrates the product and material flow through supplier to manufacturer to customer. Typical logistics decisions for the focal firm are shown. In the *logistics* concept, control begins and ends with the corporate boundaries. Each firm makes parallel decisions independently, even though they may affect the operations of the other firms in the chain.

The *strategic* view recognizes the key enabling factor – coordination among organizations. In the supply chain concept, control is extended over the entire chain, including carriers, customers, and service providers. The details of what is to be coordinated and how are left to the specialists.

Figure 1.3. Logistics and the Supply Chain

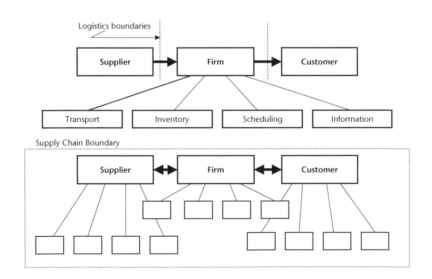

The Characteristics of the Supply Chain

The supply chain takes on characteristics that are not unique in themselves, but together present new challenges to management. Houlihan (1986) has summarized the essential attributes:

- The supply chain is a complete process for providing goods and services to final users.
- Membership includes all parties, including logistics operations from initial material supplier to final user.
- The scope of supply chain operations includes procurement, production, and distribution.
- Management extends across organizational boundaries to include planning and control over operations of other organizational units.
- A common information system accessible to all members makes coordination possible between organizations.
- Member organizations achieve their own individual objectives through the performance of the supply chain as a whole.

The supply chain both extends the logistics concept and creates an organizational system with its own attributes. More than linking operational units together, supply chain management deals with the full scope of supply activities: production, procurement and distribution. By dealing with a more complete definition of product and material flows, it recognizes interdependent behavior among member organizations. Directing this interaction becomes the purpose of supply chain management. It must take charge of all decisions that affect the chain and make decisions for the system as a whole.

The supply chain becomes an organization in its own right, a *supra-organization*, linking the operations of members. At the same time, supply membership is changeable. Individual member organizations pursue their own objectives. They may also compete for position within the supply chain, shares of profits or even entry into participation. This has important implications for the future of management in general (Mouritsen et al. 2003).

The supply chain may also share members with other supply chains. Demands by more than one supply chain on the resources of individual member firms create potential problems for competition between members. It also suggests a locus of power, the firm with a strong brand will ultimately direct the development of the chain. Examples are Microsoft, Coca-Cola, Nike, and Zara.

The supply chain presented here is normative, in the sense that we want to establish a general understanding of the underlying principles. Actual supply chains vary, affected by their own specific circumstances and evolution.

Understanding the Supply Chain

Understanding the supply chain is a prerequisite to managing it. The tasks are threefold: 1) to develop a framework for analysis, 2) to recognize the systemic nature of the supply chain, and 3) to identify the processes that are involved. Because supply chains become global in geographic scope, it is also necessary to recognize the implications of an environment with another set of influences, stemming from both factors relating to individual host countries and the phenomenon of the global corporation.

The Framework

Our understanding of the supply chain begins with a static view, freezing the chain at a particular point in time. There are three major components: 1) activities, 2) organizations and 3) processes and operations. Together they become a »long-linked technology,« a long chain of activities and decisions (Thompson 1967, Stabell & Fjeldstad 1998). They are enveloped within an internal supply chain management environment that guides and seeks to buffer the process from outside disturbance. The chain is further linked to a corporate environment that determines strategic objectives for the supply chain. An external environment of industry, competition, technology, local and global political issues, will further modify the impact of these issues. A general impression is shown in Figure 1.4.

Figure 1.4. A Framework of the Supply Chain

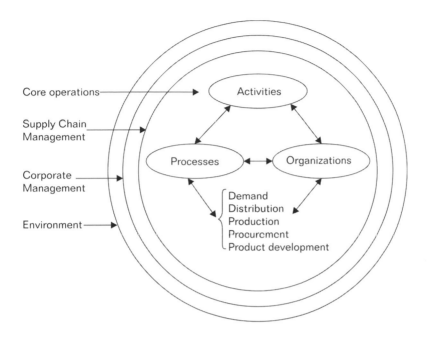

The supply chain is also a dynamic system. Activities, organizations, and processes together become the supply chain system. Activities can only be justified within the supply chain if they add value to the overall flow process. They can be reorganized by sequence, augmented, or eliminated as necessary for efficiency or effective performance. They can be shifted between organizations to improve system performance. *Activities* become the foundation. They are the building blocks of the system. Organizational units, both internal and external, perform activities. These organizations thus become a reservoir of resources for the supply chain and hold responsibility for performance of these actions. The actual operations include individual *processes* that manage and link activities, and also become part of larger sets of coordinated activities. For example, order processing is an activity that is performed jointly by a customer and a supplier. It therefore crosses organizational boundaries and requires previously agreed procedures and possible coordination. It becomes a component activity in an order fulfillment process which in turn is part of an overall supply process.

Organizations as entities can be created, expanded, contracted, or eliminated. External organizations within the supply chain can be independent, or alternatively captive to a larger organization. They require motivation and coordination as active members of the supply chain. They are also under competitive pressures both from within the supply chain and from other external competitors. The processes themselves include both actions internal to individual organizations, and those that involve more than a single organizational entity. They are changeable as a result of economic pressures, new technology, and environmental changes within the global economy.

At a single point in time, activities, organizations, and processes present a *static* view of the supply chain. A supply chain however must also be *dynamic* in the sense of change overtime. Change can come either through adaptation to a changing environment or through pro-active initiatives to gain competitive advantage. This includes possibilities to meet unrecognized customer needs, apply new technologies, and respond to potential opportunity in changing public policy. The supply chain must also initiate change to achieve competitive advantage in the market. Strategy involves thinking in terms of entire systems.

Systemic Approach

The supply chain is both a network and a system. The network properties involve sequences of connections among organizational units for product and information flow. The *systemic* properties are the interdependence of activities, organizations, and processes. As one example, transportation transit times influence the amount of inventory held within the system. In the case of global corporations, producing in Asia for delivery to North America and Europe ultimately means that transit times are either long (by surface transport) or costly (by air). These companies produce a limited number of products because each product requires inventory and the longer transit times require more inventory of each product. High inventory costs often force changes from sea to air transportation and reduced number of items. This makes the task of marketing more difficult. It becomes harder to match the specific needs of individual customers and market segments. This also forces the production task to adopt fewer and simpler product components that can be combined to accomodate product variety.

The supply chain is also part of larger networks. Competition, technological developments, and political controversies, to name but a few, influence the direction of the supply chain. These networks create an increasingly turbulent environment. As they assert their influence, they evoke management decisions that can in turn force change on the environment in ways that cannot be easily foreseen. Dealing with this uncertainty becomes an integral part of the supply chain strategy.

The decision to source in Asia to supply Western markets unleashes a chain of events and potential points of disturbance that modifies decisions in many areas. While this example identifies specific influences and consequences of the decision, it can also result in unintended consequences as different elements interact with each other.

The result is that actions in one part of the system affect other parts, in totally different areas, cause and effect become difficult to separate. Objectives of supply chain management are holistic, that isthey pertain to the system as a whole rather than to individual members. It is also possible in pursuit of global system optimization to make trade-offs between actions in one area and actions in another.

External elements become the environment of the supply chain. They essentially influence issues in technology, competition, and even corporate strategy that may result in decisions that will evoke reactions from other actors in the environment. Changes in public transport policy such as expenditures on highways, affect the transport system. Changes in costs and transit times in turn affect other supply chain decisions. In some cases, the environment must be redefined, such as supply chain actions affecting competitors, who can then retaliate with their own actions. The system can only be defined for a given set of circumstances, but systemic effects will always be present.

The supply chain structure is actually several *networks* overlaid on top of each other. One deals with the sequence of processes serving the physical flow of products. This is normally easy to identify and provides an initial step for analyzing the chain. It is generally a serial arrangement in which the order of activities is clearly defined by the requirements of the process. However, a second network of organizations and their inter-relationships will govern it. Direct interactions between two organizations may be governed by the indirect links to a third member only indirectly connected to the first.

Other networks link processes such as information flows that connect the production schedules of a supplier and an assembler, along with the operations of the connecting transport carrier. Management may exert control over the chain through this network, ensuring that all members receive and are able to take action on common information. There may also be more indirect influences by one organization on others within the supply chain through market power, political influence, or technological dominance.

Supply Chain Processes

We can visualize the supply chain from several perspectives: manufacturer, retailer, or user. The primary focus is on a complete supply chain, starting with the final user and going back to sourcing of materials to the production. Five operating processes describe the supply chain:

1. *Demand management* – Demand management includes several related activities related to the market: forecasting, customer service, customer order processing, market coordination, and sales support activities.
2. *Distribution* – Distribution provides the link between production and the market. It influences logistics through market requirements for service and efficiency.
3. *Production* – Production and related processes add value to product flow. How production takes place also influences inventory, transport, and time for delivery.
4. *Procurement* – Procurement or purchasing links stages of manufacturing together. In effect, purchasing departments become »managers of outside production.«
5. *Returns* – Close the supply loop by remanufacturing products and components, and reuse or recycle resources in the production process. How returns are organized influence value creation, transport, and waste in the reverse supply chain.

The Management Tasks

The primary task is to integrate each stage into a larger system. Individual organizations at each stage still manage resources, set objectives, and pursue individual objectives. Even within a larger corporate framework, there is danger spurred from independent decisions. Customers are remote, lead times are long, and markets change rapidly. Organizational independence invites conflict.

The concept of supply chain management is shown in Figure 1.5. *Coordination* is imperative for management. It becomes the first management task to make market demands and customer orders visible throughout the chain and direct a concerted effort to supply them. The tools are information systems and organization across normally traditional boundaries. The managers of these traditional organizations may provide the resources but the direction of operations shifts to lateral management matched to product flow. It becomes the basis for reducing the quantity of physical assets, namely inventory, that in turn reduces costs and improves response to change. In a static sense it can improve return on investment, but even more it provides opportunity for devising competitive strategy.

Figure 1.5. The Management Concept of the Supply Chain

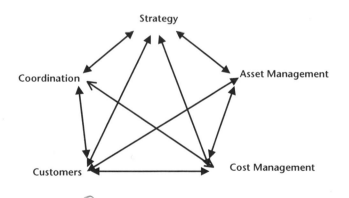

A second task is to *manage assets* across the supply chain, and specifically inventory, in order to *serve customers* and *reduce costs*. Inventory creates costs. It also creates inflexibility because obsolete inventory consumes resources and reduces the ability to respond to change. Where inventory allows individual organizations to plan their own operations, eliminating it requires coordination to substitute respective independent decisions.

The concept of the supply chain however is more than coordination and managing inventory. It has the *potential for devising a competitive strategy*, to be valued by customers because it makes their own operations more efficient and profitable. It provides a framework for resource decisions, organizational integration, and process design. It becomes a source of competitive advantage through the effectiveness of the entire chain and organizational relations. Building these relationships is difficult, but also difficult to emulate. The competitive advantage can be long lasting.

The New Corporate Environment

The emergence of the supply chain and the global corporation offers parallel changes in manufacturing enterprise. There are five fundamental themes:

The customer orientation: Customer requirements in response and product offerings have led to direct ordering and delivery to the customer, product and service customization, and real-time operations.

The decline of mass production: In many industries manufacturing has moved from mass towards customized production. This reflects the marketplace and market segmentation. Niche marketing encourages unique products and services, and short, flexible production runs. It has been further encouraged by changes computer-assisted production.

Smaller inventories: Production quantities are smaller, saving inventory holding costs while increasing flexibility in production and distribution. The trend to smaller inventories is reinforced by the concept of *lean thinking*, which emphasizes reduction of waste and a philosophy of continuous improvement (Womack & Jones, 1996).

Development of electronic commerce: Its influence on supply chain is significant. Procurement has become more efficient as companies move to Web-based supply networks. Distribution becomes more direct, with less stock between factory and market. Shorter chains are more responsive, and can be more easily tailored to different products.

Smaller organizations: Organizations are being reduced by both downsizing and outsourcing. One outcome is the *virtual organization*

(Venkatraman & Henderson 1998), a set of quasi-independent operating units pursuing a common goal, coordinated through electronic communication. It emphasizes corporate specialization and core competencies, offering their own source of competitive advantage. Other activities are performed by outside organizations. This includes many of the supporting activities of the supply chain itself such as logistics and information services. It has encouraged the development of new forms of enterprise in information system operations and third party logistics service providers, who perform the entire process of monitoring the order fulfillment and physical movement and distribution to market.

These changes expand the scope and importance of supply chain management. Supplier networks become larger and multi-tiered as suppliers themselves become more specialized, feeding other suppliers who send their product components to final manufacturing and assemblers for distribution. They place more stress on external coordination. Competition for customers increases the pressure for service and efficiency within the chain. The result is increased pressure for effective management of both internal and external connections.

A Model of the Global Supply Chain

Figure 1.6 portrays the general approach. The supply chain begins with the customer. It moves through five successive stages: distribution, final manufacturing/assembly, first tier suppliers, second tier suppliers to basic materials. In reality, the supply chain may be considerably longer. Decisions determine the choice of structure, partners, and processes. Products and materials flow forward, towards the customer. After the product is consumed, product recycling brings the material flow backward to a point for reuse or renovation. Information flows in both directions: orders and transactions move toward the source of supply. Product movement reporting, and shipping transactions move toward the customer. All of this information is potentially available to all participants in the supply chain. Transport provides the physical links between stages through transport carriers and logistics service providers. Management of the global supply chain takes place in an environment of political, economic, cultural, and social complexity.

Figure 1.6. The Global Supply Chain

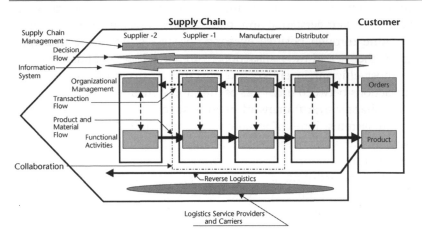

The Approach of the Book

The book follows the patterns established in this chapter. There are three parts: concepts, processes, and management issues.

Concepts

The first part, Chapters 1, 2, 3, and 4, focuses on basic concepts, the theoretical framework for describing and analyzing inter-organizational relationships, and the supporting information system.

Chapter 1 defines the concept of supply chain management and discusses various perspectives of the concept. Chapter 2 deals with the major building blocks of any supply chain: network structure, business processes, and management. Two important concepts are introduced: The postponement-speculation principle and the bullwhip effect. Chapter 3 considers inter-organizational relationships from various theoretical perspectives. Activities are performed through organizations. Organizations become reservoirs of resources, performing activities and making investments. However relationships among organizations are in transition, from market relationships to cooperation and coordination within a context of networks. This chapter introduces two different approaches to understanding organizations: networks and governance structures. The network perspective helps to understand, how relationships and trust are developed over time through positive exchange processes, while the principal-agency theory and the transaction cost analysis provide guidelines for the most efficient incentive and governance structure for exchange transactions between members of the supply chain.

In Chapter 4, a framework is introduced for supply chain information systems. The information system is directly related to decisions, operations, and coordination of product flow. How and where processes are performed, and products are delivered, become important elements of management strategy. The evolution in this area has been rapid both in software to perform transactions, plan and control operations, and in hardware and software in computers and telecommunication systems.

Processes

The second part, Chapters 5, 6, 7, 9, and 10, introduces specific processes for each stage. The emphasis here is not on individual technical issues, but on the coordination and integration of activities across organizations. Consistent with a view that the supply chain is a value-creating system, we begin with customers and distribution of goods and services to the customers. The path is from the customer toward sources of supply, and finally the return of end-of-life products to reuse or recycling.

Chapter 5 develops distribution, the link between customers and production. It includes both traditional distribution channels and new and evolving forms such as e-commerce. This chapter discusses the changes taking place in customer service. The chapter also introduces collaborative distribution models *such as Efficient Consumer Response* (ECR), *Collaborative Planning, Forecasting and Replenishment* (CPFR), and *Vendor-Managed Inventory* (VMI), both as concepts and tools for management.

Chapter 6 embraces supply chain requirements for production. Production strategy determines manufacturing processes that in turn determine inventory requirements through their degree of flexibility and time for production. It also determines scheduling, which in turn influence capacity, inventory, and the ability to meet market demand. The chapter discusses the evolution of production philosophies from mass production (Fordism) to just-in-time, lean production, flexible manufacturing, agile production, virtual manufacturing, and modular production.

Chapter 7 deals with innovation management in supply chains. The aim of the chapter is to explain how design and development of new products influence the management of global supply chains. The perspective is the requirements for material and product development for each stage of the product life cycle, from concept through design and prototype development through full production to product decline. The chapter describes platform strategies, product architecture strategies, mass customization, and supplier involvement in new product development.

In chapter 8, procurement links previous stages of production from materials and component manufacturers to final assembly. The chapter discusses the changing role of procurement, supplier relations, and various portfolio models of suppliers. Procurement strategy involves selection of critical supply relationships to develop into cooperative partnerships. E-procurement introduces new supply relationships both for on-going relationships and market-related transactions.

Chapter 9 describes the new transport environment within the European Union and the development of value-adding capabilities to the traditional transport and warehousing services. These result in creation of logistics service providers, that have gone beyond transport to include a variety of services: distribution centers, merging shipments, kitting, light production and information – related tasks such as customer order processing and fulfillment. In a global context, transport options are specific to individual regions, making generalizations difficult and not very meaningful. If there is a geographic emphasis in this discussion, it falls on the European transport industry and its influence on distribution structure.

Chapter 10 recognizes the need to conserve and reuse resources through the development of the reverse supply chain, by refurbishing or remanufacturing used products and components when possible, and recycling, and reuse of materials in the production process. It also defines the new emphasis on supply chain sustainability, corporate social responsibility, and the ecological footprint of the supply chain

Management Issues

The third section, Chapters 11, 12, 13, and 14, focuses on management issues. There are four topic areas: performance measurement and management, the role of strategy in the supply chain, supply chain planning and modeling, and the complexity of the global supply chain.

Chapter 11 discusses performance measurement and management within the supply chain. Performance measurement systems used in supply chains are often uncoordinated and internally focused. Besides, there is a tendency to focus on only a few dimensions of supply chain performance. Also issues of feedback of performance measurement in the supply chain are important. Various performance management tools are introduced, including: *target costing, total cost of ownership, activity-based costing (ABC), the Balanced Scorecard, benchmarking,* and the *Supply Chain Operating Reference Model (SCOR)*.

Chapter 12 deals with the strategy of the supply chain. The chapter introduces the resource-based approach as the theoretical foundation for strategy formulation. The thrust of supply chain management as strategy is a matching process between seeking sources of supply and matching to customer demands. The »double helix« model illustrates the long-term cycle between vertical integration and horizontal disintegration, which can be observed in several industries. The design of a supply chain is an important management issue. Two different strategies to improve supply chain performance are described. One strategy is to reduce demand uncertainty, e.g. by information sharing and supply chain integration. Another strategy is to reduce supply uncertainty, e.g. by involving suppliers in product development or shifting from single to dual sourcing. However, there must also be a broader concept of strategy to deal with the networks that become the environment, and the sense of abrupt uncertainty that goes with them.

Chapter 13 deals with models for supply chain planning. It examines the role of both descriptive and normative models. A few simple models are presented to illustrate how supply chain issues can be modeled quantitatively. The examples include: a statistical approach to sourcing strategies, modeling of inventory management by EOQ, a supply chain performance model, modeling product architecture modularization for mass customization, modeling of demand forecast, the linear programming model, and modeling of the bullwhip effect.

Chapter 14 extends the geographic scope of the supply chain. Our discussion is global, because we recognize that while supply chain practice is increasingly similar around the world, there are new influences introduced by crossing national borders. The supply chain has come under increasing criticism in some quarters because it replaces domestic labor with lower cost labor elsewhere. At the same time, global supply chains benefit both local and home economies by their innovation and its diffusion. While the general principles of supply chain management apply, each region and country of origin has its unique issues. An American firm dealing with the European market would bring a different perspective from a European-based firm dealing with the same market. The same takes place with a European firm operating in the US. These differences relate more closely to distribution and transport than to manufacturing and procurement. The impact of information technology is global and makes supply chain management into a rapidly changing but increasingly common understanding of concepts and practice.

Summary

Strategy for the global corporation is a quest for competitive advantage. Operations are being recognized as a source of advantage and profitability. There are three fundamental processes that determine the course of a business enterprise: product development, customer relations, and the supply chain. They are interdependent processes, which must be coordinated and directed to achieve successful performance of strategy for the organization. Our focus on the supply chain emphasizes the flow of physical material and products.

The supply chain is both unique and an extension of the logistics concept. The uniqueness stems from its systemic framework embracing the entire set of supply operations. The logistics concept goes part way, but is oriented to the actions and objectives of the individual firm. The key element is supply chain integration, not necessarily by ownership but by coordination of operations and decisions.

There are many ways to describe the supply chain. We begin with a three-part framework: activities, organizations, and processes. Activities are the foundations, organizations are the building blocks, and processes become the mortars to bind the chain together as a system. Processes include product design, production, procurement, distribution, and demand management. This however is a static interpretation. The supply chain is also a dynamic process. Management must seek adaptation and innovation as part of the quest for competitive advantage in the market place.

The issues of the supply chain are necessarily global. Materials and production capacity can be located virtually anywhere in the world. Markets are located wherever they can be found. The central issues of a global supply chain are not necessarily international, but are inherent in the structure and operations of the supply chain itself.

2. Structure and Process

»*The fundamental distinguishing dynamic of enduring great
companies is that they preserve a cherished core ideology
while simultaneously stimulating progress and change in
everything that is not part of the core ideology*«.

Collins & Porras (2000).

Supply chains are processes, and possibly, the most dominant processes in business. They stretch from basic resources to final markets,
and involve networks of organizations manufacturing products and
providing services to meet the demands of customers, often on a
global scale. They are both flows of products and information.
Processes of the supply chain begin with customer demands, transmitted to a chain of activities that are ultimately matched to market
preferences. Customer decisions on products, delivery, and other
service preferences should logically shape the organization of the
supply chain and determine its performance requirements.

Figure 2.1 provides an orientation to the general theme of this
chapter. The supply chain is a process that transforms materials into
products and delivers them to customers through specific activities.
Activities are attached to organizations that supply, produce, distribute, manage, and support them. Activities, more than organizations, are the building blocks of the supply chain. While there is a
necessary physical order to production and distribution, where they
are placed within these organizations depends on economic and
management considerations. The fundamental issue is the relationship between the process of the supply chain and organizational
boundaries. Organizations manage and supply resources, but activities must include both coordination and physical operations to operate the supply chain. The management task is to specify the necessary operations and select their organizational location to realize the
performance of the supply chain as a whole.

Figure 2.1. Activity Flow and Supply Chain Structure

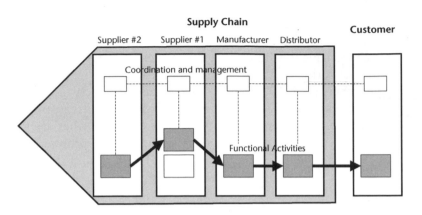

The challenge of supply chain management is to organize and manage a process through a potentially worldwide supply and distribution combination of networks that deliver product variety and services for customers in global markets. Through their supply chains, companies struggle to gain competitive advantage through sourcing, product development, production, and delivery in complex networks on a global scale. These networks extend beyond corporate boundaries to connect to suppliers, distributors, service providers, and customers.

How these networks are organized involve strategic decisions encompassing procurement, production, distribution, transport, telecommunication, and information systems, not only as individual functional networks but also as integrated systems connecting these networks in pursuit of a common goal. We begin with a discussion of Michael Porter's (1985) value chain model and value systems. We then turn to the alternatives within the supply chain structure. Because activities are performed through organizations responsible for their own performance, the initial task is to determine how these activities should be organized for optimal performance.

Accompanying this task must be decisions whether to internalize, or to outsource, letting partner organizations manage and perform activities as part of a coordinated effort. The management task therefore becomes two-fold: to design the process to link activities, and to coordinate these activities to make the supply process possible. Outsourcing has become a significant option for many operations within the supply chain. Organizing across organizational boundaries becomes important as corporations focus on their core activities, those that provide strategic value, leaving other less crucial activities for other firms to perform.

This chapter focuses on three components of supply chain management: network structure, business processes, and management issues (Lambert et al. 1998). When determining the network structure it is necessary to identify 1) what activities are necessary, 2) who should perform them within the supply chain, 3) what are the structural dimensions of the network, 4) what types of process links should be established in the network, and 5) how should the business processes be managed across the supply chain. A business process can be defined as »a structured and measured set of activities designed to produce a specific output for a particular customer or market« (Davenport 1993), or as »a collection of activities that takes one or more kinds of input and creates an output that is of value to the customer« Hammer and Champy (2001:38). The Global Supply Chain Forum (Lambert et al. 1998) identified several business processes that extend across the supply chain, including order fulfillment, product development, and customer relationship management. The management component encompasses both physical & technical elements and managerial and behavioral issues. Business processes differ in detail between companies, but they have a common structure in their general configuration.

The Value Chain and the Value System

Porter (1985) developed the concept of the *value chain* to describe a general sequence of value-adding activities for product flow within the firm:

Inbound logistics→operations→outbound logistics→sales and marketing→service

It includes both physical product flows (logistics and operations) and marketing (sales and marketing, and service), adding value as the flow moves toward the customer. Value results from any activity that makes the final product worth more to the final customer. It can include the production of tangible products, rapid delivery, physical positioning of a product for availability, or supporting after-sales support and service. He also envisioned a *value system* where individual firms and their activities are linked to become a larger chain. This opens possibilities for reconfiguring the value chain for greater efficiency through eliminating redundant activities or shifting activities between stages.

Figure 2.2 describes a conventional supply chain that might be found in Porter's value system. Each stage in the process represents a separate organization, and products are passed between organizations for processing by specific activities. Each organization is independently managed. The interfaces between organizations require connections for transfer and become potential barriers to information for coordination and product flow. For independent organizations, these barriers may also involve redundant functions at each stage, such as marketing and procurement, negotiating transfers of product ownership and responsibility. Each stage manages its own inventory and production separately. One objective of supply chain management is to reduce the total costs of product flow by eliminating this redundancy and integrating operations through close coordination. A second objective is to enhance the value of the final product by making the system, as a whole, more responsive to customer preferences.

Figure 2.2. Activities and Organisations in the Supply Chain

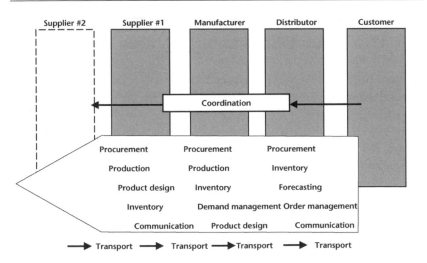

While the ultimate customer becomes the final judge of value, each stage incurs costs. Value at each stage is determined either by, the market for these intermediate products such as basic manufactured components or transport services, or by negotiation based on costs. Final value is established only with the final exchange transaction where the product comes closest to matching the specific needs of customers. Redundant activities or activities add that costs but do not add value for customers and should be eliminated. At the same time, activities that add value should be included even at an increase in cost. As the characterization of value creation changes, supply chain management must respond through reexamining and reconfiguring its activities.

The Structure of the Supply Chain

In the past, activities defined their parent organizations. The term »manufacturing« includes multiple activities involving products, their design and transformation into tangible outputs. Similarly, »distribution« traditionally includes order processing, inventory management, and transport management. However these roles are changing. The supply chain activity sequence defines a process of product flow embracing multiple activities. Supply chain management must be concerned not only with individual activities, but also with their organization and their collective output. It must be able to shift activities between organizations, changing the characteristics of these organizations in a search process for new sources of market advantage and higher financial returns. In practice, these shifts are becoming commonplace.

To demonstrate the issues, we introduce a hypothetical computer manufacturer, Elektra Electronics. Their conventional supply chain is described in symbolic terms in Figure 2.3. The purpose is to recognize that functional activities are modular building blocks that can be combined, reduced in number, or shifted between organizations. The logic behind this approach is the subject of the discussion later of the chapter. We use generalized designations of activities to avoid encumbering the discussion with detail. However, individual supply chains will use different specific activities to meet their own requirements.

Figure 2.3. Activity Deployment in the Supply Chain

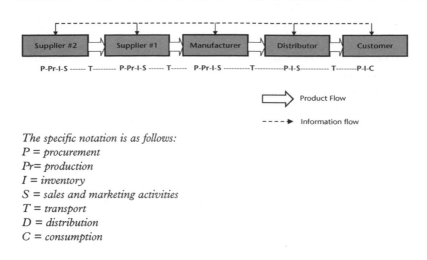

The specific notation is as follows:
P = procurement
Pr= production
I = inventory
S = sales and marketing activities
T = transport
D = distribution
C = consumption

The conventional supply chain includes procurement, inventory, and sales activities at each stage, and production in three stages, although dealing with different levels of the process. Sales and marketing are included here only to complete the value system. Orders are passed through sales and procurement to become product requests, entering into production schedules of the manufacturer who also orders from suppliers. There is a lack of central direction to this process, evident in the redundant activities and the separation of stages. The general tendency is to build inventories based on forecasts of demand, a *push* inventory environment where inventories are planned and positioned at each stage in advance of sales.

One objective of supply chain management is to reduce cost by eliminating all unnecessary inventories. Inventory serves two useful purposes: to protect the supply chain against unpredicted demands, and to protect intermediate stages against unpredicted delays and other failures. In Figure 2.4, inventory is concentrated as finished products at the distributor level. This places it close to the market where orders can be filled rapidly. At the same time, orders for inventory replenishment are filled directly from production, both from manufacturers and their suppliers. This may be possible with stable demands and simple product lines. This system *pushes* inventory to the market, but individual interactions between stages allow suppliers to produce directly to manufacturers' orders or forecasts of demand, a process also identified as *speculation* (Bucklin 1965).

Figure 2.4. Activity Shifting in the Supply Chain

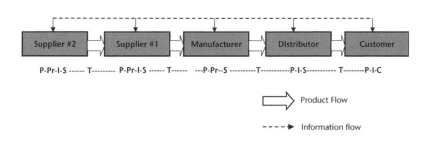

If customers are willing to wait for delivery, it may be possible, in theory, to avoid inventories altogether, producing to orders all through the supply chain. This is a *pull* system, the order pulls the product through the supply chain. Success depends on the speed of production and stable demands. The well-publicized Toyota's just-in-time production system is one example. Production is delayed until orders are received, a process of *postponement*. If we can increase coordination, we can remove inventory.

Figure 2.5. Activity Shifting in the Supply Chain

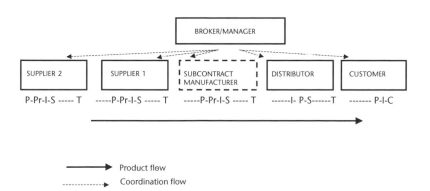

Another set of design options comes through *activity shifting*, shown in Figure 2.5. In this case, the »manufacturer« no longer manufactures, but subcontracts it to other companies that specialize in production. The manufacturer now only engages in product development and solely, designs and markets the product. This is essentially what Nike does with athletic shoes, the garment industry with clothing, and the electronics industry with both finished products and components. It is not only confined to manufacturing but can include any activity contained within the supply chain. For example, express companies, such as UPS and FedEx, have taken on order processing and after-sales service support activities.

Companies that were formerly only transportation companies offer now other services such as inventory management, light production, after-sales services and order processing (see Chapter 9). Known as third party logistics providers, they now take on activities because the combinations are more profitable than transportation alone, and can provide these services at lower cost or to higher standards of service than their clients. What this suggests is that institutions traditionally defined by their customary activities are now transforming themselves into entirely new combinations for new purposes.

Figure 2.6. Customized Order Supply Chain

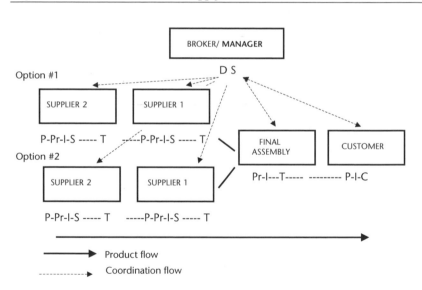

An extension of this process becomes customized ordering, shown in Figure 2.6. This alternative, related to the postponement process, involves the customer directly in the order process, selecting options and even variations of a basic product. One approach produces as orders come in, close to the market to reduce time-in-transit, with suppliers responding to specific customer orders, possibly delivering on short notice. Dell Computer follows this pattern and it is now a widely recognized model for customized manufacturing. A second approach avoids the final stages of manufacturing, shifting them forward toward the market and processing the final stages at the last minute to meet customer demands. It has the advantage of reducing inventory, but it usually depends on modular product design made specifically for this purpose. It allows for a wider range of products by combining modules.

The Concept of Postponement

In broadest terms, postponement (van Hoek 2001:161) is »an organizational concept whereby some of the activities in the supply chain are not performed until customer orders are received«. According to Lee (1998) postponement delays the timing of crucial processes in which end products assume their specific functionalities, features, and identities. Customization takes place after obtaining key information about customers' specific needs or requirements at the time of the order. The logic behind postponement is that risk and uncertainty costs are tied to differentiating products by form, place, and time during manufacturing and logistics operations. The opposite of postponement is speculation, where both product form and market place are made at the earliest possible time to obtain economics of scale in manufacturing and minimize the risk of stock-out situations.

Pagh and Cooper (1998) distinguish between three types of postponement:

- Manufacturing postponement
- Logistics postponement
- Full postponement

In *manufacturing postponement,* the final manufacturing process does not take place until the customer order is received. Instead, modular components are produced to an intermediate, generic form. They are later assembled, packaged, or otherwise completed, in some cases, at a downstream point such as a distribution center, or distributor. Using manufacturing postponement adds flexibility because modules can be combined in numerous variants to extend a product line, or match product features to individual customers. Maintaining component inventory levels controls production, but customer orders control final assembly. The advantages lie in reducing finished product inventory, being able to meet individual customer requirements, extending products in different forms to new markets, achieving economies of scale in component production and economies of scope in developing multiple products from a single design. The principal disadvantages lie in the time delays for final stages of production, risk of stock-outs, and a potential loss in control over production.

Manufacturing postponement as a strategy requires pre-planning in product development to specify modules and the choice of place and partners for final production. An example of manufacturing postponement is the mobile phone industry, where the final assembly of mobile phones often is carried out by a third party logistics provider, who has an inventory of mobile phones, manuals, SIM cards, and peripherals. When the third party logistics provider receives the specific customer order, the components are assembled, packaged, and shipped directly to the customer within a narrow time window after the order is received.

In *logistics postponement,* manufacturing is based on speculation, and the downstream supply chain is based on postponement. The finished products are stocked at a central location, e.g. a regional distribution center, to serve multiple local markets. It may lengthen transit times for local delivery, but modern transport systems can often provide equivalent service. It is speculation in the sense of holding inventory, but is postponement in avoiding distribution of the finished products to local markets, until the customer orders are received. The advantage lies in reducing inventories, although a central stock must be larger to accommodate more volume, and hold local product variations. The principal disadvantage lies with delivery over a longer distance. An example is Ford's European Distribution Center near Cologne, which delivers spare parts to dealers and garages across Europe with transit times from 24 to 48 hours.

Full postponement is a combination of the other two types. The customization of the product is delayed until the customer order is received. The delay must be considered on a continuum from manufacturing postponement with partial assembly to production of components as part of the customer order. It represents a shift toward more postponement and less speculation. Some components can be produced in advance, although usually only to a generic level of low financial commitment. The major difference lies in production at a central point with shipments made directly to the customer. The advantage obviously lies in low inventory of finished goods and the complete flexibility to meet individual customer orders. The principal disadvantages lie in a higher production costs and a longer time requirement to meet orders. An example of full postponement is the Danish audio-video manufacturer Bang & Olufsen (B&O). It assembles, tests and delivers customized products directly to the final customers' locations in Europe within five days, using both a central factory and adaptation to specific customer requirements.

Building Structure

To develop supply chain structure involves a series of steps:

1. Determine activity requirements to match the objectives of the supply chain.
2. Analyze the cost structures of these activities to establish potential economies of scale, scope and specialization.
3. Determine the optimal configuration of these activities in sequences and possible combinations in terms of market response and cost
4. Define the core competencies of the firm in terms of their ability to achieve competitive advantage.
5. Identify and select organizations and their subcontractor organizations with the capability to manage these activities
6. Negotiate with candidate firms to manage activities in logical groups to serve the supply chain as a whole.
7. Determine organizational requirements for coordination, measurement and control.
8. Determine forms of coordination that participating organizations will use, including management teams and information technology.

The first three steps define the tasks. The product and its related supply process determine activities. The choice of service or cost minimization objectives force differences in activities. The service objectives and cost structures of individual activities dictate location and whether economies of scale or scope are relevant. Using activities as modular building blocks permits them to be shifted and be combined with other activities for more effective response and lower costs. These steps provide the functional organization of the supply chain.

Steps 4, 5 and 6 determine the organizational »ownership« of these activities. The key is to identify the core of competitive advantage, an area of ambiguity. The core itself has two definitions. The first includes those activities that have a superior ability to compete. The second includes tasks requiring critical coordination such as information system design, or product development may be included within the lead organization boundaries.

Steps 7 and 8 prescribe the management tasks. Negotiation defines firm boundaries for both the lead and partner firms. The task, the technical characteristics of the organization, and the boundaries determine the needs and the extent and the means of coordination.

There is a difference between working with an established supply chain versus designing a new supply chain. In an ongoing supply chain, these activities are already established within partner organizations. Configuration then involves of shifting activities, evaluating and possibly replacing partners. These steps create a new supply chain organization.

There are also differences between stable supply chains where partners have been long-term associates, and flexible supply chains where partners change in response to different products and customers. Partnerships in this setting are activated in response to particular requirements, becoming inactive again after the project is finished.

The Bullwhip Effect

In a traditional supply chain, information about the final customer's actual demand is often distorted from one end of the supply chain to the other. This phenomenon is called the bullwhip effect (Lee et al. 1997) or the Forrester effect (Forrester 1961). Distortions in demand information often occur as we move further upstream in the supply chain, because each member makes decisions based on the information it receives from the subsequent member in the supply chain. The supplier will purchase and produce on the basis of incoming orders from the producer. The producer will arrange its production planning on the orders received from the wholesaler. The wholesaler will replenish inventory based on the orders from the retailer. The retailer will place their orders based on the actual demand of the final customer. All links in the supply chain will have their own ordering routines, based on reorder points and order quantities. The result is that orders to the upstream members in a supply chain show greater variance than the actual demand of the final customer. In Chapter 13 is shown, how the bullwhip effect can be modeled. Distorted information in the supply chain can lead to excessive inventory, out-of-stock situations, inefficient production schedules, and larger expediting costs. The bullwhip effect is illustrated in Figure 2.7.

Figure 2.7. The Bullwhip Effect

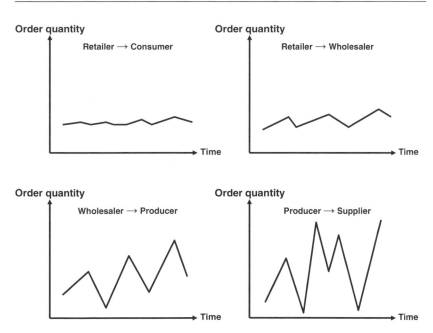

Lee et al (1997) identified four major causes of the bullwhip effect:

1. *Demand forecast updating.* Many firms use simple forecasting methods, such as exponential smoothing, based on the order history from the firm's immediate customers. If the customers' demand increase, the next upstream player will not only replenish the stocks to meet the requirements of future demand, but also increase the safety stock.
2. *Order batching.* Due to economics of scale in ordering and transportation, many firms accumulate demands before issuing an order. The further upstream we move from the final customer, the more erratic the batch ordering becomes. The result is long order cycles, which contributes to the bullwhip effect.
3. *Price fluctuations.* Sales promotions, like price discounts, quantity discounts, and coupons, encourage customers to purchase larger quantities than needed, when prices are low, and then stop buying until the products have been consumed. Therefore, the customer's demand is not reflecting the actual consumption patterns, and results in a bullwhip effect.
4. *Rationing and shortage gaming.* Sometimes, product demand exceeds supply and the manufacturer has to ration its products to customers. If the manufacturer allocates the scarce products in proportion to the amount ordered, the customers will order more than they actually need, hoping to secure a larger proportion of the scarce products. The effect of »shortage gaming« is that the manufacturer does not know, what the real demand is for these products, and therefore creates a bullwhip effect upstream in the supply chain.

Holweg et al. (2005:173) have analyzed the consumption of a washing detergent in a major Finnish grocery retail chain. The weekly variability of the consumers' purchases was less than 10 percent. The retail shops were all replenished from a distribution center, operated by the chain. However, the aggregated orders from the shops to the distribution center were 26 percent higher. The major detergent manufacturers typically used focused plants (one plant for each product group) to produce detergents for all markets in Europe. When the detergent manufacturer got the orders from the Finnish retail chain, the demand variability was amplified nine times between the local demand and the European manufacturing plant, due to the aggregation of purchase order, consolidation of shipments, and production orders into larger batches.

Information sharing and close collaboration across the supply chain can mitigate the consequences of the bullwhip effect considerably. Strategies and concepts for supply chain collaboration is an important theme in this book.

What are Activities?

Specialized activities define a system of product flow. They should only be included within the supply chain if they add value to the final product. Their collective scope extends to all tasks of the supply chain from product design to the final customer and return as recyclable material, although their individual tasks are narrowly defined.

As building blocks, activities take on a specific set of characteristics (Bucklin 1960):

- They should be related both to each other and the objectives of the supply chain as a system.
- They must be manageable as individual units, capable of standing alone or as part of other organizational units.
- They must be economically significant, adding value and incurring cost.
- They must have economic characteristics that create incentives for firms to specialize in them:
  - Economies of scale (volume)
  - Economies of scope (products)
  - Specialization in specific tasks
  - Specific operational factors
  - Their specific function should not be duplicated within the supply chain.

Most activities under this definition can be located at any of several different stages within the supply chain. One option is to assume their traditional location, such as production within a manufacturing organization. Another is to combine them with other activities as part of other organizations such as a distribution center operation within a manufacturing organization. An alternative is to outsource activities such as final assembly to another organization, such as a distributor/wholesaler that could also perform this function. A third alternative is to create another organization to perform this operation as a specialized task.

Core Competencies and Outsourcing

Core competencies drive the enterprise. The concept defines activities that an organization should retain for competitive advantage. They create opportunity for prices and profit margins that exceed the market. Other activities should be retained or outsourced depending on the logic of the individual situation and whether the activity earns competitive returns. This logic is tied to the value chain through a combination of three factors: customer importance, technology clockspeed and competitive position (Fine et al. 2002). *Customer importance* reflects the power of the brand to hold customer loyalty through product identification. *Clockspeed* indicates the rate at which the product life cycle evolves from origin to obsolescence. *Competitive position* indicates the uniqueness of the component in the market. Each product design becomes a core competency because of its competitive value. Therefore a car manufacturer could outsource product components to external manufacturers where there is no competitive advantage but has potential cost reduction, but retain those of high value to the company. An example to illustrate the process is an evaluation of automobile engine design from the General Motors Powertrain Group (Fine et al. 2002). Individual components require separate decisions. At one extreme is the engine block, an iron or aluminum casting with subsequent machining. Many different suppliers around the world can emulate this process. At the other extreme is the electronic engine management component system, which is specific to each car manufacturer.

This type of evaluation should not be bound to manufacturing alone but extended to every aspect of corporate operation. Deciding on the core competencies of an organization is often difficult. Prahalad & Hamel (1990:83-84) proposed three tests to identify core competencies in a company.

- First, a core competence should create unique and significant value to the final customer. Honda has a core competence in small engine design and manufacturing. Sony has an expertise in miniaturization. Federal Express has a core competence in logistics and customer service.

- Second, a core competence provides access to a wide variety of markets beyond the established product. Nokia, originally produced rubber boots and tires, but developed new core competencies in manufacturing mobile phones and radio base stations by using new innovate technologies. The Danish company Bang & Olufsen, a high-end stereo and television manufacturer, has a core competence in design that is applied in other product groups, such as medical devices, components for luxurious cars, and telephone equipment.

- Third, a core competence should be difficult for competitors to imitate. The more complex the mixture of capabilities and resources, the more difficult it is for competitors to imitate. Sources of competitive advantage: knowledge of unique technologies, skills in management coordination and execution and strong brand loyalty require close examination. The core is a shifting target, as competition changes and new technologies emerge, new activities become the core, and other activities can be shifted to other partners. Nokia is an example. It started producing rubber boots and ended up being the world's most innovative mobile producer. Goodyear is another example. Its core competence is still in producing quality tires, but it has also developed in house vendor-managed inventory. Goodyear not only manages its own tires at the customers' premises, but also competitors' tires on a fee per transaction basis. Long-established activities within an organization often have no advantage that commands a higher price in the market. Many firms would be left with only a few activities, contracting for the rest with outside partners.

Core competencies and outsourcing are complementary concepts. While the core deals with sources of competitive advantage, outsourcing shifts activities that do not add competitive value to other organizations that can perform them at least as efficiently. Outsourced activities release management and capital resources that can be better used to pursue core opportunities. Outsourcing also builds flexibility, non core suppliers can be changed as markets or supply conditions change. Companies that outsource can concentrate resources on areas that give them advantage, where they can earn higher rates of return.

Outsourcing creates external supply chains. Instead of internalizing activities to manage them within a single organization, they are performed by other organizations, leaving the focal organization with less direct control over the outcomes. It requires both careful selection of business partners and a need for inter-organizational management.

At the same time, other companies annex activities that they can combine with others to build their own competitive advantage, building new institutions. A relatively new industry within the supply chain, third-party logistics providers, combines transportation with warehousing, order processing, and even final stages of manufacturing to create new combinations of service. The objective is to meet the specific needs of supply chain users, while at the same time creating higher revenues and customer loyalty towards the logistics service providers.

The explosion of telecommunications and information technology favors outsourcing. The ease of internet-based communication and the widespread implementation of enterprise resource planning systems make it easier to coordinate across organizational boundaries.

Outsourcing is now becoming a competitive necessity. One organization cannot be efficient and competitive in every area. Competition between supply chains forces them to seek new solutions to what were once internal issues within the organization. Changes in many markets occur with rapidity, leaving these organizations with capabilities that are mismatched to their markets and requiring flexibility to acquire new capabilities. Fine et al (2002:69) note: »competitive advantage is at best a fleeting commodity that must be won again and again.«

Components in
Supply Chain Management

Lambert et al. (1998) proposed that supply chain management can be divided into three highly interconnected component categories:

- Network structure
- Business processes
- Management

Figure 2.8. Supply Chain Management Framework

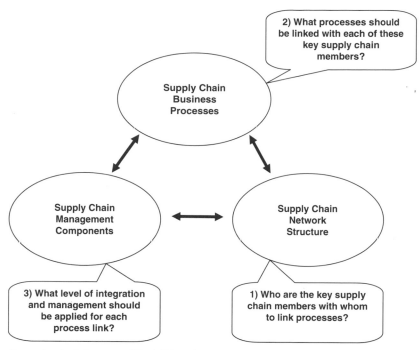

Source: Lambert, Cooper, and Pagh (1998:4)

Network Structure

The network structure involves collaboration between the most important partners in a supply chain, as well as the relationships between these partners. It is neither possible nor desirable to establish a SCM cooperative network that includes all participants in a business network. It would be complex and demand entirely too much management attention. Moreover, it is important to focus available resources on relations of strategic importance for the competitiveness of the business. As a corollary, management must consider the choices carefully for cooperative partners of the business. For other active but less significant members of the supply chain, the business can adopt more traditional arm's-length forms of cooperation.

In selecting business partners, relations can be divided into four principal categories (Lambert et al., 1998)

1. Relationships that the business in focus wishes to manage and coordinate. For a final assembly factory, a typical example would be relations to systems suppliers and customers in the next link of the supply chain.
2. Relationships that are not critical by themselves but essential for operations, and still should be monitored as part of the network. Examples include transport and storage/warehouse activities contracted out to a third party.
3. Relationships involving routine procurement of standard items from one or several different suppliers. These transactions can be based on arm's length relationships and need not to be monitored tightly.
4. Relationships to other supply chains. One company can supply several competing supply chains. These relationships are not part of the internal relationships within the supply chain but can influence the supply chain's effectiveness and competitiveness through common technologies, scheduling and capacity issues. Several writers (e.g. Miles and Snow) suggested that suppliers should also sell to competitors to avoid becoming captive within the supply chain and to ensure that the supplier remains competitive and innovative.
5. Relationships to competitors. Firms that are in a supply relationship for some products might also be in competition with each other in other products. Brandenburger and Nalebuff (1996) called it co-opetition, a blend of competition and cooperation. Cooperation with competitors producing complementary or related products might lead to expansion of the market and establishment of new business relationships.

In figure 2.9 is shown an example of mapping the various types of relationships in a supply chain.

Figure 2.9. Types of Inter-Company Business process Links

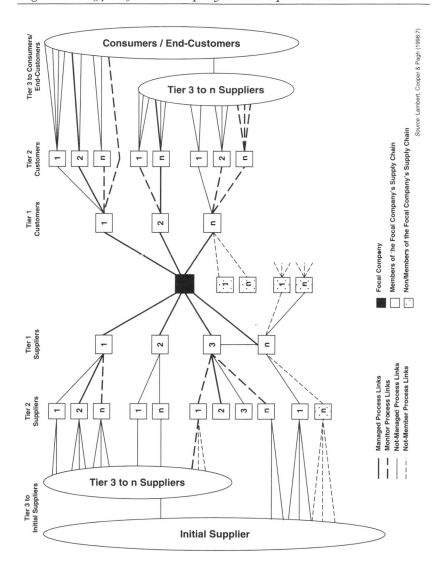

Business processes

Business processes encompass the activities and flows of information that are connected with conducting materials, products, and services through the supply chain and on to customers. Examples include:

- Order-to-Cash
- Customer Service
- Time-to-Market
- Procure-to-Pay

Each of them becomes a system of their own. The questions of how many and which processes exist, is of critical importance. They may even conflict with each other. Therefore, coordination and integration is not only of value but necessary to avoid internal conflicts. The quantity and precise nature of these processes will vary with each supply chain. As a result, the choice of which processes are to be in focus, as well as the level and depth of integration in a given supply chain, is important.

Order-to-Cash

This business process includes all activities that are tied in with expediting customers' orders: placement of the order including transmission, receiving the order, as well as the credit check, fulfillment, pick-and-pack, shipping, distribution, and the final stage, the customer receiving, invoicing, and payment. The total time elapsed between the customer placing an order until the customer receives the desired goods is often referred to as the *order cycle time*. Order placement, order confirmation, and invoicing are increasingly handled electronically. In this way, the administrative tasks as well as the transaction costs of the order-to-cash process are significantly reduced.

Customer Service

The term »customer service« includes a number of services before, during, and after the actual sales transaction. Pre-services can, for example, be advising, a flexible and easy ordering process, and easily accessible product information. Service possibilities during the actual order process include a short order cycle, warehouse service, and electronically accessible delivery information (track-and-trace, proof-of-delivery). Service after the transaction may encompass customer support, including installation and assistance in the use of products, maintenance service, guarantees, and return services in the event of error or deficiency.

Time-to-Market

Time-to-market includes activities connected with the development of new products to be launched on the market. Time-to-market also measures the speed at which a company is able to transform product ideas into saleable products. This time span is determined by a number of factors, for example: the industry, the resources the company has available for R&D, the speed at which technological developments are processed, and the speed of changes in the preferences of the customers. In the biotech industry, time-to-market can range between 5 and 10 years, while in the electronic industry, time-to-market is often less than six months. Fine (1998) used the concept »clockspeed industries« to characterize industries with a short lifecycle. They include multi-media, electronics, and telecommunication.

Previously, product development was carried out in isolation from production. Today, though, product development normally involves close communication with ongoing production. This tendency is demonstrated through such terms as *concurrent engineering*, which involves the initiation of production in parallel with continuous improvement of working processes and procedures. Nonetheless, there is often a key supplier, who is included early on in the product development sequence as a partner during prototype development, and to assist in choosing components and materials. In addition customer focus groups test for functionality and market relevance. This process ensures that non-viable product ideas are eliminated early in the development process, increasing the probability of success.

Procure-to-Pay

The procure-to-pay process encompasses all activities from procurement of goods and services, receiving of invoice, and payment to the supplier. The objective of the procure-to-pay process is to standardize and integrate activities related to strategic sourcing (e.g. supplier selection, evaluation, and monitoring), tactical purchasing (e.g. purchase requisition created and submitted, convert requisition into purchase orders, dispatch to supplier), goods receiving and control, and accounts payable.

Management Components

Several management dimensions define business processes, and the roles of participants in the supply chain. These elements are important for the successful completion of a supply chain project, because they guide individual processes and their integration.

Lambert et al. (1998) divide these components into two major groups:

- Physical and technical systems
- Operational and behavioural systems

The physical and technical management systems can be further divided into:

- Planning and control systems
- Process structure
- Organisational structure
- Information distribution
- Production flow

Planning and control systems are the core of a supply chain. Planning and control include not only activities in the individual company, but also cooperative planning and control of activities and processes across the supply chain. Cooperative planning ensures that the supply chain moves in the desired direction, while control ensures that the actual results for the entire supply chain can be compared against projected goals on an ongoing basis.

Process structure indicates how the company executes its activities and assignments. In this way, a general perspective can form the basis for common routines for activities within the supply chain. The degree of process integration between companies within the supply chain indicates how oriented the supply chain is toward co-ordinated operations.

Organisation structure determines how are different functional departments are linked within the business, as well as the extent of integration between participants in the supply chain. The existence of cross-disciplinary teams within the focal business and inter-organizational teams across the supply chain, demonstrates the degree of process coordination. This orientation can be exemplified in temporary transfer of employees between cooperative partners in the supply chain. Another could be the existence of cooperative development projects that share resources and capabilities.

The structure of information flow has great influence on the supply chain's effectiveness. Information exchange between relevant departments and companies is decisive to obtain development and adaptation of cooperative resources and goals. Therefore it is relevant to ask questions such as: How dense, i.e. how well connected are partners within the supply chain, both by the number of links and the frequency of communication? What categories of information are shared with other participants? How often and how precisely are these partners informed? Finally, how is information technologically transmitted across the supply chain?

The structure of product flow defines the complexity of control. Does the product go through a large number of stages or are the stages of production and distribution few and simple? Are there many different suppliers of components and processes? Are product development and the commercialisation of new products integrated as an ongoing process? Are suppliers and other relevant cooperative partners involved early in the product development process?

Operational and behavioural components include:

- Management principles
- Power structure
- Incentives

Management principles encompass the company's style and, management methods and philosophies that dominate the businesses in focus. If, for example, the company's leadership support a strong hierarchical decision-making process, with formal procedures and a clear definition of responsibility and duties, it is difficult to alter these principles to a more cooperative cross-functional structure.

The power structure in a supply chain conveys the potential to affect the participants in a given direction. In practice, there will often be a dominant company within a supply chain, which will take the initiative to implement the SCM concept. The dominant company can use their position of power to impose desired changes upon their cooperative partners. However, the business can also choose constructive cooperation, where all involved parties can share in the benefits of the SCM concept. The implementation of the SCM concept becomes a basis for establishing a form of cooperation for all motivated participants to exchange their experience and knowledge, even while a dominant company controls the goals and initiatives of the chain as a whole.

Incentives should support and not conflict with the process orientation. Functionally oriented companies often have budgets and result targets, which emphasize efficiency within individual departments. Supply chain performance depends on motivating employees across organisational boundaries, and performance goals should concentrate on processes rather than functions. The reward structure should parallel the processes of the supply chain, reflecting performance, resources, and risks involved in SCM cooperation. Supplier incentives include long-term contracts, a larger share of the purchasing budget, or mutual competency development. Customer incentives include higher levels of customer service, vendor-managed inventory, faster response time, cooperative development projects, and lower total costs.

However, incentives can also create distortions (Narayanan & Raman, 2004). In 2001, Cisco, the world's largest network-equipment manufacturer, wrote off approximately $2.5 billion in subassembly boards and semiconductor inventory, because incentives became too effective. Cisco had passed orders to contract manufacturers, who in turn stockpiled semi-finished products because demand for Cisco's products usually exceeded supply. They had incentives to build buffer stocks, Cisco rewarded them for rapid delivery. When demand slowed down in year 2000, Cisco found that it could not cut off supplies quickly. Since Cisco had not specified responsibilities and accountability for its component suppliers, much of the excess inventory ended up in Cisco's warehouses.

Concluding Comments

Supply chains have evolved historically based on established trading relationships. The movement to supply chain management has encouraged reexamination and reorganization of the process. Structure is the starting point, because it determines what has to be done and which organizations will do it. The orientation is systemic, looking at the process as a whole, crossing functional and organizational boundaries. It lays the foundation for inter-organizational relationships and the management of sub-processes in customer relationships, distribution, production, and procurement.

The natural tendency is to examine structural change from a cost perspective, where measurement is more possible. However, the market demands flexibility and response, and using value, as a measure is more difficult and subjective, depending on the customer's perception of needs. If the customer ultimately determines the supply chain, we must be concerned not only about supply, but their needs and how the supply chain can respond. We now begin to look at supply chains and potential change from a different viewpoint: the ability to deliver new products and expanding product lines, to meet new and changing demands from customers. Supply chain structure becomes part of a larger perspective in corporate strategy.

3. Inter-organizational Relationships

»...A company is its chain of continually evolving capabilities – that is, its own capabilities plus the capabilities of everyone it does business with«

(Fine, 1998:71)

Management attention has moved from competition between firms to competition between supply chains, which encompass all firms from raw materials supplier to end customer. Management's capability for trust-based, long-term relationships with customers, suppliers, third-party service providers, and other strategic partners is crucial in competition. Increased integration and collaboration within the supply chain increases the complexity of management and control. It requires new management skills in terms of developing inter-organizational relationships with strategic partners.

Figure 3.1. Inter-organizational Relationships

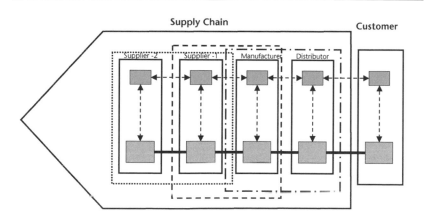

The discussion in the previous chapter presented activities in the supply chain as a network. In this chapter, we want to expand on this concept by recognizing organizational relationships. Activities define the scope of the organization, but the relationships of organizations within this network define the supply chain. Understanding supply chains is difficult, not least because the supply chain itself appears to be in continual flux.

The key appears to lie with inter-organizational connections. Business practice evolves rapidly in response to market pressures and new technology, but the most difficult issues come from management dilemmas in inter-organizational relations. The most promising approaches emanate from theories about organizational behavior that allow for identification and evaluation of the forces acting on their relationships and therefore providing a basis for prediction. This chapter presents a theoretical framework for developing and managing business relationships within a supply chain.

Theory allows us to look at inter-organizational relationships from different perspectives. First, we examine supply chains as industrial networks, how they evolve in response to their roles in economic exchange. The focus is on the interaction and positions among firms within the supply chain, developed by the so-called IMP-School (Industrial Marketing and Purchasing), supplemented from the field of social networks. A network of organizations operates not only in response to economic issues but behavioral and political issues. The focus is on relationships, describing immediate connections to other firms as interactions, such as between suppliers and buyers as dyads. It extends to the entire supply chain, such as the triadic interaction of suppliers, transport carriers, and buyers, or the chain of suppliers acting in successive stages of production.

A second aspect concerning the relationship comes from new institutional economics: primarily principal-agent theory and transaction cost analysis (TCA). *Principal-agent theory* is concerned with problems that arise when one party, the principal, delegates work to another party, the agent (Zsidisin & Ellram 2003). *TCA* is rooted in neo-classical economics (Coase, 1937), and provides guidelines for the most efficient governance structure for exchange transactions.

Trust versus control becomes an important issue in managing supply chain relationships. A high level of confidence allows partners to exchange sensitive information and to rely on informal agreements and incomplete contracts. Conversely, a low level of confidence requires control mechanisms to protect against opportunistic behavior by the other partners. We will discuss different perceptions of trust in a variety of relationships. We will also examine how trust develops over time as a result of positive business exchanges. Finally, we examine different types of industrial networks requiring different control mechanisms for different confidence levels.

Relationships from a Network Perspective

Relationships among firms are imbedded within a broader network of interdependent relationships. It is fundamental to the network perspective that individual firms depend on resources controlled by other firms. Individual firms gain access to these resources through interaction and collaboration. We discuss networks from two perspectives: the industrial network, which provides an overall orientation, and social networks describing the structure and behavior of firms within these inter-relationships.

Industrial Networks

Industrial networks provide an overall perspective on relationships within the supply chain. (Gadde & Haakansson 2001, Haakansson and Snehota 1995, and Ford 2003). It relates firms, their actions and resources as a set of linked networks. The players, individuals or organizations, invest in relationships with other players, gaining both knowledge and physical capabilities from their network partners. The network, as it evolues over time, has an inherent tendency to strengthen and stabilize these connections.

The network perspective is closely associated with supply chain management. Harland (1996:S64) emphasizes the association as »the management of a network of interconnected businesses involved in the ultimate provision of product and service packages required by end customers«. Instead of considering it as organization within a pipeline of vertically inter-linked firms, Harland considers it as management of a complex network of organizations involved in exchange processes.

The network approach involves three components and their mutual relationships, shown in figure 3.2 (Haakansson and Snehota 1995):

- Activities
- Actors
- Resources

Figure 3.2. The Network Approach

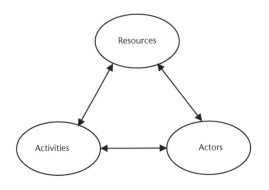

The organization of the supply chain follows a general pattern developed by Haakansson and Snehota (1995). *Links* serve individual firms by defining opportunities and constraints through connections to other organizations and their resources. Relationships among *actors* (organizational partners) may lead to formation of teams to combine resources that achieve more than individual firms could achieve individually. The combination becomes a *quasi-organization*, directed toward a common goal. Links build networks with both direct and indirect connections. Firms are affected not only by their own operations and those of partner (dyad) organizations, but also by other organizations to which they may be connected only indirectly such as triads and beyond. Haakansson and Snehota (1995:41) comment that:

> »The network is usually seen as a structure of actors. However a challenging idea is to set it at a lower level [e.g. resource ties]. Then the position of all elements (actors, activities, resources and their bonds, links and ties) is given by the existing relations.«

And a little later, after discussing the evolution of networks toward new forms,

> »The emergent structure has in any given moment a limiting effect on its actors at the same time as it provides the base for future development.«

A framework for analysis, particularly relevant for the supply chain, summarizes this network development in Table 3.1.

Table 3.1. Framework for the Analysis of Network Relations

	Company	Relationship	Network
Activities	Activity Set	Activity Links	Activity Pattern
Actors	Organizational Structure	Actors Bonds	Web of Actors
Resources	Resource Collection	Resource Ties	Resource Constellation

Source: Haakansson and Snehota (1995:45)

The individual firm itself is a structure of activities, organizations, and resources. Bonding among actors, creates a connected network that enables it to achieve its goals. This network of organizations is the underlying basis for the visible supply chain. At the same time, it is bound by the potential opportunities and constraints of its resource network.

Supply chains as networks (webs) evolve through interaction of these activity links, actor bonds, and resource ties that become sub-networks of their own. Resource ties often determine the selection of actors and activity links. A useful element for strategy development is to map the resource structure, to identifying potential actors, their capabilities and constraints, and then to establish the activity links to enable the system to function.

Activities are the commercial, technical, and administrative functions of individual firms that we discussed in the previous chapter. In a supply chain context, they become tasks that must be linked together to create the supply chain. They would include procurement, product development, in- and outbound transport, production management, inventory control and order processing. They are connected by information and physical flows between stages, the *activity links*. The premise of the supply chain is that managing links determines the performance of the supply chain as a whole. The supply chain in its entirety is therefore a network of linked functional activities.

Actors include both organizations and individuals. We will generally consider organizations as our principal focus, although individual managers make the decisions that shape the supply chain. Actors hold decision-making power. Actors in the supply chain include suppliers, distributors, customers, and transport and logistics service providers and other intermediaries. These actors (firms) encompass stages of activities and determine the connections to other actors. *Actor bonds* align organizations into a network of organizational relationships, determined by contract, informal connections and marketplace transactions. The supply chain itself depends on the development of these relationships. They involve mutual identification and commitment, leading to the development of trust.

Resources include tangible resources of manpower, equipment, financial capacity and production capacity in addition to intangible resources of knowledge, organizational learning, market image, innovative capabilities and patent rights. *Resource ties* connect organizational capabilities as combinations of resources for new opportunities as well as constraints on freedom to act. The resource structure determines the arrangement of the supply chain. Control over resources defines the actors and their activities, and becomes its motivating force.

Activities

The choice of activities involves two opposing forces: economy and effectiveness. Economy involves a search for efficiency, favoring standardization and scale economies. Effectiveness is the ability to deliver differentiated performance to match the requirements of other activities within the supply chain (often referred as alignment).

Activity links among firms in a network develop through two separate, but closely linked processes:

- Exchange
- Adaptation

Exchange processes involve mutual transfers of information, goods and services, and social processes. Adaptation as a set of processes adjusts requirements and accommodation through technical, legal, logistics and administrative elements and personal interactions. Processes can convey a sense of uniqueness, ultimately resulting in some supply chains as customization to match individual customer requirements. The parties gradually build mutual trust through social exchange processes. In addition to efficiency and adaptation, activities are inter-related through activity links that synchronize operations. As these links connect to others, they become an activity network connecting resources. They are governed through relationships between organizations.

Actors

Actor bonds recognize that all firms are integrated into a network context. Individual firms have specific attributes, but they achieve identity in their role in relation to other firms through mutual orientation. Through adaptation of activities, they achieve trust that leads toward commitment. These bonds and perceptions become a basis for future development. Bonds must necessarily be limited because internal resources are limited. Close relations between a buyer and its suppliers only become possible with a few extensively developed links.

The process of adaptation by actors is important for several reasons. First, it strengthens bonds between the parties. If a supplier has adjusted his production process or products to the needs of a particular customer, they both become mutually dependent. Second, the adjustment process signals that their mutual relations are stable and enduring, and not governed by short-term considerations. Examples include mutual modifications, administrative systems, and production processes to achieve more efficient utilization of resources.

Through interaction, the parties in a network develop various kinds of mutual bonds that tend towards long-term relationships. Haakansson and Johanson (1990) distinguish between:

- Technical bonds, attached to processes applied by the firms
- Social bonds established through personal trust
- Administrative bonds resulting from administrative routines and systems
- Legal bonds from contracts between firms.

Networks can be simultaneously both stable and dynamic. New relations are established, and old relations come to an end. Some relations are strong, others are weak, and existing relations will change over time. Thus, a network has a *dynamic nature* that does not seek an optimal equilibrium, but is in constant state of change. In a supply chain, a firm could have loose and changing relations with a large number of potential suppliers but strong, long-term ties with a limited number of key suppliers and key customers.

Resources

Resources in the context of the supply chain have value only through use in combination with others. Resource ties enable the organization to secure those that it does not already have available. Through adaptation, they are combined within a resource constellation to produce unique outcomes. Links can become more important than possessing resources per se and can change to match new opportunities. Managing resources requires continuing investment and experimentation as a search process for innovation and optimal allocation.

Networks and Structure

We have discussed networks and relationships, but we have yet to touch on the inherent structure of networks (Schary 2006). Most of the theoretical discussion lies beyond the scope of this book, but it does raise important points. Networks lie between hierarchy and the market. In the supply chain, they can take a linear form for processing physical flows or more complex forms for information and decision, with forward loops for anticipating the future, or backward loops for orders and control. They can be centralized in star configurations between e-hubs and satellites, or a buyer with multiple suppliers. They can be sparse, with only a few links or densely connected in clusters.

There is a tendency of networks to cluster, such as small world networks with strong dense connecting links. Information is restricted to small groups of decision-makers, even becoming insular in their outlook. This presents a dangerous situation, as new information is restricted. Product development with close collaboration is one example. The solution is to loosen the network ties to allow connection to other networks. Granovetter (1973) called it: »The strength of weak ties«. Procurement policies will sometimes avoid complete dependence on a single supplier, and require suppliers to take on other customers in order to maintain links to other sources of information.

Networks also tend to concentrate linkages around key nodes as centers of power. This leaves the network vulnerable when key nodes fail. Distributed centers create redundant paths. The disadvantages are the network complexity and difficulties of making decisions. Realistic solutions lie in limiting decisions, controlling the flow of information and delegation of authority to decentralized centers as a form of federal organization. Another solution separates operating units with interdependent operating decisions from strategic decision-making.

The Social Implications of Networks

In any given network there is a power structure in which individual players have different relative strengths as a basis to act and influence actions of other players. The power structure determines the role and position of the individual firm in relation to other firms in the network. The perception of the firm's role and position in the network defines the firm's strategic identity as it is shaped and developed through interaction with other firms. This power structure, combined with the players' common interest and contradictions influence the development of the network. Common interests could be product development for successful introduction in the final market. Contradiction is expressed in conflict, such as buyers and sellers negotiating for price and profit margins. Thus, there exists a condition of mutual interaction between the strategic identity of a firm, development of the firm's own industrial activities and its relations with other firms in the network.

A specific network is one of a large number of possible structures. By establishing new relations, finding new candidates or making new investments, the firm will strive to use the network to create a competitively advantageous position. In a network strategy, a central element is the ability to influence both direct and indirect players through the direct partners. Thus, firms in a supply chain not only influence suppliers and customers, but also their suppliers' suppliers and customers' customers. The performance of a firm depends not only on how efficiently it cooperates with its direct partners, but also on how well they co-operate with their own partners. The network connects players who may also belong to other networks so there may also be influence from resource and market competitors.

Haakansson and Johanson (1990) distinguish between *formal* and *informal networks*. This distinction is relevant for the management of supply chains for several reasons. First, formal cooperation between firms in a network is visible both to the firms involved and to outside observers.

Second, informal but less externally visible cooperation is based on trust developed through social exchange processes. Informal cooperation develops as a consequence of mutual interests from business transactions. It fosters a climate of cooperation, which gradually develops from repeated transactions into a single sourcing arrangement, often without a formal contract. In formal cooperation, visualization comes first through specific agreements, but the actual cooperation depends on trust between the parties. For example, formal cooperation with a third-party logistics provider begins with a contract, but gradually may turn into a more informal trust relationship.

Third, informal cooperation often develops between personnel directly involved in operations, whereas formal cooperation often is established at a strategic management level. Both formal and informal relations can create »entry barriers« against new external players, as well as »exit barriers« for the partners involved.

From network theory, a firm's relations with other firms often constitute its most valuable resources. Access to complementary resources in other firms becomes an important asset. Nelson and Winter (1982) point out that invisible assets (tacit knowledge) play a central role in sustaining the competitiveness of a firm because of causal ambiguity and difficulties in imitation. Causal ambiguity exists when the link between the resources controlled by a firm and a firm's competitive advantage is difficult for other firms to understand and imitate (Barney 1999). The invisible assets are often created internally and cannot be separated from external relations. If the network is broken, the invisible assets also disappear. This becomes an important reason for network relations to become stable over time.

The premise of the network perspective is that the firm's continuous interaction with other players becomes important in developing new resources and competencies. It changes the focus from how the firm allocates and structures its internal resources towards relating its activities and resources to those of other players in the supply chain. Network theory makes an essential contribution to the understanding of the dynamics of inter-organizational relations, emphasizing the importance of »personal chemistry« between parties, the build-up of trust through positive long-term co-operative relations and the mutual adjustment of routines and systems.

However, there are also paradoxes within the network perspective (Haakansson & Ford 2002, Gadde et al. 2003). The first is related to how a firm becomes embedded in its network. The more investments the firm and its partners have committed to the network and the stronger the ties to other actors in the network, the less freedom the firm has to act. The network as a resource constellation may create inertia that limits innovation, but may also create a platform for new development. A change in a network involves changing the interconnected firms and their relationships. Therefore, a decision by a firm wanting to change its logistics system is dependent on approval and actions of others. The costs and time involved in building relationships with other firms in the network makes it difficult for a firm to achieve change by seeking new partners. The knowledge and mutual understanding that has developed over time in existing relationships will disappear if the firm choose new ones. Therefore, it is often more cost-effective to implement changes in existing relationships than to establish new relationships.

The second paradox reflects a firm's relationships as a result of its strategy and actions, but at the same time, the firm itself is a result of the history of its relationships with other firms. Thus the firm and its network have a mutual influence on each other. This paradox emphasizes the importance of choosing the right partners. »No business is an island« (Haakansson & Snehota 1989). It also means that the strategy process of the firm is interactive, evolutionary, responsive, and developed in conjunction with its partnerships.

The third paradox is related to controlling the network. Each firm tries to control its surrounding network and manage relationships with the other actors in the network to achieve its own goals. However, the more the firm succeeds, the less effective and innovative might be the network. A dominant firm in a network might control its partners to an extent that the network becomes a hierarchy and other firms effectively disappear. A controlled network cannot develop faster than the firm that controls it. The automobile (e.g. SMART Car) and fashion industries (e.g. Benetton and Zara) are examples of networks tightly controlled by the dominant firm. In these networks, actions of other participants depend on the decisions of the focal company.

Transactions

Networks establish a framework for inter-organizational relationships. These include a wide range of behaviors, from simple buyer-seller market transactions to long-term collaboration that lead to innovation and close integration of operations. The first is straightforward: it is focused on single exchanges without necessarily implied continuation beyond the immediate event. Anything else however involves mutual obligations, sometimes bound by contract, other times by implied agreements, and reinforced by continued relationships.

The concept of a transaction bears some explanation. While the acts of buying and selling become a transaction, we mean here a relationship beyond a simple exchange, the nature of the link between two parties. It is more than a single act at arm's-length, but a continual sequence of acts. This point needs emphasis in an electronic age when simple exchanges are almost costless.

In this discussion, we begin with the nature of contracts. We then move to transaction cost analysis (TCA), which provides the basis for analysis of inter-organizational relationships. The models under discussion are founded in theory, but they provide a platform to illustrate possibilities in arrangements.

The Firm as a Nexus of Contracts

Principal-agent theory focuses on the optimal contract between a principal and an agent. The simple model assumes goal conflicts between the principal and the agent, an easily measured outcome, and an agent who is more risk averse than the principal (Eisenhardt 1989:60). It can be applied to many relationships, e.g. employer-employee, buyer-supplier, and shipper-third party logistics provider. The contract is the basic unit of analysis, and the firm is considered as a nexus of internal and external contracts (Reve 1990).

The most efficient contract governing the principal-agent relationship depends on a wide range of variables such as outcome uncertainty, self-interest behavior, goal conflict, bounded rationality, information asymmetry, measurability of outcomes, task programmability, relation length, difference in risk preferences, and whether information itself is a commodity to be purchased (Eisenhardt 1989:58).

There are two important aspects of the agency problem: Moral hazard and adverse selection. *Moral hazard* refers to lack of effort on the part of the agent that has been agreed-upon in advance, e.g. a distributor, who is not advertising and selling the principal's products according to the contract. *Adverse selection* refers to a situation where the agent claims to have certain skills, when the contract is agreed-upon, but the principal cannot completely verify them at the time the contract is signed or while the agent is working. An example is a subcontractor, who claims to have the necessary competencies to produce a specific component for the principal but fails through lack of skills or knowledge. In supply chains, principal-agent theory has been applied in multiple areas, such as designing successful outsourcing relationships (Logan 2000), and managing risks in supply chains (Zsidisin & Ellram 2003).

The optimal contract would align *incentives*, which are outcome-based or behavior-based to the objectives of the contract. Outcome-based incentives are used when outcome uncertainty is low and measurability is high. Behavior-based contracts are used when uncertainty is high, the agent's risk aversion is high, and the principal's risk aversion is low. Also in situations when task programmability is high and information systems can reveal the agent's behavior to the principal, and when principal and agent are engaged in a long-term relationship behavior-based contracts are preferable.

Boundaries and Governance

Managing the supply chain, and its governance, is determined by organizational structure, which is in turn determined by the boundaries of individual firms within the supply chain. Defining boundaries is therefore the point of departure. Which activities should be performed within the boundary of each firm and which activities should be outsourced? Boundaries and product definition are closely related. TCA (Williamson 1975, 1985, 1996) presents an economic approach for determining boundaries, based on characteristics related to the transactions. Williamson distinguishes among three different governance structures for managing business exchanges: markets, hierarchies, and hybrid organizations. The most efficient governance (organizational) structure minimizes transaction costs.

Transaction costs are »the costs of running the economic system« (Williamson 1985:18). These costs can be divided into two categories – ex ante and ex post costs. *Ex ante costs* involve searching for and evaluating business partners and the costs of drafting, negotiating, and safeguarding an agreement (contract costs). *Ex post costs* include enforcing agreements, negotiation to correct misalignments and mechanisms associated with solving disputes between the parties.

An example illustrates the difference. A firm has to find a new supplier for a specific component. In order to find the right supplier, the firm searches among potential suppliers, evaluates, and selects the most appropriate one. Then, the firm negotiates and creates a contract acceptable to both parties. These are *ex ante* costs. After the contract is signed, there may be costs from differing interpretations, enforcement, and procedures for conflict resolution. These are *ex post* costs. However, there is a close relationship between ex ante and ex post costs. Logically, careful performance during the search and contracting stages can reduce ex post costs substantially.

TCA rests on two basic behavioral presumptions about management perception:

- Bounded rationality
- Risk of opportunistic behavior

Bounded rationality results from insufficient information, limits in management perception or limited capacity for information processing. The actors may try to act rationally, however their intellect or inability to communicate their knowledge or opinions to others restricts their ability to foresee or act. The concept is particularly relevant to complex and uncertain environments such as product development in high technology. In an ex ante situation with bounded rationality, management may not be able to identify and consider all potential options, future risks, and opportunities as the contract is negotiated. In addition, control in the ex post phase only provides limited capacity to control the results.

This may lead managers to adopt opportunistic behavior. Williamson defines it as »self-interest seeking with guile«. He does not presume that all players act in an opportunistic way, but that some players sometimes will behave opportunistically, it is difficult to predict who will be opportunistic and when it will occur.

Williamson further identifies three characteristics related to transactions, which determine the most efficient governance structure:

- Asset specificity
- Uncertainty
- Frequency

Asset specificity is considered to be the most influential factor on governance structure. An asset becomes specific as it relates uniquely to a specific transaction, with a limited value in alternative applications. Williamson identifies several types of asset specificity: physical specificity (e.g. customized tools and investment in research and development), site specificity, (referring to location of successive but immobile production stages close to one another (e.g. a seat supplier, locating their plant close to a car assembly plant), human specificity (e.g. employee training dedicated to specific customers' requirements) and reputation (e.g. brand loyalty).

Figure 3.3. Governance Structures and Transaction Characteristics

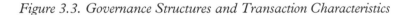

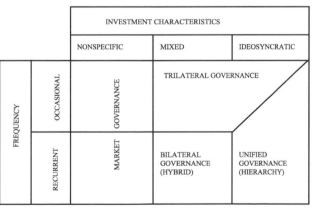

Source: Williamson, 1985, p. 79

Hierarchy (vertical integration) may be the most efficient governance structure in situations characterized by great uncertainty, high transaction frequency, and high asset specificity. This structure favors complex decision-making and a high volume of communication and absorption of risk from uncertainty and specialized assets. For lesser specificity, Williamson recommends »hybrid« governance structures that mix elements both of markets and hierarchy. When asset investments are not tied to specific transactions, the market becomes the most efficient mechanism. Figure 3.3 shows alternative combinations of transaction frequency and asset specificity and presumes that all transactions take place under uncertainty.

The reality is that in a world of costless exchange and freely available information, vertical integration through ownership may not be absolutely necessary. Suppliers and buyers can deal jointly with technical and management problems over the net with e-mail and specifically focused software. Suppliers may even work in a buyer's production facility.

Williamson assumes that transactions often begin in an »ex ante situation« with many potential business partners (large numbers bargaining). The bargaining position of the buyer is strongest at that point. A »fundamental transformation« with selection and negotiation, leads to an »ex post« situation with only a few partners (small numbers bargaining). After having established close relationships with some suppliers and invested in relation-specific assets, switching costs and risk may be high.

To protect against opportunistic behavior, Williamson advocates »safeguards« to ensure that the other party does not take advantage of the situation. These safeguards may take on two forms:

- Legal ordering
- Private agreements

The first implies that the parties enter into a formal contract covering as many aspects of the relationship as possible, sometimes denoted as a *relational contract*. In case the contract is violated by one of the parties, the court solves the dispute. The latter form presumes that the parties will try to reach a balance of reciprocity. In case of disagreement, the dispute is solved by direct negotiations between the parties or via third party arbitration, accepted by both parties. The parties may also enter into joint ventures, exchange stocks, or make specific investments in the relationship (credible commitments). As a metaphor Williamson talks about the exchange of »hostages«. An example is a buyer and a supplier, who exchange employees in order to solve problems in inter-firm relations. In other contexts, these become boundary-spanning or liaison positions.

The assumptions and implications of TCA have been examined by several economists and management theorists (Noorderhaven 1995, Barney 1999, Cox 1996, Ghoshal & Moran 1996, Zajac & Olsen 1993). The major discussion points are taken up below.

- TCA is essentially a static theory
- The behavioral assumption of opportunistic behavior excludes business relationships based on trust
- TCA focuses solely on cost efficiency and does not take into consideration the mutual value creation in the relationship
- Asset Specificity based on »Sunk Costs«
- Too costly to develop or acquire the specific assets

Static versus Dynamic Boundaries

TCA implicitly assumes in the long run that only the most efficient governance forms survive, but the theory does not explain transition from one form to another. For example, what happens if technology or the competitive environment changes? Noorderhaven (1995) has set up a dynamic model for shifts from one governance structure to another. The model is shown in figure 3.4. The development of specific human assets often takes place gradually and almost imperceptibly in the relation between two parties. For example, a relationship between a manufacturer and a supplier might develop into a trust relationship over a long period of time, where the partners gradually learn to know its others' preferences and administrative routines. Thus, it is not always a question of abrupt and fundamental transformation, as in the case of investing in physical assets (machines, buildings). Therefore, the parties are not always aware of a need for safeguards, as the changes take place incrementally.

Supply chain relationships often develop over years of experience. Often, business exchanges may rely on informal contracts and personnel of the organizations involved have acquired an in-depth knowledge of procedures, routines and personal preferences of each other. Formal safeguards such as detailed contracts may be unsatisfactory or are often not even available.

Figure 3.4. Dynamic Model of Governance Structures

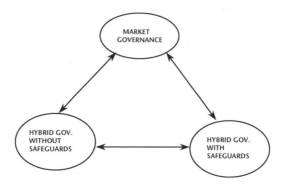

Changes can take place between three principal forms of governance structures: Market mechanism, hybrids with built-in safeguards, and hybrids without safeguards. One example of a hybrid structure with safeguards is collaboration between a manufacturer and a component supplier based on a long-term contract with penalty clauses for quality and delivery defaults. A hybrid without safeguards could involve informal collaboration relying on mutual trust.

Noorderhaven (1995) makes several propositions about this transition. One is that a *rapid build-up* of specific assets will lead to a hybrid with safeguards. A *slow build-up*, on the other hand, will lead to a hybrid without safeguards. A rapid build-up could involve a multinational company entering the European market and establishing a Pan-European delivery contract with a third-party logistics provider. A slow build-up could involve the transfer of tacit knowledge between two partners about administrative routines.

Is Transaction Cost Theory »Bad for Practice«?

Ghoshal & Moran (1996) criticize Williamson's opportunistic behavior as »bad for practice«. Assumping opportunism can become self-fulfilling, causing opportunistic behavior to increase along with sanctions and incentives imposed to curtail it, and creating a need for stronger and more elaborate sanctions and incentives. An exaggerated emphasis does not encourage employee initiatives, cooperativeness, and motivation. It may even stifle the elements that could increase the competitive ability of the firm.

Long-term efficiency, including innovation and collective learning, becomes the deciding criterion. Innovation is often characterized by high uncertainty and ambiguity, relying on strong trust and commitment. Collective learning in a supply chain is only possible if the partners have developed trust and are willing to share knowledge and experiences. The original TCA is only useful in a limited set of business relationships, with stable business environments and stagnating industries. When firms are in dynamic and innovative environments – then they must rely on trust.

TCA Focuses on Cost Efficiency

The efficiency criterion is based on minimizing transaction costs for the individual firm and fails to consider the joint value of long-term cooperation instead of cost minimization for one party, the efficiency criterion should maximize the *joint transaction value* of a given transaction for the parties involved (Zajac & Olsen 1993).

Transaction value includes transaction costs as a subset of the total costs of inter-organizational cooperation. These costs in turn must be compared against the total advantages from cooperation to assess the overall result. Thus, transaction value is broader than transaction costs alone and includes the joint values and transaction costs associated with inter-organizational cooperation.

High asset specificity does not necessarily lead to increased transaction costs (Dyer 1997). Williamson argues that higher asset specificity leads to complex contracts and safeguards. However, Dyer compared supplier-auto assembler relationships in the USA and Japan, finding that Japanese automakers had lower transaction costs, even though the Japanese made higher specific investments in supplier relationships. Japanese car manufacturers do not control opportunism through legal contracts as do their US counter partners, but instead rely on other self-enforcing safeguards such as relational trust and stock ownership. According to Dyer, these safeguards might have high initial »set-up« costs but once established they have relatively low transaction costs.

Asset Specificity based on »Sunk Costs«

Cox (1996) criticizes TCA from a more strategic perspective. His major criticism is that the concept asset specificity is based on »sunk costs«. When assets of high asset specificity have been embedded in the firm, the related transactions should be internalized. However, Cox states that companies are then likely to hold to one operating structure and therefore not able to respond to strategic changes. The sunk costs of past transactions should not lead to stagnation, but whether or not the skills, knowledge or assets contribute to creating sustainable advantage.

Thus, asset specificity relates to competence and revenue. High asset specificity is directly connected to *core competencies* and therefore should be kept internally. For medium asset specificity, the skills, knowledge and technology become *complementary competencies* and can be provided by external partners. Low specificity becomes *residual competencies*, and can be acquired on market terms because they are standardized, from a large number of suppliers.

Too Costly to Develop or Acquire Specific Assets

Barney (1999) criticizes TCA for not considering the relative capabilities of a firm and its exchange partners. In a situation where the firm does not possess all the capabilities itself, it has three ways of gaining access:

- Cooperation with firms that possess the capabilities it needs.
- Try to develop the capabilities internally (hierarchy)
- Try to acquire another firm with these capabilities (hierarchy)

The choice should depend on the level of transaction-specific investments. With high investments, the firm should either develop its own capabilities or acquire another related firm, i.e. hierarchical governance. If this proves too costly the firm might use other governance structures, even with a high risk of opportunism.

The Internet, e-commerce and other forms of telecommunication present a new limit to TCA. Formal organizations are above all devices for communication through personal contact, bureaucratic procedure, and documentation. Modern information and telecommunication systems (ITC) replace the need to internalize many activities within the firm with external coordination. The complexity appears to be comparable. When messages are transmitted electronically, transaction cost decreases, with incentive to outsource activities to other organizations.

Modern management delegates decision-making to autonomous units within an organization for flexibility, supporting outsourcing. The supply chain appears to be characterized by arrangements that involve close cooperation between independent firms. This change does not always lead to market solutions, but in some cases to integration without the necessity for ownership.

Perceptions of Trust

The concept of trust is central in understanding how inter-organizational relationships develop. At the same time, trust is a diffuse concept, defined in different ways, depending on whether the perspective is psychological, sociological, anthropological, or economic. Thus, there is no generally accepted definition of the concept of trust.

Williamson (1993) defines three forms of trust: personal, calculative, and institutional trust. He decided that personal trust is not relevant in business, although personal relationships across organizational boundaries become a building block for other relationships.

Calculative trust (or risk) is based on the penalties of acting opportunistically exceeding the expected benefits. Each party is assumed to calculate the costs and benefits. *Institutional trust* relates to the specific environment of the transaction. It might be culturally based, the meaning of trust in Japanese business relationships differs from that in Western business relationships, »differential trustworthiness is rarely transparent ex ante. As a consequence, ex ante screening efforts are made and ex post safeguards are created«. Thus, trust is founded on an assumption that the other party acts from self-interest by not acting opportunistically.

Sako (1992) proposes a different conception of trust. She identifies three types:

- Contractual trust
- Competence trust
- Goodwill trust

In *contractual trust,* the trade partners can expect written or oral promises to be kept. This is important in all market transactions where a buyer relies on a vendor to deliver according to prior (ex ante) agreements. *Competence trust* means having confidence in a partner's ability and resources to carry out a specific task, e.g. the carrier's capability to transport the goods from A to B without damage or delays.

Goodwill trust is more diffuse and difficult to define, reflecting a willingness to go beyond formal agreements to do whatever is required, such as exceeding the customer's expectations, offering preferential treatment or additional help when necessary. Supply chain management assumes the existence of goodwill trust, supplemented by contract. The parties are expected to share both gains and risks equitably. It is not an immediate reciprocal relationship, but one of a common vision and long run reward.

Barney and Hansen (1994) discuss how trustworthiness becomes a source of competitive advantage. They define trust as »the mutual confidence that no party to an exchange will exploit another's vulnerabilities.« They also distinguish between trust and trustworthiness. Trust is characteristic of relations among parties, while trustworthiness is a *characteristic* of the individual partners. A partner is trustworthy when he is worthy of other people's trust. Barney and Hansen establish three types of trust:

- Weak (limited possibilities of opportunism)
- Semi-strong (trust through regulations)
- Strong (»hard-core« trustworthiness)

Situations of weak and semi-strong trust can usually be regulated through the market with adequate economic and social safeguards. In situations requiring strong trust, trustworthy behavior usually rests on values, principles, and standards, internalized in the parties to a commercial exchange.

Barney and Hansen's principal thesis is that the vulnerability in strong trust situations is so great, relative to the opportunism of the other party that it is not possible to establish ex post economic and social governance structures. If the parties have sufficiently strong trust in each other, they can establish a competitive advantage over other partners without such a high level of interpersonal trust. Consider a firm considering cooperation with a rival firm to develop new, advanced technology, with great risk, but also large potential earnings if they succeed. Firms that develop strong mutual trust with partners have greater opportunities from cooperation for competitive advantage than firms that must protect themselves through safeguards. In supply chains where innovation plays a major role, strong trust is essential for developing inter-organizational relations.

Authority (hierarchy), price (market exchanges) and trust (hybrid) represent three different modes of governance mechanisms. Authority means monitoring through commands, rules, and procedures. Price regulates the market. Trust on the other hand implies monitoring through social norms, sanctions, and personal relationships. Governance of supply chains becomes a combination of control, market mechanisms, and trust. According to TCA, the actors secure their interests by developing formal structures as safeguards. In the network approach the actors secure their interests by developing trust relationships.

Developing Collaborative Relationships

Trust evolves over time. Most business relations have started as arm's length exchanges, and have only gradually changed into collaborate relationships. Ring and Van de Ven (1994) have developed a model that describes the different phases, which the parties undergo in developing inter-organizational cooperation. The model is shown in figure 3.5.

Ring and Van de Ven describe a three-phase iterative process:

- Negotiation
- Commitment
- Execution

Figure 3.5. Process Model of Interorganizational Relations

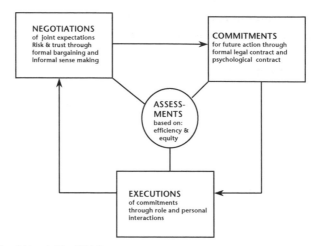

Source: Ring & Van de Ven (1004)

Each phase is rated regarding both efficiency and equity between parties. The duration depends on the level of uncertainty involved in each particular case, the degree of trust and the role of relationships between the parties.

The Ring and Van de Ven model from cooperation emphasizes the importance of a balance between formal and informal relations. If informal relations are overemphasized, there is a risk that the business relationship depends too much on relations between competencies of individuals. If one or more of these individuals should leave the firm, the business relationship risks falling apart. Conversely, focusing on formal contracts that try to allow for any conceivable situation may involve the risk of disintegrating cooperation, as trust within the relations is lacking. The relative weighting between formal and informal relations changes over time. Formal relations weigh in more at the beginning of inter-organizational cooperation, but informal relations increase in weight as personal and social relations develop between the parties.

The Ring and Van de Ven model describes, how inter-oranzational relations develop over time and why relations cease to exist. Thus, the model supplements the network perspective, which is largely concerned with the initial development of these relations.

Conclusion

The network perspective on supply chains requires a holistic approach. It recognizes the interdependence not only of immediate partners but also among the entire network of relationships. The movement of organizations toward network relationships places new challenges on management: 1) to define the core and establish the boundaries of the firm, 2) to create the most effective governance mechanisms and 3) to develop the most appropriate relationships with partners. The success of the supply chain depends not only on defining these relationships, but also on managing and developing them over time.

Trust relationships are a necessary condition in supply chain management. Without it, partners will not share information or commit to specific high-risk investments. Establishing trust is essential to collaboration. It is time-consuming and is based on building positive experience. In the turbulent world of the supply chain, however, formal relationships cannot deal with its full complexity. Devices such as relational contracting may be the only feasible course, where the details are left for later decision.

The essential characteristic of the supply chain is its inter-organizational relationships. The ability to develop and manage the supply chain becomes a core competency, along with product technology, knowledge, and market access these relationships govern future actions of the corporation.

Illustrative Case

Benetton's Supply Networks[1]

The Benetton family founded Benetton S.p.A., the Italian-based fashion retailer and manufacturer, in 1965. It has become one of Europe's largest clothing companies. Today, the Benetton Group is present in 120 countries around the world. Among its brands is

---

1. Material for this case came from www.Benetton.com, Harrison 1994, Jarillo and Martinez 1994, Jarillo and Stevenson 1991, Ketelhöhn 1993, Rovizzi and Thompson 1992, and Camuffo 2001.

casual *United Colors of Benetton*, fashion oriented *Sisley*, leisurewear *Playlife* and streetwear *Killer Loop*. The Group produces around 115 million garments every year. Its retail network of 5,000 retail stores around the world generate in 2005 a total turnover of approximately 1.8 billion Euros. The Benetton production system is co-ordinated by a high-tech facility in Castrette (Treviso), covering more nearly 1.2 million square feet. This facility is one of the most advanced clothing-manufacturing complexes in the world.

The development of Benetton's commercial organization has been supported by a major programme of investment in megastores, some of which are directly managed by the Group. These stores are characterized by their large dimensions, their prime site locations in historic and commercial centers, and by the high level of customer services they offer. The new Benetton megastores carry complete casual womenswear, menswear, childrenswear and underwear collections, as well as a wide selection of accessories. However, most of the stores are own by independent store managers, who have signed franchise agreements with Benetton.

A global information system links stores, sales agents, distribution center, manufacturing, suppliers, subcontractors and carriers.

The structure of Benetton's supply chain is shown in Figure 3.6.

Figure 3.6. Benetton's Supply Chain

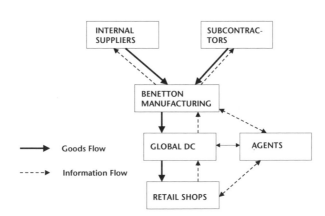

DC: distribution centers

Measurement of all items are kept in a CAD/CAM system, so if a store in San Francisco were to run out of a hot-selling pink sweater, the store would call the US sales agent, who would send a replenishment order to the mainframe computer in Italy. If the sweater is in their automated distribution center, it will be picked by a robot and shipped to the store within a week. If the sweater is not in stock, its measurements are transmitted to a knitting machine, and it is produced and bar-coded with a code containing the address of the store and sent to the distribution center. From there it is consolidated with other orders and shipped directly to the store. Benetton can produce and deliver garments anywhere in the world within 10 days of orders being taken. The rapid replenishment cycle enables stores to postpone ordering until the trend of sales is determined.

One »secret« behind Benetton's flexibility and response to changes in the market place is its supply chain organization. Benetton outsources most of the production processes to over 500 subcontractors, 90 percent of them located in the Veneto region of northeastern Italy. Benetton supplies raw materials and in-process goods, generates production plans and materials requirements, and provides technical and administrative support. Benetton also occasionally takes the investment risk away from the subcontractors by providing them with highly specialized knitting machines with a high risk of obsolescence. The only production processes that remain in-house are grading, marking, dyeing, and cutting operations where scale of economies can be realized or that require special skills or technology. Dyeing is one of these processes. It involves complicated chemical processes, and cutting is performed through advanced CAD/CAM systems.

Benetton performs most of the design work. Purchasing of raw materials is also centralized to obtain the benefits of buying power and knowledge of commodity markets. The Benetton Group is the largest producer of wool in Patagonia, Chile, and is able to control the production cycle from »sheep to sweater«. Benetton only uses 10 percent of its own production of wool, but running the sheep ranches enables the firm to improve the technology of wool production and to strengthen its negotiating power with suppliers.

Benetton has recently moved to more upscale clothing and transformed its global network (Camuffo, 2001). Upstream, they have gradually increased vertical integration of textile and thread suppliers to ensure direct control over the supply of materials and exercise quality control sooner. Benetton can then send the materials directly to the production facilities without further checks and thereby reduce both transport costs and production lead times. Downstream, they have set up a number of mega stores throughout the world owned and managed by Benetton itself. This allows Benetton to get closer to end customers and collect data on their last-minute needs and expectations. At the same time, Benetton has reduced the basic product assortment and increased the number of flash seasonal collections to respond faster to changes in market trends. In other words, as Benetton transforms its product line from relatively more functional products to relatively more fashionable clothing, it is restructuring its organization from an intermediate governance structure consisting of close cooperation with key suppliers towards a more hierarchical governance structure resorting to vertical integration.

Benetton's production network has surprising similarities to the Toyota System. Benetton has a few family-owned plants, all located within the immediate region of Benetton's headquarters in Treviso. Benetton also owns its own spinning mills. However, most labor-intensive and low-wage work is performed by subcontractors, organized in a hierarchical network similar to the supplier structure found with Japanese car manufacturers. The first-tier suppliers are medium-sized subcontractors who work closely with the Benetton plants. These contractors in turn manage their own relationships with lower-tier suppliers located in the same industrial regions in southern Italy or in other low-wage regions abroad. Lower-tier subcontractors are typically small, family-owned firms, highly specialized, employing unskilled, non-union workers. The lowest tier consists of small workshops and »cottage industry« workers. This evolving production form is sometimes called »decentralized Fordism« or *concentration without centralization* (Harrison 1994). The structure of Benetton's production system is shown in Figure 3.7.

These production networks provide Benetton with clear advantages compared to competitors with more traditional in-house production. If demand increases more than expected the subcontractors will work over-time and weekends, avoiding the costs and union problems of in-house production. The subcontractors will often have less than 15 employees in order to save on social security costs. It is also easier to increase or reduce capacity, because these small entrepreneurs are more flexible and often capable of performing a variety of working processes. Benetton also divides orders among a large number of subcontractors to minimize individual risks. Benetton guarantees work for these subcontractors throughout the season. On the other hand, Benetton expects the subcontractors to be willing to carry the set-up costs associated with short-term shifts in the production mix. An additional benefit to Benetton is the effect of continuous improvements in efficiency by the subcontractors.

Figure 3.7. Benetton Production System
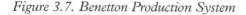

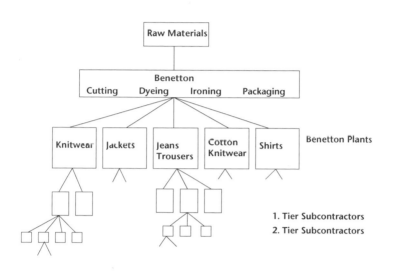

The subcontractors could run major risks by investing in new machinery. In the past, subcontractors have been stuck with knitting machines that were useless because of changes in fashion trends. Benetton facilitates change of outdated machinery both by buying it and by giving the subcontractors wide margins on some orders, which allow them to re-invest in new machines.

Benetton has a policy of encouraging employees to start and run their own subcontracting units. In return, it requires exclusivity. This clearly imposes problems with decreasing demand because they have no alternative customers. However, many subcontractors are closely interrelated through family or business relationships and share workloads. The relationship between Benetton and its network of subcontractors has been described as an »umbilical cord.« Benetton's plant managers know each subcontractor and his or her

family personally. Manufacturing people visit subcontractors frequently and have daily communication with them by phone. This
allows them to solve problems quickly and to make adjustments to
production plans.

Most competitors within the garment industry have moved the
manufacturing to low-cost countries in eastern Europe or East Asia.
Benetton still concentrates most of its manufacturing within northern
Italy. The company has set up manufacturing plants outside Italy,
e.g. in France, Scotland, Spain, and the USA, primarily to bypass
trade barriers in these countries. In the future, Benetton expects
rapid increase in sales to Asia and South America. This will move
production to joint ventures in countries such as Japan, China, India,
Argentina, Brazil, Mexico and Turkey and add complexity to the
supply chain.

4. The Information System for the Supply Chain

»Information has economic value if it leads to the satisfaction of human desires. A small portion of that is final goods, which derive their value from supply and demand. By far the larger portion is intermediate goods that derive their value substantially from the value of the goods and services to which they lead.«

(Dertouzos 1997: 236)

Introduction

SCM is more than managing the flow of goods. Managing information is essential for process, planning and control. Information networks both parallel and extend beyond physical operations to reach organizations that do not actually become directly involved with product flow. (See Figure 4.1).

IT has changed business operations through the flow of information, control over operations remote in distance and across organizational boundaries, and by automation of processes. IT also shapes the future development of the supply chain with Internet technology, that currently offers fast and easy ways to transmit complicated information and has considerable future potential. IT is no longer driven by a search for efficiency alone but as an enabler of new opportunity. No business can ignore the power of IT to transform operations and strategy.

The most important contribution is to bring visibility to the entire supply chain. The challenge of SCM is to deal with a complex process, coupled with exposure to tremendous uncertainty in the environment. Companies at one stage in the chain might not be aware of actual customer demand, they may face late deliveries from suppliers. The result is often out-of-stock situations or unreliable deliveries. The solution to reduce uncertainty historically was to buffer resources through inventory or capacity, a costly practice that has been traditional in industry. In the case of the US-American consumer goods industry or the textile industry, studies have shown that excess inventory in the total channel was in the region of approximately US$ 30 billion in consumer goods and about US$ 25 billion in textiles (e.g. Kotzab 1999).

Figure 4.1. The Information System

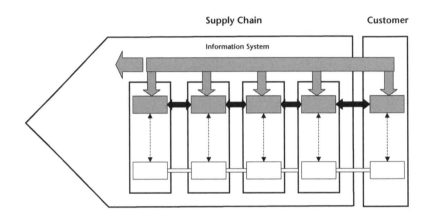

An alternative is to improve the ability to handle information and establishing cross-functional coordination (e.g. Galbraith 1977). Application of IT within the supply chain reduces unnecessary inventory, leading to substituting information for inventory. IT enlarges the scope of management and allows managers to make informed operational decisions in a variety of areas where information was previously lacking. IT becomes a vehicle to monitor and control operations without regard to geographic location. IT also allows supply chain partners to coordinate operations using common data.

Information technology can automate processes such as documentation and internal operation routines. Orders can be processed and result in complete fulfillment without human intervention. Automation, however, has limits. There are inherent dangers of supply chains going out of control from data errors and incomplete decision rules when they are left to their own devices and not subject to human supervision (Wilding 1998). Small data errors become amplified and potentially create havoc over time.

The information system becomes the glue of the supply chain. Visibility through operating data coordinates operations, either through automated tasks or management surveillance. IT can provide managers with overall direction for strategic decisions, to match market requirements with resource allocations to optimize the system. IT is the basis for developing the supply chain as the extended enterprise (Tapscott 1995) or even borderless company (Picot et al. 2001). The concept of the supply chain as a network of separate organizations becomes the foundation for redefining the concept of the enterprise as we enter the age of the network economy.

The promise and the danger of IT comes from the rapidity of the changes now taking place. Much of the description of the supply chain information system is transitory. The transition from stand-alone applications to direct inter-functional and inter-organizational communication created the supply chain. The movement to real-time operation has forced functional integration to execute operations. The transition from relatively fixed to flexible networks will change from permanent to more temporary structures.

This chapter focuses on several distinct areas:

- Logistics information
- Information exchange
- Information and operations
- The concept of a supply chain information system
- Elements of the information systems
- Software systems

Logistics Information

Logistics as well as SCM are defined as the management of the flow of goods and related information, which we call logistics information. Gudehus (2005:462) differs between various types of logistics information that can mainly be grouped into logistics master data and logistics transaction data based on its stability. A fraction of logistics information that exists in logistic systems is shown in Table 4.1.

Table 4.1. Characteristics of logistics information

Logistics information	
Logistics master data	Logistics transaction data

• Article- and order-based data
  ° Addresses
  ° Article numbers
  ° Measures of units
  ° Prices
	• Article- and order-based data
	  ° Delivery quantities
	  ° Delivery times requirements
	  ° Number of delivery units
	  ° Number of shipping units

• Location-based supplier logistics data
  ° Shipping dock information (number of doors, areas, buffer capacities, shipment control)
  ° Delivery channels
• Location-based operation logistics data
  ° Receiving dock information (number of doors, areas, buffer capacities, incoming control)
  ° Shipping dock information (number of doors, areas, buffer capacities, shipment control)
  ° Inventory areas (storage types, capacities and marginal performance of given storage systems
	• Location-based supplier logistics data
	  ° Delivery addresses
	  ° Delivery times, shipment times, operating times
	• Location-based operation logistics data
	  ° Picking information (types, capacities, marginal performances)
	  ° Number of used logistics units
	  ° Operating times, collection times, standard delivery times

• Logistics unit data
  ° Identification number
  ° Technical-functional name
  ° Measures
  ° Sizes
  ° Weights
  ° Restrictions coding
	• Logistics unit data
	  ° Number of logistics units and packaging units
	  ° Number of loading equipment and transport means

Logistics information can be grouped according to its functionality into (Bowersox et al. 2002: 192, see also Figure 4.2):

- Transactional information (formalized, standardized and routine information that records individual logistics activities and functions)
- Management control information (information on performance measurements)
- Decision analysis information (information that helps to identify, evaluate and to compare strategic and tactical logistic alternatives)
- Strategic planning information (information for wide-range business planning and decision-making models).

Figure 4.2. Logistics information pyramid

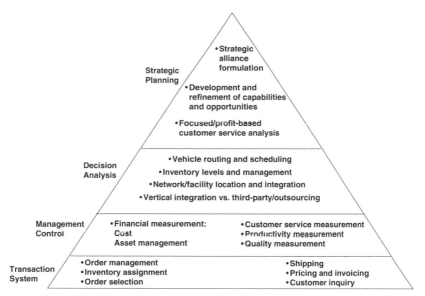

Source: Bowersox et al. (2002:192)

We stress this differentiation as more and more of the current literature suggests that implementing logistics information management systems provides suppliers, located upstream, the information required from their customers' to plan according to real demand, and to avoid forecasting with highly inaccurate data. Based on the presented differentiation, this can be a complex task which is therefore more frequently organized in an automated manner by the use of ERP systems using SCM-software (e.g. Simchi-Levi et al. 2003: 284).

However, the underlying hypothesis within the field is the more information exchanged, the better the outcome of a logistics system in terms of time, quality and speed. We have to differentiate and acknowledge that information can flow within the firm (intra-firm information flow) and between firms (inter-firm information flow). When it comes to inter-firm information flow, standardization issues are especially relevant. The most common tool is known as Electronic Data Interchange (EDI) (Hsie & Lin 2004). Today, new standardised applications, which rely on the use of the Internet, have been a driver that has improved companies' abilities to better handle information from other companies in supply chains (Premkumar 2000).

Information Exchange

The information flow in a traditional supply chain setting refers to the simple moving of orders which represent information often decoupled from real (independent) demand. This traditional way turns real (independent) demand into distorted dependent demand with the consequence of upstream amplification of order quantities.

From this point of view, the need for transparency or visibility, as well as exchange of information, becomes obvious. The power of information sharing and exchange is shown in Figure 4.3. The upper part of the figure shows the traditional information flow between the different stages of a supply chain. Information flow refers to orders that are sequentially passed from one stage to the other. No stage has visibility or transparency on the processes of the previous or subsequent stage.

The power of information visibility within the supply chain has already been emphasized (Forrester 1961, Bowersox 1969). In the last 10 years, Lee et al. (1997) presented the bullwhip-effect as a consequence of an obscured supply chain, where real demand is hidden, and results in wide aberrations in reported demand. The solution is to make real demand visible to the entire supply chain with minimal delay and distortion.

Figure 4.3 Information Flow in Traditional and Modern Supply Chain Settings

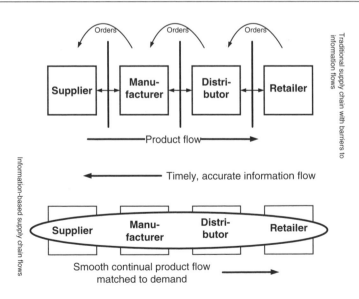

Information and Operations

The basic requirement for optimizing the total supply chain is to integrate information processing involving all supply chain actors. This requires inter-organizational integrated information systems (Hansen & Neumann 2005: 733). Even under current conditions, such integrated chains are possible. The concepts have already been introduced as Computer-Integrated-Merchandising where retail-based scanner cash desks are connected directly with manufacturer MRP-systems (Kotzab 1999).

All operations within the supply chain are activated by a series of transactions that trigger the movement of products and materials. Some observers (e.g. Marbacher 2001) divide the supply chain into supply management and demand management, where supply management covers the flow of material and products from production back to sources of supply. Demand management encompasses the span from customer order to production. The critical link is the production schedule. Supply chain operations begin with a customer order. In many industries and product lines, the order is actually point-of-sale bar-code data scanned at a retail checkout counter or inventory stock location, aggregated by the retailer customer and transmitted to its supplier.

In other cases, orders come directly from the sales force, or electronically from Web sites. Sales data becomes orders either transmitted to a distribution center for order fulfilment, to production scheduling or serve as input data to forecasts by customers, users or within the supply chain itself in anticipation of future orders to become a basis for the production schedule. In the case of push distribution, distribution center inventories are replenished by production based on forecasts.

Production scheduling determines when orders will be fulfilled using one of several approaches. Feasible solutions include MRP or priority-based, chronologically based or optimized schedules randomly generated by computer. Setting a production schedule becomes a basis for releasing orders automatically to major first-tier suppliers, who then release their own orders to second-tier suppliers. With non-critical or standard items, the system monitors inventory and dispatches electronic agents to business-to-business exchanges to procure items in a process similar to auctions or to vendor catalogs.

Complete customer orders release electronic advance shipping notices to customers, notifying carriers, producing electronic bills of lading and other documentation. The carrier's data system tracks the shipment to the point of delivery. Electronic proof of delivery triggers the billing and payment systems, using automated payment systems to transfer funds electronically.

The transaction system is supplemented by other electronic data and information systems. Transaction data held in the system creates records of performance for later analysis and planning as part of decision support systems. This support is provided through database query, modeling and optimization tools. In addition, drawings and other technical data can also be transmitted between partners. Joint discussions can also be facilitated by groupware and e-mail, allowing dialogue and simultaneous access to common databases. Ultimately, negotiation can also take place through the information system, culminating in offers, transfer and acceptance of legal documents that obligate partners to perform agreed services and other actions.

These elements of the information system are now in place, although not universal and not always incorporated in the same supply chain. Other elements such as the transport market should also be recognized as part of the information system. Current interest lies in transaction systems, with management and decision support getting secondary emphasis. The ability to implement and utilize these systems has become a major management challenge.

The Concept of a Supply Chain Information System

The essential role of the information system is to bind the entire chain together as a single integrated unit. The underlying framework is shown in Figure 4.4. It has both an intra-firm dimension that is largely vertical and hierarchical and inter-functional (and inter-firm) dimensions that are horizontal, following the transaction flow. The intra-firm system is highly developed, following a traditional management orientation. The inter-firm system is emerging slowly, restrained not by technology as much as by relationships among organizations in the supply chain. With current technology, real-time supply chain management as »information at your fingertips« (Liekenbrock 2006: 22), becomes reality.

Figure 4.4. Different Information Flow Levels within a Supply Chain

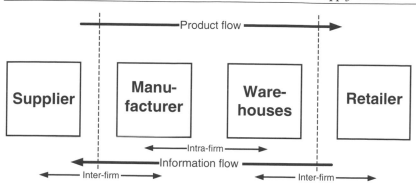

The Intra-firm Information System

With a hierarchical orientation, top management deals with strategy and strategic direction. From this follows planning to implement strategy, and the specific decisions necessary to direct operations. The work of the organization comes from execution, functional activities performing the tasks determined through the flow of transactions. Transactions flow horizontally across functional and organizational boundaries from customers, external partners and suppliers. At a higher level, functional activities must be coordinated between organizations and intra-organizational units. Higher levels become involved with joint planning and strategy, negotiating the terms of partnership, and participation.

The source of activity is the transaction flow. There has been a migration from paper (hard copy) documentation to electronic, computer-compatible data. The entire information system is vulnerable to data problems. There are potential problems of compatibility in the form of data and computer formats, although these barriers are being overcome more easily now. In terms of information systems, execution involves internal operations systems such as vehicle scheduling, warehouse management or production scheduling. These operations may involve automated processing, with precise decision rules, flagging of deviations and the ability to manage exceptions manually. Although they may have external connections for guiding delivery and production priorities and schedules, their principal focus is on the utilization of internal resources. In the course of operations, they generate data that can be reported and stored for use at higher levels.

The role of coordination is to synchronize operations between separate functional activities, to supervise ongoing processes and to balance capacity. The first level of operations is closely linked to transaction flow. Planning though is involved in operations and in strategy. The operational level uses transaction flow data to project activity levels and to anticipate facility capacity and process requirements. This includes optimization and forecasting. Planning also establishes monitoring and control systems. It also provides a reporting function to inform management of the state of operations. At a strategic level, it also deals with capacity, process and optimization, although at a more aggregated level.

Both execution and planning deal with established processes. In contrast, the need for strategy also calls for less predefined activities. It includes environmental scanning, the development of alternative scenarios for the supply chain and reaction to new situations. The key is to make tools and data easily available to management for data access and analysis. The decision support system is designed to promote this ease of use, characterized by the contingent question: »What if?«.

The data sources also show this difference. Internal operations use and generate data relating to specific activities. This becomes input to local operations planning. Higher levels of planning may also use this data, although usually in more aggregated form. At a strategic level, outside sources of data are corporate planning, external product and supply markets. These data would be selective, project-oriented and gathered to meet a specific need.

The intra-firm information system in the Internet-driven business will be better known as intranet which can be defined as a private network within a single organization that utilizes Internet standards in order to allow internal information sharing (Chaffey 2004: 576).

The Inter-firm Information System

The central management problem of the supply chain is coordination of operations. In concept, the information system enables this to take place, integrating operations of separate organizations into a unified system capable of responding to customer orders, changes in market and supply conditions and changes in corporate direction. Figure 4.5 displays a framework in simplified form. It includes a first-tier supplier, the lead enterprise and one customer. Each firm includes the framework of the intra-firm information systems discussed above. The central concerns are the connections and coordination. Transactions between organizations activate the supply chain. Executing operations in these organizations generates performance data which are shared with other operations and planning units. Linking operations requires coordination. This can involve routine data to signal between activities, routine reporting, e-mail, complex messages including visual elements and non-standard multimedia communication.

Figure 4.5. The Supply Chain Information System

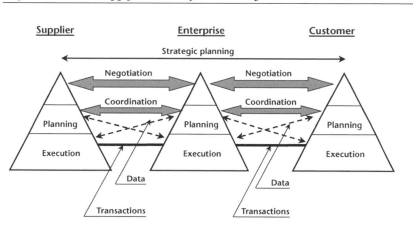

Establishing or changing the terms of this coordination requires negotiation, again utilizing multimedia. Further, as supply chain strategy becomes a collective activity among partners, there are further demands for multimedia connection. All of this requires broadband connections that require a technical solution within the information system.

The information system involves both hardware and software systems. While we treat them as separate topics, they are closely linked. Advances in hardware such as computers or the connecting links, enable software development towards more sophisticated programs. Similarly, the complexity of software influences the development of computer and connecting links.

The inter-firm information system in a web-based system is known as extra- and Internet, where the extranet is an extended intranet between a company and its suppliers and customers (Chaffey 2004: 574).

Interface Optimization

Interface optimization is needed in order to link intra- and inter-firm information systems which are parts of the internal and external physical flow of goods. Based on a study of information integration in transportation processes, Clausen et al. (2006) show that there are three information system optimization issues (see Figure 4.6).

Figure 4.6. Software optimization within a transport system

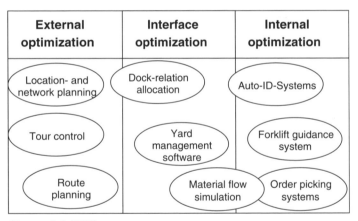

External optimization	Interface optimization	Internal optimization
Location- and network planning	Dock-relation allocation	Auto-ID-Systems
Tour control	Yard management software	Forklift guidance system
Route planning	Material flow simulation	Order picking systems

Source: Clausen et al. (2006)

External optimization refers to inter-firm information systems coordinating operations of separate organizations within the supply chain, internal optimization seeks to increase efficiency and effectiveness of internal flows. However, interface optimization is needed at those locations where the intra-firm system meets the inter-firm system, which is where internal flows become external flows.

Elements of the Information System

Visualize the information system as a web of connections. The power of this system should not be understated. The ability to control and make decisions about the supply chain depends on the capabilities of this system. Within this web are three major components: computing power (hardware), connecting links and software. These are interrelated, and the driving force is difficult to isolate. Hardware is the collective term for all the physical parts of a computer (Hansen & Neumann 2005). The hardware consists of input devices, memory, central processing units as well as output and storage devices (Chaffey 2004: 574).

The governing dimensions are the organizing system and communication. The power of the computer in the supply chain comes from its connections. The expansion of network communication through broadband capacity increases the power of computer networks which, in turn, is limited by the computing capacity available within the network. The capacity of the system and the accompanying software form a symbiotic relationship in which either one places demands and stimulates the other.

On-demand Computing

Where computing power resides in the system, is becoming less important over time. Multiple computers can be linked together to perform calculations that exceed the capacity of any single computer, ultimately as *grid computing* where these connections become a matter of course. The Web also makes possible computation remote from the physical system as computer utilities, performing routine processing literally on-demand, or as specialized applications such as transport scheduling through *application service providers* (ASPs).

The significance lies beyond its obvious advantages in specialized knowledge, and reduced capital cost, but in the ability of supply chain partners to send data directly to a common point of entry into the system. Supply chain information processing can become standardized within a given supply chain, although it may present problems in dealing with data entry systems of different suppliers or customers.

Software Systems

Software is the collective term for all computer programs (Neumann & Hansen 2005) and as much as the hardware, software defines the supply chain information system. To date, it has emphasized transactions and operations in real time more than planning and strategy. The collective thrust of development has been towards connecting and integrating operations across the supply chain. This reflects a current management focus, but development is also taking place in strategic areas.

The worldwide market for supply chain software in total according to AMR Research is $5.6 billion (ARC 2006). Supply chain software has branched into two orientations. One is specialized, focusing on specific tasks. The task is to link them together as a coherent system. The other is broad, which immediately becomes complex and difficult to install and use. Compatibility among proprietary software programs becomes a critical problem. Another problem is time, there are problems of data entry into the system. Enterprise resource planning is a case in point.

Enterprise Resource Planning (ERP)

The first specific development in software for managing supply chain information took place in ERP systems. These systems manage financial, human and material resource transactions within the boundaries of a single organization. Originally offered as mainframe applications, they are now available for client–server applications on the Internet, typically using Java as the language. Typically offered in process modules, they are oriented towards operating processes rather than particular functional areas, crossing functional and departmental boundaries. Enterprise resource planning systems typically utilize process engineering, matching the work flow across the organization. They parallel the development of the lateral organization. Typical modules include accounting, financial payments, human resources, inventory and order processing. Table 4.2 presents the evolution of ERP over time as Lawrence et al. (2005: 9) outline it.

Table 4.2. An ERP time line

Evolution of ERP				
1960s	1970s	1980s	1990s	2000 and beyond
Inventory management	Material requirements planning (MRP)	• Manufacturing resource planning (MRP II) • Distribution Requirements planning DRP)	Enterprise resource planning (ERP)	Next generation integrated applications
• Bill of materials processor	• Complex manufacturing operations • Process efficiency	• Integration of departments • Suply/ Demand chain	• Resource optimization (RO) • Supply Chain Management (SCM)	• E-Business • Customer Relationship management (CRM) • Business • Intelligence
Planning the business	Tracking the business	Understanding the business	Improving the business	Predicting the business

Source: Lawrence et al. (2005:9)

Some of the most well-known standard ERP vendors today are SAP, Oracle Applications and Microsoft Dynamics (Formerly Microsoft Business Division).

By managing and documenting the execution of transactions on computer, ERP offers precise control and potential elimination of paper documentation within the organization. Data generated from operations can be held in databases for reporting and analysis. In the past, ERP has been difficult to implement because of the sheer size of the task, initial data requirements and compatibility with other systems.

Enterprise resource planning is currently limited to the boundaries of the firm, but the open architecture of many systems permits connections to external applications. Enterprise resource planning is a foundation for managing interfunctional supply chain processes within the firm. By itself, it is inadequate to manage the supply chain beyond organizational boundaries, without supporting applications linked to external partners. Boundaries mean that transaction data do not always reflect immediate inputs from on-line connections. Data is fixed at the time of entry and therefore requires updating. As one observer notes, ERP systems alone do not deal well with logistics. These systems normally do not accommodate special orders or customer inventory positions. They do not deal with global logistics problems easily, such as the timing of invoices in relation to customs clearances.

Software for Supply Chain Management

Supply chain software can be differentiated into supply chain planning, supply chain execution and supply chain coordination systems (Hansen & Neumann 2005: 734, Frost & Sullivan 2004). Supply chain planning refers to strategy and planning while execution refers to the transaction level of the supply chain information systems.

This software is linked to sales force automation software, because of the stress on data for forecasting. These modules are also typically offered as additions to ERP, although they are also offered as a separate, linked coordination system. The supply chain software market is complex, obscure and heterogenous (RECO 2006). Typical vendors are independent while others have alliances with ERP vendors for specific functions and levels of interaction. Further, some offer vertical market, industry-specific supply chain software. Most interest has come from distribution-oriented demand chain users, rather than the supply chain.

Figure 4.7. Classification of SCM software systems

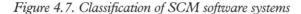

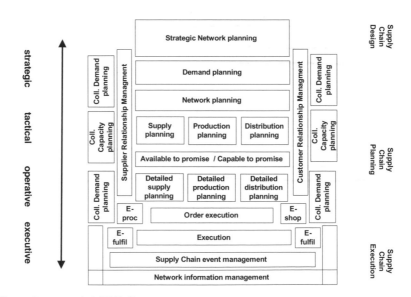

Source: Lawrence et al. (2005: 9)

Kuhn and Hellingrath (2002) provided a functionality-model of a SCM software system. This model divides all supply chain tasks into planning and control tasks and shows the necessary specifications for SCM software. Wannenwetsch (2005: 82) classifies SCM-software systems in relation to Bowersox et al.s (2002) information pyramid into strategic, tactical, operative and execution software (see Figure 4.7).

The individual components can be described as follows (based on Kuhn & Hellingrath 2002, Wannenwetsch 2005, Stadtler 2004):

- Supply Chain Design (SCD) is also known as the configuration level which provides the necessary information and restrictions for the supply chain planning and execution activities.
- Strategic Network design aims at the long-term oriented optimal design of the supply chain based common network goals in order to decide on investments, allocation and rationalization efforts as well as location issues.
- Supply Chain Planning, also known as Advanced Planning Systems, include all operative and strategic planning modules which help to improve the efficiency in the total chain. These modules include:
  - Demand planning – sales volumes of products and product groups
  - Network planning – allocation of available sourcing, production and distribution capacities
  - Supply planning – required parts for meeting demand requirements
  - Production planning – optimal production plan for each individual production location in the supply chain
  - Distribution planning – optimal inventory planning and customer-oriented distribution
  - Availability and capability – planning customer requirements
  - Detailed supply, production and distribution planning – short term optimization of these activities and release of supply, production and distribution orders

- Supply Chain Execution including all functions which are needed to execute the operative processes such as Order Management, Inventory Management, Production or Transport Management.
- Supply Chain Event Management is the activity control of the execution of supply chain processes and also serves as emergency center if activities are not performed as outlined.

The major challenge of this model is to integrate information flows amongst organizations, not only to optimize the internal information flow and tasks as formerly performed by MRP systems and later on by ERP systems. Whether existing SCM software is capable to do this has been analyzed by Wannenwetsch (2005: 77). A list of these capabilities is shown below:

- strategic network design
- demand planning
- network planning
- procurement planning
- production planning
- distribution planning
- Order promising – ATP (Available-to-promise)/CTP (capable-to-promise)
- monitoring
- alert management
- technical questions
- general questions

Heidrich (2004: 131) compared selected SCM software solutions based on certain criteria (see Table 4.3 that includes only a selection from his analysis).

Overall, software vendors can be characterized by their offerings (RECO 2006: 6):

- Integrated SCM and e-business suites including Advanced Planning and scheduling functionalities (e.g. the SAP APO).
- Specific SCM-suites that offer specialized solutions for specific application planning areas.
- Expanded functional ERP-systems where SCM is an extension of the existing production planning systems or ERP systems.
- Niche solutions for supply chain planning which focuses on specific parts of SCM such as flexis or supply solutions
- Chain executive suites or software to control, process and manage supply chain activities, sometimes supported by IT and e-commerce websites.

Table 4.3. Comparison of different SCM-soft-ware

	iBaan	Manugistics	J.D.Edwards	PeopleSoft	Synquest	SAP	i2-Technologies
				System technology			
Type of system	Expanded ERP system	Strategic planning tool	Expanded ERP system	Expanded ERP system	Strategic planning tool	Expanded ERP system	Strategic planning tool
Type of system	Expanded ERP system	Strategic planning tool	Expanded ERP system	Expanded ERP system	Strategic planning tool	Expanded ERP system	Strategic planning tool
Interface concept	Data exchange by ASCII-files or JAVA coupler application or by CORBA middleware	Open Application Integration with Auto-P ug-In and configurable Network content for internet application	Extended Process integration with ASCII-files, Oracle, Sybase, AS 400, DB2-data bases	Data management in relational data bases, Oracle data can be accessed with SQL-servers	Direct access to Oracle and Sybase data bases, other integration with ACII/flatfiles	Semantic synchronization between Planning and ERP systems in infocubes, application link enabling	Access to Oracle and SQL DB and ASCII files with SQL, TradeMatrix link for data integration
Database	Oracle, Informix	Oracle	Oracle Sybase, AS 400, DB 2, ASCII	Oracle, MS SQL Server	Oracle	SAP DB, DB 2, UDB, DB2/390	Oracle, ASCII, Flatfiles
Operating System	Unix, Windows	Unix, Windows	Unix, Dec, Windows	Windows	Unix, Windows	Unix, Windows	Unix, Windows
				Functionality			
Industry applications	Automotive, procedural industries, airline, electronics, consumer goods food, medicine, telecommunication	Automotive, chemical, pharmaceutical, textile and clothing, electronics, high tech, consumer goods food and noon-food, retail, transportation	Automotive, chemical, pharmaceutical, paper and printing, consumer goods food and noon food, retail	Automotive, automotive supplier, high tech, semiconductor, consumer goods, retail	Automotive, automotive supplier, furniture, airline, paper and printing, semiconductor, telecommunication	Automotive, chemical, pharmaceutical, engineering and construction, high tech, airline, consumer goods, media, telecommunication, printing, oil and gas, mining, banks, insurances	Automotive, automotive suppliers, metal, electronics, high tech, semiconductors, transport, consumer goods, airline, paper and printing, machinery, oil and gas, textile and clothing

Source: Heidrich (2004:131)

General Application Areas for Supply Chain Information Systems

Software for supply chain management has followed on the development of ERP, specifically to solve problems of external coordination. It presents a more holistic view of the enterprise than ERP, embedded in a network of suppliers and customers. The overriding concept is coordination with customers, suppliers and service providers to create a single integrated transaction system both inter-organizationally and inter-functionally. Worthen (2002) characterizes supply chain software as the »most fractured group of software applications« as there is no single software solution available that can manage all the different supply chain tasks. Software is offered in suites of modules dedicated to specific processes such as order processing, demand management (including joint customer-vendor forecasting), transportation management, purchasing and supplier coordination. A map of supply chain software applications as of 2006 is shown in Figure 4.8 including Warehouse Management Systems, Transportation Management Systems, CRM, Demand Management, Order Fulfilment, and Procurement.

Figure 4.8. Software in the Supply Chain

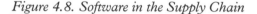

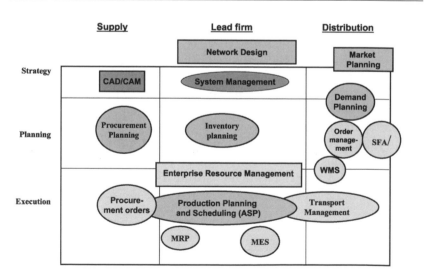

The variety of applications for particular tasks in supply chain management is impressive. There have been aggregations of functions as suites of programs to be configured to individual organizational requirements. What follows here is an overall description of some of the possible applications, recognizing that this is a highly changeable landscape. The sequence begins with the demand chain and leads to the supply chain and supporting services such as transportation.

Distribution management

A typical program is linked to customer orders either directly or through automated sales programs. Some will perform sales allocation and assert control over inventory and shipments through distribution centers. Some will also include warehouse management capabilities, although ERP and supply chain programs may have links to software for warehouse management systems.

Warehouse management systems

Warehouse management systems (WMS) embrace a variety of modules for distribution center operation in a real-time environment (Wolf et al. 2006, Trunk 2000, *Modern Materials Handling* 2000). The German Fraunhofer Institute for Material Flow and Automation has published a report since 2000 that includes the analysis of about 70 WMS-solutions. The »standard« WMS includes data files on stock locations in the distribution center, inventory management, communications modules for radio frequency contact with pickers, generation of packing slips, internal vehicle routing for stock picking and advance shipping notices. Some systems offer pick-to-voice and RFID interfaces. Some systems also handle partial shipments converging from multiple distribution centers. The Internet makes tighter control imperative over DC operation, with B2C retailing order fulfillment, processing of direct shipments passing through DCs, continuing pressure for inventory reduction, and a new culture within the supply chain for customer-specific inventories and mass customization (see also www.ware house-logistics.de).

Order management

Order management software provides a path for customer orders into the supply chain. Typical modules assume a customer-pull environment, managing contacts with the customer, providing customer service with the ability to manage complex orders from different locations with large numbers of products and with differing service requirements. It also provides access to customer credit, product and inventory status, plus proposed shipping dates. In addition, some software permits customers to have access to trace order status, with further links to carrier data systems to enable tracing shipments after the order has been shipped.

Demand planning

Supply chain software has become important because of the need to take in customer order data from the point of sale, or sales orders directly from the source, and to forecast future sales. Typical programs include sales planning, forecasting, customer commitment, order delivery promising, and customer demand data from the point of sale or orders. Some may include pricing data as well. One example for customer collaborative workflow management can be found in CPFR where each involved partner produces a data flow that is translated to standardized message formats (VICS 2002, see also chapter 5).

Production planning

The most difficult technical problem for IT in supply chain operations is probably production scheduling. Orders are now processed and scheduled in real time, requiring reformulation of the scheduling process. Materials requirements planning (MRP) and master production scheduling (MPS) preceeded ERP (see also Chapter 6). Even MRP II with an improved scheduling program and data processing capabilities now associated with ERP production planning and scheduling, has not been adequate to the task. MRP was developed in an era of stand-alone computers and programmed in COBOL, a now arcane language. It has not proven to be adaptable to this new environment of on-line processing. New production planning programs under the name *advanced planning and scheduling* have been developed to replace MRP and master production scheduling within the supply chain (Stadtler & Kilger 2004).

Procurement

There is divergence among purchasing applications. One approach assumes a pre-existing relationship with major suppliers, emphasizing coordination of operations to ensure that products are delivered as needed. The other assumes procurement of standard items, open markets with an emphasis on search and selection, involving business-to-business (B2B) markets. This process lends itself to automation of procurement through the use of electronic software agents and optimizing choices based on price, delivery costs and related variables. Some applications involve development of large-scale Web-based catalogs of pre-qualified suppliers for non-critical items, using standard protocols and data codes, previously established within the buyer's own network. All of these may operate simultaneously in parallel to meet various procurement needs (see also Chapter 8).

Transportation

Transportation management systems (TMS) refer to transport scheduling, tracking & tracing, dispatch management, transport cost management, fleet management, route planning, documentation such as bills of lading or invoicing of transportation (see www.transport-it.net). Vastag and Kellermann (2006: 9) showed that the application of TMS helped companies to improve the utilization of the fleet by 70 to 90 %. Optimized route planning also helps to minimize travel time and distances, and therefore diminishes energy consumption.

Collaboration

One purpose of supply chain software is to promote collaboration across organizational boundaries. Collaborative software has developed as a general category utilized for a variety of purposes. Some applications in supply chain management have been developed in customer relationship management, forecasting and transportation management. The next wave will be to align software to underlying business processes. One program allows for free exchange of data in multiple message types between the supplier and customer. It allows partners to share planning data and requirements.

Product Life Cycle Management (PLM)

Product lifecycle management (PLM) is, according to Cicekoglu (2005), a business process and a technology architecture that captures and maintains specific product information across the total product life cycle. PLM is a special software solution for collaborative product design, engineering, development and project management (SAP 2007). One example of such software is CATIA (Computer Aided Three-Dimensional Interactive Application), which is used in the engineering industry (e.g. automotive or aircraft construction) (Catia 2007). Another example is mySAP PLM that is built as an open framework so that all industry standards can be applied. It contains the following features and functions (SAP 2007):

- Life-cycle data management – Provides an environment for managing specifications, bills of materials, routing and resource data, project structures, and related technical documentation throughout the product life cycle
- Program and project management – Provides advanced capabilities to plan, manage, and control the complete product development process
- Life-cycle collaboration – Supports collaborative engineering and project management, employing XML-based Web standards to communicate information such as project plans, documents, and product structures across virtual development teams
- Quality management – Provides integrated quality management for all industries throughout the entire product life cycle
- Enterprise asset management – Enables project managers, maintenance engineers, and others to manage physical assets and equipment, from first investment idea to retirement of the asset
- Environment, health, and safety – Provides a solution for environment, health, and safety issues by enhancing business processes to comply with government regulations.

Communications

The backbone of the supply chain is communication. What distinguishes supply chain management from earlier supply systems is the potential for instantaneous communication, presentation of data, analysis, and the ability to react with speed to changing situations. The emphasis in supply chain strategy is on information to be substituted for the physical product wherever possible, such as coordination between stages to avoid excess inventory. It has the potential to influence the development of organizations in three areas: 1) the physical tasks, 2) internal information handling, and 3) interorganizational relationships.

The ability to manage the supply chain depends on 1) the capacity to handle the volume of individual transactions, 2) the speed with which these transactions and their accompanying data can be processed, 3) the visibility of operations to participants, and 4) the complexity of communication. Technology provides an increasing ability to handle the requirements of these tasks, information will play an expanding role in supply chain management.

The information system is limited by bandwidth, in multimedia messaging with high-speed data transfer. The foundation is the telephone system (telecoms). It progressed to direct data communication via electronic data interchange (EDI) and now to the Web. Beyond this lie broadband and wireless services. Each has particular characteristics that define its use.

Electronic data exchange in a web-based supply chain is based on communication technologies such as WAN (wide area network), LAN (local area network), TCP/IP (transmission control protocol/internet protocol), HTTP (hypertext transfer protocol), SMTP (simple mail transfer protocol), POP (post office protocol), IMAP (internet message access protocol) or FTP (file transfer protocol) (Wannenwetsch 2005: 32). WAN is a computer network covering broad geographical areas. Computer networks covering a local area are called LAN. FTP connects two computers over the Internet and allows data transfers from one computer to the other. File commands also can be performed on the other computer. The IMAP though makes it possible for a local client to access e-mail on a remote server. POP allows the retrieval of e-mail from a remote server over a TCP/IP connection, which is a protocol suite that supports the most popular Internet applications. The SMTP is the most common standard for e-mail transmission over the Internet and HTTP transfers or conveys information on the world wide web.

Electronic data interchange (EDI)
EDI is the meta-term for a multitude of different electronic standards allowing computerized and highly structured low-error communication (Kotzab 1999, Hsieh & Lin 2004, Emmelhainz 1990). EDI enables paperless communication between organizations in a supply chain through standarized messages. It was originally intended to provide mainframe-to-mainframe computer communication. Computers operated as stand-alone systems, and EDI protocols had to be adapted to each system. Supplier-to-customer connections were individual, and required individual programming support.

EDI generally utilizes value-added networks (VANs) to carry EDI messages to ensure connectivity between partners, separate from the Internet. Major firms continue its use because it offers data security and compatibility with legacy data systems. It is sometimes used in parallel with more current Web-based systems that currently offer less security. Many companies use a combination of both conventional EDI for security of data and internets for more general use.

One outcome of EDI was the development of standardized messages (transaction sets), based on common standards such as ANSI X.12 for the United States and EDIFACT in international use. The cost of installing and programming has been high enough to confine it to major corporations and their partners, restricting the number of installations and thereby limiting potential competitors. Large customers made EDI a prerequisite for suppliers. Specific industry initiatives led to the development of EDI-based supply networks with standard messages for procurement transactions such as the UCS (Uniform Communication Standard). A subsidiary set of transactions was developed for public warehouses serving the industry as a whole.

EDI is vulnerable to competition from the Web, especially from open standards (Hsie & Lin 2004: 75). The web will compensate especially the disadvantage of an limited bi-lateral connection of EDI based on the specific EDI-standards. Due to the wide spread of EDI within global businesses, some organizations like the GS1 work on the development of a global standard that is based on the EDI but keeps interface problems as low as possible, as e.g. XML promises. This means, that in future there might be a co-existence of EDI and XML, especially when it comes to electronic data exchange among large and small/medium sized companies (Wannenwetsch 2005: 35).

XML

Another advance in electronic information exchange can be seen in XML (eXtensible Markup Language). This standard was introduced by the World-Wide Web Consortium in 1998. The XML-standard was recommended as the standard for exchanging information over the web and can be seen as a further development of HTML (Hypertext Markup Language) that also allows computers to process the content of websites (W3C 2002)). XML is an an open and flexible standard to store, publish and exchange information in an Internet setting (Daum & Horak 2001: 18).

As specific Web-based networks have developed, it has been necessary to define access for specific groups of users. Intranets and extranets are contained within corporate networks, accessible only by using passwords or specific identification. Intranets are the basic corporate communication system, with a variety of communication modes from text to graphics to voice and video. It extends the reach of the organization, and serves as a vehicle for disseminating knowledge, experience and managerial judgment across the organization. Extranets serve similar purposes but embrace suppliers, customers and others linked to the supply chain beyond corporate boundaries.

One example of such networks is RosettaNet, which was specifically developed by GS1 for the electronics industry. The specific RosettaNet Partner Interface Processes (PIPs) define the electronic transmission of information and electronic transactions amongst the net members and help to simplify complex supply chains (RosettaNet 2007).

Automatic identification systems
Automated data collection is essential to the supply chain and takes place through machine-recognizable labeling and identification systems. The two most prominent systems are bar codes and radio frequency identification (RFID). They have been normally used to identify individual items, unit loads, vehicle loads and equipment, but they also enable control over operations beyond the ordinary reach of the computer. More recent developments have applied bar coding to product and shipping documentation and special handling instructions. Automatic identification is passive in that it only supplies data when interrogated by a scanning device or radio frequency transmitter.

Bar codes
Bar codes provide a common information system for the entire supply chain, from retail through manufacturing. Retail products are commonly labeled by the Universal Product Code (UPC) in the United States and the European Article Numbering (EAN) system in Europe, from which the manufacturer and the product are identified. The EAN system holds one more digit than the United States system, useful for identifying special characteristics such as pack size or special promotions, but introduces problems of compatibility across the Atlantic. UPC and EAN generate point-of-sale data that

are useful in establishing sales trends, setting forecasts and production schedules, and even serving as a substitute for replenishment ordering in addition to their initial role of automating part of the sales process.

The next level, distribution coding, introduces its own problems. The shipping container is often scanned by laser beams at a distance, requiring high readability. Codes are also used to designate shelf and pallet locations. The result is a special code, UCC/EAN Code 128, developed jointly in the United States and Europe. The objective is to link to automated warehouse scanning and picking systems.

Manufacturing introduces a different set of problems. Component parts may have more elaborate coding because they enter into multiple products. They require special codes with additional capacity to encompass more information.

Two-dimensional bar codes provide the ability to hold extensive information. Linear bar codes such as UPC or EAN or even UCC/EAN 128 are limited in information. Additional information such as documentation, routing or special environment instructions attached to individual items could serve a useful purpose. Two-dimensional bar codes were introduced to solve this problem. One label can carry from 50 to 100 times more data than a conventional bar code. They can also be read under poor lighting conditions. At present, there are at least 14 separate codes.

RFID

Some radio frequency identification systems have the ability to write changes in labels, giving them more flexibility than standard bar code labels. In these »smart« labels, as an action takes place on an individual item, the label updates the new status on a magnetic strip or embedded microchip, similar to »smart« cards now entering the consumer market.

Smart radio frequency identification tags may become an alternative information system, accompanying the objects to which they are attached. They have the advantage of accompanying packages and unit loads beyond the boundaries of the formal computer-based information system, providing new information through the label. The danger is that the formal system becomes uninformed about current status and out-of-date, requiring close to instantaneous, periodic links between the two systems.

Radio frequency identification labels have not been widely used in the past, largely because of cost, but the technology presents new opportunities. A radio frequency identification label is fundamentally a transponder, interrogated by a radio transmitter and reflecting back data such as product identification (Mill 2005). There are two forms: active and passive. Active radio frequency identification labels are battery-powered labels and can be identified at a distance, such as vehicles passing at high speed. Passive tags must be read from short distances and can be used in distribution center and retail store environments. They have the advantage of now being low in cost, down to 25 cents per unit. They augment control by indicating product location and status. Several labels can be read in a single action (rfid-handbook.com 2004). All of this increases productivity by enabling faster and more immediate status reporting by item or vehicle.

The European Union has recognized the power of RFID and invested about € 312 million into RFID-technology research. About 35 % of this funding is used for research in the field of SCM (EU 2006). The application areas for RFID are however not limited to traditional logistics or SCM but to many other fields such as baggage and passenger control at airports, speed- or skipasses, libraries or public transport tickets (GCI 2006). There has even been discussion about radio frequency identification replacing bar code labels. With the introduction of the EPC/RFID technology by ECPGlobal, which is a joint venture between EAN International and UCC, when the two coding technologies were merged and a global standard was created (Verisign 2004). By December 2006, more than 1000 companies in 12 major industries and 51 industry segments use this technology.

The two global retailers, Wal-Mart and Metro, can be seen as RFID-innovators and drivers for this 'revolution'. Metro started its first pilots back in 2000, and had a major launch in 2004 with their »Future Store« concepts, which introduces the new way to operate a retail business based on RFID technology. RFID is not only used in the store but at all stages within the total supply chain (GCI 2006). Wal-Mart also started a pilot program in 2004 with 150 stores and clubs in and around one of their largest logistics centers in Dallas, Texas. The objective was to test the effects of RFID by tracking items from manufacturers to distribution centers and then to the stores. By October 2005, the following effects were identified: reduction of out of stock items by 16 %, RFID-tagged items were replenished three times faster than non-tagged items. It was also possible to reduce excess inventory and to reduce manual orders by 10 %. By the beginning of 2006, about 9 million tagged cases and more than 80 million EPC reads had taken place. By 2007, Wal-Mart is expected to have about 600 suppliers utilizing RFID (Wal-Mart 2007). However, there are already some researchers working on the next coding solutions, such as building RFID-tags based on polymer structures (e.g. Overmeyer 2006).

As a final note on bar codes and RFID, two developments hold promise for the future: first, »smart bar codes« that can change coding as operations take place on the objects where they are attached, and second, the ability of RFID to identify individual items allows process control to become granular, to control these items through production and distribution processes. This may carry customization to a new level.

Concluding Comments

Discussion of information systems never ends. The continual change in technology opens the door for new possibilities while destroying the old order. The Web-based information system enables the virtual supply chain and changes the assumptions behind more traditional models. The virtual supply chain offers new flexibility. Partners may be connected for limited periods of time electronically for short, even customized production and distribution, although recruited through prior qualification. Although the potential development and the reality are still far apart, the movement is visible. Organizational arrangements have to adapt to this new environment of electronic connection.

The professional orientation of supply chain management is also changing, from a focus on physical processes such as production, inventory management or transportation to managing information. This requires different technical knowledge. Automation of data collection, analysis and decisions relieves management of an impossible burden. IT also presents a danger of formalized knowledge without a guide: knowledge without a knower (Brown & Duguid 1998). Failure to take advantage of the information revolution presents a danger for the future. At the same time, without a human presence, the ability to manage is lost.

The future development of IT and organizations is not predictable. But, as Drucker wrote (1999: 54) citing a historical context:

> »The new industries that emerged after the railroad owed little technologically to the steam engine or to the Industrial Revolution in general. They were not its 'children after the flesh – but they were its 'children after the spirit'.«

Illustrative Case

Gillette and RFID[2]

The RFID technology enabled Gillette to get its new Fusion razor out to the shelves of 400 retail stores in USA 11 days faster than its normal turn-around time for product launches, which translates into 11 days of sales in 400 stores that the retailers and Gillette might have otherwise missed. The five-blade razor is Gillette's answer to its competitor Schick's four-blade Quattro, so it was an important launch into the razor-and-blade industry. According to Gillette, that industry totals $2.4 billion in the United States and $10 billion globally.

»Fusion is the first Gillette product that has been completely EPC-supported at the time of launch,« said Paul Fox, director of global external relations for Procter & Gamble, Gillette's parent company. This means Gillette placed RFID smart labels on all cases and pallets of the razors shipped to the 400 RFID-enabled retail locations of its two customers involved in the pilot project. Gillette also placed tags on the Fusion promotional displays it sent the retailers.

Fox attributes the swiftness of the Fusion launch to the added visibility the tagged goods provided the company. This visibility began as the goods arrived at the retailers' distribution centers and ended at the retailers' box-crushing machines, where reads of the Fusion case tags allowed Gillette to infer that all contents had been placed on shelves. In cases where the retailer's EPC feedback net-

---

2. Adapted from Mary Catherine O'Connor: Gillette Fuses RFID With Product Launch, RFID Journal, March 17, 2006.

work showed the Fusion razors or promotional displays had reached a retail store's back room, but no read events were recorded showing the goods being brought to the sales floor in a timely manner, Gillette contacted the managers of those stores and requested the razors and displays be brought out.

Gillette forecasts a 25 percent return on its RFID investment over the next 10 years, through increased sales and productivity savings. The company's success at getting the Fusion razors onto shelves 11 days faster than normal indicates the significant impact RFID can make as an enabler of more efficient supply chain operations. Gillette's decision to tag and track the Fusion product concurrent with the launch is part of P&G's EPC Advanced Strategy, which the company developed to provide product-by-product guidelines for rolling out EPC tagging.

The strategy divides products into three categories: RF-friendly products presenting a clear business case for RFID tracking, products on which tags are not easy to read, and products on which RFID tags are very difficult to read. Another part of the EPC Advanced Strategy involves testing the latest RFID technology so the company can identify the hardware and software applications that might help it and its supply chain partners reap as much supply chain visibility and efficiency as possible from its EPC systems.

5. Distribution

»Are you tough enough to manage your channels ...»
Bucklin et al. (1996):

Distribution is the final stage of supply chain management, as successful distribution makes the final products and services available to the ultimate customers (see Figure 5.1). Distribution activities refer to the downstream parts of the supply chain that links the customer. Distribution is an integral part of the marketing mix, built upon two major processes: sales and physical distribution.

Sales processes refer to the acquisition part of distribution and deals with order management. Physical distribution refers to the logistical order completion.

Figure 5.1. Distribution

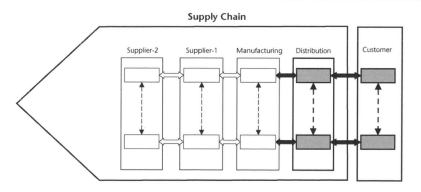

Distribution involves a wide variety of flow activities. Distribution differs with every product and market, making generalizations difficult. One division is between consumer and industrial products. Industrial product distribution is linked to procurement, see Chapter 8.

In a traditional marketing channel, distribution is a series of stages with interdependent enterprises making separate decisions about products and inventory, in loose coordination at best to deliver products to a final customer. Such a system requires heavy investment in inventory for sorting and stock holding for product availability. The result may be high inventory cost and often a lack of responsiveness to changes in the market, if no interaction and/or information exchange occurs within such a channel.

In a supply chain perspective, such traditional multi-stage distribution is too inefficient to survive. The fact that the costs of finished product inventory is too high is only part of the problem. Responsiveness to customer demand has become the key factor rather than product availability. Both are important and respond to a more systemic treatment. The distribution landscape is changing rapidly under pressures from the market, new technologies and competition. At the same time, it presents new opportunities for meeting customer demand through rapid response, customizing orders and global coverage via the Internet.

Distribution plays an essential role in the supply chain. Beyond its functional role of product delivery, it makes the supply chain sensitive to the market. If the customer drives the supply chain, distribution translates it into effective product demand, sometimes through forecasts and at other times through direct orders. One of the major changes taking place is the entry of real-time orders directly into the production schedule. Some ordering systems permit and even encourage choices in product features and options that customize production. Another is the coordination of production with demand to reduce inventory requirements. A third is increasing flexibility to take on new products and replace the old. A fourth is a change in the institutions themselves, as the role of intermediaries is changing and especially retailing is under a permanent change.

This chapter considers six topics:

- International markets
- The complexity of distribution
- The Marketing channel
- Major channel decisions
- Global retail distribution
- E-commerce and the supply chain
- Collaborative distribution models

International Markets

Several issues in international business that influence distribution are unresolved. One is the role of regional or global organizations versus local country control. Parallel to this is whether products should be localized or global. The changes brought by the European Union point directly to these issues.

The Structure of International Distribution

The issues for distribution structure are whether local sales should be served by local or more centralized distribution. Picard (1983) finds there are two underlying solutions, to either decentralize distribution to local subsidiaries, with their own distribution centers or to concentrate inventory in regional distribution centers. He further suggests that there are four basic models of product movement (Figure 5.2).

Figure 5.2 Basic Patterns of International Distribution

Classical System   Transit System

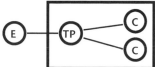

Direct System   Multicountry DC System

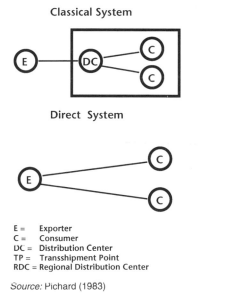

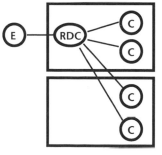

E =   Exporter
C =   Consumer
DC =   Distribution Center
TP =   Transshipment Point
RDC = Regional Distribution Center

Source: Pichard (1983)

In the classical system, the local subsidiary completely manages its own distribution to customers. There may be a supporting regional supply organization, but the subsidiary or a local distributor holds local inventory and delivers to customers. This system was typical for most multinational companies in Europe up to the mid-1980s.

- In the transit system, the local subsidiary shares responsibility at a higher level in the organization. The parent or regional unit holds inventory and fills orders, which are then processed through the local subsidiary, for local delivery. A recent application of this system is cross-docking, where products are transshipped through a network of terminals belonging to a third-party provider.
- The regional distribution system uses one central distribution center within a region to fill orders and deliver to customers. This system is especially useful within trading blocs such as the European Union or the North American Free Trade Agreement. Many firms in Europe rely on one or a few distribution centers servicing all customers within a time window of 24–72 hours, depending on the location of the customers.
- In the direct system, products move directly from production to customers without using intermediaries or intervening inventory points. Many multinational companies in Europe now use this type of distribution system, a result of low-cost and efficient transportation and communication systems. The upsurge of e-commerce will accelerate the importance of direct delivery to the final customers.

From a supply chain perspective, the central question is the extent of control by local sales organizations over distribution. The classical system gives autonomy and control to local operations, but it also separates important elements of the supply chain. It may lead to multiple inventories and problems of phasing in new products and phasing out old products. It reduces the potential for integrating the supply chain. The other three systems offer more integration but at a cost of additional complexity. In practice, companies often combine systems, by centralizing slow-moving items and placing fast-moving items in distribution points close to the markets.

Global Marketing

International marketing managers deal with a changing world. Some product preferences have traditionally varied by individual country, supported by the classical distribution system. Recently, other technologically based, standardized global products reach customers unaltered across national boundaries, supported by transit and direct distribution. More recently, there has been a shift towards regionalism, in which »Euro-products« are developed, modified or packaged for European preferences, as opposed to North American or Asian preferences. However, there are also developing market segments that reach selectively across borders to customers in many countries. In keeping with the dynamics of marketing competition, these segments are constantly emerging, developing and recombined (Halliburton & Hünerberg 1993).

The implications for distribution are strongest in inventory management. Every product is defined by adaptation of specific features or packaging for each market. It becomes a separately managed stock-keeping unit for forecasting, storage and delivery. Products proliferate with national (local) markets, reducing the efficiency of both production and distribution. At the same time, pressure for expanding market segmentation increases their number. On a global scale, the problem becomes so immense that it must be controlled through product line simplification. Further, long lead times for production or transportation require narrower lines for efficiency. The investment in safety stock inventories and the lack of control favors high-volume, stable-demand items. The net effect is that product lines in distribution must be actively managed in parallel to supply chain capacity.

Products are the objects of distribution within a marketing strategy. They can be global, regional or national. Product markets determine the distribution process through competition and the resulting price margins. Pricing is the most locally oriented element of an international marketing strategy, based on local competition and supply costs. Distribution with high revenue margins has greater slack for extra services than with low margins, where competition is intense and emphasis on efficiency is high.

The Complexity of Distribution

TheMajor Elements of Distribution and its Requirements

Distribution is one out of four marketing P's referring to the place dimension of the marketing mix. The place dimension refers to sales and logistics processes, where the sales processes refer to the acquisition of orders, which is the transaction function of the channel or the economical and legal authority to design sales processes. Sales refers to the legal, economic, informational and social relations between the distribution partners. Sales starts with identification of the final demand for products and services. It is the stage closest to the customer, so it interprets consumption patterns and preferences and transmits external customer orders. These external orders may come directly from the ultimate customers or indirectly from intermediary institutions (Gudehus 2005). These orders are then translated into specific supply chain activities such as order processing, distribution center operations, inventory holding and control and delivery. In some cases, it may go even further to include the final stages of manufacturing.

Succesful sales processes create both customer loyalty and the performance of the chain itself. Logistics processes include the design of the physical distribution process, order processing and delivery. Logistics here refers to all decisions to be taken in order to organize the flow of finished goods and related information.

Any changes in the market environment might influence distribution. These changes refer, according to Srivastava et al. (1999), to focusing on customer functionality instead of product. The need for customized solutions is increasing as customers do not accept traditional product differentiations any more. There is also a tendency to have closer relationships instead of pure transactions within a channel as most of the markets are in a mature or evendeclining phase. The traditional cost-leadership attitude may also not work, especially through the application of new technology, economies of scale as well as economies of scope and returns (differentiation) can be obtained simultaneously.

As distribution can be seen as the final link to the ultimate markets, it is obvious that distribution decisions are of strategic character (e.g. Cespedes 1988) although this characteristic is evident since

Drucker's famous observation in 1962 on the 'dark side of the continent'. The concept of a link between distribution and the supply chain is still not universally accepted as distribution is often considered as a separate entity.

The requirements for distribution are similarly varied, with specific product preferences, institutions and business practices. There are shorter product life cycles, more frequent promotions, increasing price pressures and changes in the patterns of demand and intermediary practices. The task is to supply the requirements of final customers while protecting the supply chain against too much product variety and variation in local distribution channels. While there are some cases in which marketing strategy has changed to recognize problems that it has created in distribution, that is, how distribution becomes either an advantage or a hindrance.

However, when distribution links directly production to customer or when production schedules are driven by point-of-sale data from major customers, the relationship management cannot be ignored. Srivastava et al. (1999) have therefore recognized distribution as a major part of the core business processes of a firm besides product development and customer relationship management.

Deficiencies of Traditional Distribution and Distribution Dynamics

The traditional distribution activities of making a product available by transporting, and by holding stock by specific institutions is changing. The realm of post-production processes presents uncertain demands and new intermediaries that specialize in a variety of tasks: inventory holding, sorting and delivery under a wide range of business practices. Governments and trade associations often intervene to protect specific sectors such as retailing and transportation. The very presence of the supply chain threatens intermediaries and the scope of their activities. This is therefore, not surprising, as the outcome of distribution is always dependent on the interplay between all the institutions that are involved in the process (Frazier 1999). That is why distribution decisions are unique. Cespedes (1980) interprets distribution management as a general management task as distribution has an substantial impact on a firm's performance and its image. In fact, all distribution decisions are long-term oriented and expensive, as distribution must service markets wherever there are customers that have needs, which distribution has to serve in times of quantity, quality, time and space. Coughlan et al. (2006) call this translation of customer needs into distribution actions, the concept of the service output demand that a firm has to consider when setting up its distribution channels.

The pressure on production to be more flexible in order sizes, reduction of process times or the elimination of unnecessary inventory is also important and must be recognized in the field of distribution. More and more retailers use point-of-sale data to drive the production schedules of their suppliers, which certainly indicates the need to integrate distribution and manufacturing, Linking actual sales to the final consumer market becomes a formal order process.

Figure 5.3. The Environment of the Distribution Channel

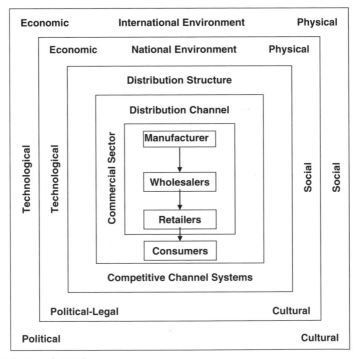

Source: Stern et al. (1996)

While traditional distribution may be organized from a single company's point of view, today's distribution decisions have to be made in collaboration with all involved actors (Frazier 1999). Distribution complexity arises also from the variety of requirements on the distribution system, that is increasingly being influenced by external factors as Figure 5.3. shows.

It is therefore very important to recognize that distribution is not a static function but a dynamic function which evolves in a dynamic environment (Stern et al. 1996). This framework, which describes the channel as a processing subsystem within the environment, is especially valuable when setting up international distribution channels. Standardized distribution channels may not be possible to implement. A lesson that some successful companies had to learn such as, Toy'sRUs when entering the Japanese market, or Wal-Mart Stores when going to German and the UK.

Internet technology may offer a lot of new possiblities, however there are also certain challenges to be considered, as Lego found out when planning a web-site for their Lego-Mind Storm. The most evident change of Lego's distribution system was the shift from B2B to B2C. Lego then found out that there are differences in the technological infrastructure around the world, different consumer spendings on toys and differences in the delivery modes. The use of Internet Technology, as a means of obtaining orders, is not a »one size fits all« solution for distribution needs. Lego underestimated the need for different channel information as Lego's customers had, more or less, always been retail outlets (Damsgaard & Hørlück 2000).

The strategic framework of marketing imposes overall specific requirements on distribution. International marketing must make decisions about products and customers in the context of varied markets with the product preferences of individual customers. Due to today's Internet technology, increasing number of manufacturers have to consider global market introduction rather than step-by-step product development, where the experiences from one country market may be used for other country markets.

Another issue refers to the increasing concentration of retailers which resulted in a power shift from manufacturers to fewer retailers as major intermediate customers. The retailers bargaining power requires suppliers to adapt to customer operations, including information systems, order quantities, inventory and delivery practices and other characteristics of operations. Supply chain operations must contend with multiple variations by customers.

The supply chain must also adapt to rapid adaptation of technologies not only within the supply chain but also by customers. Not all customers proceed at the same speed, so that there should be several different levels of performance, relating to the specific technology employed.

Push versus Pull

The roles of marketing and the supply chain are interconnected. Both are concerned with process and serving the customer as the focus. The supply chain is becoming a market-driven organization, responding to market pressures. Where the supply chain anticipates customer demand, it is a *push* orientation, placing inventory at the point of sale. This concept is shifting to an orientation where the customer order *pulls* the product through the supply chain.

The push concept produces to demand forecast in order to meet projected sales targets. It requires inventory at the point of sale, due to lead times required to produce and distribute products to the market. A push system is exppensive due to inventory costs and the danger of missed sales by not having the right product available. It does not respond rapidly to market changes.

Pull strategies treat orders individually. The supply chain only operates on the basis of orders received. Products are made to order, accompanied by direct coordination with suppliers. It is possible to configure orders to individual customers, to create micro market segments, as small as one individual customer. In theory, it is more responsive, with production matched to individual customer orders. In practice, even the most responsive system must anticipate the general direction of demand and respond by organizing the supply network and capacity. The ultimate impact on supply chain structure would be a virtual supply chain of suppliers, assembly and distribution created for a single order.

The Marketing Channel

The connection of the production of goods and services with the consumption of these goods and services is called distribution. Distribution can be defined as the total sum of all activities and related institutions, which are necessary to guarantee a successful connection between production and consumption. The way these interdependent institutions are connected, how they interact and how they make a product available for a customer is called the marketing channel. A marketing channel describes the path or the route goods and services take while they move from production to final consumption.

Any socio-economic system can be seen as the interplay between three main activities: production, distribution and consumption. While production refers to the making of a product and consumption refers to the use of such products, distribution lies in between: making products available to be consumed. Distribution refers to a compensation of distance differences, as points of productions and point of consumptions are normally not situated at the same location. It is the central objective of distribution to overcome the differences related to time, quality, quantity and spatial differences, through the main leading distribution activities:

- Break bulk – refers to the adaptation of the produced amount of products and services to the customer desired number of units of a product or service (i.e. time dimension of the channel).
- Spatial convenience – refers to the linkage between the location of the production and the location of consumption (i.e. spatial dimension of the channel).
- Assortment/variety – refers to the adaptation of what kind of products and services are offered to the customers and what kind of products and services a customer wants (i.e. quality dimension of the channel).
- Delivery/waiting time (also known as order cycle time) – refers to the time period a customer has to wait between ordering and delivery of a product (i.e. timely dimension of the channel).

Distribution activities are called flow activities and these flows can be executed by different actors as producers, intermediaries such as wholesalers, retailers, distributors, 3PL companies and even by end users. All distribution activities can be either fulfilled by one player or by all players. If one channel member is eliminated from the channel, another member has to take over the flow function (Coughlan et al. 2006). The channel performance is therefore the result of the interdependent execution of the channel flows.

Major Channel Decisions

Sales Decisions

The management of marketing channels encompasses to two basic areas – sales and logistics. Typical distribution decisions on the sales dimension deal with the question of 'how to get to an order' and mainly refer to:

- Control
- Degree of differentiation
- Channel selection
- Level of task sharing
- Geographic decisions
- Relational issues
- Governance structures

Control refers to the number of stages between production and final consumption and deals with the question whether distribution channels should be set up directly or indirectly. While there are no intermediaries involved in direct channels, different institutions are involved with distribution activities in order to make the connection successful. Direct channels are also called zero-stage-channels, while indirect channels can be multi-stage-channels.

Degree of differentiation deals with the question whether one channel should serve all customers (single track) or multiple channels (multiple track) should be set up.

Channel selection focuses on decisions whether the channel should be universal, meaning that all possible intermediaries are used for distribution or selective, where only selected intermediaries are used. Cespedes (1980) distinguishes between exclusive, extensive and intensive distribution depending on the type of product.

Level of task sharing concentrates on the issue of centralization or decentralization. In case of central distribution, all distribution functions are consolidated under one organizational unit. In case of de-central/local distribution, similar distribution tasks are completed by more organizations.

Geographic decisions deal with the question whether a distribution system is set up on a global, national or local level.

Relational issues refer to the horizontal or vertical integration of a marketing channel as well as competition or collaboration structures within the channel.

Governance structure refers to the question of who should be responsible for the distribution set up, either the manufacturer, the retailer, the consumers or others. This issue refers also to power and the concept of the channel captain, which is the institution with the keenest interest that a channel acts as it should act.

Physical Distribution Decisions

When it comes to logistics, decisions on the design of the physical distribution process have to be taken. The main driving force here is 'how to get the products where they are needed?', which means that the central objectives can be found in the execution of orders and the delivery of the products. Physical distribution decisions focus on the management of the flow of goods and the related information in the final stage of the supply chain. This means that logistics at this stage aims at inventory management, transportation and handling of (mainly) finished products.

The traditional distribution channel involved inventories in the retail store and at local distribution centers, supported by additional inventory held by central distribution centers and possibly at the end of production. This multi-tiering channel was necessary to ensure product availability for the ultimate consumer, while also protecting local decisions. The result was a system that was slow to respond to changes in demand, produced low levels of service and was often out of stock on high-demand items. Further it was costly, inventory turn-over was low, resulting in high holding costs, obsolescence and mark-downs.

This older system is being replaced as the need for more variety, faster service and lower costs is becoming more evident. Supply chain requirements have become more demanding: faster service to customers, faster response to change, more product variety, even customized products, matched to lower costs for lower prices. Inventories are becoming centralized in fewer stock locations, minimizing in-store inventories, eliminating local distribution centers in favor of central distribution centers holding complete inventories and direct distribution from factory to store and, in some cases, to final consumers.

Fisher (1997) introduced the concept of efficient and responsive channels based on demand characteristics of products that can either be innovative or functional (see Chapter 12). While demand for innovative products is difficult to predict, demand for functional products is easy to forecast. Functional products should then be available where they are needed and inventory has to be reduced at all stages except at the point of sales. Innovative products though would need responsive channels, meaning that inventory should be kept at a low level at any possible location but fast connections and visibility should be guaranteed.

Figure 5.4 Total Cost of Distribution

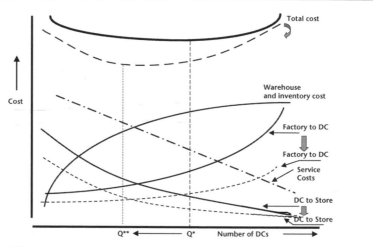

DC: distribution centers

Assume a prospective reduction in transport costs affects both trunk costs from the factory to the distribution centers and distribution costs from DC's to the stores. Q* is the optimal state of the distribution system prior to a shift in costs. Q** is the optimal state after the shift takes place. The movement from Q* to Q** then indicates that the minimum total cost, including implicitly service costs from lost sales, is shifted toward a network with fewer distribution centers than before the cost change.

Decisions about the distribution center network, including how many distribution centers and their locations, are complex because of the number of elements to be considered. The total distribution cost approach provides one answer to the »optimal« number of distribution centers, but it must be supplemented by less tangible service variables.

Typically, the following cost components are included in the total distribution cost (Figure 5.4) (Abrahamsson 1993, Gudehus 2005):

- transport costs
- inventory costs
- warehousing costs
- service costs.

Transport costs involve two separate but interrelated systems: 1) a primary system of transport from production facilities to distribution centers and 2) a secondary system of delivery from distribution centers to customers. The primary system involves a regional scope, usually with regionally matched carriers. Typically, transport costs from plants to distribution centers are expected to decrease with fewer distribution centers, because there might be economies of scale in transporting to fewer distribution centers. In contrast, the secondary system would normally be dedicated transport, either contracted or privately owned. Transport costs from distribution centers to customers would increase because having fewer distribution centers increases the distances to customers. The sum of the transport cost curves would be minimized as the two cost elements are balanced. The typical decision to be taken is to choose between different modes of transportation that have different costs and different delivery time variability.

Changes in the transportation system during the last decade, however, have altered this balance. Establishment of the European Union and deregulation of motor carriage have intensified competition and lowered transport costs (see also Chapter 9). International transport and forward companies have established fast and cost-efficient hub-and-spoke systems across Europe. Transport costs and transit time from factory to distribution centers and from distribution centers to customers have declined. The effect is to flatten the transport cost curve, and to reduce the penalties for long transport times thusp ermitting more weight to other elements. These other elements in the decision include inventory costs, the costs of distribution center operations, service and the expanding capabilities of telecommunications. The net effect is to pull the optimal solution towards fewer distribution centers (Abrahamsson 1993).

Inventory costs include handling costs, and costs of capital tied up in inventory. Inventory has two components: cycle stocks that pass through the distribution center to satisfy demand and safety stocks that serve as insurance, a buffer against unexpected demand or interruptions in supply. Safety stocks would decrease as the number of distribution centers is reduced. The change in inventory can be approximated through the square root law, which estimates the reduction in safety stock investment (Maister 1976).[3] The law states that safety stocks can be reduced by the square root of the number of distribution centers expressed as follows (Gudehus 2005):

$$\frac{S_c}{S_d} = \frac{\sqrt{n_c}}{\sqrt{n_d}}$$

or

$$S_c = S_d \cdot \frac{\sqrt{n_c}}{\sqrt{n_d}}$$

Where S_d and S_c are safety stocks in the two systems, n_d and n_c are the numbers of distribution centers. The subscripts d and c denote decentralized and centralized networks, respectively. For example, moving from a distribution network with ten distribution centers to centralization with only one distribution center would reduce the safety stock requirements by 68%.

The square root law assumes that each individual distribution center serves an exclusive market area, demand varies randomly and safety stock levels are statistically determined. Concentrating inventories in fewer locations aggregates demands, but safety stock requirements only increase as the square root of variation in demand.

---

3. Cycle stock, which is passed through the system, is considered to be unchanged.

The square root law formula can be used under the following assumptions:

- All distribution centers maintain the same level of safety (buffer) stock protection. This assumption is consistent with the practice of many companies that seek to standardize product availability across the market.
- Demands at each distribution center in the decentralized system are not correlated. This assumption is questionable when customers do not accept supplier-defined market territories: when they can get products more easily and cheaply from other distribution centers. International customers with multiple locations may order their total requirements from the most convenient location, taking advantage of price differences.

The formula is a simple rule of thumb to estimate the potential reduction in cost. However, many other variables should be considered as part of the decision, such as access to the full assortment, options of postponing distribution to the latest possible point of time, the ease of phasing products in and out, economies of scale and service requirements.

The further cost of distribution center operations includes fixed assets, such as buildings, trucks and sorting equipment, and fixed and variable costs for distribution center personnel, systems administration, heating, electricity, etc. Centralizing distribution centers to one or a few sites would normally introduce economies of scale or networks, with lower building costs or rental costs per unit of space, the ability to take more advantage of automation in distribution center operations, easier coordination and control through the use of advanced information and communication systems and lower costs of damage, pilferage and obsolescence. The cost curve for distribution centers is therefore expected to decrease by reducing the number of distribution centers (Gudehus 2005).

The centralization of warehousing and holding inventory is a major trend in today's distribution channels. A further advantage from centralizing operations is provided by possibilities of postponement that are easier to perform in a centralized system. Final assembly or packaging and labeling for individual customers or commitment to local markets can be delayed later than in a decentralized system. This problem is especially serious because of the cost of change or repackaging for other markets, when products must be adapted or packaged for specific markets or individual customers. Postponing commitment of stock to individual markets reduces the risks of misallocation from incorrectly estimating demand or misrouting products (Pagh & Cooper 1998). Service considerations involve order cycle time, access to inventory and stockouts. All of these can result in lost sales to customers. Traditionally, these costs would be higher in a more centralized distribution system. The traditional argument has been that it would take longer to serve the customer because of longer distances. However, this argument is less important now with improved transport service. The question is not geographic distance but elapsed time. Air transport and fast and efficient road transport systems enable delivery to most customers in Europe within 24-48 hours. Although transport costs may be higher, the ability to provide delivery service may increase sales or, conversely, reduce the costs of lost sales. Service costs might well be higher in a decentralized distribution system than with one pan-European distribution center.

A further argument is that the customers get access to the full product assortment. In a two-echelon inventory system, only fast-moving items are normally available at the local level, whereas slow-movers are held at a central stocking point. If customers demand products that are not stocked locally or are out of stock, they must wait for back-order fulfillment and delivery from the central distribution center, which can result in longer lead time.

A flexible approach to centralization might be appropriate to avoid premium transport for all shipments. One alternative is to use third-party providers for physical stock-keeping and distribution, sharing facilities and networks with other shippers. If the third-party operator has regional distribution centers, it may be possible physically to locate the inventory strategically close to the customer and still manage and control the inventories centrally.

Global Retail Distribution

Retailing as a Supply Chain Function

Retailing takes place, whenever a manufacturer has opted to outsource the final distribution of finished products to special intermediaries, who sell goods and services to the ultimate consumers. Retailing can be defined as a function or as an institution (e.g. Levy & Weitz 2004, Liebmann & Zentes 2001). Retailing is a set of functions that adds value to products and services that are sold to end users, while retailing as a specific institution within a marketing channel refers to the execution of specific retail functions. These functions are typical exchange activities, which help to connect a point of production with a point of consumption and represents distribution as described earlier. This understanding refers to three different retailing core competencies or core processes (Kotzab 2005):

- Marketing processes/competencies including all activities that provide a customized set of products and services as demanded by customers.
- Logistics processes/competencies containing all activities that help to transfer this specific set of products and services to the markets.
- Support processes/competencies refering to all activities that facilitate the purchase.

In the case of having a retailer involved in the marketing channel, interaction with manufacturers is needed. This interaction is based on co-productive relationships (Normann and Ramirez 1994), as the interactive combination of the three generic retailing processes creates value not in a sequential, but in a multi-directional level. Normann & Ramirez (1994) call the result of such an inter-connection, *value constellation*.

Retailing exists in many variations which are known as retail formats. These formats should be seen as results of a demand side positioning strategy as they are all combinations of the various service output demands. The most dominant retail formats are store-based formats, but non-store formats are becoming more important.

Consumer goods retailing is especially undergoing radical transformation due to the efforts of some outstanding retailing companies, such as Wal-Mart, Metro, IKEA, Tesco, Zara and Hennes & Mauritz. Competition among those giants has become intense, with increasing concentration of ownership in fewer chains. New and renovated institutions change the task requirements. Technology, especially in information and telecommunications, has manifested itself in new processes for managing operations. Lean retailing

(Abernathy et al. 1999), a combination of information technology, transportation and simplified processing, is becoming a new model for distribution.

Grocery Retailing

Food retailing has been moving towards larger units, requiring larger volumes of goods. At the same time, retail power has been projected through private label branding. For distribution, the change occurred in stock control and delivery practice. In the United Kingdom, Tesco's, the largest retailer in Europe, shifted from direct store delivery to central distribution centers with consolidated daily store deliveries. The expansion of private label gave them stronger control over suppliers. Automated ordering processes reduced processing costs and both in-store and distribution center inventories.

The relationship between Wal-Mart, the world's largest retailer, and Procter & Gamble, the world's largest grocery package goods manufacturer, further illustrate some of the changes taking place. Point-of-sale data from the cash register has become the basis of ordering replenishment stocks and the basis for production schedules. The manufacturer now manages the retail store shelves for its products as category management. At the same time, delivery is accomplished by delivery from factory to retailer's distribution center for cross-docking and direct delivery to retail stores.

Several initiatives within the grocery industry are now underway. Most notable are vendor-managed inventories and Efficient Consumer Response that we discuss further in this chapter as operational processes in customer relationship management.

Garments

Clothing has normally been sold with long-interval reorder cycles. Department stores would normally order once per season, forecasting demand and building markdowns into the pricing structure to clear away excess inventory. Supply issues only entered into consideration during the initial buy. Lead times were long, not only for retail buyers but also for the entire manufacturing process, making the system unresponsive. Intense competition brought change. Fads and fashion can change rapidly, forcing retailers to seek faster ways to change their own operations.

Some retailers have now set up their own logistics operations to manage inventories and supplier deliveries. Others have contracted with outside operators to perform this service. There was also an initiative instituted by a textile supplier, Quick Response, to compress the time interval through more effective data communication.

The need for faster ordering and delivery leads to changes not only at the retail level but in manufacturing as well, to shorten production cycles for better response. The movement emphasizes a point that retailers recognize and are taking charge of their own supply chains, managing production and delivery of products to the store.

Global Retail Logistics Operations

The changing demand patterns of consumers have favored one-stop shopping. Large retail stores with a wide assortment of both grocery products and other consumer goods have increasing shares of the market, while small and medium-sized stores are in decline. Another trend is the rapid growth of discount stores offering a limited assortment with high turnover rates and low prices. However, the success of these stores depends on product availability at the point of sale (POS), which according to Sparks (1999), is a question of successful logistics and Supply Chain Management. Retail logistics has gained importance since the 1990's (Fernie et al. 2000, Sparks 1999, Paché 1998, Kotzab & Schnedlitz 1999) and it refers to multi-echelon logistics systems, meaning that there are many nodes from the original supplier to the final store destination (Toporowski 1996, Kotzab 2004, Schnedlitz & Teller 1999). As a consequence, retail logistics presents itself as a very complex logistics system whose flows of goods and related information depend strongly on external as well as internal factors (see Figure 5.5). Gudehus & Brandes (1997) recognize logistics as the core competence of retailing.

Figure 5.5. Factors influencing retail logistics

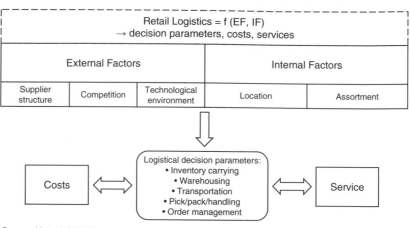

Source: Kotzab (2004)

Mulhern (1997) presents automation as a major driving force in retailing, which has also influenced retail logistics a lot, especially when it comes to the automation of the flow of information. The overall flow of information within a retail supply chain is usually managed by integrated retail logistics information systems, which are able to extract individual consumer specific purchase patterns based on real time POS data. Retail merchandise information systems allow an inter-organizational, SKU-specific, fully automated order management, that can be transformed into demand driven flexible manufacturing and order delivery systems as well as synchronized replenishment systems (Zentes 1991, Srivastava et al. 1999). Whenever a consumer buys an item, this information is immediately scanned and sent through the system, so that production planning can be set up in a real-time manner.

Economies of scale in retail outlets influence the physical store distribution systems. An increasing number of shipments go directly to the retail stores or are cross-docked at retailers' distribution centers in full pallet loads or even container loads. This allows the suppliers to simplify handling and transportation by utilizing standardized unit load modules. It also furthers the development of transport modules, which can be used as display units in the store itself. Traditional retail warehouses are transformed into zero-inventory transit terminals, where inventory processes are replaced by transportation and sorting activities. The main objective is to avoid inventory at the distribution center level.

E-commerce and the Supply Chain

The Attractiveness of a New Channel

E-commerce has created major changes in the structure and processes of distribution. The value chain is oriented towards two market processes: business-to-business (B2B) and business-to-consumer (B2C). B2B is also involved with procurement (see chapter 8). Of the two, the B2B model promises the greatest immediate potential, but B2C is expanding at a rapid pace as the market develops. The value chain involves two closely intertwined processes: 1) demand creation, resulting in customer orders and post-delivery satisfaction and 2) supply and fulfillment. The boundaries between them are unclear, but they interact strongly.

E-commerce usually consists of a Web site combined with a fulfillment system. To the customer, the Web site is the visible part of the process. Demand is created through advertising, branding, recommendations and personal referrals. The site itself plays a role in influencing demand and focusing customer choice. Once the order is in the system, the supply chain becomes paramount. How the order is fulfilled influences further purchase actions.

Fulfillment involves communication with the customer about the order, delivering the product from a supplier or distribution center to the customer, providing status information en route and any follow-up or post-sale support information. Payment can also be included as part of the fulfillment system, although we do not discuss it here.

The enablers of Internet shopping have been the postal services (e.g. Royal mail, US Post, and La Poste), the express package delivery services (UPS, Federal Express, TNT, DHL), fulfillment centers and the development of Web-resident software applications. Fulfillment centers differ from distribution centers in the order sizes that they experience. Ordinary distribution centers deal with pallet or case unit loads. Fulfillment centers service individual product orders, often with a wide variety of items. The Internet offers scalability, the ability to handle a wide range of volumes, limited only by the physical capacity to handle it. One limiting factor has been software, including installation, data, training and operating costs. By making software Web-resident, it becomes available to enterprises of any size, reducing the cost of installation, replacing it with contract or transaction-based charges.

The Case of Grocery E-tailing

Orler and Friedman (1998) recognized the importance of grocery e-tailing and introduced the Consumer Direct Services as a possible way to sell grocery goods over the Internet. Consumer direct services refer to all online-services for food and grocery items, where private users use electronic means for ordering purposes (e.g. Corbae & Balchandani 2002). This is an additional form to existing distance shopping possibilities, out of which mail order still plays a major role (e.g. Berman & Evans 1998).

The business concept behind consumer direct is that certain groups of consumers appreciate the value that consumer direct offers as a handy way for a lot of consumers to shop their groceries, as the majority of shoppers are not satisfied with their shopping experience (e.g. Siebel 2000). The different segments demand consumer direct services in a different manner (see Table 5.1), and the demand is predicted to increase.

Table 5.1. Typology of home delivery target groups

Consumer direct consumer typology after Orler & Friedman (1998) and Corbae & Balchandani (2001)		
Consumer direct consumer group	Characterization	Consumer direct attractiveness
Shopping avoider/ passive shoppers	Dislike grocery shopping, lack time but are technology-friendly	High
Necessity users	Unable to go to the store	High
New technologists/ modern responsibles	Young and technologically interested, have no time for shopping	Medium
Time starved	Dual income household with kids, time pressed	Medium/high
Responsibles	Have time but shopping is part of their 'job'	Low
Traditional shoppers	Technology avoiders, enjoy shopping, mainly housewives, high shopping frequency	Low

The example of 'tesco.com' seems to strengthen this argument from a practical point of view. With a turnover of about £ 1 billion in 2006, tesco.com is today the world's largest online retailer and shows grocery competition of how to implement electronic distribution channels (O'Connor 2004). Tesco.com in 2006 has 750,000 customers with more than 200,000 orders a week and holds a share of 65 % of the UK online grocery market (Tesco Annual Review 2006).

However, the challenging part of this channel remains logistics. Prockl & Pflaum (2002) have summarized all possible logistics models when it comes to consumer direct logistics, which is also known as the »last-mile-problem« (see Table 5.2).

Table 5.2. Last mile logistics solutions

Flow	Process	Design problem	Design alternatives				
Information flow	Order entry	What kind of order is accepted?	Conventional media (e.g. fax)	Call center		Electronic data communication	
Fulfillment flow	Picking and packing	Where is the picking and packing done?	Retail outlet	Local warehouse		Central distribution	
		Who is doing the picking and packing?	Own people	3rd party			
Reverse flow	Receiving	How is the shipment getting back to sender?	By consumer	Via parcel service	By delivery driver		
		What can be returned?	Items with refundable deposit	Rented items	Damaged and perished goods	Recyclable items	
		What is happening in case of returns?	Immediate refund	Credit for next order	New delivery of the same/other product		
Payment flow	Prizing	What pricing model is chosen?	Minimum order volume and charge	Minimum order volume	Service charge	Monthly membership fee	No charge

The Structure of E-commerce Fulfillment

Fulfillment systems have several different forms. The rapid pace of innovation in both B2B and B2C makes this into a partial list, subject to additional configurations as the market develops.

The Dell model. The Dell model takes customer orders for products directly into the assembly line. The customer order activates the supply chain. Customers can individualize their products from a list of options that can be incorporated into a production schedule. The order then initiates a flow of component parts from suppliers to be assembled into a final product, turned over to a logistics service provider, merged-in-transit with a monitor from another source, manuals from a third source, and delivered to a final customer. The system avoids holding finished product inventory, providing both lower cost and more product variety.

Automobile companies have begun to experiment with variations of this model. Car dealers currently must hold large inventories to meet specific customer preferences. Factories must produce to forecast, which results in excess inventories to clean up through heavy discounting at the end of the model year. In the North American market, both Ford and General Motors are developing processes for direct ordering to the factory. They allow customers to designate their own choices of options and colors. This model demands production systems capable of converting on-line orders into production schedules. It also makes the dealer's role uncertain in selling the vehicle. The advantages lie in inventory reduction for both the factory and dealers and broader availability for customer choice. Final assembly is driven by firm orders and not forecasts of demand.

Several alternatives are in use for e-commerce fulfillment, as shown in Figure 5.6.

Figure 5.6. E-Commerce Fulfillment Models

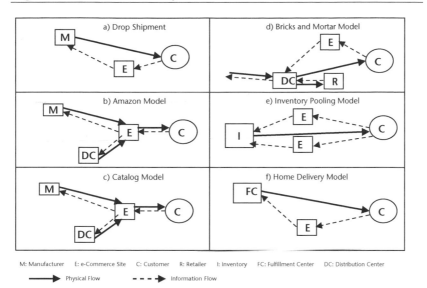

M: Manufacturer E: e-Commerce Site C: Customer R: Retailer I: Inventory FC: Fulfillment Center DC: Distribution Center

───────▶ Physical Flow   ─ ─ ─ ▶ Information Flow

M is the manufacturer, *E* an e-commerce site, *C* the customer, *R* the retailer, *I* a common inventory pool perhaps even owned by the users, as in a spares inventory holding, and *FC* a fulfillment center, a specialist separate from the retailer or the manufacturer. The dashed line depicts the order transaction flow, and the solid line is the physical product flow.

The drop shipment model. The drop shipment model follows a traditional channel pattern, the vendor takes orders, passes them to a manufacturer who then delivers to the customer. While the method of communication is new, the structure of the channel follows a well-worn path. The advantage is the absence of inventory. The disadvantage is the loss of control by the Web site operator.

The Amazon model. The Amazon model refers to the original concept of a virtual bookstore, promoting books and then transmitting orders electronically to the two largest book distributors in the United States. Books would be shipped to Amazon for subsequent delivery to the customer. More recently, Amazon opened its own distribution centers to handle books with high sales volume to provide better service. The publisher ships books not carried by Amazon or the distributor to Amazon for subsequent delivery to the customer. Amazon thus constitutes a hybrid distribution model.

The catalog model. The catalog model is also traditional. Hard copy catalogs have long been used in mail and telephone-order sales systems. This application merely shifts the catalog to electronic media. Orders may either be fulfilled from the vendor's own distribution center or drop-shipped, in a process similar to Amazon's.

The bricks-and-mortar model. The bricks-and-mortar model combines a distribution channel of distribution centers supporting conventional retail stores with a Web site that feeds orders to the same distribution centers. There are potential economies of scale, but these distribution centers may need to accommodate substantial differences in order size: individual product units from broken lots versus pallet loads.

The inventory-pooling model. The inventory-pooling model is especially important where competing customers, such as airlines, use common spare parts. Competitors draw from a common inventory pool controlled by one Web operator, such as MyAircraft.com. The advantage is that a single carrier does not have to carry a complete inventory but can even request a part from a different location.

The home delivery model. The home delivery model is currently subject to experimentation. Consumers place regular orders for grocery items with a Web-based service that routinely delivers directly to their door. One version involved actual shopping in response to a customer Internet order in a retail supermarket and then delivering to a household. This has been replaced by one where orders are filled in a traditional distribution center that also serves bricks-and-mortar stores. Another version substitutes a specifically organized distribution center and delivers to a lock box at the customer's household or drop the goods at a petrol station convenient located for the customer. The major advantage is customer convenience, and that the operators of these services avoid establishing conventional retail stores. The major detriment is the cost of serving individual households.

Elements Shaping E-commerce

The structure of e-commerce fulfillment may be developing, but specific elements will have considerable impact on its future. One is the development of package delivery systems. A second is the emergence of a specialized institution, the fulfillment center, a third is the development of contractual validity on the Web and, finally, Web-resident programs.

Express package delivery has become the most visible part of e-commerce, thanks to FedEx and UPS. They compete almost directly with government-owned postal services. UPS has become the largest transportation company in the world. It also provides Internet services for small businesses. B2C e-commerce requires home delivery, which has turned out to be a costly service. One solution is to establish consumer pick-up locations, which are now being tried experimentally.

The fulfillment center is a specialized distribution center for individual consumer orders. Whereas conventional distribution centers deal in case and pallet load order sizes, the fulfillment center deals in small orders for individual consumers. The parameters are so different that they become separate institutions and do not mix easily. Specialized enterprises have already appeared to perform this fulfillment role.

Establishing customer validity becomes important for consumer confidence and security. Several services are now being offered to perform this task. This should have the effect of reducing transaction costs because the risk element is substantially reduced. Specialized validation services are also beginning to appear as part of other Web sites.

Web-resident software is significant for the development of retailing. Because it resides on application software provider servers rather than at user sites, the cost and delay of software installation is reduced to training and data entry, in addition to licensing and/or transaction fees. The cost of entering into e-commerce is reduced. The connection to suppliers is enhanced because both parties can use the same software.

The implications are interesting. Lower costs reduce the barrier to market entry. We can envision more small, specialized e-commerce channels without being at a disadvantage against larger competitors. The access to common software, accompanied by standardization of data codes and processes would encourage flexibility in forming new supply chains to support marketing efforts.

Collaborative Distribution Models

»The new economic order is a relationship economy dominated by services in combination with new information and communication technologies.«

(Morgan 1998: 5)

Market-driven organizations (Day 2000) include the identification of individual customer requirements, the development and the supply of matching products, the coordination of the entire order process and the capturing of orders at a very early stage and their direct transmission to production. Advantage comes from responding precisely to customer needs and reducing cost by minimizing inventory in the supply chain. Certain vertically integrated companies such as Zara have all these stages incorporated in their company. Other companies such as those who operate in the fast moving consumer goods markets have to coordinate their activities with each other. Collaboration is needed in order to offer the required service output levels. We observe the building up of strategic trust-based alliances that control the dependency of the involved partners. The underlying theme is to match products and services to individual customer needs. The new combination of technology and organization requires getting as close as possible to the specific requirements and the time of need, but it also enables involving the customer directly in the operations and even the configuration of the supply chain itself.

The supply chain begins with the customer. The ultimate aim is to deliver products and services to satisfy customers. Customer preferences determine what is produced and when and how it is delivered (Blackwell 1997). Preferences ultimately result in decisions about structure, organizations and processes.

Depending on who the customer is, different marketing channel setups are possible. A consumer-oriented supply chain is a direct retail marketing and delivery system. It deals with small quantities, and service focuses on product inventory and delivery. Transactions produce data that can be utilized directly in the order process. Strategic possibilities include Internet retailing.

A trade-related supply chain is both simpler in operation because it handles larger order quantities, and more complex because it places an intermediate step between consumption and production. The simplicity reflects the structure of the traditional marketing channel of manufacturer to wholesaler to retailer, but the lack of direct contact with the final market makes forecasting difficult. Collaboration between retailers, distributors and manufacturers becomes important for production and inventory planning. These relationships generate data useful both within the relationship, and for long-term strategy in customer selection and retention.

Trade relationships can be both strategic and transaction-oriented interactions. Strategic relationships deal with negotiation, usually with partial or full visibility of supply chain data and linked production schedules. The scope can involve component and product design, selection, production and delivery schedules. Non-strategic relations involve routine order transactions of standard or limited product and service configurations with limited discretion, and the primary concerns are administrative efficiency, inventory and price.

Supply chains within specific industries have taken steps to develop stronger coordination ties among members. The general thrust has been to shift towards a pull orientation responding to customer orders. A true pull environment where customers wait for custom-ordered products is usually not possible, especially in mass production industries such as consumer package goods. The closest solution is to gain information about demand so early, that supply follows closely on demand.

The most prominent efforts in coordination has lately now in the grocery industry, the Efficient Consumer Response (ECR) initiative which is a collection of independent initiatives with a common theme of reducing inventory within the grocery industry. Two current outcomes are Vendor-Managed Inventory (VMI), extending the supply chain to the retail store shelf and Collaborative Planning, Forecasting and Replenishment (CPFR), an initiative to provide focused inter-functional communication between supplier and customer.

Efficient Consumer Response (ECR)

ECR is suggested to be a strategy of »how partners in the supply chain can best synchronize the flow of product through the distribution pipeline from point of manufacture to point of final sale» (Martin 1994: 377). ECR aims at building up strategic partnerships in the distribution channels of the grocery industry in order to increase the performance of the consumers (Kurt Salmon Associates 1993).

Svensson (2002) translates ECR as a business philosophy that centers explicitly on a vertical marketing channel perspective.

The simple message of ECR is the following: When facing stable or decreasing sales volumes, the implementation of ECR standards within the industry leads to great savings potentials. The vision of ECR is to set up a consumer-driven distribution system in which production is managed by the consumers' POS-activities. The basic notions of ECR refer to harmonization and cooperative adaptation of commonly agreed upon norms and standards that are formed to fit logistics (supply side) and marketing (demand side) business processes that avoid the duplication of costs. Supply and demand side includes the 'involved' departments (e.g. procurement, logistics, marketing and sales) at both retailer and manufacturer levels.

Processes and standards represent the way business should be conducted in this channel. These areas and categories are intended to reach the end result of ECR: a better understanding between retailers and vendors in order to offer end-user required product solutions. Suggested standards are values that members agree to adopt and primarily concern various logistics and marketing activities among supply chain partners (Grant et al. 2006)

ECR differs from Quick Response, which focused on communication and bar coding, by encouraging reorganization of other processes in the supply chain: managing replenishment inventory, new product introductions, promotions and product variety. It involves customer collaboration through involvement in retail store and supporting distribution operations. It has reduced replenishment cycles by encouraging sort-and-ship movement to replace more conventional buying and storing, and cross-docking where products move from manufacturer to store shelf, stopping only for intermediate sorting before moving to individual retail stores. For many product lines, distribution centers were converted to cross-dock operation. It has also encouraged the development and implementation of warehouse management system software to provide closer real-time control over distribution center operations.

Vendor-Managed Inventory

Vendor-Managed-Inventory is one outcome of ECR following continuous replenishment. The major difference is that, in continuous replenishment, the customer takes responsibility for inventory at the point of sale, whereas in Vendor-Managed-Inventory the supplier manages the process. In some cases, the vendor is selling on consignment and owns the inventory up to the time that the product is sold to the final customer. In effect, the supply chain »rents« the store shelf from the retailer and manages merchandising and replenishment across the store shelf in response to forecasts. Responsibility and control shift from the retail store to the manufacturer. Because it is based on forecasts, it extends the push system one step further, to the point of sale. It has also been widely adopted outside of the grocery industry.

Reduced inventory is one of the most compelling arguments for Vendor-Managed-Inventory. A simulation study by Hewlett-Packard demonstrated that Vendor-Managed-Inventory produced lower inventory costs for both manufacturers and retailers (Waller et al. 1999).

From the manufacturers' or distributors' perspectives, there are both advantages and disadvantages. The advantage is the logistics control that it offers over shipment and inventory. It eliminates fluctuations stemming from retail buying practices. Vendor-Managed-Inventory may accompany category management programs that allow the manufacturer to merchandise their products more effectively. The disadvantages are the difficulties in unstable order patterns and the need to prepare shipments for individual retail stores (Cooke 1998). It is most successful when the number of items in the product line is limited and demand is stable. It also fails when retailers either do not want to share point-of-sale data or do not use it themselves.

One of the criticisms of Vendor-Managed-Inventory by the major retailers has been that it has not been integrated into their own processes. Retailers conventionally order in fixed quantities. In a Vendor-Managed-Inventory system, the supplier makes shipments based on the difference between actual and maximum inventory levels, based on sales data, performing production planning on the basis of forecasts. Point of sale data are not always available and are often difficult to interpret. Withdrawals from distribution centers are sometimes used instead, resulting in lagged and distorted data. Deliveries must be precise in time and quantity, as the retailer carries no safety stocks. Retailers also complain that they have no visibility into the suppliers' system to identify problem areas.

Collaborative Planning, Forecasting and Replenishment

In 1998, the Voluntary Interindustry Commerce Standards (VICS) introduced Collaborative Planning, Forecasting and Replenishment (CPFR) as »*a collection of new business practices that leverage the internet and electronic data interchange in order to radically reduce inventories and expenses while improving customer service*« and also introduced a nine-step process model as a guideline for CPFR collaboration. The predominant part of the process consists of partners joining in a number of joint planning activities in different time horizons (e.g. Fliedner 2003). This is shown in Figure 5.7).

Figure 5.7. An overview of the CPFR Model

CPFR tries to eliminate all the deficiencies that have been presented through previous forms of collaboration (e.g. ECR, QR) (Barratt & Oliveira 2001) and can be seen as a very holistic SCM approach that tries to integrate supply chain relations at a strategic level. In that sense can CPFR be classified as a Type 3 collaboration as suggested by Holweg et al. (2005) as one forecast decision point is eliminated and the replenishment decision is merged with the planning of the supplier.

Conclusion

The supply chain starts with the customer, at the front end of the supply chain. Today, we see an increasing focus on the individual demand fulfilment as market segments become smaller and more precisely defined. The underlying trend is towards one-on-one marketing leading to one-to-one distribution. This can be translated into more product variety and supply flexibility. Simultaneously, the ability of customers to search the market for lower prices increases the pressure for lower costs.

For the supply system, emphasis on the demand chain is beneficial. Real-time order data is the goal, and Collaborative Planning, Forecasting and Replenishment, and sales force automation have compressed the supply chain and made it more transparent. Overall, the management of relations is becoming more important than the pure movement of goods.

Several other trends are changing the marketplace: Internet consumer shopping, extranet industrial purchasing, individual product configuration through mass customization, close collaboration between manufacturers and suppliers with intermediate customers such as retailers and automated sales contact. Even in situations that normally require human interpretation, more transactions will be automated.

The principal obstacle to this transformation lies with organization of the process. Responding to the market involves design of options for customers, information flow to indicate demand and flexibility in response. Interfunctional coordination is a traditional hurdle. When inter-organizational coordination is added, the problem is compounded. Strategy can only be successful when the supply chain can sense the direction of the market as change takes place.

Illustrative Case

ECR by Triumph International in Germany[4]

Triumph-International (TI) is a family run private company and was founded in Germany in 1886. It is one of the leading underwear producers in the world and in 2003 had an annual turnover of 1.6 billion Euro, and 38,691 employees. 49 % of the sales volume comes from the Overseas-Department that includes the most important Asian markets and 35 % stem from 10 Western European countries except Germany. Triumph-Germany who is headquartered in Munich, Germany, achieved, with about 2,000 employees approximately 13 % of the total sales volume. The remaining three percent come from Triumph-Eastern Europe that includes seven country markets.

The multinational manufacturing and marketing organization operates in 120 countries around the world. Triumph's reputation as an innovative, resourceful and caring company has been maintained since its earliest days. Ever versatile, Triumph has kept up with, and often led, fashion trends through the years, from the corsets made for ladies of society in the late 19th century to its wide range of fashionable styles for today's markets in underwear, nightwear, swimwear and sportswear.

With a market share for the brand Triump of 27 %, TI is the market leader in Germany. Market research has shown that 45 % of all German women have products from TI followed by Schiesser (42 %), H&M (25 %), Esprit (15 %), Sloggi (14 %) and Bee Dees (14 %). TI can certainly be recognized as the leading company in the German corsetry and underwear market. Market developments are not promising. Traditional linen retailing does not grow anymore and increased globalization leads to increased concentration and aggravated competiton. Textile retailing is increasingly becoming vertically integrated and the assortments are blurring. Consumers are spending less money for underwear and fulfilling their re-

---

4. Adapted from Kotzab, H. & Walenta, C. (2006): ECR/EDI – Strategische Allianzen mit den Handelspartnern bei der Triumph International AG, in. Müller-Hagedorn, L. & Mesch, R. (ed.): Efficient Consumer Response in der Praxis, Frankfurt am Main: Deutscher Fachverlag, pp. 27-56

quirements in other retail stores than in textile stores (e.g. grocery stores or discounters).

TI initiated their first ECR-trials in 1997 as the company recognized that ECR is an efficient answer to consumer demand. Knowing the consumer is key! Their ECR approach includes all major ECR areas as outlined in Figure 5.8. This approach is currently applied amongst more than 500 business partners of TI in Germany.

Figure 5.8. ECR by Triumph International

Efficient assortment	Efficient sales	Efficient product introduction	Efficient Replenishment
• Assortment optimization • Inventory optimization	• Innovative presentation of the merchandise • Space optimization • Sales promotion	• Optimization of introduction activities and information	• Automated ordering • Never-out-of-stock • Fast replenishment • Cross docking • EDI

←-----------------Category Management-----------------→

←------------------------------ECR--→

Category management refers to the joint optimization of assortments. Both, retailer and TI have to identify the link to the consumer. TI therefore developed a space management approach that identifies the optimal assortment for any store size. The store space is divided into style-areas that include TI products as well as products of the competitors. Layout deficiencies as claimed by consumers can be eliminated. The results of this approach include improvement of the shelf productivity as well as increased turnover rates, a minimization of out of stocks as well as elimination of over capacity in the shelves.

All of TI's retail partners had the application possiblities but due to lack of knowledge, electronic communication was not used. TI helped their retail partners to use their computer facilities so that electronic order transmissions, shipping notification and invoicing were possible. The simple use of existing EDI-standards helped to reduce the order administration by 7.5 hours for an order of 120 pieces. Using the TI-generated bar codes (EAN) and not retail specific barcodes helped with savings up to € 125,000 a year. TI truly acted as a channel and category captain!

6. Production
Issues for the Supply Chain

*»The more advanced or modern the production process, the
longer and more complicated the chain of linkages.«*

S. Cohen & J. Sysman (1987, p. 14)

Production is the operational center of the product flow process, as
shown in Figure 6.1. It becomes the dividing point of product flow.
From this point forward, product flow is determined by actual customer orders or by forecast demand. Behind this point, product
components and materials move towards production either in response to customer orders or in quantities determined by forecasts.
As both actual and anticipated orders enter the production schedule, the speed of the production process determines how much inventory must be carried downstream towards the market. It also
determines the rates at which suppliers must respond. Further, production efficiency and quality along with product design determine
the ability of the supply chain to compete in global markets.

Figure 6.1. Production

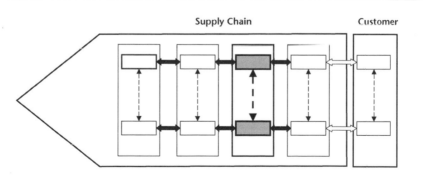

While this chapter is concerned with processes inside the factory, it
is important to recognize the position of production within the sup-

ply chain. First, the factory is linked to both suppliers and customers. It does not operate either in a vacuum or in a one-way flow. Both the customers and suppliers interact with production, changing schedules, modifying products or even influencing design. As we have noted in Chapter 2, companies have been under pressure to outsource major parts or even all of production, so that inter-organizational relations and capabilities become important considerations.

This chapter focuses on production issues that have had, and continue to have significant impact on SCM. We begin with a discussion of some major trends and philosophies in the production arena that have shaped the competitive landscape of SCM. Then we describe how some of the current and emerging production strategies are setting the stage for the future of SCM.

Supply Chain Requirements – A chain of Processes

The global nature of production is important in developing the supply chain. Investment in factories becomes a strategy, of timing and access, where new investment decisions recognize opportunities across the globe. Factories must be located close to markets, sources of technology or low labor cost. Production technologies have been diffused around the world, so manufacturing in the global marketplace must operate with comparable efficiency if they are to remain competitive. Plant managers have to be familiar with current factory technologies, even when modified to meet local conditions. In fact, many new production concepts are introduced in newly built plants in developing countries where no legacies exist from older production systems.

A global production system is a network. Logistics becomes important for connecting the production process, both within host countries and externally. The transport system ultimately determines lead times for orders and the ability to respond to change. Some factories are deliberately located in local markets despite higher labor costs to respond quickly to local product demands.

Production may take place in successive or in parallel stages. Semiconductor production had often began in the United States, flowed to Malaysia or other points in Southeast Asia for hand assembly and then returned to the United States for finishing. Similarly, garment production often has the following processes: (1) cutting fabrics with computer-controlled laser cutting machines in Europe or North America, (2) sending the pieces to Southeast Asia for labor-intensive assembly, and then (3) return to the United States for sale. The current emphasis in global companies is on regional production to serve local markets. In addition, plants may specialize in specific products, taking responsibility for design, global production and distribution.

Global networks are accompanied by pressures to create local supply sources, both to satisfy employment needs and to transfer technology. Before it started producing automobile engines in the United States, Toyota supplied complete engine assemblies from its plant in Japan to its United States plant in Kentucky, in order to take advantage of economies of scale in production. This also works both ways, United States electronics companies operate in Japan to take advantage of technology. Components are procured locally, but the real motivation is to learn about technological advances.

Plants also vary by factor costs, principally in labor wage costs. The garment industry, with its high commitment to manual work, has pursued low-wage economies across Asia. As one country or region develops higher wages and skills, factories either move or change to automation and even to participation in product development.

Two other factors should be noted: infrastructure and culture. These terms, however, are imprecisely defined in common usage. Infrastructure generally refers to transport, telecommunication and governmental support. The state of transport and telecommunications networks influences how governmental support is obtained. Governments can impose taxes, incentives and regulation to such infrastructure. Governments also influence factory decisions, sometimes forcing higher levels of factory development than the immediate market would dictate.

Culture enters in through workers' attitudes and educational levels and the general business climate. Motivation and capabilities in the labor force play obvious roles in determining the success of production ventures. How factories are received within the local community becomes an important determinant for a successful operation.

Management Concepts in Production and SCM

The management of the supply chain has changed since the birth of *mass production* (sometimes referred to as *Fordism*) with Ford's Model T. Mass production involved the full use of the assembly line by rearranging the functional organization of the factory into a moving line where each worker had a specific task to accomplish. When it was introduced for the first time (in 1913) to assemble the Model T, the amount of labor time spent making a single car reduced from 12 hours and 8 minutes to 2 hours and 35 minutes. As the production volume increased, the price also fell from 800 USD in 1908 to 360 USD in 1916 (Pine 1993). The characteristics of mass production are summarized in Table 6.1.

Table 6.1. Principles of Mass Production (Pine 1993)

Principles of Mass Production
• Interchangeable parts
• Specialized machines
• Focus on the process of production
• Division of labor
• Flow
• Focus on low costs and low prices
• Economies of scale
• Product standardization
• Degree of specialization
• Focus on operational efficiency
• Hierarchical organization with professional managers
• Vertical integration

The adoption of the American mass production system in Europe took place during the 1930s. European car manufacturers, however, modified the American system to tailor to the different geographic cultures and needs. For instance, European cars were smaller and had smaller engines. During this time, European manufacturers such as Jaguar, Mercedes Benz, Porsche, BMW, Saab, Volvo, Rover and Ferrari, entered the U.S. market with 'specialist' or luxury cars.

The evolving production environment has introduced new elements into manufacturing operations. They include the change in orientation from push to pull, real time interaction with customer orders, wider product ranges with more emphasis on designing modular products, customization, expansion of computer and information technology in production planning, execution and control, quality and new production technologies. Since 1960, various management concepts have emerged, from Forrester Effect to Collaborative Planning, Forecasting and Replenishment (CPFR), as illustrated in Figure 6.2.

Figure 6.2. Management Concepts since 1960.

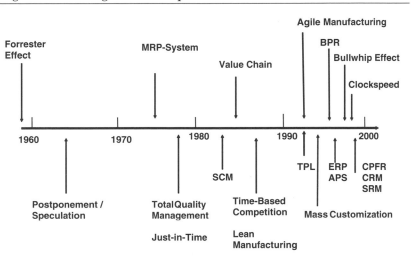

Just-in-Time and Lean Manufacturing

The *just-in-time* (JIT) and *lean manufacturing* (sometimes referred to as *lean production*) concepts have their origins from the Toyota Production System (TPS) – Toyota's philosophy on operations management. TPS was developed to improve quality and productivity, as a result of two philosophies that are central to Japanese culture: elimination of waste and respect for people. According to Toyota, there are seven types of waste (Suzaki 1987):

- Waste from overproduction
- Waste of waiting time
- Transportation waste
- Inventory waste
- Processing waste
- Waste of motion
- Waste for product defects

In order to eliminate waste, the following elements were introduced (Chase et al. 2004):

1) *Focused factory networks* – These are small specialized plants that are designed so the operations can be run more economically.
2) Group technology (GT) – GT groups machines and processes together to make a part.
3) Quality at the source – When a quality problem is found during the assembly process, the worker is obligated to stop the line.
4) JIT production
5) Uniform plant loading (or *heijunka* in Japanese) – It means to distribute volume and different specifications evenly over the span of production.
6) Kanban production control system – Kanban means 'signboard', 'sign' or 'instruction card' in Japanese.
7) Minimized set up times

JIT production coordinates the movement of parts through the production system and the supply chain to meet customer meets. The use of kanban is to signal the preceding process that more parts are needed. The basic idea behind JIT is to produce goods when they are needed. This means the buffer inventory that exists with the traditional approach is eliminated, as illustrated in Figure 6.3.

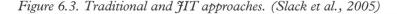

Figure 6.3. Traditional and JIT approaches. (Slack et al., 2005)

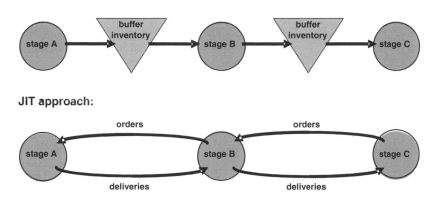

JIT brings materials and components to the specific point and time where they would be immediately used in quantities to match the production schedule. This creates immediate advantages to the receiving firm in the form of reduced inventory and factory space, reduced material handling, and quality control through smaller lot sizes. For suppliers, JIT means 1) stable production, 2) inventory on-hand, shifting the inventory cost from manufacturer to supplier or 3) flexible production processes that can produce on demand. It requires close coordination between manufacturer, carrier, and supplier, including telecommunication links.

Intelligent use of JIT requires buffer inventory to account for delays, although not in the quantities required before JIT. From the standpoint of total supply chain costs, it also requires supplier development to improve production processes. The principal value of JIT is more than just to reduce inventory. Inventory hides problems. Taking inventory away exposes problems so they can be solved. Applying JIT throughout the supply chain would reduce inventory for the entire pipeline. Buffering, however, has advantages where demand or supply conditions are unstable.

Although JIT is primarily a Japanese approach, Western companies quickly adopted the philosophy. In the West, JIT became synonymous with the following terms:

- Continuous flow manufacturing
- World class manufacturing
- High value-added manufacturing
- Stockless production
- Low-inventory production
- Fast-throughput manufacturing
- Lean manufacturing
- Short cycle time manufacturing
- Lean production

The term 'lean production' is used by Womack et al. (1990) in *The Machine that Changed the World*. Lean production had a tremendous influence on mass producers, mainly the American automobile industry. During the 1980s, for instance, the Big Three (i.e. Ford, Chrysler, and GM) 'transplanted' the JIT thinking into their operations. The New United Motor Manufacturing Industry (NUMMI), a joint venture between GM and Toyota, was a clear indication that JIT techniques could be transferred and implemented in the West. According to Lamming (1993) lean producers assume the benefits of JIT, total quality, total employee involvement, and build a global strategy on that basis. Slack et al. (2005) summarize the lean philosophy of operations as the basis for JIT techniques that include JIT methods of planning and control, as shown in Figure 6.4.

Figure 6.4. The Lean Philosophy summarized.

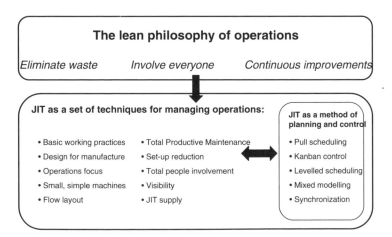

Source: Slack et al. 2005

Materials Requirement Planning (MRP)

While JIT and lean manufacturing are pull systems, Materials Requirement Planning (MRP) systems are push systems. MRP is driven by the master production schedule, which indicates the exact timing and quantity of orders for all components.

MRP consists of a production schedule and a bill of materials (BOM). The underlying logic is that a forecast determines a production schedule, projected on a specific time schedule. Each product has a BOM, composed of the product components and materials that enter into this final production schedule. MRP requires the development of three steps: 1) the master production schedule, 2), the BOM and 3) the master production schedule together with the BOM to create input requirements. The number of units in the production schedule combined with the BOM determines the number of component units that will be required. The MRP must take into account the lead time and order quantities for these components. It also takes into account BOM for component units and their subcomponents in the same manner. It is logical to think of the BOM in terms of levels. Products (level 0) are assemblies of components. Each component (level 1) also has assemblies (level 2). Carrying the product materials beyond three or four levels is impractical, as it requires too much data, especially if schedules change.

We demonstrate the process with an oversimplified example in Figure 6.5 on bicycle production. There are three components: frames, wheels, and tires. Assembled bicycles are at level 0. Frames and wheels are at the final assembly level (1) and wheels at one level lower at level (2). First we introduce the bill of materials for a single bicycle. Note that we include order information for components.

The production schedule calls for these numbers of bicycles per week. To further simply the problem, we will assume that they can only be made in batches of 30 units at one time.

The production schedule as seen at the start of week 1 therefore calls for 30 frames and 60 wheels in week 1. These wheels require 60 tires. Leaving the frame out for still further simplicity, we concentrate on the wheels and tires. Note that we start the week with 80 wheels on hand. These will take care of week 1. We anticipate delivery of an order for 200 wheels that we placed one week before our start date in time for assembly in week 3. We further anticipate production of 60 bicycles each in weeks 5 and 6. In week 3, we have 10 wheels on hand, receive 200 more and use 60 for a net inventory of 160. Again, there is enough on hand to cover week 5, but we anticipate having only 40 on hand at the end of the period. We need to place an order in week 3, to arrive in week 6. The same process will be followed for tires. The tire requirement is driven by the wheel requirement and is in turn by the assembled bicycle production schedule. Note that the lead-time for tires is 2 weeks and the order quantity is 300. At this point, the production planner has a view over the entire forecast period.

Figure 6.5. Materials Requirements Planning (MRP)

Master Production Schedule - Bicycles

Weeks	1	2	3	4	5	6
Requirements	30	-	40	-	50	-

Order quantity = 200 units   Lead time = 3 weeks   **Component Plan - Wheels**

Projected Requirements	60		80		100	
Scheduled Receipts			200			
On hand, End of Period 100	40	40	160	160	60	60
Planned Order Release				200		

Order Quantity = 300 units   Lead time = 2 weeks   **Component Plan - Tires**

Projected Requirements				200		
Scheduled Receipts			300			
On hand, End of Period	0	0	0	100	100	100
Planned Order Release		300				300

The documentation needed for MRP can be extensive, recording the production schedule for each component, scheduled receipts, inventory on-hand and the planned order releases.

There is more than one problem, however, with MRP. First, as the production schedule changes, it requires the system to pull in more component inventory, which makes the lead time a constraint. The feasible schedule becomes even more difficult to change. With the data requirements, regeneration of the entire MRP schedule requires massive amounts of computer capacity, although greater power in computers reduces that problem. Second, going below three or four levels becomes cumbersome, leaving lower level sub-components to be managed through simpler inventory systems. Third, order quantities theoretically could be matched to the requirements of the production schedule, but this may not match schedules or optimal order quantities of suppliers. Even without an environment of constant change, MRP is likely to accumulate inventory on hand. Changing requirements further compounds the problem. MRP was designed for stand alone applications on mainframe computers without input in real time. Connection to real time systems is not a feasible option. Most companies have made extensive changes to make it operate without any success.

As the manufacturing and supply chain processes became more complex, not mentioning the increasing computing capacity of computers and how products are assembled in the production lines, firms started to develop better systems. Examples of more sophisticated systems that have been evolved from MRP include: Manufacturing Resource Planning (MRP II), Enterprise Resource Planning (ERP), and Collaborative Planning, Forecasting and Replenishment (CPFR). The goal of MRP II is to plan and monitor all the resources of manufacturing including marketing, finance, and engineering. Despite these improvements, it was a sequential system, all the tasks such as master production scheduling and final production scheduling were independent of each other. Both MRP and MRP II assumed infinite production capacity. As stand-alone applications, they are not readily adapted to real-time applications and the rapid changes necessary to deal with interactive demand requirements. Optimizing solutions are often too difficult to achieve. As described in Chapter 5, CPFR is an emerging approach for analyzing inter-organizational collaboration across supply chains.

Total Quality Management

Total Quality Management (TQM) is an approach that involves the whole organization with focus of producing high-quality goods and services. The goal of TQM for many organizations is to ensure that the organization's systems can consistently produce the design of the product or service. TQM programs have four main elements:

- Leadership
- Employee involvement
- Product and process excellence
- Customer focus

Challenges of TQM Implementation

Properly implemented TQM systems have improved organizational performance of many firms in the form of fewer defects, lower inventory levels, reduced lead-times, higher flexibility, and increased employee satisfaction. However, the implementation itself can be very challenging. In a study of American companies, Salegna and Fazel (2000) identified the following obstacles when implementing the TQM:

- Lack of a company-wide definition of quality
- Lack of a formalized strategic plan for change
- Lack of a customer focus
- Poor inter-organizational communication
- Lack of real employee empowerment
- Lack of employee trust in senior management
- View of quality programs as a quick fix
- Drive for short-term financial results
- Politics and turf issues
- Lack of strong motivation
- Lack of time to devote to quality initiatives
- Lack of leadership

TQM for Supply Chain Management

With increasing outsourcing activities and globalization, the role of quality management systems has to be redefined, especially with respect to SCM. The traditional TQM systems have worked well for many firms. Manufacturers of electronic components, IT services and automotive industry, for instance, are faced with fierce pricing pressure and have recently considered sourcing in markets with low labor markets. The quest for survival has, furthermore, made matters even worse with the rising costs in Latin America, the expansion of European Union, and the increasing economic power of Asian markets.

European Foundation of Quality Management (EFQM)

TQM practices also differ between Japan, U.S.A., and Europe. While Japanese practice is mostly applied from JIT and lean management approaches, Americans tend to apply Six Sigma principles. In Europe, the European Foundation of Quality Management (EFQM) framework is widely used. EFQM was formed by 14 leading Western European companies in 1988 to recognize quality achievement (Slack et al. 2004), especially for public sectors and SMEs (small and medium enterprises). A recent study reveals that EFQM has 19 partner organizations in Europe, and over 20 000 member companies, which include 60% of the top 25 companies in Europe (Basu 2004).

EFQM is consisted of the following concepts of quality excellence (www.efqm.org):

- Results orientation
- Customer focus
- Leadership and constancy of purpose
- Management by process and facts
- People development and involvement
- Continuous learning, innovation and improvement
- Partnership development
- Corporate social responsibility

Furthermore, EFQM framework is structure around 9 criteria:

- Leadership
- People
- Policy and strategy
- Partnerships and resources
- Processes
- People results
- Customer results
- Society results
- Key performance results

ISO Standards

International Standard Organization (ISO) defines TQM as »the management approach to organization, centered on quality, based on the participation of all its members and aiming at long term success through customer satisfaction, and benefits to all members of organization and society.« The most known ISO standards are ISO 9000 and ISO 14000. The ISO 9000 series basically certify that the firm meets certain industry standards. This should enhance customer confidence about the quality of the product or service provided by the firm. In order to gain ISO 9000 certification, the company has to produce well-documented standard and consistent processes that meet certain specific standards or performance to an accredited auditor.

Six Sigma

Six Sigma was created by Motorola, and has been a tool for managing the number of defects of a production process. The purpose is to manufacture products with zero defects, measured in terms of defects per million (DPM) opportunities. Sigma stands for the number of standard deviations. Six Sigma translates to 3.4 DPM.

Six Sigma is built on statistical processes control techniques, which can be extremely complex. Currently Six Sigma has been improved to include other business functions of the firm, such as product development, finance, human resources, and services. Such an approach to TQM has been gaining popularity mainly among large corporations, such as General Electric (GE), Honeywell International, Ford, and Raytheon. GE, for example, launched the Six Sigma program in 1995. Over a four-year period, GE was able to achieve 20% margin improvement, 12-18% capital increase, and 12% reduction in headcount per year (Basu 2004). Depending on the level of expertise desired, practitioners can be trained to become: Master Black Belt, Black Belt, or Green Belt.

Two emerging developments within Six Sigma are 'Lean Sigma' and 'Fit Sigma'. Lean Sigma extends Six Sigma to include the lean production concept, such as eliminating waste and improving process capability. Fit Sigma extends Lean Sigma by integrating the following features (Basu 2004:14):

- Formal senior management review process
- Period self-assessment with a structured checklist (adopted from EFQM thinking)
- Continuous learning and knowledge management program
- Extension of Six Sigma across the whole business

Integration of Manufacturing Technologies

In addition to Toyota's TPS, various material-process technologies and systems have emerged since the adoption of JIT and lean manufacturing. Cellular manufacturing, flexible manufacturing systems (FMS), and computer integrated manufacturing (CIM) are material-processing technologies.

Figure 6.6. Integration of Manufacturing Technologies

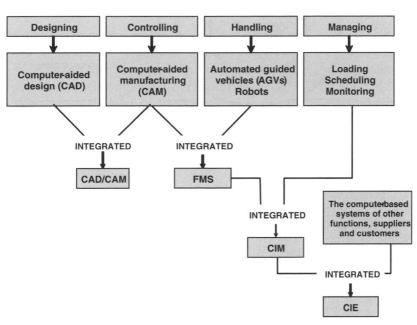

Source: Slack et al. 2005

Cellular Manufacturing

In this method, production is divided into teams responsible for producing a complete product or component, shown in Figure 6.7. Workstations are arranged in a U-shaped layout so that each team member can see the output of the team. While production tasks are different from each other, workers become multi-skilled, able to take over any specific task in the cell. Production problems are thus visible to every member of the team who takes on total responsibility for product output. Production control is thus decentralized to the team. Cellular production has been tried in a variety of industries.

Figure 6.7. Cellular Manufacturing

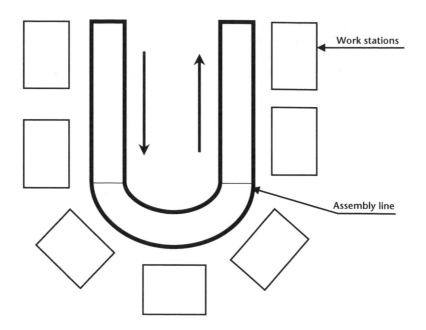

One case where cellular production actually improves production lead-time is in the garment industry (Abernathy et al. 1999). Typically, garment assembly is a piece-work business, performed either at home or at a factory where each worker receives inventory as work, performs one task and at the end of the day passes the completed work to the next station. It is not hard to visualize a lengthy production process that does not respond well to rapid change. Abernathy et al. (1999) describe a cellular production line, with responsibility for a complete garment, reducing the time interval to as low as one day. When consumer tastes change rapidly, this would seem to be an improvement. However, they noted that the industry adoption has been slow.

Flexible Manufacturing System
Different processing technologies can be combined to form the flexible manufacturing cells and systems, depending on the degree of mechanization, automation, computer control, and how flexible it is to produce a wide variety of products. Flexible manufacturing

systems (FMS) typically consist of the following technologies: computer numerically controlled (CNC) machines, AGVs (Automated guided vehicles), industrial robots to load and unload parts, and a comprehensive computer control system to run the system.

CNC machines use computers to reduce human interaction with the process. Their purpose is to increase accuracy, precision and repeatability of the process. AGVs use wires or cables that are embedded onto the floor in order to direct driverless cars or vehicles to various locations in the manufacturing plant. AGVs are often used to transport materials or components to the designated assembly area. Industrial robots, furthermore, have virtually substituted human manipulation and other highly repetitive tasks. Robots can be reprogrammed to serve multiple functions, such as welding and soldering. Some advanced robots have abilities to 'feel' and 'see'.

Computer Integrated Manufacturing
Computer integrated manufacturing (CIM) brings together all the automated technologies mentioned above via a network and integrated database. The integration of manufacturing technologies to incorporate design, control, handling, and managing is illustrated in Figure 6.6. There are three stages of integration: (1) integration between areas of activities (i.e. DAC/CAM and FMS), (2) integration of all internal activities (i.e. CIM), and (3) integration of organization's CIM activities with other functions to form the computer-integrated enterprise (CIE).

The CIM system contains computer-based software to manage the production process from design to total production (Hill 1994). The defined boundaries sometimes expand to include distribution, reflecting the integration of the entire firm with the production process. It includes computer-aided design, computer-assisted manufacturing and computer numerical control. In addition, there are computer-aided production systems that plan, schedule and control the production process. Computer-aided design has accelerated the design process that provides a vehicle for communication and also links with precise data for tooling and programming of machine tools for factory automation. Computer numerical control involves numerical control of machine tools in factory automation. Computer-aided production systems include 1) a BOM that lists assemblies, components and materials for the final product 2) a list of operations to produce each component for the BOM, itemized by time requirements for machines, tooling and labor, 3) work centers required with their capacities, 4) customer delivery requirements, and 5) components and materials available and the procurement requirements.

Agile Supply Chain

According to Naylor et al. (1999, p. 108): »agility means using market knowledge and a virtual corporation to exploit profitable opportunities in a volatile market place.« In order to be agile, an organization or a supply chain needs to be flexible. Agility as a business concept is originated from FMS.

Linking Lean and Agile Supply Chains

Agility makes the supply chain focus not only on efficiency (gained from lean manufacturing) but also on effectiveness. A comparison of lean supply with agile supply is illustrated in Table 6.2. (Mason-Jones et al. 2000, from Bruce, Daly a Towers, 2004)

Table 6.2. A comparison of lean supply with agile supply.

Distinguishing attributes	Lean supply	Agile supply
Typical products	Commodities	Fashion goods
Marketplace demand	Predictable	Volatile
Product variety	Low	High
Product life cycle	Long	Short
Customer drivers	Cost	Availability
Profit margin	Low	High
Dominant costs	Physical costs	Marketability costs
Stockout penalties	Long term contractual	Immediate and volatile
Purchasing policy	Buy goods	Assign capacity
information enrichment	Highly desirable	Obligatory
Forecasting mechanism	Algorithmic	Consultative

Other concepts within the agile supply chain include: 'agile manufacturing' and 'leagile'.

Agile manufacturing

Agile manufacturing (sometimes referred to as agile production) is not a concept in itself but a call for attention to a set of currently available technologies and their applications as a change in orientation from mass production to customized manufacturing (Sharp et al. 1999). Agile manufacturing has been labeled the competitive environment of the future (Kidd 1994). Genasekaran (1999b) describes its manufacturing processes as a customer-supplier integrated process for product design, manufacturing, marketing and support services, which requires an integration of various members of supply chain. Yusuf et al. (1999) describe it as a holistic approach to production more than a collection of technologies. Gunasekaran (1999a) furthermore defines it along four dimensions: cooperation, value-based pricing, organizational change, and investment in information. Technologies are not necessarily new in themselves, but have been grouped together to respond to the new pressures from the marketplace.

There is little consensus on a precise definition although desired outputs from production are familiar: cost, flexibility, responsiveness and quality. The inputs are equally familiar: information systems, shifts in decision location, supply chain coordination, real-time ordering, customization and virtual partnerships and rapid prototyping. Ultimately, it stresses the ability to respond rapidly to new challenges.

A model of interdependence is replacing the model of the self-contained factory with customers, suppliers, marketing, and procurement. Procurement and marketing were considered as appendages, one to secure materials and components in the open market, the other to move products out the door to customers. Information was not shared and production was an island unto itself. The new model is one of close integration to match individual customer requirements and serve strategy beyond the boundaries of production. Agile manufacturing, therefore, recognizes the need to integrate production operations into the supply chain. When developing an agile manufacturing system, the following factors should be taken into consideration (Figure 6.8): strategies, systems, technologies and people.

Figure 6.8. Components of an Agile Manufacturing System .

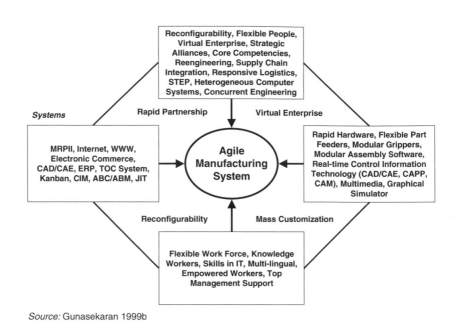

Source: Gunasekaran 1999b

Leagile

'Leagile' is a combination of lean and agile approaches combined at the decoupling point for optimal supply chain management (Bruce, Daly & Towers 2004). The decoupling point is where the real demand penetrates upstream in a supply chain (Christopher 2000), or when the inventories are transformed to be 'customized' into customers' demands. This transformation from standardized goods into customized goods is enabled by postponement strategies (Chapter 2). Christopher, Peck & Towill (2006) propose a framework to distinguish between lean, agile, and leagile supply chains (Figure 6.8), based on the following variables: products (standard or special), demand (stable or volatile), and replenishment lead-times (short or long).

Figure 6.9. Leagile classified in terms of supply and demand characteristics.

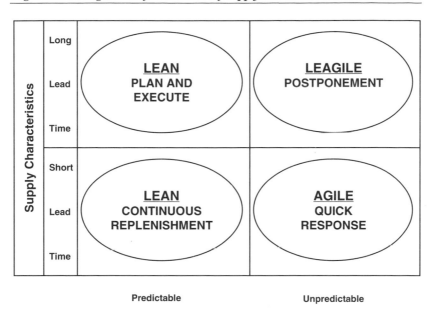

Source: Christopher, Peck & Towill 2006

Figure 6.9 suggests four supply chain strategies. For instance, companies with predictable demand, short replenishment lead times (e.g., Procter & Gamble and Wal-Mart in the USA) should pursue a 'continuous replenishment' strategy. Companies that make or source ahead of demand in the most efficient way should pursue lean supply chain (with plan and execute strategy). UK retailer Woolworths, for instance, orders one million plastic Christmas trees from China six months ahead of the season. When demand becomes unpredictable, companies should pursue either agile (short lead time) or leagile supply chains (long lead time). The Spanish fashion garment manufacturer Zara is an example of agile supply chain, as they can move products into their stores across Europe in as little as three to four weeks after they have been designed. Hewlett Packard's postponement strategy with Deskjet printers fits the leagile supply chain strategy. In this case, semi-finished printers are built then shipped to four regional centers around the world, in which they are finally configured and delivered when actual customer orders are received.

Strategic Perspectives on Production Processes and Technology

The basic choices in production processes are shown in Figure 6.10. Traditionally, these have been determined by the size of the production run progressing from the scale of a single project, through batch production to production lines, and continuous flow processes with large volumes. Manufacturing processes can be classified according to their volume-variety characteristics into five types: (1) project, (2) jobbing, (3) batch, (4) mass, and (5) continuous.

Figure 6.10. Product Volume and Process

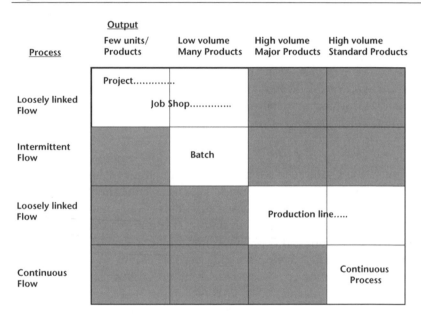

- *Projects* can be characterized as make-to-order with little standardization. One example is construction of a major building or a unique piece of capital equipment. Suppliers are called in for a specific project with no prospect of continuation on that project, although they may participate on other projects with the same contractor.
- *Job shops* deal with small-order production. They are organized around work centers with specialized activities. The work (pro-

duction) flows through a series of work centers. Job shops offer flexibility in that they can apply routine operations to several different production sequences at the same time, and their sequences can be changed to meet the specific requirements for each product. The potential disadvantages lie in the scheduling, where conflicts may result in delay in completion, need for movement between work centers and inability of workers to see the results of their output.

- *Batch processing* is similar to job shop operations in that it deals with a variety of operations, where production volume does not warrant full assembly lines. The disadvantages lie in the changeovers from one product run to another, requiring changing dies or assembly jigs, setting up machining or other special processes. Batch processing is probably the most common form of production and is sometimes combined with assembly line operations.
- *Production lines* are associated with standardized products produced in high volumes.
- *Continuous flow* is characteristic of chemical processes such as petroleum and refinery production. They are normally capital-intensive and therefore involve financial risk.

There are dangers of either over- or underinvestment. Referring to Figure 6.10, a lateral move assumes anticipation of higher volume that may not materialize, a case of overinvestment. On the other hand, if market demand is underestimated, production will be late in shifting to higher volume processes, leading to possible congestion in production and higher operating costs, a case of underinvestment. From a strategic perspective, there appears to be a narrowly balanced efficiency path between product demand and production capacity.

The demands of the supply chain modify this view. First is the problem of product variety. While component volume may justify production lines, final assembly may be done in batches with high service requirements, high inventory costs, in batch or even something approaching job shop scale. Second is customization. Depending on the stage where it takes place, it may require job shop operations throughout the production process despite high volume. Both of these involve short production runs in at least one stage. In turn, this requires flexibility in changeovers not only within the factory but also with suppliers to change over as well. Changing colors on an automobile assembly line requires changeovers not only in the paint shop but also in components such as bumpers and upholstery that are sometimes supplied through external production.

Product Design for the Supply Chain

It may be surprising, but product design plays an important role in the supply chain. There is a market role for product design in corporate strategy, but there are also supply issues involved as well. In this section, we consider modular products, concurrent engineering, design for manufacturability, and design for logistics.

Modular Products Demand of Production

Modular products give the supply chain flexibility to meet the requirements of a broad product range without the need for specialized production for individual products (Van Hoek & Weken 1998a, b). The definition of a product module also defines the scope of partners within the supply chain: how much partners will participate in the supply chain. Van Hoek & Weken identify three levels of modular production: product, product group and process. Product modules refer to individual products, product group modules mean standardized interchangeable modules across a set of products. Process modularity is the ability to change the process itself, suggesting a means to production flexibility. Modularity presents opportunities for increasing product variety and accelerating product development. It creates more flexible development processes at lower cost, decoupling design tasks to enable module development to proceed on different schedules.

Modularity also defines organizations, specifying roles to be played in the development process (Sanchez 1999). Hsuan (1999) makes the point that supplier–buyer interdependence influences the outcome: more collaboration makes for a higher degree of modular development. Interfaces and constraints should be defined early in the process.

In the computer industry, changes in chip design to incorporate more functions also change the roles of partners in designing circuit boards to adapt to the new chip design. As chips take on more circuitry, there is less need at a given level of product development for other chips to be attached to the motherboard. This may also mean that the overall product sophistication of personal computers can also change. This in turn shifts the proportions of value added and hence profitability of individual stages.

There is also inventory saving with modular product design. By pooling modules as a group, production is easier because it can be undertaken in longer production runs in advance of demand. Demand for a modular product group can be forecasted far more easily than for individual products, which have erratic demand. For this reason, production of modules is usually more stable than demand for individual products. This also has the effect of reducing finished product inventories, enabling postponement of final assembly. Hewlett-Packard builds inkjet printers in modules, with country-specific power supplies, packaging and manuals added as demand calls (Feitzinger & Lee 1997). Van Hoek & Weken (2000) report on Smart Car, development of a modular automobile by Daimler-Chrysler and SMH (Swatch). The car consists of five modules with only seven main suppliers who bring in their modules only when called by the production schedule. Modularization extends production in some cases, to the supplier and into the distribution center such as the case of Hewlett-Packard Inkjet Printers.

There are also distinct disadvantages. The entire product line must be planned with a basic platform with common interfaces for different modules. While it is possible to update modules, basic innovation involving fundamental product change is slowed. Further, modular design may be suboptimal for the performance of individual products in the line. Modularization will inevitably involve compromise, trading off production and inventory efficiency against product performance. More detailed description of the role of new product development for SCM is outlined in Chapter 7.

Concurrent Engineering

Supply chain management must be concerned with time to market: the time interval between design concept and market introduction. Automobile companies are extremely aware of the advantages of rapid product introduction. DaimlerChrysler in the United States used to take as long as 5 years to bring a new model to market. In some cases, the elapsed time has been reduced to 24 months, providing the ability to capture changing market tastes through rapid product development. Normal practice meant successive stages of development and design, performed in isolation, and then passed to the next stage, described as »throwing the project over the wall«. This has often resulted in limited communication between groups, and in some cases, product designs that were often difficult to manufacture, with low productivity and poor reliability. Concurrent engineering brings many activities of a firm (especially product development and manufacturing) from a sequential process into a parallel process. Significant gains in elapsed time and problem solution have come as concurrent engineering where designers and production process engineers work cooperatively on the same design to eliminate problems before they begin. Beyond individual products, Japanese semiconductor manufacturers encourage their capital equipment suppliers to develop processes in advance of the product itself (Methé 1992). Information technology also offers substantial time reduction. Computer-aided design offers the ability to develop and communicate designs without having to commit them to physical models (21st Century Airliner, Schrage 2000).

Design for Manufacturability

As with most manufacturing firms, savings from manufacturing is a major determinant of a firm's financial success. Design for manufacturability (DFM) is a technique used by product designers to minimize manufacturing costs. Various sources indicate that approximately 80% of a product's costs are determined at the design stages (i.e. prior to the final production stage). The DFM technique often involves the following tasks (Ulrich & Eppinger 2004, p. 212):

- Estimate the manufacturing costs
- Reduce the costs of components
- Reduce the costs of assembly
- Reduce the costs of supporting production
- Consider the impact of DFM decisions on other factors

A crucial part of DFM is related to design for assembly (DFA), which is concerned with checking ease of assembly and manufacturing to stimulate product simplification (Goffin 1998).

Design for Logistics

Logistics involves both movement and inventory. The location of product assembly affects the cost structure, order cycle time and the ability to respond to change. Modularization enters in through the point of assembly. Product complexity limits the number of possible locations, reflecting skill levels, equipment and product support.

Packaging design is dictated by the environments that the products have to be exposed to, the products' physical dimensions, and whether the products are recyclable. Environmental considerations such as outdoor exposure or need for refrigeration affect packaging requirements and cost. Dimensions affect materials handling and cost. In many industries, warehouse pallet dimensions and the number of cartons per pallet determine costs. Unfortunately, dimensions differ between countries and industries, such as the difference between Euro-pallet (1200 by 800 mm) and the United States Grocery Industry standard (40 by 48 inches), suggesting a need for more international standards. Physical density is also a problem, it reduces transport efficiency because most vehicles, containers, and aircraft tend to be limited more by space than weight. Further, bulky items are more costly to store because they occupy more warehouse space.

Value density is the ratio of product value to weight. The long-term trend has been towards higher value in relation to weight. In fact, even Alan Greenspan, former Chairman of the US Federal Reserve Board noted, »While the weight of current economic output is probably only modestly higher than it was a half century ago, value added adjusted for price change has risen well over three-fold« (Coyle 1997, p. viii). Higher value means that products are more mobile because they can absorb higher transport costs without seriously influencing total costs. This means either longer distances from production to market, or more use of air cargo, or both.

Emerging Production Paradigm – Modular Production

As we move from mass production to lean manufacturing, the more modern production paradigms take, to some extent, strategic importance of customers and suppliers. These new paradigms are based on certain principles such as: modularization to created product variety, postponement to delay customization as late as possible, and, mass customization to create individualized customization to customers. These paradigms are changing the configuration of supply chains. Modular production is an example of such a paradigm.

Modular production is a manufacturing principle that focuses on decreasing product complexity, and at the same time to offer increased product variety to customers. It is based on modularization principles, in which a complex task is decomposed into smaller portions so they can be managed independently. In modular production, suppliers are an integral part of the supply, assembly, production, and distribution processes. Such requirements force suppliers to be co-located with the manufacturing of the product. As long as the interfaces are well specified (with all the suppliers complying with such specifications), the system should function as desired when various modules are assembled together.

Although the concept of modular production has been around since the 1960's (Starr, 1965), only a handful of companies (mainly in the automotive industry) have been able to implement it successfully. One of the most notable examples is the Volkswagen (VW) truck and bus plant in Resende, Brazil. It was opened in 1996, and since then it has broken the conventional method of car production. The production flow is designed to integrate seven production modules. Each partner is responsible for controlling the quality of its module, and the suppliers receive payment only when the final assembled vehicle is approved by VW (Lima, 1997). Another popular example is Smart Car, described below.

Illustrative Case

Smart Car

Smart Car began in 1994 as a joint venture between Daimler-Benz and the Swiss watchmaker Swatch. In 1998 Swatch sold its part and the unit was reorganized as a separate DaimlerChrysler subsidiary. Smart Car is a small, plastic-bodied, two-seater city-car, measuring 2.5 meters in length, 1.51 meters in width, and 1.53 meters in height (van Hoek & Harrison 203) – a little more than the half of the length of a Volkswagen Beetle. The average fuel consumption is

3 liters per 100 km. DaimlerChrysler originally forecasted a yearly sale of about 200,000 units. It hoped to capture 7-8% of the car market and would achieve initial profits within six years (ICFAI Business School 2006). In 2004, however, only about 150,000 units were sold, and the company had lost about $5 billion since its launch in 1998.

The Smart Car is sold in 36 countries, including Germany, France, England, Canada, and Japan. In 2006 DaimlerChrysler announced that the two-seater Smart (called 'Smart Fortwo') would be available in U.S.A. Three additional models will be available in 2008. Because Fortwo's were so popular, a right-hand-drive version, a sporty roadster and a four-seater version, called Smart Forfour was launched in 2004. So far, this model has also been popular (with approximately 100,000 units sold), but DaimlerChrysler has decided to discontinue this model. The decision was based on cut-throat competition and the current economic situation.

Smart cars face major challenges at the American market including their size, pricing, and increasing competition from other fuel efficient automakers for sub-compact cars in the market. Smart cars sizes were also viewed as unsafe, in terms of crash protection for collision.

The Smart Car can be ordered from about 140 Smart Centers throughout Europe or configured and ordered via the Internet and then delivered from the nearest Smart Center. The Smart Centers are high-profile showrooms located in shopping centers or other highly visible places in big cities. From the outside the characteristic Smart tower is a landmark, which can be seen from far away. The Smart Centers have repair shop areas where body parts can be replaced quickly or new product features added. When a customer orders a car from a Smart Center, the order is submitted to Hambach, France. Special features can be added and body parts changed in the Smart Centers. The order to delivery lead-time is 2–3 weeks (Van Hoek & Weken 2000).

Smart's Production System

Smart Ville is the name of the production plant in Hambach in El-zas-Lothringen, France, where the Smart Car is assembled. In Smart Ville seven system suppliers are integrated with the Smart assembly operation. The »integrated« suppliers have co-invested in the production location and are located adjacent to the assembly hall of Mitsubishi Motors Company (Figure 6.11). The workforce at the Hambach plant is about 1800 (in 2002), of which 1100 are provided by the seven integrators. The Smart Car consists of five modules: the platform, powertrain, doors and roof, electronics, and the cockpit. The modules are pre-assembled on site and synchronized with the production schedule for final assembly. It takes 4.5 hours to assemble a car (and the plastic body panels can be completely replaced in an hour) (van Hoek & Weken 2000), with more than 400 vehicles built every day in a two-shift operation.

The outsourcing process has gone further than in most other car manufacturing companies. For example, the pressing and painting process has been outsourced to a first-tier supplier. Information systems to plan and control production and logistics operations are run by Andersen Consulting. The buildings and the sites were sold to a property company under a lease-back arrangement.

Smart Car has been a prototype for a new way to organize collaboration between the assembly plant and first-tier suppliers. The investment costs have been estimated to be about USD 1.5 billion (Ewing & Johnston 1999). The Smart Car concept is considered as a strategic learning project in the DaimlerChysler Corporation. Other car manufacturers have generally accepted the Smart Car concept as of key importance to future organization of assembly processes. For instance, General Motors has built a plant in Brazil incorporating the ideas of heavy contribution of supplier capital and a small assembly plant.

In order to stay competitive, a new 'environment friendly' factory is being built at the Smartville Energy Centre at Hambach. This factory is designed with quality of the environment in mind. For instance, all the materials used in building the factory are from environmental friendly material. Recycled, and raw materials are used in the manufacturing process of the Smart Cars.

Figure 6.11. Smart's Production Plant Layout.

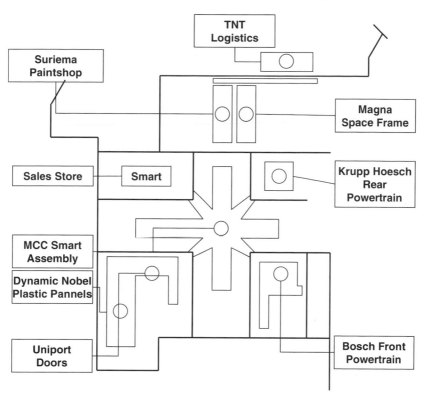

Source: www.autoIntell.com

7. Innovation Management in Supply Chains

> »*Winning in business today demands innovation.*
> *Companies that innovate reap all the advantages of a*
> *first mover. They acquire a deep knowledge of new markets*
> *and develop strong relationships within them. Innovators*
> *also build a reputation of being able to solve*
> *the most challenging problems.*«
>
> R.M. Kanter (2001)

We live in a world that is governed by technology in the form of computers, TV, mobile phones, cars, ATMs, etc. Through technological solutions, innovation in products, processes and services are created and advanced. For companies, innovation management brings various rewards, such as increased profitability, recognition, and hopefully increased market share. This chapter focuses on the role of new product development (NPD) in influencing the success and failure of innovations in shaping the supply chain. From a product flow perspective, NPD is the first process companies need to consider when developing new products or enhancing existing products, as shown in Figure 7.1.

It often takes a long time for new products to be developed, evaluated, tested, manufactured, marketed, and subsequently sold in the market. Positive return on investment of a product may not show up in corporate accounting books until many years after its introduction to the market place (Aaker & Jacobson 1994, Hodder & Riggs 1985). The high degree of uncertainty and risk inherent in new product development (NPD) projects pose enormous difficulty for managers to make rational decisions regarding technology selection of product platforms and architecture strategies for the next-generation of product families. Furthermore, the complexity of NPD and innovation management policies often extends to include other members of the supply chain. These reasons make return on investment of NPD projects extremely difficult to assess.

Figure 7.1. New Product Development in SCM.

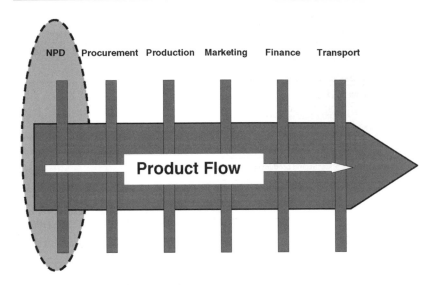

The creation of an innovation rests strongly in a firm's NPD capabilities and the ability to make technical changes, be they incremental or radical. Incremental innovation introduces relatively minor changes to the existing product, often applied to existing markets and customers. Radical innovation establishes new sets of core design concepts, and is driven by technological, market, and regulatory forces (Henderson & Clark 1990).

The most comprehensive and used framework to describe the new product development process is by Ulrich & Eppinger (2004), of which the NPD process can be divided into six phases (Figure 7.2). With an understanding of the NPD process, we can make better judgments about how the design and development of products influence the management of supply chains.

Figure 7.2. The Six Phases of NPD Process

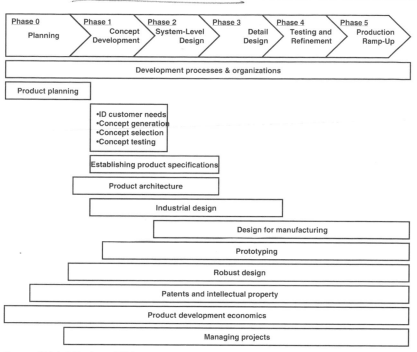

Source: Ulrich & Eppinger 2004

Phase 0 – Planning

Planning is generally referred to as the initial phase of the NPD. During this stage the designers consider possible product platform strategies. This is when new technologies should be assessed. At this stage, marketing activities usually includes the articulation of market opportunities and definition of market segments. Manufacturing identifies production constraints as well as to set supply chain strategy. In addition, research department (if it exists) demonstrates available technologies, and the finance department provides planning goals. Most importantly, the General Manager has to allocate resources for the projects.

Phase 1 – Concept Development

Concept Development Phase is when the designers investigate the feasibility of product concepts, develop industrial design concepts, and build, as well as test, experimental prototypes. At this stage, marketing department is in charge of collecting customer needs, of identifying lead users and competitive products. This means that the manufacturing department has to estimate manufacturing costs and assess production feasibility. Moreover, the finance department has to facilitate economic analysis while the legal department investigates patent issues.

Phase 2 – System Level Design

At the System Level Design Phase the designers typically generate alternative product architectures, define major subsystems and interfaces, and to refine industrial designs. The marketing department is usually responsible for developing plan(s) for product options and extended product families. The manufacturing department is responsible for identifying suppliers for key components, performing make-buy analysis, defining final assembly scheme, and setting target costs. Furthermore, the finance department is responsible for facilitating make-buy analysis while the service department is responsible for identifying service issues.

Phase 3 – Detailed Design

At the Detailed Design Phase the designers define part geometry, choose materials, assign tolerances, and complete industrial design control documentation. The marketing department typically has the duty of developing marketing plans. This means that, at this stage, the manufacturing department has to define piece-part production processes, design tooling, define quality assurance processes, and to begin procurement of long-lead tooling.

Phase 4 – Testing and Refinement

At Testing and Refinement Phase, the designers typically have to perform reliability, life, and performance testing. The designers are also responsible for obtaining regulatory approvals and implementing design changes. Concurrently, the marketing department has to develop promotion and launch materials and facilitate field testing. In addition, the manufacturing department has to facilitate supplier ramp-up, refine fabrication and assembly processes, train work force, and refine quality assurance processes. The sales department has to develop a sales plan, which can be quite complicated.

Phase 5 – Production Ramp-up
At Production Ramp-Up Phase, changes can be very costly. The design department has to evaluate early production output, the marketing department has to place early production with key customers, and the manufacturing department begins operation of the entire production system.

Platform Strategies

Increasing numbers of firms are applying platform strategies to achieve economies of scale while creating customization of their products. For example, Volkswagen produces the following car models based on a common platform (Muffatto & Roveda 2000): Skoda Octavia, Seat Leon, VW Golf, Audi A3, and Audi TT. Ford now uses the same 'luxury platform' to produce Lincoln, Jaguars and Volvos (Gartman 2004). The product price and generic strategy (ranging from cost leadership to differentiation) determine the differentiation between the models. As put by Meyer & Utterback (1993, p. 30), »a robust platform is the heart of a successful product family, serving as a foundation for a series of closely related products.« On the other hand, it has been argued that it threatens to reduce the real differences between cars that drive the niche markets (Rubenstein 2001).

According to Simon (1995), a complex system can be divided into hierarchies (consisting of few less complex stable components, each of these of a few even simpler components, and so on) that can be divided into many independent components having relatively many relations among them, so that the behavior of each component depends on the behavior of others. A great number of systems (e.g., automobiles, airplanes, computers, elevators, ships, etc.) are complex systems that can be subdivided into hierarchies (e.g., subsystems, modules, sub-modules, etc.). At the highest level of analysis of these complex systems, is the product platform that can be defined as (Meyer & Lehnerd, 1997, p. 39): »... a set of subsystems and interfaces that form a common structure from which a stream of derivatives products can be efficiently developed and produced, [and] the combination of subsystems and interfaces defines the architecture of single product.«

Product platform is, then, a collection of shared assets (such as components, processes, knowledge, and people and relationships) that are shared by a set of products (Robertson & Ulrich 1998). Product platform has tremendous implications for a firm's product portfolio management, in which sets of technologies and products are evaluated in relation to each other. How platform architecture is planned and configured, in terms of the technology composition contained in the subsystems and respective interfaces linking these subsystems, has significant impact on trade-offs between the degree of standardization and customization of product families and respective end products (Mikkola 2006).

Product platform provides the basis for the product architectures and related product families. A product family refers to (Farrell and Simpson: p. 541) »a group of related products that share common features, components, and subsystems, and yet satisfy a variety of market niches.« The basic relationship between product platform, product family and respective variations of end products is illustrated in Figure 7.3.

Figure 7.3. Product Platform, Product Family, and Product Variants.

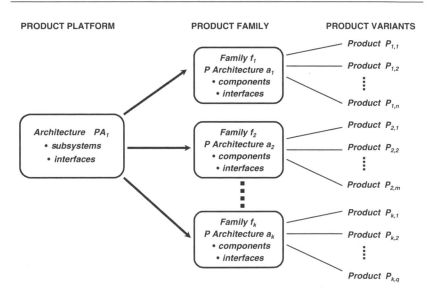

Source: Mikkola 2003

For a given product platform, a number of product families [e.g., f_1, f_2, ..., f_k] can be generated, each with its own unique architecture [e.g., a_1, a_2, ..., a_k]. Based on one product family architecture, many different products are created. For example, family f_1 with product architecture a_1 can produce n products, and family f_2, m products, and so on. For example, the platform for *Audi A4* is the basis for *VW Golf*, the new *Beetle*, and *Bora* product families (or sometimes labeled as brands) (Lung et al. 1999).

Product Architecture Strategies

In order to implement a platform strategy, product architecture strategies have to be devised (Mikkola 2003). Product architecture strategy decisions are closely related to the way systems are decomposed, the selection of components to be used and how these components are linked with one another. A great portion of the literature analyzes such strategies in terms of modularization, strategic sourcing, mass customization, and postponement.

Architectural design decisions consider various trade-offs, and there are no optimal designs. Subsequently, most optimization models offer limited insights. Hence, the focus is not to find the optimal level of modularity in product architectures, but to understand the fundamental relationships shared between components and respective interfaces as well as the tightness of coupling shared among the components. The goal is also to gain a better understanding about the role of unique components and their substitutability in product architectures (needed for long term survival of firms), which has direct implications for mass customization, and subsequently SCM (Mikkola & Gassmann 2003).

According to Robertson & Ulrich (1998), good product development means good platform development, and in order to do so, a firm must carefully align its differentiation and commonality plan through an iterative planning process. This planning process leverages the trade-offs between distinctiveness and commonality in product architectures. As explained by Ulrich & Eppinger (1995): »architectural decisions allow the detailed design and testing of [basic] building blocks to be assigned to teams, individuals, and/or suppliers, such that development of different portions of the product can be carried out simultaneously.«

Product architecture is often established during the system-level design phase of the product development process after the basic technological working principles have been established, but before the design of component and subsystems has begun. In general, changes to the elements/constituents of product architectures (components and respective interfaces) are avoided after the design-freeze stage. Depending on the interdependencies shared between the components and respective interfaces, product architectures can vary from integral to modular.

Modular Product Architectures

Modular product architectures are used as flexible platforms for leveraging a large number of product variations (Gilmore & Pine 1997), enabling a firm to gain cost savings through economies of scale from component commonality, inventory, logistics, as well as to introduce technologically improved products more rapidly. Modular product architectures typically have components with standardized interfaces, which enables mixing-and-matching of components. Some of the motivations for product change include upgrade, add-ons, adaptation, wear, consumption, flexibility in use, and reuse (Ulrich & Eppinger 1995). Modular architectures enable firms to minimize the physical changes required to achieve a functional change. Product variants are often achieved through modular product architectures where changes in one component do not lead to changes in other components, and physical changes can be more easily varied without adding tremendous complexity to the manufacturing system. Outsourcing decisions are often made concurrently with the design of modular product architectures, and specialization of knowledge is gained through division of labor. Examples of products with modular product architectures include LEGO toys, personal computers, bicycles, elevators, etc.

In modular product architectures, components can be disaggregated and recombined into new configurations, possibly substituting various new components into the configuration, without losing functionality and performance (Langlois 1992). Upgradability is also enhanced as it enables firms to listen to customer feedback and alter their systems accordingly by substituting some components while retaining others (Garud & Kumaraswamy 1993, 1995).

Integral Product Architectures

In integral product architectures, the interfaces shared between the components are coupled (Ulrich 1995), or highly interdependent. Changes to one component cannot be made without making changes to other components. Costs of customized components tend to be higher due to the integral nature of product architectures where an improvement in functional performance can not be achieved without making changes to other components. This can be prohibitively costly for complex systems. As the interfaces of the customized components become standardized, costs are significantly reduced as changes to product architecture can be localized and made without incurring costly changes to other components, making outsourcing possible.

Integral architectures are designed with maximum performance in mind. The optimization of certain dimensions of performance is achieved by combining many functional elements. In other words, modifications to any one component cannot be done without requiring the redesign of the product (Ulrich & Eppinger 2004). Apollo Computer in the 1980s, for instance, was a more integral product (compared to IBM PCs and Sun Microsystems, for instance). High performance was emphasized and the workstation was designed with a proprietary architecture based on Apollo's own operating and network management systems, and much of the hardware was designed in-house. Apollo's designers believed that it was necessary for various parts of the design to be highly interdependent for achieving high levels of performance in the final product (Baldwin & Clark 1997).

Chesbrough & Kusunoki (2001) identify three advantages of integral development:

1) Superior access to information – more information can be shared more quickly within the firm than can be shared between firms, that is, less 'impacted information' (Williamson 1975).
2) Weaker incentives to exploit temporary advantages inside the firm – individuals within different divisions that must coordinate have relatively little to gain directly from exploiting a temporary advantage over individuals in a sister division, that is, 'low-powered incentives' (Williamson 1985).

3) Tighter appropriability of the returns generated by the solutions to technical problems (Teece 1986) – divisions within a firm that work together to reduce technical interdependence complexities can be fairly certain that they will benefit from the results.

Interface Specification and Standardization

Interface specifications define the protocol for the fundamental interactions across all components comprising a technological system. The setting and development of interface specifications have a tremendous impact on setting industry standards, such as Global System for Mobile Communications (GSM), Time Division Multiple Access (TDMA), and Code Division Multiple Access (CDMA) to name a few.

The degree to which interfaces become standardized and specified defines the compatibility between components, hence the degree of modularity embedded in product architectures. Standard components have well-specified and standardized interfaces, hence product architectures comprised of standard components are considered modular. According to Langlois and Robertson (1995, p. 5), »standardization of interfaces creates 'external economies of scope' that substitute in large part for centralized coordination among the wielders of complementary capabilities. This allows the makers of components to concentrate their capabilities narrowly and deeply, and thus to improve their piece of the system independently of others.«

Ulrich (1995) classifies modular product architecture into three sub-types:

1) Slot – each of the interfaces between components is different from each other, so that various components in the product cannot be interchanged. For example, the linkage of an automobile radio to the instrument panel is different from that of a speedometer (although their interface connectors may look similar), and naturally these two components cannot be interchanged.
2) Bus – there is a common bus to which other physical components are connected via the same type of interface. Examples of bus architecture include the extension card for a personal computer, and wiring harness of a car.

2) Sectional – all interfaces are of the same type with no single element to which all the other components attach. Examples of sectional architecture include pipes, furniture (e.g., from IKEA), personal computers, etc.

Conversely, interface specifications and hence compatibility issues of unique components with other components of a given product architecture are not well understood. Consequently, introduction of unique components into product architectures reduces modularity freedom. Interface specification of such components is dependent on technological innovation available in the market or feasible for the firm to develop. It is only when the interfaces of these components become well specified and standardized, that they become standard components (Mikkola & Gassmann 2003).

In general, standardization of parts enables tasks to be performed independently, encouraging supplier specialization to take place often fostering the emergence of network organizations. The rate at which interface specifications change (which has deep implications for component integration and decomposition) influences the way product architecture is controlled, hence impacting how firms organize within the industry compete or cooperate around the new set of interface specifications.

NPD's Impact on Outsourcing

The survival of a high-tech firm is strongly associated with its NPD as well as supply chain strategies. However, the increasing complexity of technologies and shorter product life cycles, combined with the globalization of markets and aggressive global competitors, are forcing high-tech firms to reconsider their strategic thinking. Better performers also include NPD in the SCM strategic planning.

Modular product architectures require that component interfaces be loosely coupled so that functional specification and detailed engineering activities can be carried out independently. Firms engaged in pursuing modularization as a NPD strategy are concerned with cost savings gained from component standardization and outsourcing. According to Trent & Monczka (1998), increasing supplier involvement in product development during the 1990s has been one important means of achieving performance improvements. For instance, by the late 1990s, close to fifty percent of a Boeing commercial aircraft's total value was contributed by outsourcing (Fine 1998:10). Similar trends are evidenced in the PC industry. Up to 1995, all of IBM's printed circuit boards (PCB) were built in-house. Today, in contrast, it only makes about 10 % of its boards. Furthermore, it used to make 85 % of the memory chips used in computers, and in 1999 the figure dropped to 15 %. IBM used to build its power supplies and keyboards and assemble all of its own computers in-house. Today, these tasks are outsourced to contract manufacturers, including PC-assembly, manufactured notebook computers, lower-end servers and workstations, and mass storage devices. From 1986 to 1996 the proportion of IBM's revenues spent on outside suppliers increased from 28 % to 51 %. An economic outcome is that IBM has reduced the overall costs by about 20% through outsourcing (Carbone 1999). In 2005 IBM sold its PC division to Lenovo Group, the largest PC maker in China, formerly known as Legend (Kanellos 2004).

Early Supplier Involvement in NPD

In order to cope with the risks associated with component outsourcing, many firms have engaged in strategic partnerships and alliances. Firms form alliances in order to gain production efficiencies, to expedite access to technology (as well as markets and customers), to promote organizational learning, to expand strategic competencies, and so on. There is an extensive body of studies identifying partnerships and alliances with suppliers as a strategy for competitive advantage. While some focus on the importance of early supplier involvement in product development, others focus on the supplier-buyer relationship itself. However, according to a KPMG survey, 70% of the failed strategic alliances are caused by problems with respect to the relationship of the partnership (Duysters et al. 1998).

The increasing trend towards outsourcing is somewhat in concert with discussion of consolidation of the supply base and the subsequent benefits of early supply involvement in NPD as a means of shortening lead times. Intensified competitive pressures during the early 1980s have forced Western assemblers to look for further savings from their components. Many automakers tried to exploit economies of scale in parts production, which meant rationalizing their supplier structure and reducing the number of suppliers (Lamming 1993). It has been shown that every mass producer of automobiles during the 1980s, reduced the number of suppliers from a range of 2,000 to 2,500 at the beginning of the decade to between 1,000 and 1,500 at the end (Womack et al. 1990, p. 157).

Nevertheless, firms are plotting strategies to leverage the supply chain with product variety and customization. Competition will always exist when more than one supplier is involved, and product architecture modularity has a critical role in the global trend in reducing the number of suppliers. Conversely, the suppliers are gaining more bargaining power with the increasing state-of-the-art technology and process complexities embedded in the product. This suggests that a firm should start to develop a nurturing relationship with its suppliers as early as the product development stage. The customers can benefit from modular product architecture based products in the form of price, quality, accessibility, features, selection, customization, and availability of the products.

Innovation and Supplier Relationships

Innovation can require investment in highly specific assets – both human and physical. From a transaction costs approach, innovation should therefore take place in-house or through quasi-vertical integration, where the buyer has ownership of specialized equipment and knowledge. However, the transaction cost approach cannot deal with innovation, because this approach assumes efficient resource allocation with known opportunities. Innovation however involves uncertain environments and outcomes. The solution is not to use classical contracts that specify outcomes, but to enter into agreements that share risk and reward.

Sako (1996) suggests that the buyer can enhance the suppliers' incentives to create their own product and process innovation by rewarding their innovative contributions by giving them equitable proportions of the financial gains from their innovation. McMillan (1990) refers to the practice of Japanese manufacturing, where the buyer specifies a target price and a time path of price reduction targets, which remain unchanged whether suppliers enhance their efficiency or not. In some cases, the supplier can even capture 100% of the gain through operating efficiency.

Another method of improving supplier efficiency is through joint analysis of costs using established value analyses and engineering methods, sharing the efficiency gains equally. This contrasts with traditional Western bargaining patterns, where the buyer dictates both prices and equal shares of additional cost savings at the same time. In product innovation, *trust* becomes a necessary precondition for involving suppliers in the design and development process. Chapter 3 mentioned three types of trust: contractual, competence and goodwill trust. Trust must encompass all of these meanings.

Clark & Fujimoto (1991) classified motor vehicle parts in the car industry into 1) supplier-proprietary (developed entirely by parts supplier), 2) detail-controlled (assembler-developed and controlled), and 3) black-box (jointly developed) categories. Comparing the ratios of the three types for Japan, the US and Europe, they found 8:62:30 in Japan, 3:16:81 in the United States and 7:39:54 in Europe. The relatively high proportion of black box parts in Japan indicates the high level of trust prevailing in their supplier relations. By contrast, the high level of detailed controlled parts in the United States reflects low trust leading to a high degree of vertical integration.

Prahalad & Hamel (1990) argue that a firm's core competence is a source of value creation and establishing competitive advantage, and therefore should be retained in-house. The implication for supplier relationships and innovation is that analysis of resources and capabilities that create core competencies is essential to determining what processes to outsource. However, the firm still has to define and identify what competencies will be the core for the future.

The guiding principles in both transaction cost approach and strategic management for the use of subcontracting are clear: subcontract out processes and components where only small costs can be saved and the processes do not undermine the firm's core competence. However, Sako (1996) comments, »these principles may protect the innovative capability of the buyer firm, but it may be protected because of, at the expense of, or regardless of, the innovative capability of the supplier firm«.

An alternative would be to forge partnerships and strategic alliances with innovative suppliers, to create superior products and capitalize on the combined effort and resources. The prerequisites are the presence of mutual trust, a capacity to learn, and a reward for innovative contribution. Then, the firm can engage in subcontracting, conducive to innovation only if both parties have organizations that can take the advantages of learning opportunities

Transaction Cost Perspective on NPD and Outsourcing

From the Transaction Cost Economics (TCE) perspective, component outsourcing decisions change the firm's boundary decisions as well. With outsourcing a firm enters into a contractual agreement with a supplier, hence shifting the ownership and decision rights of the outsourced function to the supplier (Momme et al. 2000). Both greater product complexity and technological uncertainty favor making a component in-house because they are likely to increase the cost of writing fully-specified contracts, which would result in higher transaction costs compared with the option of doing the design and production work in-house at a lower coordination cost (Masten 1984). Outsourcing decisions should be governed by specificity of the assets required to engage in development and production of the product.

Standardization of interfaces of components in product architectures creates the option for firms to engage in component outsourcing, as it enables division of labor hence increased specialization of tasks (Langlois 1992), encouraging the firm to pursue specialized learning curves and increase its differentiation from competitors (Schilling 2000). Component outsourcing enables the firm to purchase components from multiple sources, hence decreasing switching costs. It also implies that the firm has to share its technological knowledge with its suppliers, and competitors can gain access to such knowledge, which has been a source of incentive for many entrepreneurial firms. For the assembler, this can be extremely risky as it may lose the technological control of its product architectures, especially if it takes its suppliers capabilities and management practices for granted.

One of the main purposes of outsourcing is to have the supplier assume certain classes of investments and risks, such as demand variability. Due to greater complexity, higher specialization, and new technological capabilities, outside suppliers can perform many activities at lower costs and with higher value added than a fully integrated company can. New production technologies have also moved manufacturing economies of scale toward the supplier (Quinn & Hilmer 1994). On the other hand, outsourcing is also an important cause for the continuing loss of international competitiveness by Western firms (Bettis et al. 1992). Involving suppliers early during the development process is one way to cope with the risks of outsourcing. Advantages of supplier participation in NPD include shorter project development lead times, savings in project costs, improved perceived product quality, and better manufacturability. It also brings the supplier and the firm closer in sharing not only knowledge and learning, but technological risks as well. Outsourcing and the subsequent supplier involvement is only possible when a system can be decomposed in such a way that interfaces of the components are well specified and standardized, which is a central focus on modularization strategies. How a firm decides to decompose its system is dependent on the technological complexity of the system and its NPD capabilities as well as on the suppliers' capabilities in developing the component at lower cost and faster lead times than by the firm itself (Mikkola 2003).

Component Design for Postponement

Outsourcing of product designs and/or manufacturing processes are tightly dependent on how products are designed. *Design for postponement* is one such strategy. It refers to design of the products or the processes so that postponement is possible in order to counteract the complexity and uncertainty factors that paralyse supply chains. One type of postponement closely related to modularization is *form postponement*, which calls for a fundamental change of the product architecture by using designs that standardize some of the components (hence changing the form of the product architecture) or process steps. In order for postponement to be successful, products or processes should be modular in structure (Lee 1998). In other words, product modularity requires module interface to be redesigned so that they can easily be assembled and tested as a total unit. Furthermore, because postponement strategies involve product development and many members of the value chain, collaboration becomes inevitable between multiple functions (e.g., cross-functional integration) or organizations (e.g., collaborative efforts among multiple firms).

One of the aims of the form postponement strategy is to retain product commonality as far downstream in the supply chain as possible. The degree of product commonality, or the degree of substitutability (especially when unique components are considered), is deeply rooted in the design of product architectures with respect to component composition and interfaces shared with these components. Postponement strategies are also treated as vehicles for benefiting from mass customization and vice-versa. The role of modularization with respect to form postponement is illustrated in Figure 7.4. Under the normal circumstances, the same firm produces Products X and Y. Component X goes into product X, which is sold to market X. Component Y goes into product Y, which is sold to market Y. With form postponement strategy, components X and Y are redesigned into a new component Z that can be fed to both products X and Y. The firm needs only to concentrate in producing one component serving multiple markets, hence gaining from economies of scale.

Figure 7.4. Component Design for Form Postponement

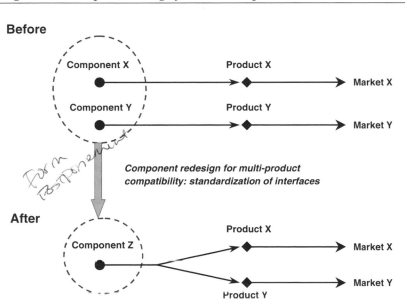

Source: Mikkola and Skjøtt-Larsen 2004

Mass Customization, Postponement and NPD

Mass customization and postponement strategies depend on technological choices in product architectures and allocation of resources. In the mass production paradigm, product variety is relatively low and customer involvement is sought through market research only to capture standard product design attributes that have wide appeal (Duray et al. 2000). Through modular designs, mass customisation has enabled firms to achieve manufacturing efficiencies that approximate those of mass production. Knowing the point to involve customers in product design influences the configuration of processes and technologies that will be used in designing and making the mass-customised product (Duray et al. 2000, Lampel & Mintzberg 1996). Although product variety is a customer-oriented objective, the customization itself is design- as well as manufacturing-oriented objective (Pine 1993, Baldwin & Clark 1997, McCutcheon et al. 1994, Salvador et al. 2002), which is dependent on the suppliers' capabilities as well.

Depending on the amount of modularization that exists in products, different supply chain structures can be found, whether to gain advantages from postponement or mass customization, as illustrated in Table 7.1.

Tale 7.1. A comparison of different supply chain structures

Opportunity for modularization	Traditional supply chain	Mass customization supply chain	Postponed supply chain
Interface compatibility effects	• Integrated vertical structure • Long development lead times	• Modular product architecture • Reduction of development lead time • Vertical coordination	• Customer decoupling points • Accurate and short customer response time
Component customization	• Design and manufacturing focus • In-house product development • Standardized components	• Autonomous innovation in NPD • Customer focus • Design for manufacturability	• Process design • Design for postponement
Value inputs	• Economies of scale • Exploiting advantages of market mechanism • Standardization of operations • Consolidation of outbound logistics	• Outsourcing • Flexibility towards specific customers' needs • Economies of scale and scope	• Reduced inventory costs and risks of obsolescence • Increased flexibility toward market needs and changes • Economies of scale and scope
Supplier-buyer interdependence	• Arm's-length at component level • Supplier involvement in development not critical • Multiple sourcing	• Early supplier involvement in NPD • Strategic partnership • Supplier as system integrator • High interdependence	• Customer relationship management • Involvement of TPL providers in final manufacturing and logistics • Direct deliveries to customers through merge-in-transit

Source: Mikkola & Skjøtt-Larsen 2004

NPD for Recycling

One of the emerging issues relating NPD to recycling is about how to design products to facilitate the disassembly tasks of products. As corporations become more conscious about the environment, end-of-life (EOL) product management is taking a serious look at how certain products can be refurbished, reused, remanufactured, or recycled (Pagell et al. 2007). For instance, the automotive recycling industry recovers 75% of material weight in EOL vehicles primarily through ferrous material separation (Williams et al. 2007). Disassembly of products is only possible when products are designed with modular product architecture configurations. For example, a manufacturer of PCs (or any company engaged in the recycling of PCs) can easily disassemble the computer into keyboards, operating system, monitor, mouse, etc., so that the functional components can be reused. See Chapter 10 for more about reverse supply chains.

The role of NPD in SCM will become increasingly more important as firms take supply chain integration issues more seriously. This is especially crucial for companies engaged in industries where the total efficiency of the supply chain has to be considered.

Illustrative Cases

Oticon[5]

Oticon, a Danish hearing aids producer, has recently launched a powerful behind-the-ear hearing aid called SUMO. There are two types of platforms at Oticon: (1) extension of existing platform and (2) new platforms. The existing platforms are expanded with new variants up to a few times per year. As the concept evolves, simulations are performed in order to minimize the risks of failure and to verify that the ideas are technically feasible. SUMO is developed based on a new mechanical platform and a new IC platform. The development lead-time of SUMO (from concept generation to final production) took a little over three years involving all competence areas of Oticon. It has been in production since 2002.

SUMO's product architecture is comprised of the following key components: housing, volume control, microphone, receiver, battery wall, switch, connecting element, and PCB where the customized IC is placed. There are about 25 components in SUMO, of which all are unique, with the exception of volume control and the

5. Case material extracted from (Mikkola & Skjøtt-Larsen 2006).

microphone. It is interesting to note that although the volume control is a unique component for Oticon, it is made from a library of combinations from the supplier, hence considered a standard component, of which the technique is also standard for the supplier.

Although there are no black-box components in SUMO (Oticon wants to have the control of its design), relatively few of the unique components are, in varying degrees, developed in cooperation with the suppliers. This is a start for Oticon to trust its key suppliers more, and to some extend, to respond to customer needs better. For instance, the design of switch and IC were carried out in-house, but the manufacturing (and assembly of the switch) was delegated to the suppliers. The receiver and the connecting element, on the other hand, are the only components that suppliers were actively involved to jointly solve technical problems. Development costs were also split between the suppliers. It is interesting to note that Oticon typically does not involve suppliers in its NPD. SUMO is one exception that illustrates how new platforms can be realized at Oticon.

Oticon is a small company making products in a limited production scale, meaning that it depends on its suppliers to deliver prototypes in relatively small quantities. In order to reach the highest possible level of quality and performance, Oticon, in some cases, involves these suppliers in joint development of components, which can result in a high degree of dependency on the supplier. For instance, only one supplier (out of a total of two possible suppliers worldwide) is currently capable of developing the receiver used in SUMO. The development of the receiver started in parallel development with the supplier. Oticon generally balances the use of the two suppliers to ensure that they are both actively involved. By this policy, Oticon also ensures a high technical competence from the suppliers.

A dual sourcing strategy is not sufficient in itself to guarantee suppliers' commitment in developing new technologies. So how does Oticon handle this challenge? Although Oticon involves suppliers in NPD, and also helps its suppliers to improve their processes, Oticon owns all the tooling (especially for plastic moulding) to ease supplier costs of second sourcing as much as possible. Oticon gives more responsibilities to its system suppliers, who assemble subsystems, such as parts of the hearing aid switch. Video conferences with their global suppliers are also held for one to two hours per week for exchanging drawings and other information.

Jeeps' Windshield Wipers[6]

Since late 1980s, Chrysler has replaced its adversarial bidding system with one in which the company designates suppliers for a component and then uses target costing to determine with suppliers the component prices and how to achieve them. Jeep Grand Cherokee was first introduced in U.S. in 1993 as a high-end utility vehicle. The commercial success of this new family of Jeeps was uncertain, as it had numerous new concepts and innovations that were not present in former Jeeps. Moreover, a great portion of the development responsibilities of these innovations was outsourced. As in this case, the wipers controller module (WIPER) was outsourced as a black-box part to a first-tier supplier. During the development the supplier faced two technological solutions: solid-state and silent-relay.

The controller used by older Jeep families applied relay-based technology which made a 'clicking sound' when switching from ON to OFF, an annoying feature that Chrysler wanted to eliminate. The supplier was asked to develop a 'quiet' WIPER controller. One solution was to create a solid-state module (with the use of standard components), where Chrysler did not have to be involved in the NPD process.

Although all the modules of the wiper system (i.e. motor, wiper arms, blades, wiper switch, and WIPER) had pre-determined interface specifications set by Chrysler, how they would function as an integrated wiper system in relation to the rest of the vehicle was not known. This uncertainty was accentuated, especially when new innovations were concurrently being developed for the new Jeeps. At one stage, solid-state WIPERs would catch fire when tested under certain conditions in the real Grand Cherokees, even though the modules worked well in lab simulations and tests. Eventually, the development of solid-state WIPER was put to a halt.

Triggered by the failure, interface specifications and compatibility issues had to be re-examined. As a consequence, the design team went back to the drawing board, and started the redesign of WIPER from scratch. During this process the silent-relay WIPER was created. However, 'silent-relay' was a component that did not exist in

---

6. Case material extracted from (Mikkola 2003).

the market. Thanks to an efficient sourcing team and close coordination with the design team, major relay suppliers in the world got to know about the new relay's technical requirements, and started to compete and innovate to deliver first-run prototypes that would meet the specifications of the 'silent relay.' At the end, a Japanese firm was chosen as the sole supplier because it was able to offer the best performing 'silent relay' with the most competitive price. The 'silent relay' proved to be the key factor for allowing economies of substitution to take place. With it, not only Jeep Grand Cherokee's WIPER became 'quiet,' it could also be used with other Jeep families (i.e. Jeep Cherokee and Jeep Wrangler families). This meant that one common WIPER could be mounted on any Jeep family without degradation in functionality and performance. The silent-relay WIPER entitled the supplier to deliver a 'quiet' module that was appreciated by Chrysler, not mentioning the savings gained from availability and economies of scale of components, universal tooling, and common assembly and manufacturing processes.

Even though the solid-state-WIPER was abandoned after several different architecture designs, it provided both the supplier and Chrysler with an unforgettable and valuable learning experience. A much better understanding of the windshield wipers system as a whole in terms of its functionality and interfaces with other elements of the vehicle was gained. Most importantly, a great deal of WIPER's specifications for the Grand Cherokee Jeep had to be redefined. This step was possible through an increased mutual involvement in NPD to solve technical and interface specification problems.

8. Procurement

*»The arm's length buy-sell transaction, use your clout to
beat up the supplier, is a highly outdated model. We also be-
lieve that to share information is absolutely key, and sometimes this requires changing a lot of norms and practices in
your company where secrets are sovereign.«*

(Martin J. Garvin, Vice President, Corporate Management,
Dell Computers, quoted in Mazel 1999)

Global competition emphasizes the sourcing of materials, products,
and production capacity around the world. The searching for and
managing the flow of materials and components becomes essential
to the international supply chain. It also becomes essential to corporate strategy as firms emphasize their core competencies, while
sourcing other components, processes, and services from outside
organizations. This has changed the role of procurement. The traditional role of procurement was achieving the cheapest price and
ensuring a sufficient flow of materials for production. Conventional
wisdom would spread purchases among several suppliers with a
large supplier base to get the best prices in the marketplace.

The new perspective recognizes that processes and links to suppliers define the supply chain. One writer describes procurement as
being on the cusp of radical change, shifting from a focus on products to supplier capabilities. Procurement becomes proactive, designing and managing networks of connections. It involves inter-
organizational relationships, utilizing the resources of suppliers, supplier development, cost management, and logistics for connecting
and processing. Purchasing management has become strategic procurement management, even shaping the strategic direction of the
corporation.

Figure 8.1. Procurement

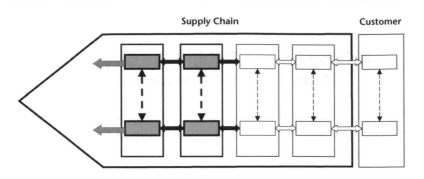

Procurement is a primary arena for inter-organizational relations. It demonstrates the usefulness of the theories from Chapter 3, especially transaction cost analysis and networks. One criterion of supplier commitment is asset specificity, specialized investments that are difficult to transfer to other uses, including capital equipment and specialized training. These incur switching costs, with financial risk in commitment by both the supplier and the customer.

There is divergence in computerized purchasing applications. One approach assumes a pre-existing relationship with major suppliers, emphasizing coordination of operations to ensure that products are delivered as needed. The other assumes procurement of standard items, open markets with an emphasis on search and selection, involving business-to-business (B2B) markets. This process lends itself to automation of procurement through the use of electronic software agents and optimizing choices based on price, delivery costs and related variables as the *Total Cost of Ownership* (Ellram 1995). Some applications involve development of large-scale Web-based catalogs of pre-qualified suppliers for non-critical items, using standard protocols and previously established data codes. All of these may operate in parallel within the same system to satisfy differing procurement needs.

In this chapter we first look at the driving forces behind the new strategic role of procurement. Second, we identify different types of customer-supplier relationships from arm's length to strategic alliances. Third, we use portfolio models as a basis for classifying purchases and purchasing strategies. The underlying assumption is that there is no one-size-fits-all type of relationship. However, within a specific relationship there may be one best fit, depending on the situation.

Driving Forces Behind the Strategic Importance of Procurement

The role of procurement in the modern corporation is changing. Gadde and Haakansson (2001) point to three decision areas in the new strategic procurement context:

- Make-or-buy decisions
- Supply–base structure
- Customer-supplier relationships.

The decision on whether to buy or to rely on in-house production has always been a major topic. However, until recently it was not considered as a strategic issue for top management attention but rather based on short-term cost considerations with a bias towards internal production. A more recent strategic emphasis on outsourcing is changing management attitudes towards external supply and production whenever the decision can be justified by cost or capacity.

The supply–base structure involves two strategic issues. One is the number of suppliers, the other has to do with their organizations. The number of suppliers is related to the classical choice between multiple versus single sourcing. Multiple sourcing is traditional, dealing with suppliers at arm's length through market transactions. Once equivalent products are available, price, quality and delivery become paramount in the decision. Single sourcing and, in some cases, dual sourcing, by contrast, involves more permanent ties and the development of closer cooperative relationships.

The organization of suppliers deals with the variety of links with other suppliers, whether in open market relationships, or as tiered networks, *keiretsu*, with supplier associations and other forms of organization. The customer–supplier relationship has become a strategic issue for two reasons. One is cost rationalization, the other is to benefit from utilizing resources and competencies of suppliers to develop new skills and innovations. Two trends emphasize the differences between market and network relations. One is the development of e-commerce, with rapid comparison of supplier offerings.

The other, the development of relationships has been fostered by the need to collaborate and capture supplier expertise, while reducing company involvement where there is no competitive advantage.

Together, the three decision areas mark a distinct, although partial break, from past practice of procurement by squeezing profit margins out of suppliers for short-term cost reductions. Several factors have influenced this development. The most important are:

- Increased outsourcing
- Global sourcing
- JIT purchasing
- Green supply management
- Information technology

Increased Outsourcing

There is a strong tendency towards buying more from outside suppliers. In the management literature, Hamel and Prahalad (1994), Quinn (1999), and Quinn and Hilmer (1994) have been influential proponents for a strategy of focusing on the firm's core competencies and outsourcing the rest to external suppliers. In the automotive and electronics industries, typically between 60% and 80% of the product value is now outsourced to suppliers. In the fashion and sports wear industry outsourcing is even more widespread. Companies such as Nike and Reebok deliberately retain only design, prototyping, and marketing in-house, while outsourcing production and distribution. Increased outsourcing changes the role of procurement from reactive to proactive, such as searching for and evaluating potential suppliers, establishing contracts and developing long-term relationships. The recent trend on outsourcing to China and India makes procurement strategies even more crucial in the context of SCM.

Just-in-Time Purchasing

The principles of JIT production have also changed the purchasing process. JIT purchasing provides materials to production just as they are required for use. The fundamental aim is to ensure that production is as close as possible to a continuous process from receipt of raw materials or components to the shipment of finished goods (Gunasekaran 1999c).

JIT purchasing is ideally characterized by a small supplier base of long-term »partners« with the buying company, incorporating production facilities located close to the buyer's plant and frequent deliveries. Supplier relations are built on a high degree of mutual trust and openness. The objective is to eliminate inbound quality inspection, establish close relationships for coordination and problem solving, deliver on time in small quantities, and arrive at an equitable price. Transportation becomes important, often requiring a carrier commitment to routings and schedules. Many relationships specify information system requirements such as manual or electronic kanban.

For JIT purchasing to work well in a production environment, demand must be relatively stable with a commitment over a term long enough to cover specific investments. Suppliers must be able to anticipate demands, both through leveling of production orders or through forecasts that allow them to plan their own capacity. Otherwise, JIT will push inventory requirements back on the supplier, with costs that will influence the cost bid for the supply transaction.

Information Technology

During the last decade, developments in information and communication technology have increased the potential to make the procurement process much more efficient. Implementation of automated and e-procurement systems and increased use of electronic data interchange have made transactions with suppliers faster, cheaper and more reliable to replenish materials and components. Bar-coding, and more recently RFID tags, for individual products, packages and pallet loads have made it easier to install and implement automatic replenishment systems, track-and-trace systems and stock location to control procurement operations and movement throughout the supply chain (see also Chapter 4).

The Internet has created further opportunity for electronic exchange, both in easier access to ordering and payment, and greater transparency of the international supplier market. E-procurement, purchasing portals, and reverse auctions are projected to increase dramatically in the foreseeable future. These developments have given procurement new opportunities to make purchasing more efficient and reliable, but have also emphasized the strategic importance of procurement. Online reverse auctions are widely used as a method to reduce the unit price of globally sourced components and materials bought by original equipment manufacturers such as the aerospace, automotive, and electronics industries. The theoretical assumptions supporting the use of online reverse auctions include (Emiliani 2004):

- Lower purchase prices result in reduced costs.
- Request for Quotation (RFQ) represents actual total costs.
- Qualified suppliers are interchangeable.
- Costs are external to the buyer, rather than internally generated.
- Suppliers benefit from participating in online reverse auctions.

A study by Smart and Harrison (2003) concluded that reverse auctions have the potential to be used in both the collaborative and competitive relationship as a means of tendering contracts. Firms with long-term relationships with key suppliers might want to test the market prices from time to time or invite new suppliers to bid. This is done through a tender or a Request for Quotation (RFQ) to a number of suppliers. The majority of buyers and suppliers interviewed in this study claimed that on-line reverse auction was an efficient method for conducting tenders, which could save time, cost, and resources. Thus, reverse auctions are considered as a process improvement tool, even if price reductions were not the main objective.

Bartezzaghi and Ronchi (2004) suggest adopting a portfolio approach to different purchasing situations. They identify four different purchasing approaches:

- Private purchase
- Supplier based
- Specific based
- Source selection

In *private purchases*, the purchasing department mainly adopts catalogs managed by their own e-procurement portals. In the *supplier based* approach, the purchasing department relies on their suppliers' initiatives and bought via electronic catalogs developed and managed by suppliers. *Specific purchase* approach uses vertical marketplaces to buy materials specific to the industry they belong to, e.g. chemicals, steel, or auto components. In the *source selection* approach, the buyers focus on the sourcing process and they used horizontal marketplaces running reverse auctions or virtual exchanges.

Recent studies (Emiliani 2004) have shown that online reverse auctions might damage the buyer's long-term relationships by creating mistrust among its key suppliers. The reason is that reverse auctions are often focused on unit price savings and do not include the extra costs of switching from one supplier to another or the value of having a long-term relationship with the suppliers. Jap (2007) examined how the buyer's auctions design, e.g. the number of bidders, the economic stakes, price visibility, and price dynamics over the course of the auction, affected its relationship with suppliers. The study showed that the larger the number of bidders, the larger the economic stakes, and the less visible the price is in an auction, the more positive is the impact on the buyer-supplier relationship. Large price reductions over the course of the auction had a detrimental effect on the buyer-supplier relationship. Besides, there was an increase in opportunism suspicions in auctions with greater price visibility.

The Variety of Supplier-Buyer Relationships

In a supply chain, many different types of relationships exist side-by-side. No one type of relationship fits all business transactions. Developing partnerships with external actors is resource-intensive in terms of time and management involvement (Gadde and Snehota 2000). Therefore, a firm can only be highly involved with limited numbers of supplier relationships. An important role of management is to decide, which type of relationship is the most appropriate for each transaction. For some, arm's-length relationships are the most effective, for others, close interpersonal ties become necessary. By managing a range of different relationships, the firm can economize on scarce resources.

Sako (1992) and Helper (1993) identified two patterns of contractual relations: arm's-length and obligational, the extremes of a multidimensional spectrum. Arm's-length contractual relations involve a single specific, discrete economic transaction. An explicit contract specifies the tasks and duties of both parties. All business exchanges are performed at arm's length, to avoid undue familiarity and personal ties. Changing trading partners is therefore easy when the contract is terminated.

Obligational contractual relations, in contrast, are more embedded in social relations between trading partners and are also characterized by a sense of mutual trust. Transactions often take place without a prior formal contract. Even when the tasks and duties of each partner are specified in a contract, both parties recognize the incentives to do more than expected by the trading partner. When one partner fails, there is a willingness to seek remedies rather than to shift to other partners.

Figure 8.2. The Range of Supplier Relationships

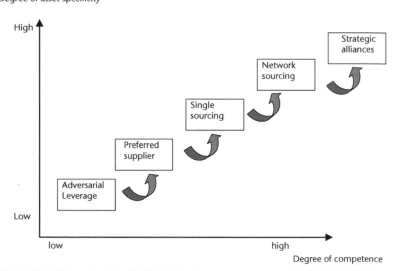

Source: Cox (1996)

Any particular relationship can be placed on a continuum between adversarial relationship and close integration. The closer a relationship is to core competencies or investment in highly specific dedicated assets, the more likely that the relationship becomes quasi-integrated. Cox (1996) proposes a typology (Figure 8.2):

- Adversarial
- Preferred supplier
- Single sourcing
- Network sourcing
- Strategic alliances.

Adversarial Relationships

Adversarial relationships or market relations have long dominated purchasing thinking and practice. Focusing on price comparisons between different suppliers as a major basis for comparison kept supplier–customer relationships at a distance. In this situation the supplier does not retain ownership rights over the goods and services provided. Arm's-length relationships offered flexibility for competitive markets. Today, the arm's-length approach is now subject to criticism because of its focus on short-term cost reductions. However, it has merit under specific conditions: in commodity markets, with multiple suppliers, low asset specificity and little market uncertainty. The market also serves as a control mechanism to ensure competitive prices. The increasing use of the Internet as a medium for product catalogs has made it possible to compare product specifications and prices across supplier markets.

Preferred Suppliers

Preferred suppliers provide goods and services that are of medium asset specificity and can be considered to be complementary to the core competencies of the buying firm. However, the products purchased have relatively low strategic importance for the buyer. Suppliers with equivalent product specifications, quality and price are limited, and the buyer typically uses a bidding process to evaluate and choose a few suppliers as preferred sources of goods and services. Preferred suppliers have some advantages over market-based suppliers. The contract period is normally longer. The suppliers are granted preferential relationship for a certain period of time. There is exchange of planning information, such as forecasts and production plans, making the planning process more reliable and predictable for the supplier while also making supply more reliable for the customer.

Single Sourcing

Single sourcing means that the buyer is supplied by a single source for a specified period of time. This type of supplier relationship refers to supply of medium to high levels of asset specificity, with goods and services linked directly to the core competencies of the buying firm. During the last two decades, there has been a debate about the relative merits of single and multiple sourcing. The proponents of single sourcing have argued that there is a need for single sourcing as JIT deliveries are becoming more widespread in many industries.

Figure 8.3 Single sourcing

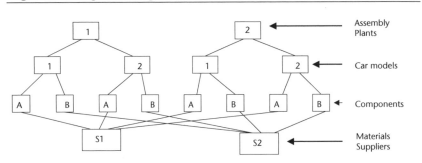

Figure 8.3 shows single sourcing even though two assembly plants are involved. Materials suppliers are linked to one component supplier, in turn linked to one module producer supplying both assembly plants.

Conversely, multiple sourcing involves two or more suppliers. Variations include both dual and parallel sourcing. Dual sourcing involves two suppliers. Parallel sourcing combines asset specificity with commitment to long-term single-source relationships and still allows for a high degree of competition among suppliers for future contracts. This system is used when a car manufacturer produces a number of models at different plants using a single source for a component of one model at one assembly plant, while another source is used for the same model at another assembly plant. The principles of parallel sourcing compared with single sourcing are shown in Figure 8.4.

Figure 8.4 Combined Single and Parallel Sourcing

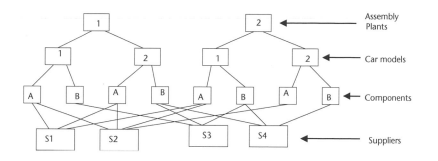

An assembler has two plants producing the same model, and component A is used at both plants. In single sourcing, one supplier supplies both plants with component A. In parallel sourcing, one supplier supplies component A for plant one, and another supplier supplying component A for plant two. Parallel sourcing ensures that two or more suppliers with similar capabilities act as single source suppliers of the same components, but they are guaranteed production for their particular model. The assembler can compare their performance and keep competitive pressure for bidding on the next model cycle. The assembler also assists the weaker supplier to compete more effectively through exchanges of technical personnel, capital assistance on purchase of new equipment and even taking ideas from the winner to give to the other supplier. At the same time, the winning supplier experiences continuing pressure for improvement, despite its previous success.

Slack et al. (2004: 453) compare the advantages and disadvantages of single and multiple sourcing:

Table 8.1 Advantages and disadvantages of single and multiple sourcing

	Single sourcing	Multiple sourcing
Advantages	• Potentially better quality because more supplier quality assurance (QSA) possibilities • Stronger relationships which are more durable • Greater dependency en-courages more commitment and effort • Better communication • Easier to cooperate on now product/service development • More scale economies • Higher confidentiality	• Purchaser can drive price down by competitive tendering • Can switch sources in case of supply failure • Wide sources of knowledge and expertise to tap
Disadvantages	• More vulnerable to disruption if a failure to supply occurs • Individual supplier more affected by volume fluctuations • Supplier might exert upward pressure on prices if no alternative supplier is available	• Difficult to encourage commitment by supplier • Less easy to develop effective SQA • More effort needed to communicate • Suppliers less likely to invest in new processes • More difficult to obtain scale economies

Source: Slack (2004:453)

The risks are clear when various sourcing strategies are compared. From a supplier's perspective, success depends on the demand for the customer's product and the performance of other suppliers in the supply chain. From the buyer's perspective, several sources become insurance against supplier failures from fire, strikes, quality or delivery problems. In addition, more than one supplier maintains the process of competition.

According to Liker and Choi (2004) neither Toyota nor Honda depend on a single source for anything. Both Japanese car manufacturers develop two to three suppliers for every component or raw material they buy. They also encourage competition between suppliers starting with product development. The selected supplier receives contracts for the life of a model, but if performance is not adequate, measured by the standards of the car manufacturers, the next contract will be given to a competitor.

Network Sourcing

Hines (1994, 1995) uses the term network sourcing to characterize the unique supplier network structure of the Japanese subcontracting system. Network sourcing combines many different aspects of cooperation between major car manufacturers and their suppliers. These include a tiered supply structure, cross-exchange of staff between buyer and supplier, relatively high asset specificity and risk-sharing, early involvement of suppliers in design and innovation, trust relationship, supplier associations (*kyoryoku kai*) and supplier coordination and development. These closely interrelated elements together constitute a complex inter-organizational network producing a competence difficult to imitate and transfer to Western industry.

The Japanese automobile industry has multiple tiers of suppliers. Final assemblers, such as Toyota, Honda, Mazda and Nissan, are at the top of the pyramid. First-tier suppliers provide key components, subassemblies and systems, such as engines, seats, electronic systems, braking systems and steering systems. Typically, there are about 200 to 300 first-tier suppliers per final assembler.

Figure 8.5 Tier Structure in Supplier Networks

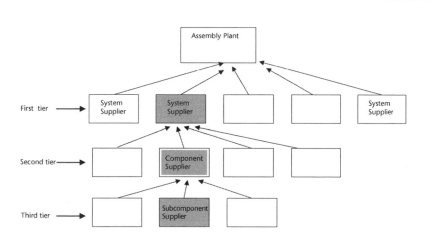

Second tier suppliers provide first-tier suppliers with components or perform specific processes, such as metal forming, painting as well as sub-assemblies. Second-tier suppliers have their own subcontractors to provide them with specialist process capabilities such as plating, casting and machining. Depending on the product and specialization, there may be several layers of subcontractors. The tier structure is illustrated in Figure 8.5.

Embedded in the sourcing network is the institution of *kyoryoku kai* or supplier association. This institution is evolving, shifting from a system of supplier dependence towards one of balanced power (Hines 1994). This is a form of external quality circle for suppliers at the same level in the tiering structure. For example, first-tier suppliers form a supplier association where they exchange ideas and cooperate in solving individual or mutual problems. The association includes both non-competing and competing suppliers. Supplier associations are also established at lower levels in the tier structure to diffuse innovations and improvements further into the network tiers. The effect is to raise the skill and sophistication level across the supply network. The success of the supply network rests not only on flexible connections but also on diffusing modern production technology throughout the entire network. As a result, participating firms have adopted computer-integrated manufacturing, product quality management programs and modern procurement methods such as value analysis, value engineering and statistical process control.

To the dominant firm, the benefits of the supply network are numerous: flexibility in production to respond to new market requirements, low transaction costs through electronic data interchange and *kanban* systems, and frequent delivery from close physical proximity. With stable membership, suppliers can be encouraged to invest heavily in new technology, take part in new product and process development, and contribute their own knowledge of production processes. Furthermore, subcontractors advance their own expertise in manufacturing as a balance against the power of the dominant firm. The source of power in the network is diffused away from the customer, the assembler or the buyer at the next stage. Flexible production capacity is allocated across the supplier network. If one supplier has utilized the production capacity 100%, the remaining production orders can be transferred to other suppliers with idle production capacity. The combined effect is to produce a network with a collective capacity and expertise greater than that of any single member.

The question is continually raised about the validity of this concept outside of Japan. One argument is that Western suppliers would not tolerate the control asserted by parent companies. Also, the parent company wants suppliers to share in the increasing costs of research and development and increase the flexibility and efficiency of the production process. Lamming (1993), however, points to a shift towards more supplier component development taking place within the European car industry. Furthermore, the United States electronics industry is utterly dependent on the development of new product components and subsystems by suppliers such as Intel and Cisco. Supplier innovation has actually become a driving force in parent company product development, such as the Intel processors used in PCs.

The management role in the supplier network has several dimensions. First, it becomes important to acknowledge the supply relationships of the first-tier supplier. Second, the potential impact of changes in performance or supply failures in second-tier relationships leads to establishing precautionary alternative network links. Third, mapping the entire supply chain network becomes important, to recognize where value is added, where capacity may be limited and the complete cost structure (Kulkarni 1996). Cost analysis indicates where functional activities can be reorganized, eliminated, combined or shifted to other partners. Fourth, it is also important to recognize the location of the source of innovation within the network, both for its direct contribution to new products and its impact for changing other components. Finally, shifting activities may also change the balance of power in the network. When suppliers communicate directly with final customers, the role of the immediate customer can be bypassed or at least diminished.

The success of the global corporation will depend increasingly on its supply networks as a source of knowledge of technology. Manufacturing location strategy often emphasizes access to new technology through its suppliers, as United States and European companies have pursued Japanese expertise by locating production facilities first in Japan, and now from China and India. The advantage of the global corporation is the freedom to source components and rationalize production around the world. Most of the motivation has been to seek low costs. Beyond costs, however, is a need to maintain parity in technology with potential competitors. The ability of the global corporation to compete is limited by the quality of the relationships that it establishes with its suppliers.

Against this is the tradition of arm's-length negotiation with suppliers as adversaries, emphasizing price over quality or service, with the resultant high defect rates, lack of incentive for suppliers to commit to capital expenditures and lack of trust. This relationship will probably hold for much of non core-related procurement, although there have cases where inter-organizational teams have developed efficient procurement processes (Banfield 1999).

Strategic Alliances

Strategic alliances are voluntary arrangements between firms involving exchange, sharing or co-development of products, technologies, or services (Gulati 1998). Strategic alliances are deeper than normal business relations. They involve complementarities: the matching of skills, knowledge of technologies, resources, and activities to complement the partners' own capabilities. In short, they add value. In the vertical context of supply chain management, they appear in both material and component procurement and in services such as third-party logistics, information, and transportation services. In a value-adding partnership, each partner performs only part of the process, focusing on one specific activity. The value-adding partnership becomes a long-term arrangement without the necessity for vertical integration by ownership.

Value-adding partnerships are especially useful in international procurement because they provide flexibility and commitment beyond normal contract relationships. Contracts are not easily enforceable across national borders, and cultural patterns often dictate personal relationships in preference to formal contracts. They establish a permanence that might not otherwise be available.

Many examples can be taken from procurement. Joint research and development is one. Subcontract manufacturing is another, the supplier's knowledge comes from superior knowledge of production processes. Shipper–carrier and other logistics relationships are also frequently used. They are symbiotic in the sense that business operations are complementary, partners become mutually dependent, but the activities can be clearly separated. They have developed because of the synergy between interrelated roles. In effect, they create extended organizations, moving away from individual transactions to form quasi-integrated units.

Portfolio Approach
to Supplier Relationships

Typically, a firm must deal with different types of suppliers and needs a model to assist in managing with several kinds of supplier relationships. Portfolio models have primarily been used in strategic decision-making to support resource allocation decisions. Some of the main advantages and disadvantages include (Mikkola 2001):

Advantages:

- It provides systematic analysis of the relationships or projects
- Relative strengths and weaknesses of the relationships or projects are revealed
- Consensus among different functions is created
- Selection criteria are evaluated with respect to business level performances
- Clear gaps and future development opportunities are highlighted

Disadvantages:

- Orthogonal issues seem to be an inherent challenge
- Interdependencies among relationships are not so apparent, hence difficult to assess
- A good understanding of the purchasing situation is needed, a task difficult for non-purchasers
- Identification of measurement indicators is difficult

One of the best-known supplier portfolio model is Kraljic's model from 1983. This model has been elaborated by several other others, e.g. Olsen and Ellram (1997) and Bensaou (1999). These models have in common a functional or product-oriented perspective. Another approach is taken by Møller et al. (2003), who propose a portfolio segmentation based on inter-organizational competence development. A comparison between the three portpolio models is shown in Table 8.2.

Table 8.2 Supplier segmentation portfolio models

Author(s)	Classification criteria	Context
Olsen & Ellram (1997)	• Importance of purchasing • Complexity of supply market	Procurement items • Strategic • Bottleneck • Leverage • Non-critical
Møller, Johansen & Boer (2003)	• Supplier's knowledge contribution • Buyer's knowledge contribution	Inter-organizational competence development • Purchased • Supplied • Cross • Transferred
Bensaou (1999)	• Buyer's specific investments • Supplier's specific investments	Supplier management profile • Market exchange • Captive buyer • Strategic partnership • Captive supplier

We briefly describe the three portfolio models that can be used to classify suppliers and provide a basis for a differentiated supplier strategy.

The Olsen & Ellram Portfolio Model

Kraljic (1983) developed a portfolio model to be used as a basis for classifying and setting purchasing strategy. His model divides purchasing transactions into four groups based on two dimensions: their strategic importance and the difficulty in managing the purchasing process. Olsen and Ellram (1997) expanded on Kraljic's model to propose an approach to analyze a firm's portfolio of supplier relationships. The first step is to identify important factors related to the two dimensions in the Kraljic model. The first dimension relates to their strategic importance:

• Competence factors describe how close the purchased items are to the core competencies of the firm and their strategic importance.

An important question is whether the purchase can improve the knowledge or the technological strength of the buying firm.

- Economic factors include the volume and value of the purchases, the possibilities of getting leverage with the supplier for other buys and the purchased item's contribution to the profitability of the finished products.
- Image factors describe how critical the purchase is to the brand names or perceived image of the firm by customers.

Factors in managing the purchase situation include:

- Product characteristics, such as uniqueness and complexity,
- Supply market characteristics such as the number and relative market shares of suppliers, their size and power and their shares of the buyer's purchases, and
- Risk and uncertainty related to the purchase transaction, such as technological risk and opportunistic behavior by the supplier.

Figure 8.6 Portfolio Model of Purchases

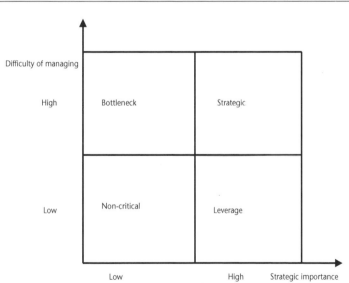

Source: Olsen & Ellram (1997)

Decision-makers in the firm identify and evaluate the relevant factors for specific transaction categories, assigning weights based on the perceived importance of each factor to the firm's operations. This part of the process is based on individual judgments. However, participants should ultimately agree on their relative rankings, and the factors provide a framework for discussion. Purchases are then classified into four portfolio categories, illustrated in Figure 8.6.

- Leverage
- Non-critical
- Bottleneck
- Strategic.

Leverage purchases are easy to manage but strategically important to the company. Concentrating purchases at one supplier might enable discounts across product groups or lower administration and transport costs.

Non-critical items are easy to manage and with low strategic importance. Here standardization and consolidation are key words. Purchase administration of these items could also be outsourced to a third-party provider.

Bottleneck items are items that are difficult to manage but have a low strategic importance to the firm. Here the key words are standardization of the purchases to keep the purchasing administration costs down and search for substituting suppliers.

The strategic category encompasses purchases both critically important to the firm and difficult to manage. This category should get the major emphasis from purchasing management. In this category the firm should consider close supplier relationships, early supplier involvement in product development and similar arrangements to integrate the suppliers in the firm's supply chain.

The Competence Development Model

This portfolio model is based on the type of competencies exchanged between buyers and suppliers. The model is essentially concerned with long-term competence development and transfer of knowledge and skills between the partners. The model suggests four different types of competence exchange relationships, as shown in Figure 8.7.

- Purchased competence
- Transferred competence
- Supplied competence
- Cross competence

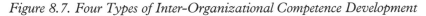

Figure 8.7. Four Types of Inter-Organizational Competence Development

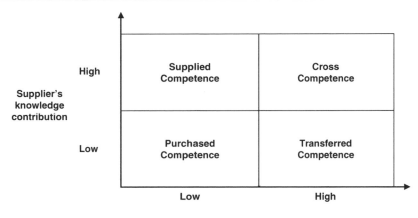

Source: Møller et al. (2003:372)

Purchased competence refers to basic competencies bought from standard suppliers in the open market. The switching costs are low. If the buyer is not satisfied with the products or services delivered, the same competence can easily be purchased from a different supplier. The sourcing concept is a make-or-buy decision.

Transferred competence refers to situations where the buyer transfers knowledge and skills to the supplier to complement the supplier's own areas of expertise. This is often the case in outsourcing situations, where the outsourcing firm transfers tools and machineries to the supplier and trains the supplier's employees in executing the outsourced tasks.

Supplied competence is the opposite of transferred competence. Here, the supplier transfers expertise to the buyer's organization. This transfer can be either direct (e.g. training of buyer's employees or demonstration of the use of the supplied product) or indirect – embedded in the supplied product. The switching costs are high, and there will be an extensive exchange of information between the partners.

Cross competence describes situations in which both supplier and buyer bring knowledge and skills to the relationship. The competencies resulting from the interaction between the buyer and the supplier are specific for this relationship. If one of the parties withdraws from the partnership, the developed competencies are lost. The dependence between the parties is very high and so are the switching costs.

The Bensaou Model

Bensaou (1999) has proposes a framework for managing a portfolio of relationships based on specific investments by both buyers and suppliers, following the transaction cost analysis model. The purpose is to give managers guidance on the most appropriate governance structure under conditions of differing financial commitments and on how to manage them to achieve maximal effectiveness. The model is a portfolio of supplier relationships based on the two dimensions of the buyer's and the supplier's specific investments in the relationship.

Examples of buyer-specific investments in a relationship include tangible investments in buildings, tooling and dies committed to the supplier's product or operations or customized products and processes using particular components procured from the supplier. Specific investment also encompasses intangible investments in educating and training personnel of the supplier in product knowledge, administration and business practices.

Supplier-specific investments might include dedicated physical assets such as plants or warehouses and specialized tools and equipment dedicated to the customer's needs. It could also include less tangible research and development projects, specific knowledge about the customer's products and processes, placement of boundary-spanning employees on the customer's premises to solve current problems and intangible investments in human assets, such as training and other methods of skill and knowledge development.

The Bensaou model classifies buyer-supplier relationships into four categories depending on the degrees of specific investments from either party (Figure 8.8):

- Market exchange
- Captive buyer
- Captive supplier
- Strategic partnership.

Figure 8.8. Portfolio Model of Relationships

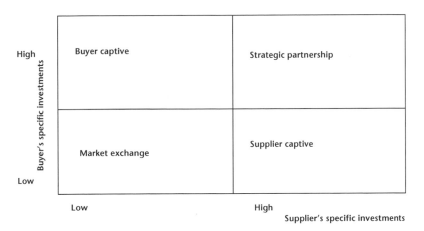

Source: Bensaou (1999)

Market exchange relationships are characterized with low specific investments from both customers and suppliers, highly standardized products, typically based on simple mature technology and well-established manufacturing techniques. Many suppliers offer these products in a highly competitive supplier market.

Captive buyer relationships involve complex components with customization, although they utilize well-known, stable technologies. The supplier adds a proprietary technology that provides a monopoly position to the seller. The supply market is concentrated, with a few large, well-established suppliers. If the buyer wants to terminate the contract, finding an alternative supplier might be difficult.

Captive suppliers make specific investments to win and keep their customers and face a threat of switching. Customers hold monopolistic positions derived from their own technology or access to markets. The relationship involves highly complex products based on proprietary technology. However, the supplier market can be competitive and the buyer often uses two or more suppliers, shifting contracts among them to keep their interest.

In a strategic partnership the technical complexity of the buyers' products is high, and suppliers' components are highly customized. The supplier is often involved in the design and development processes. The relationship becomes long-term and based on mutual trust.

Asset specificity in supply relationships must be defined in terms of specific industries. Bensaou and Anderson (1999) examined the United States and Japanese automobile industries to identify sources of credible commitment for buyers adapting to their suppliers and found eight:

- The buyer's specific investments for a supplier relationship,
- Task features that require buyer-supplier coordination, including both manufacturing task complexity, and task interdependence, reflecting the interface between the component and the vehicle,
- Supplier credentials, including size and market share, to indicate confidence in the relationship,
- Environmental uncertainty, including both predictability of volume and potential changes in the component,
- Thinness of supply market, reflecting a high concentration of the component market and non-standard resources needed to produce components,
- Relational safeguards such as the overall business done with this supplier and the age of the relationship,
- Supplier trustworthiness based on its market reputation, and
- The institutional context, differing between Japan and the United States.

Investment in specific assets by automobile assemblers (buyers) involves a risk of opportunism by suppliers, which is perceived differently in Japan and the United States. Bensaou and Anderson (1999: 476-478) note: »a significant challenge for European and U.S. carmakers will be to duplicate a Japanese style of dependence on suppliers without having to divert expensive resources to an expensive governance structure to protect themselves from opportunism.«

Bensaou (1999) separately questioned the general assumption that Japanese firms manage supplier relations primarily through strategic partnerships. Based on empirical data on supplier relationships in the United States and Japan across a representative set of components and technologies, he found that this assumption was not justified. On the contrary, he found that the percentage of strategic partnerships in Japan was lower than in the United States (19 % versus 25 %). He also found that the captive supplier relationships were relatively more important in Japan (35 %) than in the United States (15 %), whereas the captive buyer relationships were significantly higher in the United States (35 %) compared with Japan (8 %). Japanese companies appear to be better able to persuade their suppliers to invest in specific assets than are their United States counterparts.

Bensaou concluded that firms could not manage with only one design for all relationships. He recommends managers to follow a two-step approach: first, to identify the type of relationship that matches the competitive conditions surrounding the product or service exchanged, and second, to design the appropriate management model for each type of relationship.

Critique of Portfolio Models

Recently, purchasing portfolio models have been criticized with respect to the following issues (Gelderman & Weele 2005):

- The selection of the dimensions on the axes.
- The supplier's side is disregarded in most portfolio models.
- The operationalization of »supply risk« and »profit impact«.
- The subjective and equal weighting of factors on the two dimensions.
- The simplicity of recommendations based on just two dimensions.

Dubois and Pedersen (2002) argue that portfolio models use previously established products as bases analysis, which is problematic since the costs and value creation associated with developing, producing and using these products are not incorporated in the analysis. Also, whether the buyer involves the supplier in the product development or not has an impact on their relationship.

Furthermore, interdependence between relationships in the network in which they are embedded is seldom discussed in these models (Olsen & Ellram 1997). They are limited to analyzing products in a dyadic buyer-seller context, and fail to capture all of the aspects important for buyer-supplier relationships within a network perspective (see chapter 3). When firms cooperate closely, external factors cannot be easily separated from internal ones.

Strategic Partnerships

Strategic partnerships are normally established only when suppliers contribute processes, components or systems critical to the customer's value chain or that contribute significantly to product value. Strategic partnerships are limited to key suppliers. As an example, in 1999 about 85% of Dell Computer's parts requirements went to just 25 suppliers. Dell selects key suppliers and technologies well before product introduction. Many suppliers become active participants in a »virtual lab« for product development. Examples are Microsoft for Windows, Intel for microprocessors, Maxtor for hard drives, Sony for monitors, and Selectron for motherboards. Sharing technical information and collaborating in research and development allows Dell to lead in product transitions and providing an advantage in time-to-market (Vedpuriswar 2004).

Systems suppliers provide a special variation by supplying complete subsystems for final assembly into finished products, guided by prespecification of requirements. The systems supplier selects and manages component suppliers and maintains technological development within its own area (Hines 1996b). They are prominent within the aircraft and automobile industries. The concept of modular production in the car industry has encouraged this development. Volkswagen's modular production line in Brazil builds trucks, in which system suppliers are co-located in the plant with assembling and production responsibilities. Other major car manufacturers have followed the same path, e.g. Volvo in Sweden and SmartCar in France. The concept can also be applied in other industries where the finished product is composed of large numbers of components and services, such as power plants, trains, and ships.

Toyota and Honda have set up car manufacturing operations in USA since 1980s. From the beginning, the two Japanese car manufacturers encouraged the creation of joint ventures between their Japanese suppliers and the American suppliers. Both Toyota and Honda have been successful in building up deep supplier relationships following six distinct steps (Liker & Choi 2004):

- Understand how their suppliers work and respect their capabilities.
- Turn supplier rivalry into opportunity by sourcing each component from two or three suppliers and setting up joint ventures with existing suppliers to transfer knowledge.
- Supervise their suppliers and provide immediate and constant feedback.
- Develop supplier's technical and innovation capabilities.
- Share information intensively but selectively and in a structured format.
- Conduct joint improvement activities, e.g. by exchange best practices with suppliers, initiate kaizen projects at suppliers' facilities, and set up supplier study groups.

In contrast, the US car manufacturers, GM and Ford, continue to rely on arm's length relationships with suppliers, although their supply chains superficially resemble those of their Japanese competitors (Liker & Choi 2004:106). For instance, Ford uses online reverse auctions to get the lowest prices for components. Both Ford and GM source components globally, particularly from China and other Asian countries. Recently, Ford announced that they plan to reduce their supplier base by about 50 percent and to encourage their key suppliers to bring leading-edge technological innovations to Ford (Mas 2005).

Managing Sourcing Relationships

A recent approach to managing strategic sourcing relations examines both the external relationship and the internal organization under the names of »balanced sourcing« (Laseter 1998) or »strategic sourcing« (Banfield 1999). Like other approaches, it abandons the adversarial relationships of the past in favor of stronger supplier participation. However, it goes beyond partnership to take a proactive position in order to take full advantage of the supplier's capabilities, seeking mutual improvements on both sides. The new elements are 1) the addition of the customer's own capabilities through organizational change including cross-functional and inter-organizational teams, 2) autonomy of the buying organization, 3) involving the entire organization beyond the procurement function, and 4) upgrading the procurement function to top management level. It requires flexibility based on trust between partners and sharing information. It also projects new roles such as bringing partners into new product development.

Two topics bear emphasis: supplier development and supplier participation in new product development. Much has been written about the first. It comprises a mixture of activities from technical assistance, training, exchanges of personnel to specific investments on the supplier's premises. Krause et al. (1998:40) define it as:

> »... any set of activities undertaken by a buying firm to identify, measure and improve supplier performance and facilitate the continuous improvement of the overall value of goods and services supplied to the buying company's business unit.«

Krause et al. differentiate between »reactive« and »strategic« approaches. *Reactive* suggests ad hoc efforts to remedy specific supply problems, while *strategic* identifies key commodities and suppliers, to anticipate problem areas. The first ultimately leads towards the second. The key elements in a successful development process appear to be communication, formal evaluation, training and supplier award programs.

JIT purchasing emphasizes close relationships. De Toni and Nassimbeni (2000) divide development into two sets of practices. *Operational* practices include product and process development, production planning and scheduling and delivery synchronized to production requirements. *Supplier development* practices include selection and monitoring, assistance and training, contractual incentives and supplier organizational integration. They identified three types of links between supplier and buyer: logistics, quality and design. The logistics link, involving delivery and production planning, shared forecasts and packaging, dominated the quality link (information exchange, inspection of incoming goods, and certification, and the design link involved in product design.

Vendor-Managed Purchasing

Vendor-managed purchasing is an extension of vendor-managed inventory (see Chapter 5). In vendor-managed purchasing, the vendor's organization and the buying organization are very closely integrated (Christiansen 2000). This is shown in Figure 8.9.

Figure 8.9. Vendor-Managed Purchasing

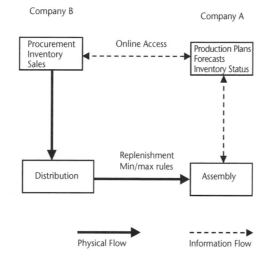

Source: Christiansen (2000)

A is a manufacturing company and B is the supplier. Company A uses vendor B as the sole supplier of a particular category of goods, typically standard items like »nuts and bolts« or maintenance, repair and operations (MRO) items. Production planning and automated inventory replenishment rules at A automatically generate orders for items that are then transmitted to B. B then fills these orders, ensures quality and ships to A. The goods are delivered directly to production areas without a need to perform incoming quality inspections.

The vendor has on-line access to company A's stock level, production plans and sales forecasts and therefore knows the requirements for future production. With this knowledge, the vendor can order the items from its own suppliers and manage documentation, transport, and payments. The customer's benefits are cost savings on purchasing administration, inventory costs, inventory management, and quality control. Thus, the purchasing organization of company A can be relieved of routine purchasing decisions to concentrate on strategic procurement. The vendor's benefits come from 1) economies of scale in purchasing 2) economies of specialization in knowing the supply market, and 3) scheduling its own purchasing, production, inventory and distribution in a more efficient manner. Customer's demand becomes visible at an earlier stage in the supply chain. It can thus reduce the bullwhip effect in the supply chain (Lee 1993).

Conclusion

Management's capability to establish trust-based and long-term relationships with suppliers and other strategic partners becomes a crucial competitive parameter (Christopher 2005). The increased integration and collaboration among companies within the supply chain increases the complexity of management and control. It requires new management skills in terms of developing inter-organizational relationships with strategic partners.

The role of procurement has changed dramatically during the last decade, from routine to strategic. Relationships between buyer and supplier have shifted from arm's length to close collaboration with key suppliers. Many companies have adopted a differentiated approach to individual procurement situations. Information technology and outsourcing to third parties have reduced the workload of routine purchases.

At the other end of the spectrum, strategic sourcing is becoming collaborative. Suppliers contribute their technology and innovative expertise to processes, components, and subsystems that become part of the final product. The buying organization can become more focused on its own core, and the final output becomes more a joint venture. The boundaries between vendor/supplier and customer become less important than the ability to manage the process.

Illustrative Case

Kolobri[7]

On November 19, 2005, Jakob Hansen, Procurement Manager at Kolibri again read the headline of an article, which one of his employees had given him that same morning: »The future supplier is electronic. New e-business technology allows companies to gain efficiency in their procurement processes«. This article seemed to verify Kolibri's current procurement strategy for indirect material since they had implemented an e-procurement system almost two years ago.

The article stated that the adaptation of new IT technology such as the Internet or EDI would revolutionize the procurement side of Supply Chain Management. Electronic based procurement solutions, which were summarized as e-procurement would help improve procurement efficiency by decreasing the total procurement costs as well as increasing the procurement services. This was exactly the reason why Jakob had decided to implement e-procurement at Kolibri. He especially wanted to obtain one particular competitive advantage of e-procurement, which was to make purchasing a strategic and competitive area, as 'the potential of e-procurement is so great that it has turned the formerly looked-down-upon traditional purchasing function into a competitive weapon' (Presutti 2003: 222).

Even though Kolibri had achieved lower purchasing and transaction costs by implementing an e-procurement system for indirect material, the current 6.000 users of the system were very dissatisfied. Many purchase transactions were therefore still done outside the system by calling the suppliers directly. The reason for this dissatisfaction was threefold: Firstly, the users found it difficult to find the items they were looking for in the e-supplier catalogues in the e-procurement system. Secondly, the information in the e-catalogues was sometimes outdated meaning that some products did not exist anymore even though they were still present in the e-catalogue. Finally, many of the users at Kolibri were unhappy with the fact that they could not call the suppliers they used to purchase from since

---

7. Adapted from Buchdorf-Pedersen and Kotzab (2006:205-214), in Arlbjørn et al. (2006)

Kolibri had started using single-sourcing when implementing the e-procurement system.

Based on these issues, Jakob felt the need to improve the efficiency of the current e-procurement solution by focusing on improving the quality and usability of the e-catalogues in the system: 'We have to find out what a state-of-the-art electronic supplier catalogue has to include and how it can be implemented« Jakob said to his e-procurement department. He looked in his calendar in order to plan a meeting where his team could present a solution to the board members of Kolibri.

Many companies that have implemented e-procurement solutions are experiencing the same problems as Kolibri is. The main focus on e-procurement implementations is usually on the more technical aspect – making sure that all IT systems are working the way they should. What companies are becoming more and more aware of is that the content and quality of e-catalogues is just as important if not more. If the e-catalogues are not of high quality, the end-users cannot find the products or services they are looking for. This is why the compliance and user satisfaction of the overall e-procurement solution will be low. This is a major obstacle for companies trying to obtain a positive return of their e-procurement investment.

What is needed is a larger focus on the qualitative aspects of e-procurement solutions. Companies – such as Kolibri– should locate the reasons for the low quality e-catalogues, as well as figuring out how to improve and implement them in their e-procurement systems.

Company Presentation

Kolibri is a Danish company, which provides purchasing services and solutions mainly for their parenting company Eagle A/S, who is a world leading company within the high-tech sector. Since December 2003 Kolibri has implemented an e-procurement solution built on SAP technology aiming at ensuring price and process related savings when purchasing indirect material.

Figure 8.10. The Kolibri Supply Chain

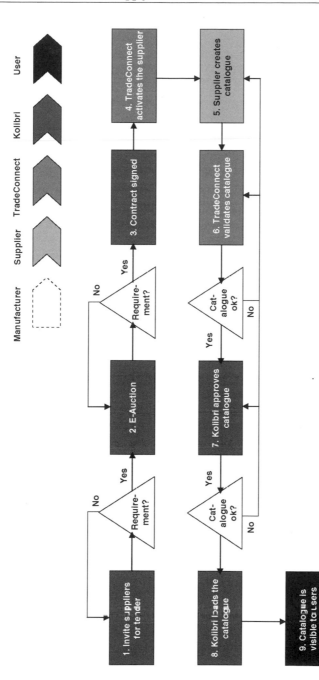

By using the current e-procurement solution, Kolibri today handles the total purchasing volume for indirect material of Eagle A/S, which is grouped into four categories: high-tech products, IT and consumer goods, technical products, and finally services. Kolibri handles approximately 3 billion DKK for Eagle A/S each year of which 70 % goes through the current e-procurement system. Kolibri has chosen to use an e-marketplace by the name of TradeConnect to handle their e-procurement solution. TradeConnect is a five-year old Swedish owned e-marketplace with offices in Stockholm, Oslo, Stavanger, Helsinki and Copenhagen. The focus of TradeConnect is to provide efficient purchasing solutions within the areas of electronic source, procure, and pay. TradeConnect today has some of the largest and most prominent companies in Scandinavia as its customers. Figure 8.10 illustrates the supply chain structure between Kolibri, their suppliers and TradeConnect.

The figure shows a complex interaction between the three companies in this particular supply chain. Activity 1 in the figure indicates that Kolibri invites several suppliers within a specific sourcing area for tendering. If these suppliers meet Kolibri's minimum requirements (e.g. quality, lead time, costs, ethics, environmental policies, etc.), they are invited to participate in an e-auction where they compete against each other based on different criteria (activity 2). The winner of the e-auction is then invited to sign a contract with Kolibri – thereby being the only supplier to Kolibri within the specified sourcing area (activity 3). When the contract is signed, Kolibri informs TradeConnect that they can 'activate' the supplier. The 'activation' primarily consists of helping the supplier in creating an e-catalogue (activity 4 and 5). When the supplier has done this TradeConnect validates the catalogue based on some pre-defined technical validations (activity 6). If the technical format of the e-catalogue is accepted, Kolibri is asked to approve the commercial aspects of the catalogue (activity 7). When this is done the e-catalogue is »set live« in the e-procurement system and the users at Kolibri are able to search and purchase items in the e-catalogue (activity 8 and 9). Kolibri today has 71 e-catalogues within the area of indirect material in their e-procurement system.

Many (so-called) experts within the field argue that the handling of e-catalogues is not as simple as it looks. This is due to the cutting-edge character of this environment and to a lack of practical experience concerning the application. This setup seems to include a lot of complex coordination and cooperation between the involved actors in the supply chain, which might not be the case when starting the e-catalogue. The catalogue quality which drives the success of the total e-procurement solution depends on the willingness to share between suppliers and buyers: »Content management poses the biggest challenge to enterprises rolling out e-procurement and it's one of the primary reasons, many IT managers say, e-procurement is making little or no change in the overall cost of buying products and services« (Hicks 2001: 51).

Jakob understood that the current supply chain setup is a step towards a virtual integration of all involved actors. All SCM processes will rely more and more on the quality of the virtual/e-based actor relations, which will be closer on one hand but less personal on the other. An e-procurement system as the one outlined in the figure above allows the individual user to directly purchase the needed product/service, which can be found in the e-catalogues in the e-procurement system. The need for a central purchasing department will therefore be reduced. Within the e-procurement system there will only be a predetermined number of suppliers, each with their own individual catalogue containing a specific range of products/services. The selection will be based on the best possible conditions each supplier offers. All transactions will be processed electronically and a total integration of the buying company's ERP-system must be guaranteed.

When it comes to the content of e-catalogues, Jakob looked at the results of one study among 55 e-business experts that has shown that three main areas should be covered in an e-catalogue: 1) product information, 2) catalogue architecture, and 3) catalogue functionality. But how do these areas refer to the dynamics within a supply chain setting and how can the information be guaranteed to be current and always updated.

Jakob and his team decided to treat the three areas as follows. Product information is the key area, as the knowledge on the right product information certifies advantages against other competitors. The suppliers have to find out what kind of product information is relevant for the e-procurement users at Kolibri. Catalogue architecture refers to the set-up of how the product information is presented. In which relevant categories is the catalogue separated and how updated is the presented information? Finally, catalogue functionality should be understood as the type of process integration between the actors and quality of the search function.

Although these issues were known within the field of e-procurement, Jakob and his team were very surprised to find that they could not find any answers to these issues. It looked as if most existing e-procurement implementations had not taken these issues into consideration. The consequential system development objective his team was therefore very obvious: »Okay, there is no time for trial-and-error. We have to find out how to implement a state-of-the art e-supplier catalogue in our e-procurement system and we have to rely on our know-how of cooperation between different actors in a supply chain.«

9. Transport and Logistics Services

»The 3PL should be viewed as an extension of the logistics department in your business and be treated in the same way as any other internal operation of your business.« Raymond McGuire, Vice President, International Services, Kellwood New England in »2005 Third-Party Logistics«

(Langley et al. 2005)

Introduction

The global supply chain relies on the effective use of transportation networks (Figure 9.1). They vary substantially, depending on the region, country, or function. Both intercontinental and regional transport becomes important in the global context of business. Materials supplied in one country, can be moved across the globe for processing, returned for assembly and quality control, and then delivered to many individual country markets for distribution. Each transport link is also a unique market, with its own options determined by its own regulations, business practices, and industry characteristics. Transoceanic transport options differ from those within Europe, which again differ from those available in North America. Transoceanic product movements utilize bulk movement, container, and air transport. According to the OECD, air cargo accounts for more than one-third of world trade in value, but only a small percentage in weight. Transport inside Europe uses motor carriage heavily, railways and inland waterways much less and air selectively. North America uses rail and air transport to a much greater extent.

This chapter emphasizes transport and logistics services available within Europe. The options and their impact on supply chains are sufficiently unique to require different management practices. We begin with structural changes in the logistics systems in Europe that have increased the importance of fast and efficient transport systems. We then look at transport policy within the European Union where the most significant contribution has been the deregulation of the transport market, the removal of barriers between member states, and the enlargement of EU in 2004 to encompass 25 member states, and also in 2007 to include Romania and Bulgaria. The majority of the chapter discusses the market for transport and logistics services. The main development has been the increasing presence of third-party logistics providers. Here, we identify different types of third-party logistics providers and present various steps in developing third party relationships. Finally, we look at the future of the transport and logistics industry in Europe and examine new developments within the transport and third-party logistics.

Figure 9.1. Transport

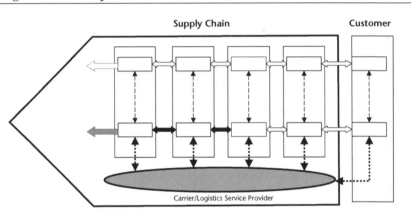

Structural Changes in Supply Chains

Major changes in both European supply chains and logistics systems, highlight the importance of solving transportation problems at a regional rather than at a national level. Changes in production methods such as just-in-time production and flexible production specialization have created the need for flexible, fast, individually tailored transportation systems with reduced shipment sizes and increased shipment frequency to reflect coordinated supplier-customer operations. Simultaneously, there has been a shift from primarily local or regional sourcing to global sourcing, with increasing requirements for fast and efficient international transport systems. The shift from standardized mass production to small-scale production of customized high-value products involves smaller shipments, a market that favors road and air, over rail and sea transport. Specialized production feeds other production facilities, sometimes located at considerable distances. Distribution has become centralized, relying on fast, flexible transport to substitute for purely localized distribution systems. Realizing the single European Market has included deregulation of transport, removal of customs clearance, and abolishing technical trade barriers.

Eliminating these obstacles has resulted in large increases in regional intra-European goods movements. Beyond removing obstacles, growing environmental awareness among people and public authorities changes the focus to the negative effects of increased road transport. A limitation on solving capacity problems through new investments in motorways and airports puts a constraint on the free movement of goods. One result is pressure to reduce the volume of road transport and encourage usage of the more environmentally friendly modes of rail, inland waterways, and intermodal transport.

Infrastructure Investment

Transportation infrastructure in Europe reflects the historic differences among European countries in geography, demography, communications systems, political and economic systems, and cultural backgrounds. The current infrastructure is still oriented more toward serving national needs than international goods transport. This is especially true for railways and inland waterways. There is a vital concern in the European Union about whether the transportation infrastructure will support the logistics requirements of business or whether it will impede the free movement of goods and services. Since 1995, road transport of goods in EU-25 has increased by about 35 percent, measured in ton-kilometers. The share of freight transport by road has increased in the past 10 years from about 68 percent of surface transport to 73 percent. The railway share has decreased from 20 percent in 1995 to only 16 percent in 2004. Inland waterways and pipelines are responsible for the remaining 11 percent (Eurostat, 2005). Airfreight has increased in market share for high-valued products but is still negligible in terms of ton-kilometers. In the past 5 years, the volume of regional intra-EU transport has been growing by nearly 5 percent per year, and there are no signs that this growth rate will decline in the future. The combination of increasing passenger vehicles and freight transport, environmental concerns, and inadequate investment in infrastructure places pressure upon the highway network. It has caused severe congestion problems around some core industrial areas in Europe: the Rhine-Ruhr Area, Greater London, Madrid, Milan, Frankfurt, and Munich.

There is a conflict between national interests in reducing the environmental impacts of increased goods transport and the EU policy of free movement of goods across Europe. An example is Switzerland, which has a strategically important position for lorries transiting to and from Italy and the Balkans. There are only a few crossing points, and this imposes a heavy burden on the fragile Alpine eco-system and the Swiss population. After a referendum in 1994, Switzerland decided only to allow foreign trucks in transit with a maximum weight of 28 tonnes, compared to 40 up to 56 tonnes gross weight in most European countries. This meant that lorries to and from Italy had to make a long detour and use other crossing points, mainly the Brenner Pass between Austria and Italy. After negotiations between EU and Switzerland the ban of lorries over 28 tonnes was abolished in 2001. In return, Switzerland was allowed to charge a tax on these vehicles.

Austria has a similar geographical situation at a crossroads between the north-south (Germany-Italy) and east-west routes, and the same sensitive state of the Alpine environment. Therefore in 1992, the European Union and Austria signed an agreement on the transit of goods by road and rail. This agreement introduced the ecopoint system to encourage international truck operators to use more environmentally friendly trucks in transit through Austria. There were restrictions on the number of eco-points allocated to each operator. The aim was to achieve by 2003, a 60% reduction in polluting emissions (NOx) from heavy goods vehicles transiting through Austria. The eco-point system was terminated in 2004 in view of EU's new policy of charging infrastructure to allow a real shift from road to rail.

In Germany the expression »Verkehrsinfarkt« (traffic infarction) has been used to characterize the current traffic situation, which has resulted in increasing congestion costs from time delays, increasing fuel consumption, and pollution. In order to reduce the truck traffic, Germany introduced in 2005 a new toll system on the 12,000 km of German autobahn for all trucks with a maximum weight of 12 tonnes and above. The new toll system, called LKW-MAUT, is a governmental tax for trucks based on the distance ridens in kilometres, number of axles, and the emission category of the truck. The tax is levied for all trucks using German autobahns, whether they are full or empty. The toll system will affect over 1.5 million truck rides in Germany and the rest of Europe. The government will use the tolls collected on road improvements and new road constructions.

With the gradual deregulation of the transport market, the European Union has focused attention on common trans-border infrastructure, notably the »Trans-European Networks« (TEN) program, which was included in the Maastricht Treaty of 1992. The programme takes into account the need to link islands, landlocked and peripheral regions with the central regions of the European Community. TEN projects have included investments in high-speed passenger rail networks in Europe, the Channel Tunnel between England and France, the Öresund Bridge between Denmark and Sweden, several new motorways and inland waterway connections. Thus far, the impact of the huge investments in TEN projects on the freight transport in Europe has been limited. Most of these investments have improved high-speed train services for passengers, but not the capacity for rail freight transport services.

Deregulation of the European Transport Market

1993 was a milestone in transport policy within the European Community. This date marks the start of deregulation of intra-Union transport. International transport of goods by road between member states was liberalized from the beginning. However, domestic or national transport of goods has only been gradually deregulated since 1993. To allow for a more efficient use of resources (less empty lorries), transport companies were allowed to perform cabotage transport in other countries under certain conditions, and with the limitation that it must be temporary. If it is permanent, the haulier is required to have a registered office in the country. Cabotage means that a carrier from one country is allowed to perform domestic transport in another country. For example, a French forwarder can pick up cargo between Munich and Basel on a backhaul trip from Stuttgart. Cabotage has lead to increased competition between the international transport and forwarding companies and the freight rates have been reduced on major traffic routes. However, road cabotage transport represents less than 1 percent of the total road transport market in EU-15 »old member states« excluding Greece (Ecorys Transport, 2004). For the new Member States, the application of the right of cabotage is still subject to transitional periods of between two and five years, except for Slovenia, Cyprus and Malta.

Railways are still state-owned and operated in most countries in Europe. However, in several countries both passenger and freight transport have been privatized and have access to perform railroad services liberalized. The competitive position of rail freight differs by country. Railways in Sweden and Germany have relatively high market shares (in ton-kilometers), although for different reasons. In Sweden, it is the result of a combination of long distances and heavy bulk goods (e.g. timber, pulp, steel, heavy equipment, and large appliances). In Germany, the market share has, until recently, been maintained through subsidies along with restrictions on road transport. In Denmark, England, Benelux, and Southern Europe, railways hold only 10 to 20 percent of the transport market.

In 1993, the European Commission put forward a directive aiming to separate the infrastructure (such as tracks, signals, bridges, roadbeds and tunnels) from train operations. This directive opened up access for private firms to establish railway companies, using the public infrastructure for private train operation. The railway companies themselves should be free to take only that part of the traffic they considered being profitable. For unprofitable traffic, special public service contracts were to be negotiated with state, regional, and local governments.

In practice there have been many obstacles to European-wide liberalization of access to tracks. Differences in electrical systems, security systems, signal systems, and educational systems in individual European countries continue as entry barriers to private train operators.

The process of changing the European railway systems into a single, commercially viable transport system able to compete with road transport will demand large investments and total reorganization of the state controlled railways. In addition, to be fully competitive, new services must be developed and tailored to individual customer requirements, they must provide on-line freight information systems, improve intermodal service across Europe and expand door-to-door service with competitive transit times and high reliability.

The EU is supporting the development of a system of key rail freight routes running across Europe on which operators will be able to compete for customers. The system is called »Trans-European Rail Freight Freeways« (TERFF). Such routes are for example established from Scandinavia to Italy and from England to Hungary.

Intermodal transport in Europe is increasing, with aggravated road congestion, and more restrictions and taxes being placed on road transport. Intermodal transport encompasses several types of rail freight systems, such as ISO containers, swap bodies and piggyback trailers.

ISO containers are standardized boxes, typically 20 or 40 feet long, used in ocean shipping and international transport. ISO containers can be transferred between ships, trains, and trucks. Often large containerships arrive at big European ports, such as Rotterdam, Bremen, and Antwerp, where the containers are loaded on feederships, trains, or trucks to the next or final destination.

A swap body is a demountable body, which can be transferred between train and truck. When demounted, legs support it. Swap bodies are mostly used in national or international transport within Europe.

Piggyback trailers are semitrailers with lifting points for transfer between road and rail. A piggyback trailer on a rail wagon is also called »Huckepack« in German. A variant is »Rollende Landstrasse« (rolling highway), where the entire truck is put on a rail wagon. Piggyback trailers offer high flexibility between rail and road, e.g. for freight in transit through Switzerland or Austria to avoid restrictions on truck transport.

The Transport and Logistics Service Industry in Europe

The market for transport and logistics services in Europe has changed dramatically since the early 1990s. Shippers now reconfigure production and distribution systems on a pan-European basis. They increasingly outsource warehousing, transportation and other logistics-related activities. The upsurge of e-commerce has increased the demand for direct, fast, frequent, and reliable shipments to customers.

The deregulation and liberalization of the transport market in Europe has changed the competitive environment. New competitors and combinations of previously traditional firms have entered the market: global express companies, postal companies and US logistics companies. Mergers and acquisitions are taking place at a speed and with geographic coverage never seen before. Strategic alliances among leading transport and forwarding companies have been established to provide pan-European or even global coverage and a wide range of transport and logistics services. Some established strategic alliances have dissolved because of acquisitions that turned former partners into competitors. Expansion of logistics concepts has also changed the scope of competition as carriers have sought competitive advantage in annexing non-transport services.

Third-Party Logistics

Since the early 1990s, there has been a pronounced change in shipper-logistics provider arrangements. While the initial driving forces were to reduce costs and release capital for other purposes, they now have a more strategic scope: to increase market coverage, improve the level of service or increase flexibility to meet the changing requirements of customers. Cooperation between parties has become long-term in nature, mutually binding and often combined with changes in both organization and information systems on both sides. Solutions are tailored to specific requirements and often include value-adding services such as final assembly, packaging, quality control, and information services. This broader, long-term, and customized, cooperative arrangement is termed third-party logistics (TPL).

What is Third-Party Logistics?

Third-party logistics has many definitions and the content of the concept is changing as the practice itself evolves. Some recent examples illustrate the broad scope of definitions: Coyle, et al. (2003: 425) define a third-party logistics provider as »an external supplier that performs all or part of a company's functions«. This is a very broad definition that encompasses suppliers of services such as transport, warehousing, distribution, IT services, and so on. However, the authors add that a »true« third-party logistics arrangement includes multiple logistics activities that are integrated or managed together, and provide »solutions« to logistics/supply chain problems.

Berglund et al. (1999: 59) also emphasize »management« as an essential element of third-party logistics in their definition: »Activities carried out by a logistics service provider on behalf of a shipper and consisting of at least *management* and execution of transportation and warehousing (if warehousing is part of the process)«. Other activities can be included, such as information services, value added activities, call centers, invoicing, and financial services. Management support can range from simple inventory management to advanced consultancy about re-alignment of supply chain management.

A more narrow definition of third-party logistics is given by Murphy & Poist (2000: 121): »A relationship between a shipper and third party which, compared with basic services, has more customized offerings, encompasses a broader number of service functions and is characterized by a longer-term, more mutually beneficial relationship«. This definition is in line with Bagchi and Virum (1998b), who distinguish between simple outsourcing of logistics activities and logistics alliances. According to their definition a logistics alliance means: »A long-term formal or informal relationship between a shipper and a logistics provider to render all or a considerable number of logistics activities for the shipper. The shipper and the logistics provider see themselves as long-term partners in these arrangements. Although these alliances may start with a narrow range of activities, there is a potential for a much broader set of value-added services, including simple fabrication, assemblies, repackaging, and supply chain integration«. In contrast to the first two that emphasize the performance of functional activities, the last definition stresses the duration of the relationship between shipper and logistics service provider, as well as the potentially wide range of logistics services included in the arrangement.

The term »lead logistics provider« is used for a third-party logistics provider, who has a single interface between the client and multiple logistics service providers. Lead logistics providers are used by clients, who want a »one-stop-solution«, and outsource subcontracting and logistics management and operational activities to one organization. The lead logistics provider signs contracts with sub-suppliers of logistics services and takes care of facility management, transport and warehouse management, performance measurement, etc.

In Figure 9.2, we have classified various types of relationships between shipper and logistics service provider according to the degree of integration and the degree of specific investments in the relationship (Halldorsson & Skjoett-Larsen 2004). It is important to note that the framework in figure 9.2 does not illustrate a dynamic progress from one stage to another. Some third-party logistics arrangements remain on stage two, others degrade from stage three to stage two, or change to in-house logistics solutions.

Figure 9.2. Types of TPL relationships

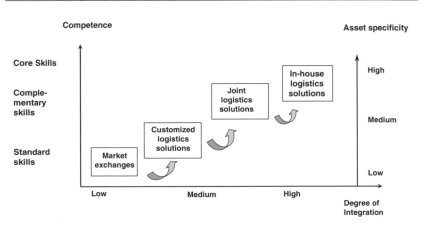

Market transactions in the lower left corner involve no specific assets or integration between the parties. The transactions can involve single or continuing purchases of logistics services, but the relationship will typically be at arm's length. Agreements are short-term and often informal, carrying no commitment beyond the specific transaction. Usually it will involve single activities such as transport. Price is a strong element in competition, although there might be special service requirements that also influence the choice. Asset specificity is low and the services offered are standard skills.

The next level, customized logistics solutions, would usually include transport and warehousing. The degrees of asset specificity and integration are relatively low. The shipper would maintain management and control internally, outsourcing operational activities to a service provider. The service provider offers a broad range of standard services from which the customer can select a combination of modules. There will only be minor adjustments to the customer's specific requirements. Asset specificity is low/medium, and the services can easily be adjusted to other clients to obtain economies of scale. The duration of the relationship is typically limited to one year or less. The price and cost savings are decisive factors in choosing the service provider.

A joint logistics solution is the third stage in the development of the relationship between the shipper and service provider. Operations of both parties are integrated, with interfaces between information systems and inter-organizational teams. Cooperation is based on mutual trust and open information interchange. Asset specificity is also relatively high. The logistics provider may invest in dedicated facilities and other tangible assets, and also in the less-tangible, personnel training. Agreements are more formalized and binding than for simple outsourcing. Services become tailored to the requirements of the individual client. Sometimes, the service provider assumes fully or partly responsibility, for the personnel, equipment, and warehouse operations of the client.

Lead logistics provider involves the highest degree of collaboration, both in the scope of services and strategic importance. The lead logistics provider offers a broad range of management and logistics services, covering not only traditional operational activities such as warehousing, transportation and value-adding services but also management and optimization of the client's supply chain, IT competencies and global coverage. Lead logistics provider often is established as a joint venture or a long-term contract between the parties. The collaboration involves high system integration and inter-organizational teams at various management levels. Moreover, asset specificity is normally high, both in physical assets such as dedicated warehouses, specialized handling equipment and human assets involving activities such as the exchange of personnel, and specialized training.

Typology of Third-Party Logistics Providers

Berglund et al. (1999) have identified three waves of entrants into the third-party logistics market:

- Asset-based logistics providers
- Network logistics providers
- Skill-based logistics providers

Asset-based logistics providers represent the first wave, originated in the early 1980s. They were typically operators of owned or leased logistics services assets, such as trucks, airplanes, warehouses, terminals and containers, they offer third-party logistics services as a natural extension of their core businesses. For example, a transport and forwarding company may provide dedicated trucks, transport management, distribution centers, and information services to a shipper. Or a distribution center operator may offer inventory management, final assembly services, and order administration in addition to basic warehousing. Declining margins and a tougher competitive environment in the traditional transport market have been the main drivers for these companies to enter the third-party logistics market. Some of these providers used the additional logistical services and third-party logistics arrangements to secure volume for their basic services. Others have entered the third-party logistics market because of higher profit margins and customer loyalty. Examples of asset-based logistics providers in Europe are Panalpina, Penske Logistics, Geodis, Schenker, and DFDS Transport Solutions to name a few from a growing list. Well-known asset-based third-party logistics providers in the United States include Cat Logistics, Schneider Logistics, Ryder Integrated Logistics, and Menlo Worldwide.

Network logistics providers date back to the beginning of the 1990s. These third-party logistics providers started as couriers and express parcels companies and built up global transportation and communication networks to be able to expedite express shipments faster and more reliably. Supplementary information services typically include electronic proof-of-delivery and track-and-trace options from sender to receiver. They include such familiar names as DHL, Maersk Logistics, UPS, TNT and Federal Express. Recently, these players have moved into the time-sensitive and high-value-density third-party logistics market, such as electronics, spare parts, fashion goods, and pharmaceuticals and are competing with the traditional asset-based logistics provider in these high-margin markets. UPS, as the largest transportation company in the world, also offers a broad range of services from shipment tracking, shipper-accessible information services, and specialized logistics services to e-commerce and financing services for overseas manufacturing.

Skill-based logistics providers are a third wave of third-party logistics providers, started at the end of the 1990s. They typically do not own physical logistics assets, but provide consultancy and financial services, information technology, and management skills to the clients. These new players are often subsidiairies or joint ventures. They may merge with players from the previous waves or use them as subcontractors. An example of a skill-based logistics provider is Maersk Logistics, a subsidiary of the A.P. Moller – Maersk Group. Maersk Logistics provides customized solutions for suply chain management, warehousing and distribution, and sea and airfreight transport.

Figure 9.3. Typology of Logistics Services

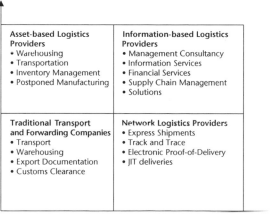

Physical Services

Asset-based Logistics Providers • Warehousing • Transportation • Inventory Management • Postponed Manufacturing	Information-based Logistics Providers • Management Consultancy • Information Services • Financial Services • Supply Chain Management • Solutions
Traditional Transport and Forwarding Companies • Transport • Warehousing • Export Documentation • Customs Clearance	Network Logistics Providers • Express Shipments • Track and Trace • Electronic Proof-of-Delivery • JIT deliveries

Management Services

In Figure 9.3, the different types of logistics and management services available are classified according to availability of competence in supply chain mangement and customization of logistics solutions. Traditional market-based solutions offer only basic physical and management services. Asset-based providers may perform extensive services but leave control with the client management. With some exceptions, network providers become more oriented toward management services but limited physical operations. Skill-based logistics providers become more comprehensive, offering both management and operations capabilities.

Driving Forces Behind Third-Party Logistics

Several forces drive the development of third-party logistics. In a global environment, logistics and supply chain activities become more complex, expensive, and capital intensive. By outsourcing logistics activities, many companies can reduce their logistics costs and/or improve their customer service performance. This parallels the trend of outsourcing in manufacturing. These companies concentrate their resources on the most vital parts of their business, performing other activities via third-party specialists.

The benefits of outsourcing logistics services to third-party logistics providers include:

* The conversion of fixed costs to variable costs
* Economies of scale and scope
* Creation of a leaner and more flexible organization
* Faster access to new markets and distribution channels
* Reconfiguration of European logistics systems

The conversion of fixed costs to variable costs. By outsourcing transport and warehouse operations, a company can free capital investment in transport equipment, warehouse buildings, and materials handling equipment and thereby transform fixed costs to variable costs and transfer the financial risk to the third party. If the demand for capacity is uncertain or fluctuating, the shipper can easily adjust costs to the scale of activity.

Economies of scale and scope. The third-party logistics company can use its assets to serve multiple clients and product groups with complementary demand patterns, and thereby obtain a better utilization of the assets. In addition, the third-party logistics operator will often have a knowledge and experience in international logistics, which exceeds that of the client. The cost savings may partly be passed on to the shipper.

A leaner organization. The shipper may be able to simplify and streamline routine logistics operations such as documentation, distribution planning, inventory control, and personnel administration. It also facilitates implementation of EDI, bar coding, and exchange of employees between organizations. Dealing with one or a few third-party operators on a long-term basis is more efficient than working with a number of independent haulage companies through individual transactions.

Faster access to new markets and distribution channels. For example, on-line retailers or e-tailers are typically outsourcing the logistics part of their business to third-party logistics operators. Instead of having to invest in »bricks and mortar« in different part of the world, the Internet retailers can utilize the third-party logistics operator's global network. That allows the many new e-commerce sites to get instant access to the global market place without having to tie up capital in fixed assets.

Reconfiguration of European logistics systems. Some companies are using third-party logistics as a transition from a decentralized to a centralized distribution system in Europe. Until recently, many international companies in Europe had a decentralized structure with sales subsidiaries and distribution centres in every EU country. Many of these companies have moved towards a centralized system with one or a few distribution centres in Europe. Examples include Atlas Copco Industrial Techniques, Danfoss, Nike, Philips Electronics, Mattel, Reebok, and Xerox. Expansion of logistics services to pan-European scale has been a strong enabling factor.

Developing a Third-Party Logistics Partnership

Outsourcing decisions are both difficult and stressful. Preparing for an outsourcing decision must be thorough. Evaluation and selection of an appropriate third-party logistics partner requires management resources, establishing trust relationships and common information systems and joint standard operating procedures. The most critical resource is time. From case studies and in-depth interviews with both third-party logistics providers and clients (Skjoett-Larsen 2000), a general guideline for the third-party logistics buying process can be developed. Similar conceptual decision models can be found in Bagchi and Virum (1998b), Sink and Langley (1997), and Magill (2000). The stages include:

- Establishing objectives and selection criteria
- Evaluating and selecting a third-party logistics provider
- Making a contract between the partners
- Implementing the partnership
- Making continuous improvements
- Renegotiating the contract

Although these stages are sequential, they can overlap in time. Outsourcing decisions are not simple linear processes, but are active search-and-learning, iterative processes, returning to previous stages as necessary. Outsourcing logistics activities has a number of strategic and organizational consequences that have to be balanced between costs and service benefits. Therefore, prior analysis of the current logistics system is an essential part of the process.

Many companies do not recognize their own actual logistics costs. Indirect costs such as capital costs tied up in warehouses and inventory are not usually identified separately in accounting systems. Transport costs can be hidden in the purchase price, when the goods are delivered with free shipment or cost, insurance, and freight (c.i.f.) terms. Comparing costs between third-party logistics solutions and current logistics costs is often difficult. The comparison is further complicated when the outsourcing decision occurs simultaneously with redesign of the supply chain processes.

In these preparations, the company must establish operational service performance criteria for monitoring and evaluation while setting realistic service objectives. It is not unusual for companies to claim substantially higher service performance from the third-party logistics provider than from their own operations. Tasks must be specified precisely to match service requirements, competencies required, and market coverage.

Evaluation and selection of third-party logistics providers must match the specific requirements of the outsourcing decision. Outsourcing warehousing and related operational activities become a relatively simple decision among many possible alternatives. As the decision involves less tangible requirements such as competencies in management skills, advanced information systems, and fast, reliable global networks, the number of potential operators diminishes. There might be few alternatives in a global market.

Typically, the shipper selects a handful of the most promising candidates. Evaluation of bidders can be complex, although it may be aided by quantitative tools, as the analytic hierarchy process to weight selection criteria (Bagchi 1989). This would be followed by qualitative evaluation with site visits.

The contract will typically have two parts. The first part includes the scope of the assignment, price agreements, service levels, length of the contract and penalty clauses for failure to meet agreed performance measures. The contract can be specific to safeguard against opportunism. This part is often a statement of intent about the scope of collaboration. The second part is a working manual for the contract, typically including detailed description of activities, performance evaluation, coordination and reporting requirements.

Implementation typically takes up to a year due to the difficulties of merging two organizations. Transmitting and sharing information both in hard data and more subjective content is the focal point. Information systems must be integrated, including computer systems, software, and data coding. In a few cases such as inventory management, the client may rely on the third-party logistics provider's own system, although clients usually prefer to maintain their own. Data links such as EDI or Internet-based systems must be established to allow fast, accurate data transmission about orders, invoices and other documents, as well as inventory status and shipment tracking.

An important part of a third-party logistics arrangement is transferring »soft« information on products and customers. This type of knowledge is often tacit and informal, but must be formalized for the relationship to operate. It includes setting up joint teams across the participating organizations, and a third-party logistics-appointed key manager to be responsible for client relationships. However, there should also be multiple levels of contacts with direct communication across organizational boundaries. One useful approach for information transfer is to introduce boundary-spanning personnel. Key client personnel can be assigned to the third-party logistics provider's premises, or vice versa.

Continuous improvement is an important part of the process. Costs and service requirements during the contract period should become targets for improvement. Incentives should be built into the contract, providing cost-based savings shared among both parties.

Renegotiations typically start after 2 to 3 years, although the period of the contact might be longer with dedicated and specialized investments in distribution centers or vehicles. The current provider normally holds a competitive advantage for renewal gained from knowledge of the client's operations. Clients do not change providers unless there are significant differences in projected performance or dissatisfaction with present arrangements. Initializing and implementation costs become high switching costs for the client.

Obstacles in Logistics Outsourcing

There are risks involved in turning over an internal logistics function to external third-party provider. First is the potential risk of loss of control over the flow of products and materials. This risk can be reduced through information systems linked to the third-party operator with a capability to track products at any time and location on their way to the customer.

A second risk is related to the third-party provider going out of business or being taken over by another company with inferior services or geographic coverage. Such disruptive events threaten the entire distribution process between the company and its customers and severely injure the customer service image of the client company. It therefore becomes essential to evaluate the financial strength and stability, along with the competence of prospective partners, before the contract is signed.

Lack of hard cost data on their existing logistics systems may also prevent companies from evaluating logistics activities for outsourcing. Few companies have adequate accounting systems with realistic knowledge of costs within their own logistics operations. Administrative costs of managing and controlling goods flows are often hidden in overhead costs. Interest on capital invested in warehouse buildings and transport equipment are seldom included.

Conflicting objectives among different internal organizational units within the shipping organization create resistance to outsourcing. A logistics department may object to a potential threat to its own activities and even its survival. The sales department may fear deterioration of customer service. The finance department may primarily support outsourcing as a tool to release capital in fixed assets.

Additionally, inter-organizational cooperation itself has inherent difficulties in compatibility of corporate cultures, data systems, and the level of employee knowledge and skills. Additionally, there may be problems with management coordination. Finally, there is an underlying problem of linking two organizations with differing goals. The result may be service failures, particularly in the initial phases of organizational learning.

Mergers and Acquisitions

Klaus (2005) estimated the market for logistics within the European community to be around 585 billion Euro. The majority of this market volume is taken by the third party logistics industry. During the last decade, The European market for third-party logistics services has changed dramatically.

The mergers and acquisitions in the transport and logistics industry have led to a few dominant players with global coverage and diversified activities, and a large number of small and medium-sized third-party logistics providers with a regional coverage and a more specialized service portfolio. The liberalization of the European post offices has resulted in a wave of mergers and acquisitions since 1996. Thus, Dutch Post Office acquired in 1996 the global logistics provider, TNT, in 1999 the Italian third-party logistics provider, Tecnologistica, in 2000 the US-based CTI, specialized in automotive logistics, and in 2005 Wilson Group, an international airfreight company. In 1999, Deutsche Post acquired the Swiss transport and forwarding company, Danzas, and later the Swedish ASG, the US-based international air freight forwarder, AEI, the global integrator DHL, and recently in 2005, the large UK-based logistics provider, Exel. All transport and logistics companies acquired by Deutsche Post are now using the common brand, DHL. The Danish haulier company, DSV, bought in 2002, the Danish DFDS Transport, and in 2006, the Dutch transport and forwarding company, Frans Maas. The wave of mergers and acquisitions is not over yet, and it can be expected that the dominant players will acquire more medium-sized and specialized transport and logistics companies in the coming years. Hertz (1998) has used the metaphor »domino-effect« to characterize the recent development on the European transport and logistics market.

In 2004, the 10 largest European logistics companies lead by Deutsche Post and followed by the Danish, Maersk Group generated a sales volume of nearly 100 billion Euro (Klaus 2005).

The mergers and acquisitions within the third-party logistics industry can be explained by the following objectives (Carbone & Stone, 2005):

- Wider geographic coverage and control of major traffic flows through the creation of efficient transport chains.
- Economies of scope to improve operating margins through commercial entry into new market segments.
- Economies of scale to cope with the high investment in physical infrastructure and information and communication systems.
- Strategic and operational synergies, through the acquisition of specialist capabilities, especially higher value-added services.

However, there are also risks involved in the merger and acquisition activity. There are cultural differences, different IT systems, different brand names, different operating procedures, etc. to overcome, when former independent third-party logistics providers merge into horizontal logistics alliances.

The Future of European Transport and Logistics

The transport industry in Europe, and in the world at large, will undergo dramatic structural changes in the coming years. Many small and medium-sized transport companies will disappear or be acquired by larger companies. Transport companies as a group are moving away from pure transportation services. Logistics service providers will assume a prominent place in serving the requirements of global clients. To do this they are growing through mergers, acquisitions and strategic alliances, and to a much lesser degree through internal growth.

Five types of logistics service providers are likely to emerge in the future:

- Lead logistics providers
- Pan-European logistics providers
- Niche logistics service providers
- E-commerce logistics providers

Lead Logistics Providers

A lead logistics provider (LLP) is an intermediary between a shipper and a number of more specialized logistics service companies or asset-based third-party logistics-providers such as carriers, warehousing companies, express companies, and regional logistics service providers. Lead logistics providers are not bound by fixed assets, but operate independently of geographical scope and functional activities. They are designers and managers of logistics solutions for their clients, subcontracting the execution to specialized carriers and distribution center operators. The advantage for the client company is that it can concentrate on its core business and has one single point of contact with the lead provider as one-stop-shopping. The benefits for the lead logistics provider are primarily broader access to the customer's portfolio of logistics activities, higher customer loyalty and a potentially long-term relationship to the customer. They are also flexible as the lead provider in dealing with customer requirements, calling in subcontractors as needed.

Global companies, largely American-based, such as CNH, Disney, Ford, Eastman Kodak, Nike, Sun Microsystems, and Xerox use lead logistics providers for their pan-European or global logistics. Lead logistics providers include DHL, Menlo Worldwide, Cat Logistics, Schneider Logistics, Maersk Logistics, and Ryder. US-based logistics service companies are entering the European scene »on the back of customers they already have in the United States«. Menlo Worldwide was asked to set up a new European distribution center for Nike Equipment in the Netherlands. Schneider Logistics started operations in Europe at the request of its US-based client, CNH. Penske Logistics was, in 2006, selected by Eaton Corporation, a diversified industrial USA-based manufacturer of electrical systems and fluid power systems for transport equipment, to serve as its lead logistics provider in Europe. The new contract builds upon a well-established relationship between the two companies in the United States.

Carbone and Stone (2005) emphasize the risk of the »piggyback« route for international expansion used by UK third-party logistics providers in the 1990s. For example, Marks & Spencer encouraged Exel Logistics, Tibbett & Britten, Christian Salvesen, and Hays to join them when they expanded their retail business at the continental Europe. Later, in 2000, Marks & Spencer retreated from the continent with adverse consequences for their third-party logistics providers.

Pan-European Logistics Providers

The pan-European logistics provider services cross-border logistics requirements on a Europe-wide basis and normally offers a broad range of services, including groupage (shipment consolidation), warehousing, forwarding, and value-added services. To control the flow of goods from door-to-door, pan-European providers must build networks of transshipment terminals covering the most important regions of Europe, along with communication systems to link terminals, network sales offices, and customers.

International clients increasingly ask for pan-European, single carrier solutions. However, only a few transport and logistics companies have complete pan-European coverage alone, but must establish strategic alliances or subcontract with other transport companies to complete their coverage. During the last few years a wave of acquisitions and mergers has altered the competitive situation of the third-party logistics market towards more pan-European and global players. Examples include DHL, Schenker, UPS, and TNT.

Niche Carriers

Some carriers have specialized their operations to specific regions (e.g. Eastern Europe), specific classes of goods (e.g. frozen foods, computers, furniture, fashion, hazardous goods, etc.) or specific services (e.g. warehousing, reverse logistics or call centers). These specialists often work in niche areas requiring unique competencies, technologies, and equipment. Competition would not be expected to be as intense as in the subcontractor basic carrier market. On the other hand, specialists become more dependent on individual customers or markets, because competence and equipment are not easily transferable to other areas.

JIT-oriented manufacturers and companies that have centralized their European distribution systems to one or a few strategically located sites, provide other niches for specialized carrier operations. A carrier offering customized, pan-European logistics solutions, including unique value-added services tailored to individual customers, can establish a niche that will provide it with long-term relationships with shippers. A specialist carrier may often be able to provide services that larger carriers are unable to perform because of the scale of their operations.

Examples of niche logistics providers in Europe include Tibbett & Britten (now part of DHL), which has developed particular capabilities and experience in the fast-moving consumer goods industry, and Cat Logistics, a subsidiary of Caterpillar, which is specialized in managing warehousing and distribution of service parts for a number of international clients.

E-Commerce Logistics Providers

The boom in Internet trade in both business-to-business (B2B) and business-to-consumer (B2C) has created an increasing demand for fast, reliable logistics service of small shipments to global customers. Global express companies, such as UPS Worldwide Logistics, TNT, DHL Express Services and Federal Express, and postal companies, such as US Postal Service and Royal Mail, dominate this new business, because they have the infrastructure needed in terms of physical network and information and communication systems. In addition, national or regional express and parcel companies have emerged to serve particular niches defined by product offerings or time. Home delivery often encounters conflicts with consumer preferences and work schedules, resulting in experimentation for new methods and institutions to hold packages for customer pickup, e.g. at gas stations or local shops.

Internet retailers are beginning to realize that logistics capabilities are necessary to attract and keep customers. It is both costly and risky to build up logistics infrastructure. Therefore, most Internet retailers outsource warehouse management and distribution to third-party logistics providers. Often, other logistics activities such as order fulfillment, inventory replenishment and returns management are outsourced to third-party logistics providers.

One of the unexpected consequences of e-commerce is to make »brick-and-mortar« DCs more important, as efficient, specialized operations become key to order fulfillment. Amazon, one the the largest e-tailers in the world, has recognized this, and established distribution centres in USA and brick-and mortar alliances with etablished brand name companies, such as Borders, the third largest books retailer, Target, one of the largest retail chains in USA, the US-based toy retailer ToysRUs, and the European Carphone, which sells mobile phones and services from major manufacturers and service providers.

Tiering Structure of the Logistics Market

A tier-system, similar to the supplier network in the automotive industry, is emerging in the transport industry. Fourth-party logistics or »lead logistics providers« operate as the first tier for multinational clients, offering »one-stop-shopping« for global logistics solutions. The first tier makes subcontracts with a second tier of asset-based logistics providers, information service providers and regional carriers to perform operational logistics activities in specific regions or business areas. The second tier might further collaborate with small and medium-sized operators in local and niche markets. A future structure is envisioned in figure 9.4.

Figure 9.4. Tiering structure of Third-Party Logistics

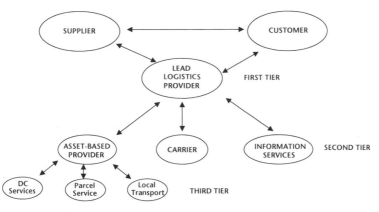

DC: *distribution center*

Conclusion

The market for transport and logistics services has changed dramatically during the last five years. There has been a trend toward broadening the scope of transport and logistics services with wider geographical coverage. There has also been a shift from asset-based to skill- and knowledge-based logistics providers. A wave of mergers and aquisitions has swept across the industry, led by Deutsche Post, TNT Post Group and leading US-based logistics companies. There has been an increasing demand for pan-European and global logistics solutions, although it is important to note that it is difficult to apply a single model on operations in different regions. Both the logistics industry at large and in Europe in particular is still a collection of diverse markets with differing customer requirements and distribution structures. One-stop-shopping and the use of lead logistics providers are some of the emerging trends in the European market for third-party logistics services. Also, a tiering structure is emerging, where the dominant players serve as the primary interface with the clients, the medium sized regional and specialised third-party logistics providers are subcontractors to the dominant players, and small and medium sized national logistics providers are operating at the local market.

Illustrative Cases

One-Stop-Shopping at Oticon[8]

Oticon is a leading hearing-aid manufacturer, part of the Danish holding company, William Demant, which incorporates the following three business areas: Hearing Aids (Oticon and Bernafon), Diagnostic Instruments, and Personal Communication. The company's headquarters with sales, marketing and R&D is located in Copenhagen (Bernafon has a similar setup in Berne, Switzerland). Oticon is a full line supplier ranging from sophisticated high end to lower priced high volume segments. Bernafon (acquired in 1995) has, in principle, the same offering, but with fewer models and reduced geographical coverage.

A condition for both Oticon's and Bernafon's hearing aid solutions is that the companies master a wide spectrum of technologies, including the design of integrated circuits for advanced processing of sound signals, the development of fitting software, the design of micro amplifiers, and the development of micro-mechanical components. The products are created in collaboration with experts having in-depth knowledge of their particular fields and through the interaction of suppliers, users and hearing-care professionals.

Three of the largest hearing aid manufacturers in the world are from Denmark. It is estimated that more than 90% of the world market share for hearing aids is dominated by six companies. Although the world market for hearing aids is relatively stable, there is still a large potential for growth in the existing market. It is estimated that less than 10% of the world's population with hearing problems have hearing aids. The hearing aids business has been consolidated during the last decade from about 100 to less than 30 manufacturers.

The supply chain focus is to minimize lead times and to reduce costs as well as the amount of tied-up capital. Hence, a high level of IT integration and efficient inventory reduction contribute to achieving this goal. The focus on the supply chain, then, is to ensure a high degree of delivery reliability compared to other companies, and to minimize the number of processes that are not strategically

8. Adapted from Mikkola & Skjøtt-Larsen in Arlbjørn et al. (2006: 1-8)

important. The entire supply chain process should become completely transparent.

Oticon introduces new products quite often. It sees itself as a maker of customized solutions rather than a maker of components, although component reusability in new designs is an important factor. 85 % of all products are introduced within the last 4 years. Some of the 15 % were introduced more than 20 years ago. The item database continues to grow even with strong focus on component reusability due to the increased pressure on shorter intervals between introductions. About 40 % of the item database is purchased items, the rest consists of a large number of hearing aid families and variants on various levels.

Oticon produces two main types of hearing aids: Behind-The-Ear (BTE) and In-The-Ear (ITE). In recent years, the hearing aid industry has worked with a new technology for manufacturing individual shells for ITE hearing aids. The technology, implemented in 2005, is based on 3D scanning of the ear impression. In the long term, manufacturers will be able to cut lead time significantly. Furthermore, new production technology will make individualization more precise than conventional technology, and may thus reduce the number of hearing aids requiring adjustment due to faulty designs. All item numbers are stored in a centralized ERP system, which tracks and traces the critical components at the receiving dock as well as the correct usage of the components. There are bar codes virtually on all products.

Oticon entered in 2001 a one-stop-shopping agreement with Wilson Group (now part of TNT Freight Management) encompassing all inbound and outbound logistics activities globally, including spare parts. The new 3D technology has also changed the distribution demands dramatically. Before, the silicone impression of the customer's ear was physically sent from the dispenser to the production plant in Thisted, where the plastic shell was produced and returned to the dispenser. Now, the silicone impression is scanned at the dispenser and sent electronically to one of the seven production centers, where the plastic shells are produced. Then, the hearing aid is assembled and sent to the dispenser. For instance, a Swedish customer visits a local dispenser in Stockholm. The dispenser takes a silicone impression of the customer's ears, sends the impression to the local Oticon company, who scans the impression by 3D technology and sends the 3D picture electronically to the assembly plant in Thisted, where the shell is produced and the components installed. Hereafter it is sent by courier service to the dispenser in Stockholm. The total lead time for this process is three days. In this setup TNT has ensured Oticon that both their services and a second source can be used to solve this traffic. This way TNT ensures Oticon the necessary flexibility of having the optimal solutions in every area of the cooperation.

One drawback of one-stop-shopping is that Oticon becomes dependent on one TPL provider and it might be difficult to change to another one. The information exchange between Oticon and TNT is based on an EDI highway solution. Thus, Oticon can relatively easily change from one provider to another. Nevertheless, Oticon emphasizes that they consider the partnership to be a long-term commitment. Oticon's IT system is totally integrated with TNT Freight Management. The integrated information system between TNT and Oticon shows Oticon's willingness to make changes in their system to gain mutual advantages.

The service requirements at Oticon differ for different product groups. As a general rule, the total lead time for ITE products is 3 days, and 24 hours for BTE products to Oticon sister companies and Oticon production centers in Europe. The agreement between Oticon and TNT is based on a win-win situation. In the partnership agreement there is an obligation for both parties to take initiatives and to focus constantly on non-value-added activities. TNT is under obligation to follow the development of the transport market very closely and select the most efficient subcontractors at any given time. In addition, they are under constant obligation to reduce costs and improve performance. Any savings made must be shared between the partners.

DHL and Sun Microsystems[9]

In 2005 Sun Microsystems selected DHL as exclusive global aftermarket services parts logistics provider. Sun's products range from low-end laptops to high-end servers and EDP-equipment. Each of Sun's contracts with their customers specifies the service levels to be

9.   www.dpwn.de/dpwn

met. Often Sun has to deliver parts within a two-to-four hour window everywhere in the world. Before the contract, Sun was using 35 different logistics providers worldwide, including transport companies, warehouse companies, call centers, and order management services. Sun consolidated its after-market logistics to improve customer service.

The contract involves 300 logistics facilities housing thousands of parts to be used for service support to 1.5 million Sun customer systems in over 100 countries. The three-year agreement is unique because of its size and scope. Only a few global companies are collaborating with only one logistics provider.

Parts orders received by Sun and DHL service centers will be routed to the most appropriate local DHL facility anywhere in the world, from where replacement components will be packed and shipped to Sun engineers in the field within the specified time-window.

As part of the agreement, DHL will co-develop an advanced global IT platform, specifically designed for service parts logistics management. This will allow Sun to eliminate a number of existing legacy IT systems and enhance Sun's ability to optimize its global supply chain, minimize inventory levels, and ensure high and reliable customer service levels while controlling costs.

LEGO Group Outsources Logistics to DHL[10]

The LEGO Group, one of the world's leading manufacturers of play materials for children, has centralized its European distribution center (EDC) in Prague, The Czech Republic, and outsourced its European operation to DHL Solutions. DHL began operating its new and customized logistics center in early 2006.

Following an analysis of its structure, the LEGO Group announced on August 2005 that it plans to discontinue its five distribution facilities in Europe and to concentrate its European distribution operation in Jirny, 10 km east of Prague. In 2006, LEGO decided also to outsource a major part of its production to Kladno, The Czech Republic. Flextronics will take over the operation of

10. www.dpwn.de/dpwn, www.lego.com

LEGO's existing plant in Kladno, and most of the production at LEGO's plant in Billund, Denmark, will be moved to Kladno. Thus, production and distribution will be closely geographically located.

The new European distribution center handles distribution to LEGO customers in Europe and to LEGO distribution centers throughout the world (except North America). The total site will be one main logistics center of total 56,000 m^2 and will be one of DHL Solutions bigger facilities in Central Europe. In full operation, in 2007, the LEGO activities will occupy 51,000 m^2.

The center's activities include inbound and outbound logistics, storage and value added services such as assortment packing and customization. The Jirny site is going to be one of DHL Solutions' strategic locations from where DHL is offering the complete range of logistics services to the market. The LEGO Group and DHL have signed a contract for 5 ½ years. The LEGO group expects to achieve significant benefits from outsourcing and centralizing their logistics operations in Jirny. The distribution center will be operated as a multi-client facility.

10. Reverse Logistics and Supply Chain Sustainability

»Product returns have long been a necessary evil.
But top companies today are managing their reverse
supply chains as a source of value«

(Lauren Keller Johnson 2005)

The forward flows of goods and services have always been the back-bone of industrial supply chains and received the greatest attention from both academics and practitioners. However, an increasing proportion of the products are coming back to the manufacturers or the importers. This is true for a number of industries, including consumer electronics, white and brown goods, pharmaceuticals, automobiles, packaging materials, clothes and apparels, and so on. While some firms are forced by legislation to take products back, others do it as part of a customer service policy (e.g. internet-based firms), or because they can recover value in used products (e.g. pho-tocopiers, tires, instant cameras, and autos).

Figure 10.1. Comparison of ReverseLlogistics and Green Logistics

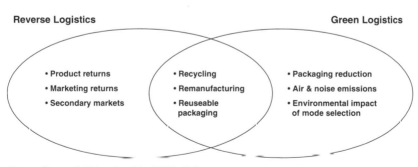

Source: Rogers & Tibben-Lembke (2001: 131)

The terms reverse logistics, green logistics, reverse supply chains, and closed-loop supply chains are often used interchangeably to deal with the reverse flows of products. There are differences between reverse logistics and green logistics but also some overlap between the two terms. This is illustrated in figure 10.1.

Reverse logistics is defined by Rogers and Tibben-Lembke (2001: 130) as »the process of planning, implementing, and controlling the efficient, cost effective flow of raw materials, in-process inventory, finished goods, and related information from the point of consumption to the point of origin for the purpose of recapturing value or proper disposal«. According to Stock (2001) reverse logistics encompasses a broad range of activities within, and outside of, logistics including: product returns, source reduction, recycling, material substitution, reuse of material, waste disposal, and refurbishing, repair and remanufacturing.

The *Closed-loop supply chain* is a wider concept, and includes, besides reverse logistics, the return product process of acquisition, test, sort and disposition, including distribution and marketing (Guide et al. 2003: 9). Closed-loops consist of two supply chains: a forward and a reverse chain, whereby the recovered product either reenters the primary forward chain or is shunted to a secondary market (Wells & Seitz 2005).

Green logistics or *environmental logistics* is defined by Rogers and Tibben-Lembke (2001:130) as »efforts to measure and minimize the environmental impact of logistics activities«. These activities include a proactive »design for dis-assembly« (van Hoek 1999) in the initial product design stage, use of environmentally friendly transport modes, consolidation of goods to increase capacity utilization of vehicles, reusable containers, and reduction of packaging materials.

We use the term »reverse supply chain« instead of »reverse logistics« to emphasize that the management of returned products cannot be limited to a single entity in the supply chain, but must encompass the entire chain. Guide and van Wassenhove (2002:25), state that the reverse supply chain as »... the series of activities required to retrieve a used product from a customer and either dispose of it or reuse it ... becoming an essential part of business«. Similarly, Kokkinaki et al. (2000) argue that a holistic view of reverse logistics complements forward logistics within a »closed loop supply chain approach«.

Major Types of Return Items

Product returns can be categorized in three major groups:

- End-of-life returns
- End-of-use returns (leased)
- Commercial returns

The product management strategies and requirements to the reverse supply chain differ by the type of returns. Taking back products at the *end-of-life* is often mandatory, regulated by EU directives or national legislation. This is the case for packaging materials, tires, batteries, cars, white and brown goods, and electrical and electronic equipment. Japan has also passed a legislation for mandatory takeback at the end-of-life for e.g. washers and dryers, TVs, VCRs, and refrigerators. Often return systems are organized and subsidized by municipality authorities or government agencies. The product management strategies for end-of-life returns are: repair and reuse, refurbish, recycle with disassembly, recycle without disassembly, and incineration. The value recovered is highest if repair/reuse is possible and lowest if incineration as fuel is the only option. Recycling with disassembly allows components to be sent back to the supply chain and reused in the production process, or recovered materials (e.g. gold, copper, and aluminum) to be sold at secondary markets. Recycling without disassembly is often carried out through a grind and sort process, where different materials are separated based on material types.

The EU has issued a Directive on Waste Electrical and Electronic Equipment (WEEE),[11] which makes manufacturers (and domestic importers/distributors) responsible for taking electrical and electronic waste back from consumers in an environmentally friendly manner. This directive will be implemented in the 27 EU countries from 2006 and onwards. The waste stream of electrical and electronic equipment has been identified as one of the fastest growing streams in the EU, increasing by 16-28% every five years.[12]

11. Europe Parliament and Council Directive 2002/96/EF of January 27, 2003.
12. IP/00/602, Brussels, 13 June 2000.

Besides, it is one of the largest known sources of heavy metals and organic pollutants in the municipal waste.

The objective of the WEEE directive is to reduce the total quantity of waste going to final disposal at landfill sites and incinerators. This can only be achieved through separate collection of electronic waste from private households. Therefore, member states must organize this collection and transport the waste to designated collection facilities. From there, the producers will be responsible to take over their share of the waste and make sure that it is further treated according to the standards set out in the directive.

The first step in implementing the new directive was to register all companies, which produce or import electric or electronic equipment in a national register. This process should have been finished in 2006, but has been delayed in most member states. The next step was to allocate a proportion of the electrical and electronic waste to the producers, based on their market share of various product groups. Then, in line with the *polluter pays* principle, producers should be responsible for organizing and financing the treatment, recovery, and disposal of waste. Most companies in Europe have joined collective systems for electrical and electronic waste recycling. An exemption is, Braun, Electrolux, HP, and Sony, which have established a European Recycling Platform (ERP) to operate a pan-European compliance scheme for the WEEE directive.[13]

End-of-use returns are often products, which are leased for a period of time (e.g. photocopiers, cars, TVs) and then returned to the lessor and if possible, refurbished and returned to a secondary market. Normally, this category is organized and managed by the leasing companies themselves.

Commercial returns (clothes, PCs, DIY products, furniture, books, etc.) as a broad category include defective products within warranty period, products that do not fit the customer, products returned because of customer dissatisfaction, or products shipped to the customer in error. The return flows can either follow a path from customer to retailers, through distributors to the manufacturer, or be outsourced to a third party operator, who collects the items at the customers' location and return them to the manufacturer's location or a dedicated return center.

13. See the illustrative case at the end of this chapter

Customer service related to a fast and flexible claim and return process and a short claim-to-pay-back period is important and can create both customer loyalty and competitive advantage. Products sold online or via mail catalogs sometimes have return rates up to 40% (Rogers et al. 2002). Many companies have discovered that they can regain value from products at the end of their normal life cycles. In some cases, the product can be repaired or refurbished and returned to the market place (e.g. photocopiers and printers), in other cases components from returned products can be reused as refurbished components (e.g. instant cameras) or as spare parts.

Most logistics research has focused on the forward supply chain with the implicit understanding that the reverse supply chain could be similarly managed. However, the reverse flows of materials and products have general characteristics and structure completely different from the forward flows. Mollenkopf and Closs (2005:34) note, »reverse logistics has often been viewed as the unwanted stepchild of supply chain management«. However, more companies now see reverse logistics as a strategic activity that can enhance long-term supply chain competitiveness. They identify five ways that proactive reverse logistics can have a positive impact on profitability:

- Increased revenues realized from »secondary« sales
- Offering new products in place of unsold or slow-selling stock
- Shareholder goodwill from acting with social and environmental responsibility
- Reduced operating costs from reuse of recovered products and components
- Higher asset turnover due to better management of returns inventory.

The Challenge of Reverse Supply Chain

Reverse flows have challenges that differ from those of forward flows of materials and products:

- Large variations in timing, quality and quantity of product returns
- Lack of formal product returns procedures
- Delayed product returns reducing their market value

- Lack of local competence in inspection, evaluation and disposition of returns
- Risk of cannibalizing new product markets
- Lack of performance measurement for return process efficiency

The variations in timing, quality, and quantity of product returns make it difficult to forecast requirements and allocate resources to return systems on other than an ad hoc basis.

Only few companies have a formalized information system and standard operating procedures for handling returns. An important problem is related to the fact that products returned by end-users are often unpacked, without barcodes or other product identifications. When the products are returned to consolidation or return centers, it is a time-consuming task to identify the product and relabel it with a barcode.

Time-to-remarket is essential for time-sensitive returns, e.g. clothes, books, mobile phones, and electronic equipment. Blackburn et al. (2004) use the term »preponement« as a strategy to make the reverse supply chain responsive by reducing time delays and promote early collection, sorting, disposition, and disassembly rather than late (postponement) process and product differentiation.

Cannibalization is a problem for companies, which take back used products or new products returned from the end-customer to be returned to the market. In some cases the products are repacked and returned to the primary market at the same price. In other cases, the products are sold on a secondary market, e.g. via a broker or an electronic auction (e-bay.com, lauritz.com, amazon.com).

While performance measurements can be routine in the case of forward flows of products in the supply chain, the return flows are rarely measured in a systematic way. However, it is important also to set up performance measures for the reverse supply chain, e.g. time from consumer complaint to replacement of new product/repaired defect product at the customer premise, time to payback the customer, quantity and quality of returns, causes of returns, costs involved in returns, etc.

The responsibility of the reverse supply chain is often fragmented among different actors, and as a result, no one takes overall responsibility. This often results in sub-optimization and inefficient solutions. By adopting centralized control over the reverse supply chain, it is possible to identify where the initiative and responsibility should lie for managing the reverse flows.

Two extreme configurations of the reverse supply chain are presented. At the one end, a centralized reverse supply chain, and at the other end, decentralized reverse supply chain. Between the two extremes are, of course, various hybrids.

A Centralized Reverse Supply Chain

A centralized reverse supply chain is a system, where one organization is responsible for collection, sorting and redistribution of returned items, cf. Figure 10.2.

Figure 10.2. Centralized Structure of a Reverse Supply Chain

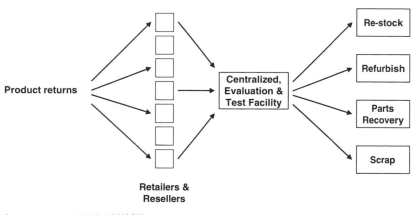

Source: Blackburn et al. (2004:13)

In this system, the gate-keeping activities of collection, inspecting and sorting are centralized within one organization. The same organization or another company at the up-stream levels of the supply chain may take on the physical processing.

The centralized reverse supply chain can be organized in several ways. It can be integrated into and managed by the company's forward supply chain. If some kind of remanufacturing of the products is needed, this activity is likely to be conducted at the upstream levels of the supply chain. Large brand-owners return systems support closed-loop recycling. An example is IBM's closed-loop supply chain, in which returned used equipment, such as PCs, laptops and printers, are used as sources for spare parts (Fleischmann et al. 2003). The efficiency may be improved by creating a pool of returned products through an industry consortium. An example is the breweries' return bottle system, which makes reverse supply chain a part of the breweries' forward distribution system or is authorized to a third party operator. Another example is Xerox-Europe, which serves 600,000 customers with 1.5 million installed machines, and makes over 1 million deliveries per year through distribution channels. Xerox introduced in 1991 its waste-free supply chain program (Guide & van Wassenhove 2003). The first step in the closed-loop supply chain for photocopiers is getting the used copiers back from customers that will serve as inputs to the remanufacturing process. The used machines are returned to one of four centralized logistics return centers, where they are inspected, tested and assigned to one of four grades: 1) repair, 2) remanufacture, 3) parts remanufacture, or 4) recycle. Repaired and remanufactured copy machines are distributed to customers through the traditional forward supply chain. The financial benefits of equipment remanufacture and parts reuse amount to several hundred million dollars a year (Guide & van Wassenhove 2003:18).

The achievement of reverse logistics efficiency is related to the make-or-buy decision. Based on the assumption that forward flows and return flows have different basic requirements, de Koster et al. (2002) discuss whether or not to combine inbound and outbound flows. The trade-off between these options depends on the economies of scale of using the existing distribution system versus the increased complexity and risks of mixing forward flows of goods with return flows. Sometimes, the reverse flows require special competencies from personnel regarding inspection and disposition of the returned products.

The reverse supply chain may also be organized and managed by a dedicated reverse logistics provider (e.g. a return system for disposable packaging materials). Spicer and Johnson (2004) view third-party collection as a promising alternative that may substitute for the manufacturers' own responsibility for products taken back.

A third option is for the return flows to be organized and managed by a TPL provider, with a return system integrated in the existing hub-and-spoke structures, or a dedicated return system for a product group or industry. An example is the German TPL provider Schenker, which manages Dell's commercial returns from the Nordic countries. When a customer has a defective product, a return order from Dell is submitted to Schenker, which arranges a time window to pick up the product at the customer's premise. As a rule, the product must be returned in the original Dell box. The box is then labeled with a barcode and a return number, so it can be identified on its way back in the reverse supply chain. All returns from the Nordic countries are consolidated at Schenker in Copenhagen with shipments twice a week to Dell's European return center in Coventry in the UK. Schenker only deals with commercial returns, not with end-of-life returns.

Up to now, most TPL providers have hesitated to offer fully integrated reverse logistics programs, but this is changing. Reverse Logistics can be viewed as one of several »value-added« services now offered by logistics providers, such as UPS, which handles laptop repairs for Toshiba America[14]. The critical mass of clients for third party (logistics) providers can play an important role in the reverse flow because it offers scale economies. Centralized return centers (CRC) are common in return processing (Rogers and Tibben-Lembke 2001), and may overcome challenges in consolidation and maintaining a »process flow«[15] (Trebilcock 2001) in reverse logistics. However, each company must decide whether to perform the activities in-house or outsource them to intermediaries. That decision requires consideration of the forward and reverse flows, and alternative use of in-house resources.

A Decentralized Reverse Supply Chain

A decentralized reverse supply chain consists of multiple organizations involved in collection, sorting and distribution of returned items. Figure 10.3 depicts a supply chain of reverse logistics processes, conduct of which is spread among various actors in the supply chain.

---

14. See Illustrating case at the end of this chapter.
15. I.e. eliminate touches, apply conveyor and sorting equipment.

Figure 10.3. Decentralized Reverse Supply Chain

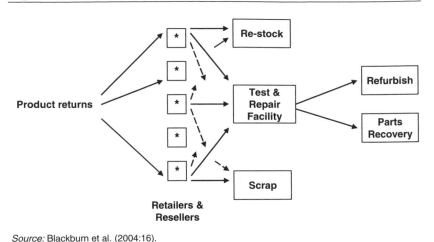

Source: Blackburn et al. (2004:16).

Note: *) Evaluation of product at retailer or reseller

Starting from the left, products or items enter the reverse supply chain at the retail level. The particular sales outlet serves the function of a »gate-keeper« that evaluates the product and sends it further on to one of the three actors in the center column of Figure 10.3.

This requires specific guidelines for determining the condition of the product, local skills to perform initial inspections, and a logistics infrastructure to pass the items further into the activities represented at the right side of the figure. The advantage is that the individual item can be sent directly to the correct form of value reclamation. This configuration favours time-based strategies (Blackburn et al. 2004), to support value reclamation efforts such as refurbishment of high-value products (e.g. consumer electronics). The choice between a centralized and a decentralized reverse supply chain is a trade-off between various factors, such as economies of scale in collection, sorting, and disposition in a centralized system versus the costs of coordinating various links and destinations, and the costs of building up and maintaining the sufficient resources and competencies needed to serve the various reverse logistics processes represented in each box in a decentralized system. The reason why more attention is devoted to the centralized structure than the decentralized, and in particular the role of third party providers, is explained by the various determinants in the following section.

The Marginal Value of Time

The flow of returned products often represents an essential value for many firms, but often the value is lost because of lack of efficient return systems or negative effects of time delays. An important concept in reverse supply chain is the »marginal time value of product returns« (Blackburn et al. 2004). Much of loss in the return stream is due to time delays in processing the return flows. A simple metric is the product's marginal value of time: the loss in value per unit of time spent before processed in the return system. This is illustrated in Figure 10.4.

Figure 10.4. Time Value of Product Returns

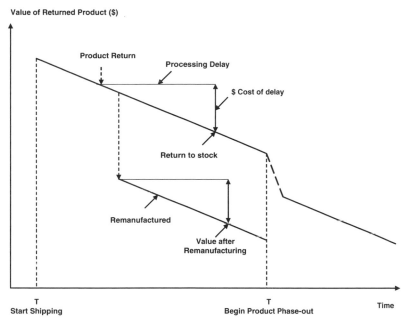

Source: Blackburn et al (2004:11).

The marginal value of time measures the value depreciation for a specified time interval. There are many reasons for value depreciation: new product introductions, technological innovations, the product becoming a commodity, and price cuts from competitive actions. The marginal value of time differs by product and different stages of the product life cycle. Some products such as reusable containers and bottles have a relatively low marginal value of time, which means that time is a lesser consideration when designing the reverse supply chain. Other products, such as mobile phones, PCs, fashion clothes, and DIY-products, with high marginal time values require reverse supply chains with fast processing.

The distinction between time sensitive and time non-sensitive reverse supply chains is similar to Fisher's (1997) taxonomy of two fundamental supply chain structures for innovative respectively functional products. The innovative products require a supply chain that is responsive and fast, while the functional products require an efficient supply chain designed to deliver products at low costs. The major difference between efficient and responsive reverse supply chains is the positioning of the evaluation, testing, and sorting activity in the supply chain. In an efficient reverse supply chains these activities are centralized whereas in a responsive reverse supply chains they are decentralized.

Stock et al. (2006) distinguish between controllable and uncontrollable returns. Controllable returns are caused by problems or errors of the company or other member of the supply chain. These types of returns can often be mitigated with elimination of picking-and-packing errors, improved forecasting, improved product handling, better quality control, and better communication with the customers. The uncontrollable returns are returns, which companies can do little about in the short run. A basic strategy would be to attempt to eliminate the root causes of controllable returns while simultaneously developing optimal processes for handling uncontrollable product returns (Stock et al. 2006:58).

Green Supply Management

Customers are now increasingly aware of the environmental effects of the products they are buying. Purchasing organizations should therefore have a solid knowledge of environmental issues, such as origins of materials, the supplier's production processes, dismantling, recycling and labor force conditions. Commentators note the importance of incorporating environmental aspects into the supplier assessment process (Bowen et al. 2001, Sarkis 2003, Simpson &

Power 2005, Roberts 2003). Low environmental concerns by suppliers may counter the high level of environmental performance achieved by a firm. A well-known example is Nike, which in the late 1990's faced a barrage of negative publicity about the working conditions in its supplier factories. Life-cycle analysis of products throughout the supply chain should determine environmental purchasing strategies. An increasing number of companies are being environmentally certified according to ISO 14001 or other international standards, and the purchasing department has an important role to play in this process.

Product Stewardship

Product stewardship is a product–centered approach to environmental protection. Product stewardship recognizes that product manufacturers must take on responsibilities to reduce the ecological footprint of their products. By rethinking their products, their relationships with their supply chain partners, and the end-user, some manufacturers can reduce costs, promote product and market innovation, and reduce the environmental impact of their products. Reducing use of toxic ingredients, reducing energy consumption and material waste, designing for reuse and recyclability, and developing take back programs are some of the opportunities to become better environmental stewards of their products. An example is Nike, which has set long-term environmental targets of eliminating waste and toxins from production processes with sustainable product design as the unifying goal. It does this by actively advocating sustainable use of resources, reducing waste, reuse and recycling within its global supply chain (www.sustainability.vic.gov.au). Another example is the US-based *Interface Carpets*, a world leader in modular carpets, which since 1994 has made a commitment to becoming an environmentally sustainable company. Interface's sustainability efforts fall into three categories: waste minimization, engineering changes, and product and process changes. Thus, Interface has implemented a closed-loop supply chain by leasing carpets, maintaining them, taking them back again, and reusing them as raw materials for new carpets and fabrics. Besides, Interface has designed a system of eco-metrics that allow them to measure the inputs and the waste outputs per unit of finished product, so they can track their progress and see, which areas to prioritize in the future (www.interfacesustainability.com).

The Triple Bottom Line and the Supply Chain

Economic prosperity, environmental quality and social justice will increasingly become the driving forces for trans-national corporations (Elkington 1998:2). However, the issues will not only affect one company, but also the management network of suppliers and distributors of companies, i.e. the supply chain.

Elkington (1998:2) foresees the importance of a triple benefit integrating economy, ecology and people, at the supply chain level, as companies »will increasingly be forced to pass the pressure on their supply chains«. This certainly gives management a new dimension when supply chain management extends beyond organizational boundaries and national boundaries and embraces the total flow of goods and information. This would mean that supply chain management could also contribute to increasing economic profit but also reduce social and environmental losses. Elkington (1998) showed with the introduction of the triple-bottom-line concept how to transfer sustainable development to a company level (Cramer 2002).

The triple-bottom-line approach consists of the following elements:

- Economy/profit
- Ecology/planet
- Equity/people

Economy/Profit: The economic dimension of economic sustainability does not refer only on profitability. Economically sustainable companies deliver at any time cash flows that are sufficient to liquidity and offer a constant return to the shareholders that is above average (Dyllick & Hockerts 2002).

Ecology/Planet: The environmental dimension has had in the past the largest impact to sustainable development, as an eco-system represents the ultimate profit line. Dyllick & Hockerts (2002) define a ecologically sustainable company as a company that uses natural resources that are consumed at a rate below natural reproduction or at a rate below the developments of substitutes. Ecologically sustainable companies do not cause emissions that harm the environment. It is a company whose managers limit the use of any type of resource as is necessary and minimize any waste as much as possible. From a company point of view, it might also be clear, that the input into the companies' production systems are often natural resources, the output is not only a final product but also pollution and other forms of waste. An ecologically sustainable company can be characterized as a company that has incorporated ecological considerations in its daily operations as well as in its strategic planning (Dyllick & Hockerts 2002).

Equity/People: The »people« dimension could be best characterized as the company's social responsibility. The social dimension refers to a growth strategy without decreased job quality and it reflects internal as well as external effects. According to Dyllick and Hockerts (2002), socially sustainable companies increase the human capital of individual partners as well as advancing the societal capital of their communities, in which they operate (Korhonen 2003). These actions are in accordance to the company's value system (EC-Commission 2001b or www.sustdev.org, www.union-network.org).

The consideration of these three elements within the supply chain management concepts will lead to sustainable supply chain management that can be defined as follows: *Collaboration among supply chain members within all activities, that are connected with delivering environmentally and socially responsible products and services to the end customer, as well as attaining acceptable profit and information in the supply chain* (Rabs & Bohn 2003).

A sustainable supply chain as outlined in Table 10.1 includes the inter-organizational dimension as well as the value-added perspective, social and environmental issues.

Table 10.1. A sustainable Supply Chain

Supply chain stages	Triple bottom line dimensions		
	Environment/Planet	Equity/People	Economy/Profit
Supply of raw materials and components	• Supplier evaluation and selection based on environmental profile, e.g. ISO 14000 • Selection of logistics service provider based on environmental profile, e.g. ISO 14000 • Consolidation of shipments • Sharing of information • Increased focus on ecological transport mode selection • Reduction of packaging • Cooperation with suppliers to reduce pollution and waste	• Supplier evaluation and selection based on social profile • Training and education of drivers and logistics employees • Ensuring codes of conduct at suppliers, e.g. safe working conditions, no child labor, and no abuse of union rights	• Transport savings • Costs of supplier evaluation and monitoring • Internal and external audits of suppliers' compliance with codes of conduct • Increased sale at sight
Production	• Elimination of waste and overuse in the production process • Environmentally friendly packaging • Less packaging • Product development either within the company or in collaboration with others • Elimination of waste in the storage process • Elimination of materials – and energy consumption • Production site choice that considers local ecology, e.g. waste from one company becomes input to another	• Automation of physical hard and heavy work • Reduction of noise from machinery • Minimization of over-specialized, repeating work • Prevention of work accidents • Challenging product development for the employees • Warehouse layout, that reduce distances • In-service training of employees • Improved staff recruitment and retention	• Improved working conditions that can promote satisfaction and thereby increase the productivity • Economic gain through resource minimization • Economical gain through new product development • Costs of certification, documentation and reporting • Savings from reducing energy, water, waste handling, chemicals, raw materials
Distribution	• Choice of environmentally friendly distribution channels • Focus on choice of environmentally friendly type of transport • Reduce the general need of transport • Information technology can further environmentally friendly distribution	• Reduced traffic congestion • Education in energy saving driving • Automation of loading and unloading	• Storage consolidation optimize storage room • Reduction of travel distances between production site and marketplace results in fewer transport costs • Savings due to higher capacity utilization of vehicles • Increased sales from enhancing a good reputation • Higher prices for eco-friendly products

Conclusion

Reverse logistics and supply chain sustainability is highly relevant for the actors in the supply chain, industrial organizations and society. First, national legislation and EU directives force producers and importers to take responsibility for their end-of-life products in a environmentally friendly way. Second, an effectively designed and organized reverse supply chain can regain value and competitive advantage for the companies. Third, reverse logistics and supply sustainability is an important element in many firms', annual environmental reports. The way companies organize reverse logistics activities, and interact in a reverse supply chain, provides new opportunities for value recovery as an alternative to mere disposal or incineration.

We have discussed two extreme configurations of a reverse supply chain: a centralized and a decentralized system. One conclusion is that time-efficiency may favour a decentralized structure, especially in the case of high-value, time-sensitive products. However, the costs of coordinating multiple links and the difficulty of establishing local competence in collecting, inspecting, and sorting returned products at various locations in the supply chain may well outweigh the benefits of a decentralized system.

Reverse logistics has significant consequences for the total supply chain. Manufacturers must carry out life cycle analyses of finished products to demonstrate the environmental impact of their products over the entire cycle of production, use, and disposal. Products must be engineered for ease of disassembly, and recycling. Manufacturers will also have to collaborate with suppliers and subcontractors to deliver recyclable materials and components. Packaging companies must develop materials to minimize weight and which can be reused or recycled without damaging the environment. Even the choice of transport mode and carrier will also be determined in part by the ability of the transport carrier to meet specific environmental standards.

Also supply chain managers have to deal with the consequences of climate changes, ecological issues, polluted air/water, children work, physical/psychic working conditions and more. These topics have gained extreme importance since the publication of the so-called Brundtland-report »Our common future« (UN 1987). The main outcome of this report showed the consequences of present economic behaviour and suggested change in business activities.

Business should provide a sustainable development or sustainability, which »is not a fixed state of harmony, but rather a process of change in which the exploitation of resources, the direction of investments, the orientation of technological development, and institutional change are made consistent with future as well as present needs. Sustainability puts economic, social and environmental elements together and, »like it or not, the responsibility for ensuring a sustainable world falls largely on the shoulders of the world's enterprises, the economic engines of the future« (Dunphy et al. 2003:10).

Illustrating Cases

Toshiba and UPS[16]

UPS and Toshiba America Information Systems agreed on a new laptop repair process in 2004. Since then, any broken laptop will be picked up by UPS and instead of shipping it to a Toshiba repair center, the laptop will be inspected and repaired in the specially set up UPS Logistics & Technology Park in Louisville, Kentucky. The 2 million-square foot campus, which specializes in high-tech support, is adjacent to the UPS Worldport global air hub. The proximity to the air hub means it is possible that a laptop can be received, repaired, and shipped back to the customer very quickly.

The overall goal of this partnership was to diminish the total repair cycle time for laptops and to increase customer satisfaction. By eliminating multiple transportation steps and by improving inventory visibility, they made the total repair process very streamlined. Whenever a Toshiba laptop breaks down, the customer can call a customer-service center toll-free. The customer will then receive the address of the nearest UPS store, where the laptop can be dropped off. From there, the computer is shipped to the repair center. This process reduces the cycle time from 10 days to 4 days, as the UPS

16. UPS (2004): *Toshiba and UPS Join to Set New Standard for Laptop Repair*, UPS Press Release, April 27, 2004.
   Moore, R. (2005): *Reverse Logistics – the least used differentiator*. UPS Supply Chain Solutions White Paper. San Francisco: UPS Supply Chain Solutions.

engineers are able to do the job faster than the Toshiba's technicians in the past.

European Recycling Platform[17]

The European Recycling Platform (ERP) was founded in 2002 by Braun, Electrolux, HP and Sony in response to the WEEE Directive and as an alternative to national recycling consortiums. The ERP's mission is to ensure cost effective implementation of the directive, for the benefits of the participating companies and their customers. In 2004, ERP contracted with the German CCR Logistics Systems and the French Geodis to manage all operational activities on behalf of ERP's founders and members, including take-back, logistics, recycling and all necessary administrative work to ensure full compliance with the WEEE Directive. CCR Logistics Systems will run the return systems as general contractor in Germany, Austria, Italy, and Poland, while Geodis will take care of France, Spain, Portugal, UK, and Ireland. These countries comprised about 85 percent of the four players' businesses. In 2006, ERP had 21 member companies, accounting for roughly 15 percent of Europe's waste of electrical and electronic equipment.

Kodak Closed-Loop Supply Chain for Single-Use Cameras[18]

Kodak's single-use cameras were introduced in 1987 to meet the needs of a specific customer base – those who wanted an inexpensive camera for certain occasions to take pictures that might otherwise be missed. The quality of the 35mm picture was outstanding, and the cameras were an immediate success. The cameras were designed to be easy-to-use, and disposable. Customers who bought these cameras had to return the entire product (containing the film) to a photofinisher in order to get their prints. However, some environmental groups raised concerns about the risk of a significant

17. www.erp-recycling.org
18. Guide et al (2003), www.kodak.com

increase in the amount of solid waste generated. At the same time, for economic and business reasons, Kodak was evaluating opportunities to reclaim the camera for recycling and re-use of parts.

The first step was redesigning single-use cameras to facilitate recycling and re-use of parts. This effort took place in 1990-1991 and has been an integral element of every new camera designed since then and involved the integration of business, development, design and environmental personnel to achieve the final results. Kodak's one-time use camera has gone through four major redesigns, with engineers meeting the same three environmental design goals each time:

- Reduce the material content and energy required in the manufacturing process.
- Increase the number of recycled parts
- Increase the number of parts that are reused in the camera.

Over the years, the Kodak cameras have been designed so that 77% to 90% (by weight) of the product may be remanufactured. Virtually nothing from the camera is sent to a landfill – all components that are not re-used are recycled elsewhere.

Kodak introduced in 1990 a recycling program, called OTUC (One-Time-Use Camera). The process begins, when the customer buys a camera and uses it. Then the customer takes the camera to the photofinisher. The photofinisher extracts the film, creates the prints, and delivers them to the user. The photofinisher batches all brands and models of one-time-use cameras and returns them in recycling bins to a centralized collection facility. The photofinishers are reimbursed for each camera returned to Kodak and shipping costs. Once the cameras have been sorted by manufacturer and model, the Kodak cameras are shipped to one of Kodak's manufacturing facilities for remanufacturing. At these sites, the front and back covers are removed and the cameras undergo a complete electrical and mechanical inspection. Since the cameras have been designed to be recycled up to ten times, most of the camera can be reused during the recycling process. However, any part not conforming to Kodak's quality standards is replaced. The cameras are then ready for fresh Kodak film, one final inspection, and outer packaging made from recycled materials. Meanwhile, any plastic parts that were removed from the camera during the remanufacturing process pass through a metal detector to be sure no traces of metal are left, and the plastic is shipped to a recycling center to be re-ground into pellets. The plastic pellets are then remolded into cameras or other uses. The labels on Kodak cameras are made from thin plastic so that they too can be re-ground into pellets.

Since the program started in 1990, Kodak has recycled more than 800 million single-use cameras. When considering competitors cameras that are also collected through Kodak's OTUC program the total number recycled exceeds one billion cameras. The recycle rate in the United States is greater than 75% and 60% worldwide. In comparison, the recycle rate in the United States for aluminium beverage cans is 63%. The portion of Kodak's manufacturing volume originating from recycled cameras is close to 90%, and increasing. The effort has been the hallmark of the Kodak's product stewardship and design-for-the-environment of initiatives.

11. Performance Measurement and Management in the Supply Chain[19]

*»The lack of proper measures for the supply chain will result
in failure to meet end customer expectations,
suboptimization of departmental or company performance,
missed opportunities to outperform the competition,
and conflict within the supply chain«.*

(Lambert and Pohlen 2001:1).

Today, measuring supply chain performance is most often treated as a non-core activity in the overall management portfolio of the supply chain. However, in order for companies to succeed in the complex modern global environment, measuring supply chain performance must not be seen as an ad-hoc tool that can be applied in some cases, but more as an ongoing activity that should be treated as thoroughly as other supply chain management activities linking and integrating the supply chain.

As discussed earlier in this book, in the early 1980s, writers from different academic fields in the social sciences started to argue that management should no longer focus only on intra-company activity, but also, and in equal proportion, be focused on management of actions outside traditional company borders. However, evidence suggests that the translation of this academic paradigm into »real« holistic management practices has been slow, and today, after twenty-five years, is still far from being convincingly embraced by all practitioners.

We argue that a major cause of this problem can be found in the lacking maturity of the performance measurement and management

19. This chapter has been written by Assistant Professor Kim Sundtoft Hald, Department of Operations Management, Copenhagen Business School.

practices in the supply chain (van Hoek 1998). We further argue that there are four major challenges in current performance measurement and management practices in the global supply chain.

First, the performance measurement systems used today, are often uncoordinated and often only measure those fractions of supply chain activity that are located inside the focal company's responsibility. However, since internally focused performance measurement systems do not provide the transparency needed to manage inter-connected activities in the supply chain, such an approach will often result in discouraging results. In short, existing performance measurement systems for the global supply chain lack a system perspective (Holmberg 2000).

Second, the definition of supply chain performance is often non-inclusive (Beamon 1999: 278). This non-inclusiveness of existing measures and measurement systems for the supply chain means, that there is a tendency to focus on only one or a few dimensions of supply chain performance. Such non-inclusiveness is problematic, since not measuring all pertinent aspects of the supply chain will result in a tendency to manage those dimensions measured and neglect the others. For instance, implementing a performance measurement system only measuring supply chain activity cost, risks de-focusing managerial attention from other dimensions of performance, resulting in a neglect of actions for improving customer service.

Third, almost all literature discussing performance measurement in a logistics or supply chain context focuses on which measures and systems to use. That is, performance management or how to adjust performance measurement activity to the supply chain, in order to improve the performance of the chain in desired ways, is assumed unproblematic. In this chapter we argue that such a neglect of performance management issues is undesirable. We discuss the different purposes or effects of supply chain performance measurement, and how performance measures need to be adjusted to the different types of inter-organizational relationships.

Fourth and finally, issues of communication or feedback of performance measurement in the supply chain is important. Such feedback is part of the chain of activities linking the measures to their inter-organizational effects. Therefore it is surprising that performance communication is rarely discussed by academics or managed by practitioners.

This chapter continues in the following way. After a short introduction to measures and measurement systems in the supply chain, we turn our attention to each of the four major challenges in current performance measurement and management practices in the global supply chain. Then we discuss a few supply chain performance measurement concepts, first those focused on cost management in the supply chain, and then those adopting a more inclusive and process based understanding of supply chain performance.

Measures and Measurement Systems

Performance measurement and management in the supply chain is a complex subject. It therefore requires a proper definition and introduction of its basic concepts. The purpose of this section is therefore to provide such a short introduction.

Neely et al. (1995) propose to define *performance measurement* as the process of quantifying the efficiency and effectiveness of actions. In a supply chain, actions that are quantified through the performance measurement process, include any activity or process (i.e. chain of activities) that is involved in the organization, and the flow of materials and other resources to produce and deliver the product to the final customer. Following from the definition of performance measurement, a *performance measurement system* is then the concrete tool designed to quantify performance. More precisely it is a set of connected measures or key performance indicators designed to quantify the efficiency and effectiveness of action. *Performance measurement techniques* such as The Balanced Scorecard (Kaplan & Norton 1992), Activity Based Costing (Cooper & Kaplan 1988), Total Cost of Ownership (Carr & Ittner 1992) and Target Costing (Monden & Hamada 1991) are examples of generalized principles on how to design performance measurement system, some of which we will discuss in a supply chain context later in this chapter.

According to Neely et al. (1995: 81) any performance measurement system can be examined at three different levels: the level of the individual measures, the level of the performance measurement system, and the level of the environment of the performance measurement system. Figure 11.1 provides an illustration of how supply chain performance measures and measurement systems are designed on top of supply chain strategy and supply chain activities/

processes (1). At the same time their purpose is directed towards influencing decisions and behaviour in the activities/processes in the supply chain (2).

Figure 11.1. Measures and Measurement systems in the Supply Chain

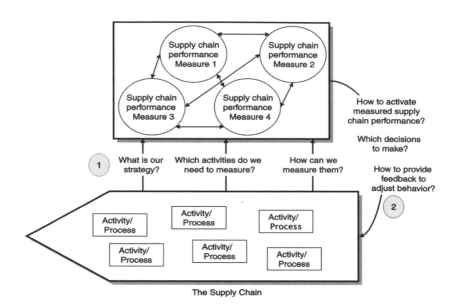

The Supply Chain

System Thinking
in Performance Measurement

There are several issues that complicate measuring and managing supply chain performance. The process of constructing these systems is difficult due to their complexity. For measurement systems to support supply chain management they need to consider aspects that cross company borders (Holmberg 1999). However, convincing a company and its employees, planners and boundary spanning managers to adopt such a system perspective is difficult (Hald 2006). First, external management and control are most often considered less important than management and control of internal activities and processes. It is natural to focus on those activities and processes that are visible and inside management reach. Second, it is also natural to focus on those activities that are controlled 100% by the company. When setting up an internally focused performance measurement system, external supplier and customers do not have to be involved. Managers are most often interested in reducing complexity, and staying with internal measures and measurement activities will reduce complexity considerably. Third and finally, if boundary spanning managers, such as the purchasing manager or the supply chain manager achieve personal performance compensation for improving the company's purchasing spend and making internal production processes leaner, as they most often do, they will act accordingly. These managers will measure those internal activities that reduce purchasing spend and production costs. As a consequence, they will not adopt a wider supply chain system in their performance management thinking.

Figure 11.2. Maturity of Supply Chain Performance Measurement

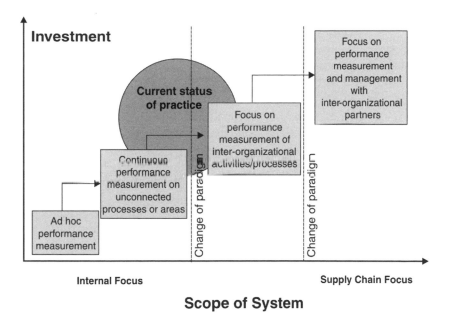

It can take several years and imply changes in underlying paradigms of practice to recognise the importance of a broadening of scope in performance measurement practices. Figure 11.2 illustrates a categorization of supply chain performance measurement maturity.

On the first level the company only uses performance measurement on an ad hoc basis. Here practitioners in logistics and supply chain functions most often only focus on required financial reporting to top management.

On the second level of maturity, companies still do not acknowledge that activities or processes outside the company's legal borders should be included inside the scope of performance measurement practice. However, on this level securing a continuous follow up on key but non-integrated aspects of intra-organizational logistic performance is implemented.

On the third level of maturity, the company, and especially the boundary spanning managers, recognize the impact of activities and processes located outside the company borders (Hald & Christiansen 2004). As a consequence performance measurement systems and practices are established that help visualize this impact, and further provides some possibility to communicate company-experienced performance to supply chain partners. However, at this level, the company sees no need to involve suppliers and customers in the implementation of the measurement system. The system that needs to be optimized is still the focal company.

Finally and at the highest level of measurement maturity in the model presented in Figure 11.2 some companies adopt a comprehensive system approach to performance measurement in the supply chain. These companies involve their supply chain partners in setting up the performance measurement systems. Measures are process-oriented and integrated across company borders. Focus is on how different dimensions of supply chain performance (see next paragraph) and the entire chain can be optimised simultaneously. Such highly mature performance measurement systems thus help identify opportunities for performance tradeoffs that will benefit the entire system, and help distribute gained increases in system performance equally among the involved partners.

The interesting question now becomes, how can a company work to reach a higher level of maturity in its supply chain performance measurement thinking? Earlier in this section we concluded that if the company agenda and personal reward structures was not aligned with a supply chain focus, implementing supply chain performance measurement systems would be near impossible. Therefore the company's personal reward structures needs to be part of the solution. For example, rewarding the purchasing manager and purchasers for last year's reduction in total cost in the processes connecting the company and key suppliers, and not just reduction in purchasing prices, would be a step towards adjusting personal reward structures to supply chain thinking. Also, and more importantly, automatically involving external partners in the implementation of performance measurement systems would help expand the focus and thus provide a platform with increased performance visibility, making it easier for managers to manage the chain and not just the company.

Inclusiveness in Supply Chain Performance

What is supply chain performance? What do companies mean when they state that supply chain performance has improved? Performance of logistics operations and more specifically, performance of the supply chain are often treated as something not needing a definition, as something given in the nature of things.

The role of logistics and supply chain management is to support the creation of customer value (Langley and Holcomb 1992). However the interesting question is how a company assesses how capable the current state of its supply chain is: How capable the setup of the supply chain is right now, or in the last period to deliver customer value? How layout and supply chain processes might be changed in order for customer value to improve? The role of supply chain performance is to answer these and other related questions.

Some contributions discuss supply chain performance as more or less equal to customer service. Others contributions discuss supply chain performance as the amount of resource utilization or cost consumed in order to deliver customer service. However in this book we argue that supply chain performance is a three-dimensional construct. For a company to measure supply chain performance it needs to consider performance in three different, but mutually supportive dimensions (Beamon 1999).

Supply chains can be assessed by means of three dimensions: effectiveness, efficiency and flexibility. This is illustrated in Figure 11.3.

Figure 11.3. The three Dimensions of Supply Chain Performance

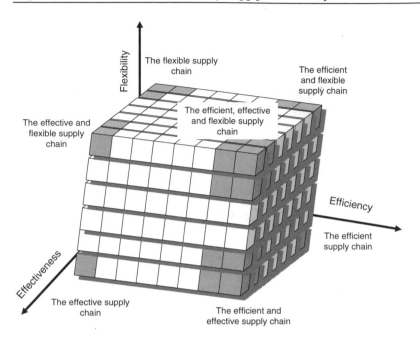

Efficiency is an »*input-oriented*« performance dimension, and it refers to how economically supply chain resources are utilized when providing a given level of end customer service. Effectiveness is an »*output-oriented*« performance dimension and is a measure quantifying the extent to which goals related to end customer service or value are meet. Finally, flexibility quantifies how able the supply chain is to adjust capacity, speed and output, to fit different external demands and changing situations.

As illustrated in Figure 11.3, combining the three supply chain performance dimensions result in seven different types of supply chains. From these different alternatives, supply chain managers need to select the type of supply chain that best fits their overall competitive strategy. However, two or more of these types can also be combined and may work in different parts of the supply chain, which might also prove to be a desirable approach. The leagile supply chain (Naylor et al. 1999, Agarwal et al. 2006) is an example: a lean or an efficient supply chain is designed to work upstream and an agile or effective supply chain is designed to work downstream.

Effects of Supply Chain Performance Measurement

An important but often neglected challenge when designing supply chain performance measurement systems is the question of their effect. Most often, companies implement performance measurement systems without being specific as to which purposes or functions these systems are designed to fulfil. Are they for instance designed to provide supply chain managers with input for decision-making? Or are they designed to motivate suppliers or designed to reach a completely different purpose?

Taking a closer look, performance measurement in the supply chain has at least eight different functions (Schmitz and Platts 2003, 2004). The performance measurement system, the measures in it, and the way these measures are communicated must be aligned with these intended functions.

1. Translate supply chain strategy into operational objectives.
2. Provide supply chain managers with information and herby giving them the opportunity to react on identified performance gaps.
3. Communicate performance expectations across company borders.
4. Clarify responsibilities and objectives between supply chain partners.
5. Support strategic decision-making and prioritization in the supply chain.
6. Align objectives across the supply chain.
7. Motivate suppliers.
8. Improve understanding of supply chain processes and how these processes are connected in a complex network of activities.

However, intended effect or function, and performance measurement design are not the only two aspects that need to be aligned. To be effective, performance measurement, and intended relational outcome must be considered in combination. Stated differently, performance measurement activity in the supply chain must be designed specifically to match the different types of inter-organizational relationships it is supposed to assess (Lamming et al. 1996, O'Toole & Donaldson 2002).

In the remaining part of this chapter we turn to discuss a few concrete supply chain performance measurement concepts.

Supply Chain Performance Measurement Frameworks

In this book we define a supply chain performance measurement framework as a method or a philosophy designed to measure certain dimensions of supply chain performance. That is, the supply chain performance measurement frameworks, often do not argue to provide complete and extensive images of end-to-end supply chain performance. These frameworks include:

- A set of measures or subjects/perspectives relating to certain types of measures.
- A description of how each of the measures or subjects/perspectives relate to each other.
- A description of how to construct the framework and/or how to apply it in different real life situations.

Several supply chain performance measurement frameworks have been proposed as capable tools for measuring and managing performance in the supply chain. Most often however, such frameworks are merely conceptual models that have not been applied in practice. In this chapter we discuss six of the most applied frameworks.

Table 11.1. Supply Chain Performance Measurement Frameworks

Name	Cost oriented frameworks	Process oriented frameworks
The Strategic Profit Model	X	
Target Cost Management	X	
Total Cost of Ownership	X	
Activity-Based Costing	X	
The Balanced Scorecard		X
The SCOR Model		X

As indicated in Table 11.1 the first four of these are concerned with measuring and managing dimensions of supply chain cost. The last two are more inclusive in their nature, and additionally look at supply chain performance from a more process oriented perspective.

All of the presented supply chain performance measurement frameworks except two (Target Cost Management and the SCOR-model) were originally developed for intra-company cost and performance measurement purposes only. However, due to their extensive intra-company success as management tools, they were subsequently suggested as capable cost and performance measurement tools in inter-organizational environments.

The Strategic Profit Model

What is the contribution of logistics and/or supply chain management to the value of the firm or to shareholder value? This question is central in selling the value of logistics and supply chain management, to top management and to other functions in the company. The strategic profit model provides an answer. The model demonstrates how asset, and margin management will influence return on assets and return on net worth (Stock & Lambert 2005: 35).

Return on Assets is calculated as net profit divided by the total value of assets used as resources to generate this profit. Improved logistics and supply chain management operations have the ability to both increase net profit and decrease the total amount of assets used to generate this profit (Figure 11.4).

Logistics and supply chain execution can increase net profit in three different ways. First, improved end customer service leads to increased sales. Second, more efficient manufacturing and lower cost of purchased materials lead to lower cost of goods sold. Finally, reduced order management costs, lower freight costs and more efficient warehouse operations lead to lower total expenses.

Figure 11.4. How Logistics and Supply Chain Management Affect Return on Assets.

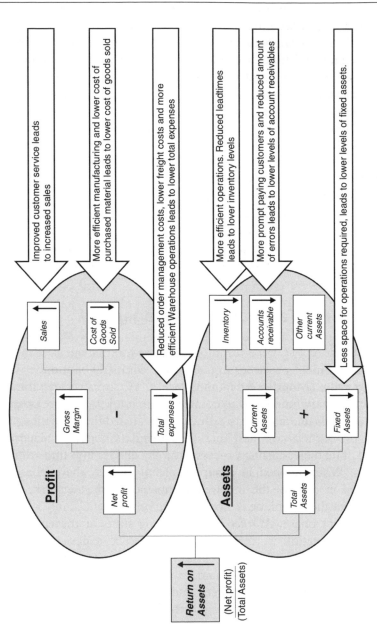

Source: Stock & Lambert (2001: 35)

Logistics and supply chain execution can decrease the total value of assets employed in order to generate a fixed amount of net profit, in three different ways. First, lover inventory levels can be achieved by running a more efficient and coordinated intra- or inter-organizational transformation process and in addition, by minimizing process and lead-times. Second, more prompt paying customers and a reduced amount of errors in the document and invoicing process will reduce the amount of accounts receivable. Finally, less need for in-process inventories, and a more lean production process will result in fewer requirements for space, and if used properly, in lower levels of fixed assets.

All in all, the strategic profit model provides and excellent opportunity for identifying and assessing the effect of specific supply chain management practices in a firm. Stapleton et al. (2002) applied the model to six different firms in the footwear industry. The study demonstrates how the strategic profit model can be applied across a sample of competitors as a tool of comparison (benchmarking), helping to identify opportunities for supply chain improvement.

Target Cost Management

Target costing (TC) is a technique designed to manage cost in product development processes in and across company boundaries in the supply chain (Monden & Hamada 1991). TC supports lean thinking, and its primary function is to communicate market pressure upstream the supply chain, in order to reduce non value adding activities and to align production cost and market demand (Cooper & Slagmulder 1999). The target costing process naturally divides into three different phases. When applied in a supply chain context, these phases are repeated in each of the involved companies in the network, and in such cases the technique is labelled »*Chained Target Costing*«.

The first phase, *Market-Driven Costing* starts at the end market level. Its function is to transmit the pressure experienced by the company in the market, to its product designers and ultimately further upstream the supply chain to its suppliers. In market-driven costing the focal company first calculates the target selling price for the new product by considering: competitive offerings (relative functionality, price), customer characteristics (perceived customer value, customer loyalty) and its own strategic objectives (corporate image, market share, long-term profit targets). It then decides on its target profit margin and subtracts it from the target selling price to reach at the allowable cost.

The second phase, *Product-Level Target Costing* works as its name indicates on the product level. Its overall function is to secure that the product cost stays below the allowable cost. First, the current cost using existing production processes to produce the new product is calculated. Then, how much production cost can be reduced (the target cost reduction objective), through aggressive design improvements and value engineering efforts, is identified. These efforts often include both internal capabilities and supplier capabilities. Therefore this phase integrates the cost management activities of the focal company with its upstream suppliers. Subtracting the target cost reduction objective from the current cost equals the product-level target cost, the cost that the new product can be produced at. If the reached product-level target cost is above the allowable cost, the gap (the strategic cost-reduction challenge) represents the inability of the firm to earn the target profit margin for the new product. In order for the target costing process to work as intended the magnitude of the strategic cost reduction challenge must be carefully managed. Preferably, no new product should be produced when the strategic cost-reduction challenge is positive (Cooper & Slagmulder 1999: 171-173).

The third phase, *Component-Level Target Costing* links the cost reduction objectives of the final product in the focal company, to its component suppliers upstream. The overall function of this phase is to foster communication and coordination of cost targets, cost reduction capabilities and opportunities across company boundaries. First, the cost target objectives of the final product is broken down into its different major functions or modules (i.e. engine and chassis) then the allocated target cost to these functions or modules are further broken down into target cost for their components. In this process, when allocating the target cost for the different functions and components, profit is implicitly distributed among the participants. Therefore, the component-level target costing phase involves an element of negotiation. Figure 11.5 summarizes the concept of target costing in a supply chain context.

Figure 11.5. The Target Costing Process

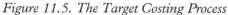

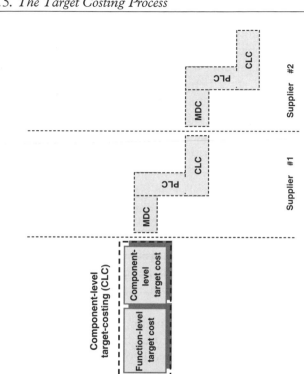

Source: Adapted from Cooper & Slagmulder (1999)

Total Cost of Ownership

The total cost of ownership (TCO) model is a total cost approach, the primary function of which is to provide new insights into the *»true cost«* of sourcing and supply. It recognises that the purchasing price is only a fraction of the cost associated with the acquisition of material. Other costs which are not traditionally measured, but which are significant to the long-term sourcing decisions exist. Failing to include such costs will ultimately risk hurting bottom line profitability in the involved organizations (Krause et al. 2001). For instance, when a supplier fails to meet quality, delivery and reliability requirements, additional costs are incurred by the buying organization, ultimately impacting the bottom line, and possibly the end customers' value experience.

TCO is thus a philosophy designed to shift purchasing away from a unit-price-oriented focus to a total cost-based focus. Figure 11.6 illustrates how the different activities involved in the cross company purchasing process are part of the total cost involved in executing purchasing.

Figure 11.6. The total cost involved in a purchase

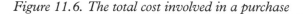

Source: Adapted from Ellram & Siferd (1993)

Take delivery for instance, few firms monitor how much it costs when an incomplete order is received. Such costs normally include follow-up on the problem, expediting, higher freight costs, duplicate paper work and changing the schedule to accommodate the shortage (Ellram & Siferd 1993: 169-170). It might even include cost from lost production caused by the incomplete delivery from the supplier. The determination of cost categories to be included in the total cost of ownership requires a good knowledge of the different processes within the company, and is often subject to political discussions.

In four different but related studies by Ellram (1994, 1995) and Ellram & Siferd (1993, 1998) the functions and benefits of the TCO philosophy were explored. These studies found that the TCO approach supported four major groups of functions and benefits:

1. The supplier selection/volume allocation decision
2. The ongoing supplier evaluation and feedback process
   - Clarifies supplier improvement potential
   - Provides an opportunity to compare suppliers (benchmarking)
3. The focal company in negotiations
   - Cost implications of supplier performance is visualised
4. A change in purchasing culture and behaviour
   - Purchase performance assessed not only on price
   - Easier to involve other internal functions in purchasing

Several different types of TCO models exist. On the most aggregated level, these types can be classified into what is called standard and unique models. Standard models are as their name indicates, TCO models that can be used across a range of different situations. Such models therefore require little or no modifications. A unique TCO model on the other hand is one that is created specially for the analysis of the total cost related to a specific item, or a specific and non-repetitive purchase. Unique models appear to generate a higher level of user support, compared to standard models, because the users of these models are able to have their own concerns incorporated in the model (Ellram 1994: 184-185).

On the more specific level, depending on the specific modelling approach used, TCO models can be classified into what is called a dollar- or currency-based approach, and a value-based approach. The currency-based modelling approach to TCO requires the gathering or allocating of actual cost data for each of the involved cost categories and processes/activities (Ellram 1995: 11). The advantage of this approach is that real costs are included in the model. The disadvantage is that such cost data often is either hard or time consuming to gather or even impossible to find. The value-based modelling approach to TCO combines cost data with other performance data for which cost information is unavailable. The advantage of this approach is that it is more flexible and easy can be adjusted/ modelled to strategic objectives and further, that it can be implemented and used even if real cost information is unavailable. The disadvantage is that it is often hard to explain since currency and other performance information is mixed together and transformed in the model.

Studies exploring the practical use of TCO models have pointed towards four major difficulties in implementing TCO models (Ellram & Sifers 1998). First data can be hard to gather. Second, TCO models are considered complex. This complexity leads to implementations that require large initial cost and time investments, and models that are hard to explain and to understand. Third, it is difficult to change the price centric focus and get buyers away from the price mentality. Finally, it should be noted that TCO models are not the proper approach for all buys. Failing to recognize that risk will destroy users confidence in TCO as a capable supply chain performance measurement framework.

Hurkens et al. (2006) reported on a TCO model implementation in Carglass, a leading vehicle glass repair and replacement expert operating in the after-sales market. First, Carglass mapped the relevant business process for which costs had to be assessed. Then, process costs was calculated for each process step and finally the model was implemented in a spreadsheet. The model could be broken down per supplier into a cost comparison across different cost categories. In 2004, the TCO model was used to guide and monitor two strategic drivers for supplier improvement: reduction of time-to-market and the reduction of stocks. It was also used in discussions with individual suppliers to explain volume shifts toward other suppliers, to trigger process improvements and, to a lesser extent, to negotiate price reductions.

Activity-Based Costing

Processes in the supply chain are series of activities linked together to serve customer requirements. The rise of customer power emphasizes processes, often hidden from management in organizational and functional units, with accounting systems that do not show costs of individual activities, let alone the driving forces behind these costs. The pursuit of more precise activity costs has led to *activity-based accounting (ABC)* and *activity-based management (ABM)* to identify and utilize these costs along with non-cost metrics to identify opportunities (Cokins 1996). Conventional accounting systems are of little help, they hide more than they help. ABC offers a more useful approach, a logical framework to trace the specific costs of serving individual customers (or groups of customers) and activities and the total set of costs of providing individual products and services. It fits a process orientation through its capacity to provide end-to-end costing.

Cost accounting systems serve four purposes: 1) to determine costs of processes and products, 2) to track changes in costs over time, 3) allocate costs for financial statements and 4) to evaluate alternative decisions. (Johnson & Kaplan 1987). Conventional cost accounting is developed in labor-intensive factory environments. Overhead costs were distributed to products on the basis of manhours directly incurred for the production of individual products. Other costs were absorbed into overhead. This approach has become inadequate to meet the needs of modern industry where labor costs are a small part of the total cost of a product, and other costs enter in a more significant way. Conventional cost accounting fails to meet these purposes even within a single organization, let alone the supply chain, as the most important resources are often classified as overhead costs.

The supply chain adds further difficulty. Comparison among partner organizations is difficult using conventional methods. Each organization has a different set of activities and cost structures. Further, the supply chain as a process is oriented toward a flow of products and materials, adding value through the application of resources to activities in ways that are not always related to the convention of direct man-hours. Approaches using other singular measures such as machine hours or space utilization are also inadequate to the task. Further, the systemic nature of the supply chain involves trade-offs between functional costs or between costs and service levels where a change in one activity area affects costs and performance in other areas. (Pohlen & LaLonde 1994).

Each activity, such as order processing, product assembly or materials handling utilizes different sets of resources and costs change in response to different measures of output, such as numbers of orders processed, numbers of units assembled or numbers of warehouse pallets handled. Under conventional accounting, this cost behavior is hidden under overhead costs. A partial solution is offered through activity-based accounting.

Financial accounting fails to provide cost control. In response, two other measurement systems have emerged: operational control and activity-based accounting (Cooper & Kaplan 1998). They operate under different procedures, collect different data and perform different roles for mangers. They are incorporated into ERP systems to provide managers with direct measures of operating performance. *Operational control* provides continual feedback about individual unit performance. It uses highly specific cost data that employees can directly influence or control. Because it reflects daily performance, it will necessarily produce variable results. Activity-based costing plays a more strategic role.

The System

Activity-based accounting (ABC) is part of a management shift towards managing businesses as a set of processes, called *activity-based management*. It recognizes a flow process: resources to activities to products. The flow is the core of the system, linking a series of activities and their costs. It is strategic in orientation, relying on statistically determined cost drivers. By following the flow of operations, the development of ABC parallels that of the supply chain. ABC serves strategy and management decisions. In ABC, all costs become variable but stable. The scope includes the entire value chain. Where conventional cost accounting would include inputs at their purchased price, ABC would carry the impact of these inputs to vendors' resources.

Costs originate with the quantity of a specific resource committed to a process activity (or function). They become cost pools within activities, allocated on the basis of the quantities consumed and the related costs, such as man-hours x hourly wage rates. Each activity has its own cost characteristics, based on the nature of the activity. These become *cost drivers:* »any event or transaction that causes the incurrence of cost in an organization« (Garrison & Noreen, 1997, p.82). Costs for individual products are then determined by resource consumption in processing the product.

An activity-based costing system is designed in a series of five steps:

- Analyze process by value
- Identify activity centers
- Assign costs to activity centers
- Select cost drivers
- Apply to products

Process value analysis follows a procedure outlined in Chapter 2: identification of value adding as opposed to non-value adding activities within material and product flow. It is essentially process engineering, designed to increase efficiency through improved process design.

An *activity* is any event or transaction that drives a cost. They should have clearly defined boundaries. However, if two adjacent activities have the same cost drivers, it makes little sense to separate them. Boundaries should be clearly identified. The danger is in data collection and management in too much detail so that the costing system becomes cumbersome in use.

An *activity center* is any part of a process for which management wants a cost. Activities are combined into activity centers to simplify the reporting process. Materials handling in a distribution center could involve several different activities that are aggregated into a single activity center. The reporting level depends on the purpose, and could focus on individual product units, batch, product category or facility. Assigning costs to activities should recognize only those costs directly incurred by the activity center and that vary with the volume of activity. Costs that influence cost behavior in a facility may not be relevant at a product unit or batch level. This also excludes overhead costs that cannot be assigned to activities or products.

Selecting *cost drivers* may be the most difficult part of the design process. A cost driver is the event that incurs the cost for the activity. In a given activity, there may be more than one driver and one advantage of ABC is the ability to include multiple drivers. The first step is to find the dominant characteristics that influence costs of the activity, through statistical analysis or as a last resort informed judgement. These however are limited by availability of data for measurement. Further, the measurement should reflect resource consumption of the activity. There may be several layers of cost drivers. The cost assignment path may go from general accounting ledger drivers to intermediate drivers that collect data in a particular functional area followed by a final activity driver that combines cost flows from different sources related to the characteristics of individual activities (Cokins 1996). Assigning costs to products at this point becomes straightforward. As products move through the supply chain, they will pass through a series of activities, incurring costs determined by the individual activity drivers. As products and materials flow through activities, they incur costs on the basis of the activity cost drivers.

A simple example will demonstrate the process, shown in Figure 11.7. We have a DC with two activities: materials handling and storage. Materials handling is performed by automated machinery. Storage involves the use of space within the building. In the first stage, the cost of performing the operation as a whole is calculated. For materials handling, this is based on costs of operation for the materials handling system. If more than one product is involved, the costs of individual products should be separated, tracing the proportions of use if necessary. For storage, it would be calculated on floor space occupied. These costs flow through activity centers (cost pools) where they would be combined with other costs related to the activity. These activities are linked by cost drivers to the number of units handled for materials handling. The cost of storage is related to the proportion of space utilized. Both costs then flow through to the supply chain process where the cost per unit handled and the cost of storing are combined and attached to the specific activity. Every activity involves a similar cost measurement procedure. The total cost of the process is the summation of all the individual activity costs. Only those costs that can be separately identified are included. ABC assigns general overhead costs as far as possible to specific actions based on logical and measurable associations between cost drivers and activity levels.

A further addition is proposed by van Damme and van der Zon (2000) to make ABC into a decision support system: adding factors that influence drivers, and tracking the system on a continuing basis for changes in operations. Using a three-tiered set of drivers for resource, process and product, they would incorporate additional factors to allow for critical dimensions. For example, resource drivers would deal with equipment age or vulnerability, process would deal with quality levels and product factors would look at batch size.

Figure 11.7. Activity-based Costing

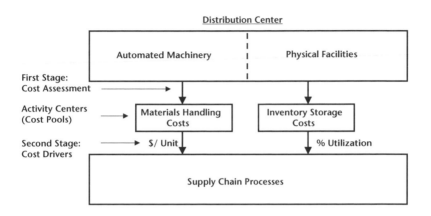

For the supply chain there is an additional problem. Cokins (1999:5) notes that ABC has been practiced as »an inward looking focus« being tied to conventional accounting systems. Members of the supply chain behave as a single organization. They incur costs for each other through their own decisions. The advantages of ABC for the supply chain are that the costs of every activity can be measured. As long as every partner uses ABC, the costs of these activities can be used to decide on courses of action for the supply chain as a whole. Cokins emphasizes the role of ABC in boundary spanning at the »touch points,« where the impact of a supplier's actions impinges on the customer, or vice versa. Management should be concerned with the total costs of actions such as changing delivery frequency for a supplier versus inventory holding costs for the customer.

The Balanced Scorecard

The Balanced scorecard is a measurement system that can provide managers with a framework to translate a company's strategic objectives into a set of performance measures. The original method was proposed by Kaplan and Norton (1992), which focused on four processes with respective purposes:

- Translating the vision – Purpose: clarifying the vision, and, gaining consensus.
- Communicating and linking – Purpose: Communicating and educating, setting goals, and, linking rewards to performance measures.
- Business planning – Purpose: Setting targets, aligning strategic initiatives, allocating resources, and, establishing milestones.
- Feedback and learning – Purpose: Articulating the shared vision, supplying strategic feedback, and, facilitating strategy review and learning.

The first process links vision and strategy to the following four perspectives (Figure 11.8): financial, internal business process, learning and growth, and customer.

Figure 11.8. Translating Vision and Strategy: Four Perspectives

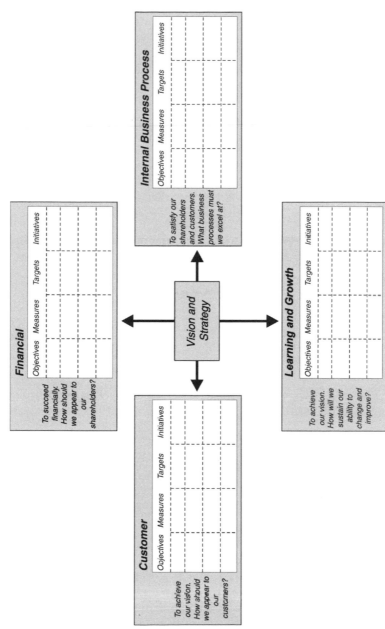

Source: Adapted from Kaplan and Norton (1996)

The Balanced scorecard has been extended and/or modified to analyze corporate performance in many perspectives. From a supply chain management perspective, Brewer and Speh (2000) propose the following model (Figure 11.9).

Figure 11.9. Linking Supply Chain Management and the Balanced Scorecard

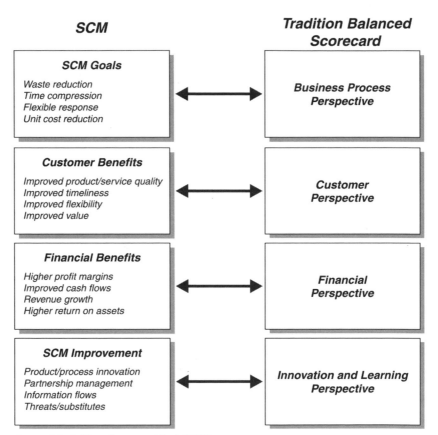

Source: Adapted from Brewer and Speh (2000)

Each of the four perspectives (i.e. customer, innovation and learning, financial, and business) is complemented with examples of goals and measures. Firms using the balanced scorecard typically tailor the goals and measures to suit their business strategies.

The SCOR Model

The Supply Chain Operations Reference (SCOR) model is a process reference model that the Supply Chain Council developed and endorsed as the cross-industry standard for supply chain management. The Supply Chain Council (SCC) is an independent non-for-profit organization founded in 1996 (SCOR Overview 2006). Today the SCC is supported by over 650 member organizations. Since its establishment, the SCOR model has been developed in successive steps, and it is now in its 8.0 version.

According to SCOR's own definition, the SCOR model integrates the well-known concepts of business process reengineering, benchmarking, and process measurement into a cross-functional framework (SCOR Overview 2006). Using a standard terminology, the SCOR model uses a language of common metrics with associated benchmarks and provides a platform for best in class comparisons and inspiration (Huang 2004). The SCOR model is further designed to assist firms in increasing the effectiveness of their supply chains, and to provide a process-based approach to SCM (Stewart 1997). Even more specifically, the model contains a standard description of management processes, a framework of relationships among the standard processes, standard metrics to measure process performance, management practices that produce best-in-class performance, and a standard alignment to software features and functionality (Huang et al. 2005).

The SCOR model is structured into five management processes or decision areas: Plan, Source, Make, Deliver and Return.

1. In the PLAN process, resources are balanced with requirements and plans are developed, communicated and integrated across the entire supply chain. Plan includes »*Processes that balance aggregate demand and supply to develop a course of action which best meets sourcing, production and delivery requirements*« (SCOR Overview 2006: 7).

   - Purchasing plans
   - Production plans
   - Delivery and distribution plans
   - Return scheduling plans

2. In the SOURCE process, upstream activity is designed and executed. Source includes *»Processes that procure goods and services to meet planned or actual demand* (SCOR Overview 2006: 7).

- Sources of supply is identified and selected
- Supplier agreements are designed
- Supplier performance is assessed
- Incoming products are received
- Raw material inventories are managed

3. In the MAKE process, products are designed and transformed from raw material into finished products that can be sold to end customers. Make includes *»Processes that transform product to a finished state to meet planned or actual demand«* (SCOR Overview 2006: 7).

- Finalize engineering
- Produce and test
- Manage in process products
- Design and manage equipment and facilities

4. In the DELIVER process, downstream activity is designed and executed. Deliver includes *»Processes that provide finished goods and services to meet planned or actual demand, typically including order management, transportation management, and distribution management«* (SCOR Overview 2006: 7).

- Customer order management
- Loading and shipping og products
- Transportation
- Customer invoices
- Finished goods inventory management

5. In the RETURN process, both the return of raw materials to suppliers and receipt of returns from end customers are managed. Return includes *»Processes associated with returning or receiving returned products for any reason. These processes extend into post-delivery customer support«* (SCOR Overview 2006: 7).

- Identify product condition
- Request product return authorization
- Schedule product shipments
- Return products
- Authorize product return
- Schedule return receipt
- Receive returned products

For each of these five management processes or decision areas SCOR 8.0 contains three levels of detail (Table 11.2). The SCOR model is flexible, in that on each of these three levels, components from the model can be selected and de-selected to fit the specific supply chain in question.

Table 11.2. The three levels of detail in the SCOR model

LEVEL OF DETAIL	DESCRIPTION
Level 1: Top level (Process types)	Defines the scope and content for the Supply Chain Operations Reference-model. Which of the five management processes are included? What are the aggregated performance targets for the supply chain?
Level 2: Configuration level (Process categories)	Configures the supply chain from a list of core process categories. Companies implement their operations strategy through the configuration they choose for their supply chain.
Level 3: Process element level (Decomposed processes)	Defines a company's ability to compete successfully in its chosen markets. On this level companies »fine tune« their operations strategy. Details included on this level are: • Process element definitions • Process element information inputs, and outputs • Process performance metrics • Best practices, where applicable • System capabilities required to support best practices • Systems/tools

Although the SCOR model at presently only includes the three levels described in Table 11.2, it recognises a fourth level – the implementation level. At this level companies implement specific supply chain management practices. The rationale for the exclusion of the implementation level is that the SCOR model is designed as a tool to describe measure and evaluate any supply chain configuration. Thus, firms must implement specific supply chain management practices based upon their unique set of competitive priorities and business conditions to achieve the desired level of performance (Lockamy & McCormack 2004).

Following the logic of the SCOR model, a process is composed of process elements that are, in turn, composed of tasks and major categories of activities. Tasks are in turn a set of activities standardized for comparison between supply chains. For example, the source process procure materials and services to meet demand. These, in turn, become process categories that identify the characteristics of the process, such as whether the components are standard or unique. At the configuration level, these categories become the basis for selecting processes such as procuring or dividing into elements such as scheduling deliveries, receiving and verifying and transferring inventory.

One of the major features of the SCOR model is that it provides opportunities for benchmarking between companies and supply chains. Besides its definition of best in class standard processes and decomposed processes, it provides an excellent opportunity for comparisons on a quantitative level. More specifically a set of performance attributes is defined. These performance-attributes range from high level measures that cross multiple SCOR processes to very specific metrics that are designed to assess the performance of a specific process element. Table 11.3 illustrate the high level measures.

Table 11.3. Performance Attributes and Level 1 Metrics

| Level 1 Metrics | Performance Attributes | | | | |
| | Customer-Facing | | | Internal-Facing | |
	Reliabilty	Responsiveness	Flexibility	Cost	Assets
Perfect Order Fulfillment	✔				
Order Fulfillment Cycle Time		✔			
Upside Supply Chain Flexibility			✔		
Upside Supply Chain Adaptability			✔		
Downside Supply Chain Adaptability			✔		
Supply Chain Management Cost				✔	
Cost of Goods Sold				✔	
Cash-to-Cash Cycle Time					✔
Return on Supply Chain Fixed Assets					✔
Return on Working Capital					✔

Source: SCOR Overview 2006, p. 8

In summary the SCOR model focuses on transactional efficiency rather than relationships with customers and suppliers (Lambert et al. 2005). Therefore the model cannot be used in isolation. It needs to be used together with other supply chain frameworks and concepts (Ellram et al. 2004).

Concluding Comments

In this chapter the emphasis has been on performance measurement and management in the supply chain. Supply chain performance measurement and management is a challenging task, since such processes involve the activities, goals and objectives of two or more companies.

Four major challenges in current performance measurement and management practices in the global supply chain can be identified. First, existing performance measurement systems for the global supply chain lack a system perspective. Second, the definition of supply chain performance is often non-inclusive. Third, measurement activity in the supply chain is too narrowly focused on selecting measures and not on designing the effect of these measures, and adjusting them and their activation to specific situations, such as with different types of inter-organizational relationships. Finally, issues of communication or feedback of performance measurement in the supply chain is important, but often completely omitted as an integrated part of the process linking supply chain performance measurement and management activity to its inter-organizational effect.

Over the years, different Supply Chain Performance Measurement Frameworks have been proposed as capable devices for measuring supply chain performance. In this chapter we presented and discussed six of the most applied of these frameworks. In each of their special ways these frameworks provide insights into certain aspects of total supply chain performance. However, we recommend that none of them be used in isolation, since as explained in the introduction to this chapter, such an approach will risk de-focusing managerial attention from other dimensions of performance, resulting in a neglect of actions for improving customer service.

12. Strategy and the Supply Chain

»Although most executives would like sustained advantage,
they are forced to operate as if it does not exist. The chal-
lenge is coping with not knowing whether such an advan-
tage actually exists – except in retrospect«

(Eisenhardt, 2002).

The concept of strategy for the supply chain is a paradox. On the one hand, the supply chain is organized around a focal firm and serves to execute a supply strategy for delivering a product to a customer. On the other hand, the supply chain can be the central product providing elements for customer satisfaction, where the focal product itself becomes a commodity. These two contexts require different orientations.

Strategy is a set of decisions made today about what to do in a specified future time period. It assumes predictability and an attainable goal matched to available resources. Most discussion of strategy in business deals with a single firm in isolation. The characteristics of the supply chain force a different perspective in which individual decision-making firms must be brought together to accept a common set of objectives whilst also simultaneously satisfying their own stakeholders.

Supply chains require communities of organizations for action. No single firm can undertake to operate the entire supply process as a separate organization. It is the collective decisions that create the entity and each firm becomes a node within a network. The network includes not only the immediate supply chain, but other supply chains in which it is engaged, competitors at its own level and also at other levels as well. The links become connections of varying intensity in a network. Supply chain strategy must involve configuring the network, define the information requirement and the physical flows, and define which of these flows can be permitted or should be restricted.

The supply chain is also a system of interconnecting organizations that have additional links outside of the supply chain to other organizations. Furthermore, actions taken within the supply chain may have connections with other organizations and markets, and other elements in the global environment. Interconnections also create interactions. Intended actions within the supply chain involve system trade-offs, one element gains while another loses, for the benefit of the system as a whole. Some external developments may have unintended consequences and disruptive effects on the supply chain. A general statement describing a supply chain strategy is to achieve optimal results while protecting the system against potential problems and disasters.

There is also a hierarchy of decisions, beginning at the corporate level concerning products, markets, or both. This challenges the environment in which the supply chain operates. The next layer involves partner relationships, choosing organizations for collaboration and coordination. A third level involves inter-organizational coordination at a functional level, such as setting production schedules for the supply chain as a whole to minimize the amount of inventory within the system. Finally there are functional decisions within particular disciplines such as determining transportation routes to minimize transport costs. The boundaries separating these levels are not absolute. A limit on production capacity has potential consequences for inventory and transportation and customer relations. The opportunities for unique advantage at the corporate level must be weighted against the constraints of the supply system.

Is a supply chain strategy even viable, given all of the interdependencies within the supply chain as a network? Even if we accept the notion of strategic choice, can we make precise decisions on which to plan? We make the following assumptions here that strategy can set a general direction, and even indicate decisions within limits, such as choosing among general alternatives. A long-term strategy and planning in a dynamic world may not be possible. Some writers would even discredit long-range planning (Mintzberg 1994, Geus 1997). At a minimum, strategy could become contingency planning within the well-recognized theme of »what if?«

Strategy and the Supply Chain

The two roles of supply chain strategy at a corporate level can be divided into: a source of competitive advantage in itself, and as support for products and markets. In the first arena are Dell as a manufacturer, and Wal-Mart as a major retailer. Both have set standards through their respective supply chains in their respective industries that their competitors have had to follow. In the second, Apple as a manufacturer and Target as a retailer in the USA, have both delivered unique products and merchandising that assert stringent requirements on the supply chain.

Beyond their position in decision-making, strategies have two roles to play in the organization. By providing a vision of the future, they establish a *focus* for partners in the supply chain, so that they may recognize and participate in the system. Focus provides motivation. A second role is *organizing* the supply chain, providing direction for all subordinate decisions, acting to coordinate actions.

Supply chain strategy can be further divided into active and reactive strategies. Active strategies serve and protect the core of the organization, to enhance revenues, reduce costs and to generally maintain the position of the focal organization in the market. Reactive strategies are intended for response to changing conditions in the market or supply. The objective here is to provide stability, to protect the system against unforeseen events and conditions.

A supply chain is part of a larger network, a system of interconnections. The center is a *directed system* designed to accomplish a specific set of tasks. This is what we normally think of as the supply chain. The boundaries defined by the operational interactions that enable supply and fulfill customer orders. Only when competitive pressures appear or catastrophe occurs do we sense a larger set of connections.

A *larger system* of competing suppliers, service organizations, and customers surrounds the supply chain. They have their own connections and competitive pressures that exert influence on the collective decisions and operations within the supply chain. Mapping the supply chain provides an initial view of the directed system but it only describes indirectly the influences that shape these decisions. Influences not only require response, but also suggest ways to seize opportunity.

There is also a third layer from the *environments* in which the supply chain operates. The environmental system includes technologies, the global economy, government policies, the labor market, and other public issues. Technologies such as IT are highly volatile and have the power to change the performance of the system. The global exposure of the supply chain makes it vulnerable to the economic and political currents that circulate in this environment.

Strategy in the context of these systems requires not only an operational focus striving for continuous improvement within the internal systems of the supply chain but also a sensitivity to change and the ability to react rapidly. These reactions are in the form of risk management and agility.

Strategy must also contend with the phenomena of *complex adaptive systems*. Generally, these would be associated with environmental conditions in a turbulent environment. New connections to the environment suddenly appear as emergent systems, operating without possibility of control, reflected in expressions such as »It just happens.« Strategy under these conditions must involve sensing change and developing tools to counter them.

Technological changes in the Internet such as on-demand processing and RFID have profound and unexpected effects on the supply chain (see Chapter 4). The first might give a new level of flexibility allowing supply chains to switch connections to different suppliers. The second could ultimately provide a level of individual item control that would extend customization into industries where it has not been present before. This speculation is merely intended to provide hypothetical examples. The inability to anticipate outcomes as the full panoply of the supply chain environment will create a need for flexible response and an inevitable drift towards new forms of organization and structure.

Objectives and Outcomes

Strategy in the supply chain takes on both external and internal aspects. The external aspects of strategy are clear: supply chain versus other supply chains and meeting customer requirements. Internal strategy takes place within the network.

The objectives of external strategy are the now-traditional ones of market share and increased revenues and profits. Supporting this is cost reduction to support pricing freedom to meet competition. In addition, meeting customer requirements include customer relationship management and consistent performance to meet and exceed customer expectations for product and service delivery. None of these however can be achieved without internal decisions. These include decision integration, time management, risk management, and agility.

Networks and Systems

A supply chain is both a network and a system. The core of the supply chain is a network, a process, and sets of relationships. The function of this network is to convert resources to finished products (including services) delivered to final users/customers. The boundary of the supply chain network is both arbitrary and permeable. Outside of this demarcation is considered to be the environment. While the boundaries of the supply chain network are established by intended interactions, the actual network in which it is embedded is infinitely larger. There are threats and pressures from external forces such as competition for markets and resources. Organizations have ties to other supply chains. External pressures from their own environments threaten them. Technology, global markets, corporate policies, and societal influences further influence this network both positively and negatively.

A supply chain is also a system. Systems are specified by their interactions. The system becomes *dynamic* because of changes, which are made both by managed decisions and actions and by external forces unleashed by the network environment. Because of these inevitable connections, the system becomes both non-linear and dynamic. The system is non-linear in that the efforts to adapt to these forces reflect feedback loops. System theorists point out that even small changes in the starting conditions (the stability of normal operations) can create complex results for the system.

The initial conditions for the system are not known at any one point in time. The exposure of the supply chain to all of the inputs from its environment creates constant change, requiring processing new information and energy to adapt. This is characteristic of a complex adaptive system. Change is constant, requiring continual adaptation, but a major event, characterized as *a strange attractor,* can throw the system off balance or even into cataclysm. If the system is sensitive to new influences, then it will ultimately change to meet the challenge.

Management occurs at the edge between stability and chaos. Stable systems do not change and hence become vulnerable to forces that will overwhelm them, such as a distribution system delivering to small shops, when large superstores begin to replace them. Chaos on the other hand has extreme turbulence in which no planning can take place, where the only possible management action is to react. Meaningful adaptation can only take place at the edge of chaos (Brown & Eisenhardt 1998).

Sanders (1998:70) summarizes:

- Our world is made up of non-linear dynamic systems.
- Underneath a world of disorder is a self-organizing pattern called order.
- This pattern of organization is created by the elements of the system.
- The relationships and interactions are not always visible
- Non-linear systems are sensitive to unknowable initial conditions
- Complex adaptive systems create change through adaptation.

Resource-Based Strategy

There is a question as to whether a supply chain has a strategy of its own. It serves other masters: products and markets. Originally perceived as an afterthought, the supply chain has flourished and come into its own in numerous cases, and threatened the survival of its dominant members in others. It is not an organization comparable to a single corporation but a network of organizations, and with connections to other supply chains. It is influenced by technology, competition, global politics, economic policies, and society at large. Therefore, there is a question as to how free the supply chain is to create its own destiny.

Corporate strategy has been a subject of endless debate. Mintzberg et al. (1998) summarized several different schools of thought about the topic. The fit of any directly to supply chain management is not strong. The supply chain is a collection of autonomous and quasi-autonomous organizations, each defining its own processes, and making its own decisions. The links across borders can vary from loose to tight. Yet, corporate strategy provides a point of departure.

The strategic objective of any supply chain is to secure the necessary resources to accomplish its mission of material and product flow from origin to final delivery. During the last two decades the Resource-Based View (RBV) has developed as an important perspective focusing on the resources and capabilities of companies. The idea of looking at firms as bundles of heterogeneous resources and capabilities goes back to the work of Penrose (1959). The resource-based view of the firm was reintroduced by Wernerfelt (1984) and has since been adopted by many researchers, e.g. Grant (1991), Barney (1999), Eisenhardt & Martin (2000), and Helfat & Peteraf (2003). It is an important theoretical framework for understanding how competitive advantage within firms is achieved and how that advantage might be sustained in the long run.

Resources and capabilities are key concepts in the resource-based theory. The firm's resources can be defined as *»stocks of available factors that are owned or controlled by the firm«* (Amit & Schoemaker 1993: 33). Resources are inputs into the production process. Capabilities refer to a firm's ability to achieve desired goals by coordinating and synergizing its collection of resources. Capabilities involve complex patterns of coordination between people and other resources, and between people themselves. However, the two concepts overlap, and in practice it is very difficult to distinguish between resources and capabilities. A firm's resources and capabilities include all financial, physical, human, and organizational assets used by a firm to develop, manufacture, and deliver products or services to its customers (Barney & Hansen 1994). They can create a sustainable, competitive advantage for a firm if they are *valuable* for the customers, *rare*, *inimitable* and *non-substitutable,* the so-called VRIN attributes, according to Eisenhardt and Martin (2000).

Resources and capabilities must add value to the products. When answering the question on value, the internal analysis of resources & capabilities must be combined with an external analysis of environmental opportunities and threats. Resources and capabilities are *valuable* because they can be used to exploit opportunities and neutralize threats. Another important condition for creating a competitive advantage is *rareness*. If resources and capabilities are available to many competitors at the same market, then they will be a competitive necessity for being on the market. If they are valuable and rare at the same time, the firm may be able to create at least a temporary competitive advantage. The more difficult it is to *imitate* them, the more likely it is that the firm can create sustainable competitive advantage. Capabilities and resources are difficult to imitate if they are a combination of both tangible and intangible assets. Finally, they should not be *substitutable* with other capabilities and resources with similar or even better properties.

There are several reasons why capabilities may be difficult to duplicate. First, capabilities may be developed as a result of the firm's history (path dependence) and therefore related to more specific circumstances and events. Second, skills are influenced by many small decisions and irreversible choices, which are invisible and difficult to understand for outsiders. Finally, capabilities are often the result of complex social interaction, embedded in the organization and not visible and tangible for people outside the organization (tacit knowledge). Trust between a firm and a key supplier is an example of invisible assets, which cannot be traded or easily replicated by competitors. Trust is embedded in the relationship and developed over time as a result of previous exchanges and experiences between the partners.

Resources and capabilities that are rare, difficult to imitate and valuable are called *strategic assets* (Amit & Schumacher 1993), or *core competencies* (Prahalad & Hamel 1990) The challenge for business managers is to identify, ex ante, a set of strategic assets as grounds for developing the firm's competitive advantage. Examples of strategic assets include: fast product development cycles, trust-based buyer-seller relationships, access to exclusive distribution channels, and short order cycle time. There are many examples within the supply chain area. The success of Ikea is closely related to logistics efficiency in packaging, handling, storing, and transport. Wal-Mart's quick-response system with Procter & Gamble has enabled Wal-Mart to minimize inventory levels in the supply chain and reduce stock-outs. Dell Computer's direct business model of customized computer equipment has given the firm a competitive advantage both in terms of distribution costs and delivery lead-time. Many competitors in the PC industry have tried to copy Dell's business model but failed, because the secret of Dell's model is embedded in both tangible and intangible capabilities in the supply chain spanning from procurement, product development, order processing, inventory management, production planning, to customer relations management. Recently, the resource-based view has been developed into a *dynamic resource-based view* (Teece et al. 1997, Eisenhardt & Martin 2000, Winter 2003). Dynamic capabilities involve adaptation and change, because they build, integrate, or reconfigure other resources and capabilities.

Establishing a supply chain core leads to a strategic sequence of planning and adaptation. While corporate planning is no longer preeminent as a bureaucratic exercise, it is absolutely necessary for a closely coordinated and integrated process. The fact that much of this process is controlled through information technology with software makes planning even more important.

Planning however is vulnerable to a changing environment. The boundary between chaos and stability within systems requires continual adaptation (Brown & Eisenhardt 1998). Change originates from many causes. The need to adapt then requires modifying or even replacing plans. However the logical precision of software requires equally precise planning. The direction of strategy becomes more obscure as it evolves as an emergent strategy.

Organizational learning becomes the key to adaptation. Starting with solutions to immediate problems, it evolves incrementally toward »mutual adjustment« (Lindblom 1959). Nelson and Winter (1982) observed that change comes from interaction among routines. Mintzberg et al. (1998) added that although routines create stability, they interact with new situations to create learning and hence changes in strategy.

Both strategy and planning, through adaptation, take on different characteristics than they held in the beginning, a form of organizational drift for the supply chain as a whole. This is necessary for their survival and their parent organizations. This makes the supply chain into a form of adaptive system, but with human guidance. More subtle changes in the environment may create less visible changes in the supply chain, even as self-adaptive systems.

From Vertical Integration to Horizontal Disintegration

Charles Fine (1998) introduced a concept of 'clockspeed-based' strategies for supply chains, to help in understanding the dynamics of fast-moving industries. The premise holds structure to be the key to both supply chains and corporate strategy. The choice of suppliers determines not only the direction for the future but also which capabilities become important for competitive advantage. Capability, however, can be temporary. Supply chain structure can change rapidly, depending on the industry. Some industries, such as electronics, multi-media, and biotech face rapid evolution, driven by the pace of their technologies. Others, such as household appliances, furniture, and automotive industries change at a slower pace. Thus the rate of change is not as pronounced.

Fine argues that:

> *»... a company's real core capability – the inner core, if you will – lies in the ability to design and manage the supply chain in order to gain advantage, albeit temporary, in a market where competitive forces may change at lightning speed.«*

(Fine 1998, p. 76)

Two characteristics of supply chains determine the design of supply chains:

*   Amplification of demand volatility (the Forrester effect), which increases as demand moves upstream, such as the variation in demand through internal order disciplines and the industry demand cycle.
*   Amplification of time volatility, which increases as products move towards the market, such as the rate of change of products as they move from material and component levels through final product to final user.

Together they argue for short, direct channels with high interdependence in industries with rapid rates of change. Strategy begins by mapping the chain to identify members and their characteristics: clockspeed (rate of change), the driving factors and profitability. The scope of supply chain management involves product design, process engineering, and organization. It also involves what to outsource and with which suppliers. This decision determines the balance between independence and reliance on suppliers.

Fine's Double Helix Model

Fine proposes »The Double Helix« model (shown in Figure 12.1), which shows how a supply chain structure oscillates between vertical integration (integrated architecture) and horizontal disintegration (modular architecture). It describes a cycle of transition from vertically integrated to fragmented, and specialized supply chains and back again. The forces of change propelling the supply chain from internal ownership towards an outsourced structure stem from 1) increasing competition, 2) products becoming almost undifferentiated commodities, 3) the entry of niche competitors and 4) the inability of large, hierarchical organizations to respond to rapid change. When companies are in competitive markets, they tend to subcontract activities that can be performed equally well or better on the outside. When companies have unique new technologies, they will integrate to capture profits and control their future direction. These companies seek to combine the new elements with other subsystems to create more value for the customer.

Figure 12.1. The Double Helix

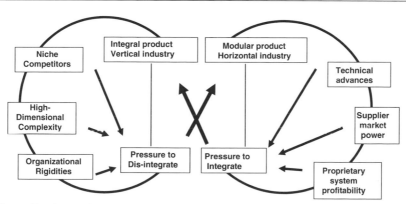

Source: Fine (1998: 49)

The forces of disintegration that push toward a horizontal/modular configuration include:

1. The relentless entry of niche competitors hoping to pick off discrete industry segments.

2. The challenge of keeping ahead of the competition across the many dimensions of technology and markets required by an integral system, and
3. The bureaucratic and organizational rigidities that often settle upon large, established companies.

Conversely, forces of vertical integration of product architectures include (p. 50):

1. Technical advances in one subsystem becoming a core competency, giving market power to its owner,
2. Market power in one subsystem encouraging bundling with other subsystems to increase control and add more value, and
3. Market power in one subsystem encouraging engineering integration with other subsystems to develop proprietary integral solutions.

Matching Product Uncertainties with Supply Chains

The product fit becomes a crucial decision. Commodity products with stable demand would require different supply chain design than high-tech products based on innovative designs. Based on the differences in demand, Fisher (1997) provides a framework to classify products as functional or innovative. Functional products, such as the fast moving consumer goods sold in grocery stores, have stable, predictable demand and long life cycles. Innovative products (such as products with high innovation content), on the other hand, have unpredictable demand and short product life cycles. Table 12.1 summarizes a comparison.

Table 12.1. Functional versus Innovative Products

Aspects of Demand	Functional (Predictable Demand)	Innovative (Unpredictable Demand)
Product life cycle	more than 2 years	3 months to 1 year
Contribution margin*	5 % to 20 %	20 % to 60 %
Product variety	low (10 to 20 variants per category	high (often millions of variants)
Average margin of error in the forecast at the time production is committed	10 %	40 % to 100 %
Average stock out rate	1 % to 2 %	10 % to 40 %
Average forced end-of-the-season markdown as percentage of full price	0 %	10 % to 25 %
Lead time required for made-to-order products	6 months to 1 year	1 day to 2 weeks

* The contribution margin equals price minus variable cost divided by price and is expressed as a percentage. Source: Fisher (1997).

Supply chains for innovative products should be responsive in order to respond to unpredictable demand. On the other hand, functional products require efficient and stable supply chains to maintain high utilization rates of manufacturing. These characteristics are illustrated in Table 12.2.

Table 12.2. Efficient versus Responsive Supply Chains

	Physically Efficient Process	Market-Responsive Process
Primary purpose	Supply predictable demand efficiently at the lowest possible cost	Respond quickly to un predictable demand in order to minimize stock-outs, forced markdowns, and obsolete inventory
Manufacturing focus	Maintain high average utilization rate	Deploy excess buffer capacity
Inventory strategy	Generate high turns and minimize inventory through the chain	Deploy significant buffer stocks of parts or finished goods
Lead-time focus	Shorten lead time as long as it doesn't increase cost	Invest aggressively in ways to reduce lead time
Approach to choosing suppliers	Select primarily for cost and quality	Select primarily for speed, flexibility, and quality
Product-design strategy	Maximize performance and minimize cost	Use modular design in order to postpone product differentiation for as long as possible

Source: Fisher (1997).

However, Fisher's framework deals only with demand character-istics of the products. Lee (2002) suggests a framework, which in-cludes uncertainties evolving around the supply side of the products. Thus mature technology, several supply sources, few quality prob-lems, few process changes, and reliable suppliers characterize a sta-ble supply process. On the other hand, an *evolving* supply process is characterized by rapidly changing technologies, limited choice of suppliers, potential quality problems, and an immature production process. The difference between stable and evolving supply charac-teristics is shown in Table 12.3.

Table 12.3 . Stable and Evolving Supply processes

Stable	Evolving
Lean breakdowns	Vulnerable to breakdowns
Stable and higher yields	Variable and lower yields
Less quality problems	Potential quality problems
More supply sources	Limited supply sources
Reliable suppliers	Unreliable suppliers
Less process changes	More process changes
Less capacity constraint	Potential capacity constrained
Easier to changeover	Difficult to changeover
Flexible	Inflexible
Dependable lead time	Variable lead time

Source: Lee (2002)

When supply side and demand side uncertainties are combined four different supply chain strategies emerge. This is shown in Figure 12.2. On the vertical axis is shown two extremes of supply uncer-tainties for stable versus evolving supply processes. On the horizon-tal axis is shown Fisher's two extremes of demand uncertainty for functional versus innovate products.

Although, functional products often also have stable and mature supply process, this is not always the case. For example, innovate products such as fashion clothing or pharmaceuticals might have a stable, and reliable supply process, while functional products such as coffee, wine, and oil, might have evolving supply process due to weather conditions or political events.

Figure 12.2. Demand and Supply Uncertainty Strategies

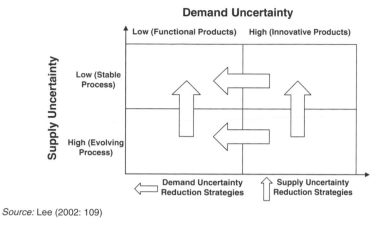

Source: Lee (2002: 109)

According to Lee (2002), firms can follow two different strategies to improve supply chain performance. One strategy is to reduce demand uncertainty, e.g. by information sharing or close collaboration in the supply chain. Wal-Mart's and Procter & Gamble's CPFR arrangement is an example. Another strategy is to reduce supply uncertainty, e.g. by going from single sourcing to dual sourcing, by involving suppliers in new product development, or by sharing safety stocks of critical items with suppliers. Dell has, for instance, thus built up a supplier park near its assembly plants in Limerick, Ireland, where the major suppliers (e.g. Intel, IBM, Cisco, packaging materials companies, and others) have built-up stocks to replenish Dell's assembly lines with short notice.

Supply Structures for Customization

Customer requirements for flexibility, agility, cost efficiency and product variety force companies to reconfigure their supply chains to focus more on collaboration with external partners. The design of a supply chain influences how a manufacturer of complex products organizes and coordinates a stream of innovative products through supply chain and architectural design strategies vis-à-vis sourcing, manufacturing, and distribution strategies. Visionary firms, such as

Dell Computer and Cisco, have developed product design and supply chain restructuring as a means to achieve mass customization and direct access to customers. There are three interrelated and complementary strategies for designing and managing supply chains: mass customization, postponement, and modular product designs.

The Dell Direct model becomes a prototype of an extended company incorporating these strategies. Dell maintains a very low work-in-progress inventory to minimize excess and obsolete inventory. Key suppliers are expected to maintain safety stock close to assembly and deliver to Dell to fulfill individual customer orders. The process is enabled by modularity in the computer design, and common industry standards that allow complete component interchangeability (Dell 1999).

Mass Customization

Mass customization emerged as a concept in the late 1980s. Generally, it emphasizes the need to provide products to meet customers' individual needs through unique combinations of modular components (Feitzinger & Lee 1997, Gilmore & Pine 1997, Kotha 1995, Pine 1993, Pine et al. 1993, Yovovich 1993, Greene 1999). The goal is to produce customized products (to achieve economies of scope) at low cost (to gain from economies of scale). It allows companies to penetrate new markets and capture customers whose special needs could not be met with standard products (Lee 1998).

Product variety is driven by customer demand. The capability to design and to produce products in collaboration with customers provides mass-customizing firms with the ability to capture valuable new knowledge. Pine (1993) argues that the best way to achieve mass customization is to create modular components that can be configured into a wide variety of end products and services. High commonality of modules lowers inventory levels and reduces risks of obsolete inventories, lowering inventory costs (van Hoek & Commandeur 1999). Mass customization has been implemented with computers, Levi's jeans, bicycles, Nike shoes, and Smart cars, to name a few well-publicized cases.

Customization has a balancing point where a customer order shifts into a more aggregated form for production, to achieve economies of scale in manufacturing and procurement. Without customization, orders are considered en masse, products are standardized and delivered in large quantities to industrial users or retailers as customers. One step further, orders are delivered directly to customers in individual quantities or with special processing as logistics postponement. If we allow customer orders to go one step further, products can be customized in manufacturing as manufacturing postponement. A further step would make changes in components. The point of postponement is how far upstream the customer order will penetrate the supply chain.

Supply Chain Integration

In a seminal work, Lawrence and Lorsch (1967) defined integration as, »the quality of the state of collaboration that exists among departments that are required to achieve unity of effort by the demands of the environment«. While this definition refers specifically to organizations, our emphasis here goes beyond the firm to encompass external organizations within a supply chain.

Stevens (1989) identifies four stages of organizational integration. Stage I describes fragmented operations within the individual company. Stage II focuses on limited integration between adjacent functions, e.g. purchasing and materials control. Stage III is the internal integration of the end-to-end planning in the individual company. Stage IV represents the true supply chain integration, including both upstream to suppliers and downstream to customers.

Lee (2000) outlines three dimensions of supply chain integration: information integration, coordination and resource sharing, and organizational relationship linkage. Information integration refers to sharing information and knowledge among supply chain members, including sales forecasts, production plans, inventory status, and promotion plans. Coordination and resource sharing involves realignment of decisions and responsibility in the supply chain. Organizational relationship linkages include communication between members, performance measurement, and sharing common visions and objectives. Here we confine supply chain integration to information and organizational integration.

Information Integration

Information integration permits management to make decisions for the operations of the organization as a whole and not as fragmented, isolated functions. Similarly, supply chain participants can be linked by information technology, thereby facilitating trans-organizational decisions and operations, such as logistics activities, inventory management, order fulfillment, production planning, and delivery planning and coordination.

Integration coordinates the disparate functions among supply chain partners in organizationally and geographically dispersed locations. Information integration involves sharing knowledge and information among members and may involve sharing design and manufacturing data among suppliers, focal manufacturers, and customers. It may also include sharing forecast and delivery scheduling data among the focal company, suppliers, carriers, and other supply chain members.

Suppliers and customers may be invited to participate in product design teams to resolve issues in product and process design. Information integration makes inventory and production visible throughout the supply chain resulting in a more congenial climate for collaborative planning and forecasting. Supply chain members, as a result, can reduce inventory buffers by postponing costly value-adding operations, provide better customer service, with more flexible responses to customer demand, and reduce uncertainty.

Electronic communication infrastructure becomes prerequisite for timely and efficient information exchange among partners. It enables manufacturers to provide immediate access to information about production requirements, giving vendors and transport providers access to planning and control systems to arrange deliveries without transcribing transactions. With on-demand computing, all parties are able to use common software without data re-entry, simplifying the coordination process. This infrastructure also facilitates and reduces the cost and time for financial transactions.

Other tools, such as bar codes, RFID, electronic messaging, and conferencing, and electronic data interchange (with a level of detail never thought possible even a few years ago), have transformed coordination of the supply chain. It has unleashed gains in productivity and rapid response and made the supply chain a dominant form of business organization. The fruits of information integration, such as reduced cycle time from order to delivery, increased visibility of transactions, better tracing and tracking, reduced transaction costs, and enhanced customer service offer greater competitive advantage for all participants in the supply chain. A summary of the characteristics of information integration is shown in Table 12.4.

Table 12.4. Characteristics of information integration in a supply chain

What goes on	How Accomplished
• Information and knowledge exchange takes place regarding: • Design and development • Process management • Planning/control • Technology exchange and adaptation • Resource and risk sharing	• Information sharing often using same or compatible systems and procedures • Linking computer information systems using new information and communications technology including EDI/XML/RF etc. • Pooling resources among supply chain partners (PLM) • Collaborative planning, forecasting and replenishment (CPFR) • CAD/CAM • Learning from one another

Source: Bagchi & Skjøtt-Larsen (2003:92)

Organization Integration

Inter-organizational integration encourages partners to become more entrenched as members of a network, instilling a sense of identification and enables trust as the essential element of a partnership in an integrated supply chain. Trust in turn promotes collaboration and decision delegation, and reduces independent organizational behavior among supply chain members, thereby reducing the need for protective strategies such as safety stocks and individual searching for alternative strategies. An additional objective of organizational integration is not merely to resolve conflicts, but to recognize and avoid potential conflicts and/or divergences of interest in advance and devise preemptive governance to forestall them. The objective is to create a supra-organization where individual members of the chain behave more as a unified entity sharing ideas, skills, and culture alike. Organizational integration among partners is crucial to long-term survival as a supply chain.

Supply chain management requires actors –decision-makers at all levels of the hierarchy in multiple organizations to work together to achieve a common goal. Managing coordination among managers therefore assumes significant importance. Organizational integration facilitates information-sharing both within and across firms. The supply chain as a process also requires a process orientation rather than the traditional hierarchical structures of individual organizations. The main characteristics of organizational integration are shown in Table 12.5.

Table 12.5. Characteristics of organizational integration in a supply chain

What goes on	How Accomplished
• Risk, cost, and gain sharing • Sharing ideas and institutional culture • Shared decision-making • Skills sharing • Building trust • Creation of bonds	• Extensive communication at all levels • Joint design teams • Process and quality teams • Incentive realignment • Exchange of personnel • Joint performance measurement and problem resolution • Managing coordination among supply chain members • Participation in joint technical and management forums • Decision delegation—chosen member in the supply chain deciding for the whole supply chain • Joint cultural programs to achieve better bonding

Source: Bagchi & Skjøtt-Larsen (2003:93)

Other Forms of Strategy

There are other general strategies for the supply chain but the two that have received the most attention are time and risk management.

Time management emphasizes reducing the time cycles for order processing, the supply cycle and product development. The logic is straightforward, the shorter the cycle, the less inventory and the greater the ability to respond. The means to achieve time compression include on-line information system, rapid transport modes, JIT and lean production, and even elimination of process stages such as the point-of-sale data collection and cross-docking procedures of Wal-Mart that eliminate inventory at the distribution center. These strategies usually involve more than a single discipline. The case of cross-docking requires information and coordination with production, carrier trailer loading and the distribution center to coordinate activities: for example to coordinate the sequence of store deliveries as products flow from factory to distribution center to store.

Risk and agility management are closely related in that they anticipate the unexpected. The difference lies in the magnitude and duration of the event. Agility is the ability to adapt to essentially short-term occurrences, such as changes in customer orders, responding to production failures and weather. Risk management involves contingency planning to avoid failures such as inadequate or excess inventories leading to financial exposure. More significant is the prospect of more permanent system failures such as the lightning strike in 2000 in New Mexico (USA) on a semi-conductor factory (Lynn 2005). It led to a production stoppage for two customers: Ericsson and Nokia. Ericsson had relied on the New Mexico plant as a single supplier and could not build its new cell phone without the chip. The company faced a shortfall in revenue of $450 million for that year. However, Nokia had lined up a backup source of supply and was able quickly to ramp up production elsewhere and gain market share from Ericsson.

The strategic solution is to plan for these events in advance. The difficulty lies in anticipating possible events. Some like weather have a measurable probability of occurrence. Others have a systemic characteristic of unanticipated effects. Perrow (1984) calls them *normal accidents*, leading to unintended consequences. One solution is to establish second sources for critical components, or to establish an alternative supply chain for other suppliers to step in and restore operations.

Toyota encountered a supplier failure that was more than threatening to its production line and other suppliers in the keiretsu stepped in to produce the components, cooperating, sharing information and knowledge. The risks of supply chain disruptions are growing in a modern world characterized by political and economic turbulence, highly specialized manufacturing, demand and supply uncertainty, short product lifecycle, and a fast technological pace. When firms are outsourcing a large proportion of value creation to external partners, who on their side are outsourcing to specialized subcontractors, it is often difficult for the original firm to know, who actually are producing the outsourced components.

An illustrating example was a one-minute long earthquake in 1999 in Taiwan, which resulted in a severe disruption of the supply of semiconductors to the electronic industry all over the world because most of the semiconductor production was concentrated on this island.

Strategy of Functional Areas

Supply chain strategy often takes on a limited perspective, bounded by specific disciplines either singly or in limited combinations. The view is limited by the circumstances or position of the decision-maker seeking to establish long-term cost savings or services. At this point, we examine a few of these strategies and the questions they raise under the guise of information technology, manufacturing distribution and logistics.

Information Technology

Except possibly as users, most supply chain managers do not deal with information systems technology. In dealing with information technology, the technical side often appears to be overwhelming. However, this technology also presents social issues that must be resolved. It also changes organizations, perhaps more than any other area of the supply chain. Information technology has requires establishing common practices in inter-organizational systems, starting with coding and reporting systems. On-demand software such as a single ERP system utilized by all members under common rules becomes a unifying force.

For the strategic use of information technology, managers must confront four questions:

- *Who?* Referring to the person/role and organizations with access to the system, whether suppliers, customers or service providers.
- *What?* Is the information content, whether raw data, selected input to software, inter-organizational verbal communication, or even face-to-face contact in electronic conferencing? In the case of data, there must be agreement on common coding across an industry, as in Rosetta.net for the electronics industry.
- *How?* Indicates the method of transmission, transitioning or probably usually via the Internet. This involves net congestion, message security, and protection against unauthorized intrusion. It also should be concerned with redundant pathways in case one should fail.
- *When?* Should data be available immediately to all users or stored in a common database so data for the same event will be consistent

when it is accessed? Globalization also presents timing problems, particularly when human contact is required. When Asia is a 12-hour clock difference from Europe, it can be an advantage when engineers can work on the same project around the clock, from both ends of the earth. However it can also strain the normal workday cycle.

Procurement

Procurement as we have learned is involved increasingly with collaboration and networks. The more closely that suppliers are bound to each other and the focal firm, the closer the supply chain is to becoming a supra-organization. The advantages lie in strengthening the community with its ease of coordination. However there is also a disadvantage in that suppliers may become captives of the system. A counter-strategy would maintain supplier independence through active pursuit of additional external business connections.

Opposed to this is the rise of the virtual organization, where chains can be connected for one specific product, then dissolved afterward or to remain latent until another opportunity appears (Chandrashekar & Schary 1999). The Internet facilitates this with its ease of connection. Rules for engagement can be established in advance. The effect is to create extreme flexibility, at the expense of long-term collaboration and integration. The limitation is that suppliers dealing with several supply chains may be forced into different procedures and processes for each relationship.

Manufacturing

Manufacturing strategies such as lean manufacturing and just-in-time are well-covered in the literature. Where the supply chain becomes important to manufacturing lies in its network role. There are several issues.

Supplier relations have product boundaries. The migration from components to subsystems creates uncertainty about where one product begins and ends. The impact is not only on the production task but also in the relationships. The subsystem imposes its own standards, requiring careful product specification and coordination.

Outsourcing has created production networks, where what was formerly performed in house is now outsourced. It reduces capital requirements for the focal firm, shifts responsibilities, and increases flexibility in selecting other sources of production. It changes the nature of manufacturing from single plant operation to coordination of delivery. That is how lean production is kept across organizational boundaries.

Flexibility as we have stressed is essential in the supply chain. Flexible production is an important component of a flexibility strategy. Tracking to coordinate processes, rapid changeovers and managing a complex component flow are part of this strategy. Economies of scale remain important but smaller order sizes and product ranges require an economic balance while meeting the need for the flexibility of the marketplace.

Location is traditionally an effort to minimize transport costs and time for delivery both for inbound materials and components and for outbound production. It is subject to local restrictions and taxes. In a global economy, it also becomes a way to capitalize on low-wage labor, take advantage of local expertise, to meet minimum requirements to do business in particular markets or to avoid tariff charges and restrictions. It may involve political risk and restriction such as local content rules. Individual factories may become part of rationalized global production networks, each specializing in particular products, but supplying a global market. An almost universal shift toward higher value products makes transport costs less important relative to other factors making location a multi factor decision.

Distribution

Surprisingly, distribution strategy has been neglected in much of the discussion about supply chain strategy. The supply chain is also a demand chain. Customer orders trigger the actions that energize supply.

The decision whether to serve customers directly or indirectly through distributor or retailer intermediaries affects the configuration of the supply chain. Direct distribution of small orders requires specialized distribution centers, known as *fulfillment centers*, oriented toward individual customers. These are distinctly different from conventional distribution centers, which handle products in pallet loads and are oriented toward efficiency. The same division also applies to carriers affecting the size of shipments and the number of delivery points for a given vehicle. Seldom can the two operate from the same facilities, and therefore require separate operations. However, it should be recognized that some companies would operate in both markets.

The conventional retail scene has also changed with the advent of »big box stores.« The quantities taken in require material handling operations at the store level. The chain stores that dominate this sector force high levels of logistics service along with low prices. Materials handling in a distribution channel also forces the development of packaging and unit load strategies to carry the product from production directly to the retail shelf, even to the point of utilizing the unit load as the display shelf. Package and load initiatives have originated with retailers that have sought to minimize their own costs at the expense of their suppliers.

The Internet has changed distribution. Consumers can compare prices and product availability directly, putting pressure on prices and forcing cost reductions on retailers. Even high cost items such as cars, TVs, and computers are sold over the net, with delivery and set up as an adjunct service. Retailing over the Web emphasizes direct shipment, but some retail operations will combine them by encouraging customers to order over the Web, but deliver at the store.

The Internet has also changed customer relationships, with a new field, *customer relationship management* (CRM), emerging to manage orders and inquiries. The concept is still developing, but CRM becomes the first and usually the only point of contact between the customer and the entire supply chain. CRM has demonstrated the power to shape product demand through suggesting changes to customer orders to guide decisions towards products in stock. It can also make the supply chain transparent, indicatings progress in processing and inventory in stock.

Logistics

Logistics is dominated by decisions made elsewhere in the supply chain. Shipment size is determined in marketing by the type of customer being served. The speed of delivery is determined by product value and factors such as urgency and perishability surrounding the order. The traditional view is a trade-off between inventory and modal choice in transportation. High value products go by air because of distance and value where transport costs are a small proportion of product value. Low value products use slower, more economical modes such as ship, truck, or rail because there is usually less urgency at a lower cost.

Routings can also become strategic decisions influencing the choice of carriers. Routings that avoid changes of carriers or terminals are preferable because of difficulties in managing the process, delays in movement and controlling individual shipments. Some routings are used to avoid delays such as port congestion or vulnerability to weather or disruption.

Functional shifting can become advantageous in logistics. An industry, third party logistics providers, has emerged to provide services that shippers find it more costly or less effective to provide for themselves. The transit time itself can often be combined with processing en route, such as merging components from various sources into a complete product. Some express companies will perform marketing tasks such as operating websites and performing product support services.

Conclusion

The supply chain is a set of networks, making a discussion of strategy different in perspective than for any individual organization. It is more exposed to external influences, because it is a collective of individual organizations. It is a combination of a functional task network, a relationship network, an information system, and a logistics network. It is also part of a larger network of influences from competitors, technologies, and other elements in the environment. It also reflects the industry in which it is embedded, evolving from growth to maturity and from fragmentation to vertical integration.

Strategic initiative from the supply chain depends on the context. It may create competitive advantage or become subordinate to product and market. While most discussion of strategy in the supply chain has been internally oriented, it is important to be aware of shifts in the external world. The supply chain will change as a result of these forces along with internal actions by management.

13. Supply Chain Planning
– Modeling Considerations

*»Despite 50 years of study in operations research models and
methods, plus numerous examples of successful modeling
system implementations, we are still in the early days of
applying them in a pervasive and enduring manner
to a range of supply chain applications.«*

(Shapiro 2001: 55)

Designing and managing the supply chain requires the evaluation of
system changes before they are implemented. The supply chain has
a large number of potential trade-offs, over many variables and
many different states. Planners require a comprehensive view to ask
»what if« questions. Planning for supply chain management involves
two stages: the corporate plan and the supply chain plan (Rushton
& Saw 1992). Corporate planning becomes the basis for supply
chain planning and strategy development. At the same time, supply
chain planning should contribute to corporate planning. The initial
stages of the supply chain plan establishes the decision environment:
external elements of supply structure, markets, country and regional
constraints including exchange rates, customs duty, transport capability and capacity, options in information technology and internal
elements of production capacity, customer service policies and corporate organization. It should also identify objectives, product characteristics and sourcing constraints.

These elements become the basis for quantitative strategy planning
models to evaluate strategic options. The role of these models is to
provide a rational basis for developing and evaluating strategic options. The analyst, in effect, has a dialogue with the model. A good
planning model represents enough features of the situation to permit
the planner to investigate alternatives and to test their sensitivity to
underlying assumptions. To use models well, however, managers
should have a general understanding of how models are developed,

their relationships, as well as the problem setting. Models should be used to gain insight into the problem and possibly to narrow choices. Although outputs may indicate solutions, the results should be balanced by judgments that assume familiarity with the methods.

The dilemma of supply chain planning lies in defining the scope of any proposed model. Scope determines the extent of the model. It means the extent, how many stages in a complex supply process should be included, and the level of detail necessary to shape the direction of the system. Few models have the capacity to span both production and distribution networks within a single structure. Furthermore, no model can be comprehensive enough to replace other more detailed planning models and processes within the supply chain.

Models are essential for planning the supply chain (Figure 13.1). Potential actions have uncertain outcomes. Environments are turbulent. There are too many potentially actionable variables. The only prescription where there are no guidelines for managers is to experiment (Eisenhardt & Brown 1998), testing variables to see what happens. Models provide a selective representation of reality, they provide a means to experiment, without endangering the organization. Models also have a subjective dimension. As Schrage (2000) points out, we shape our models and they shape our perceptions.

Figure 13.1. Supply Chain Modeling

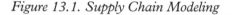

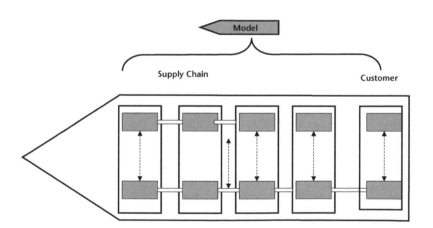

Models have several uses in supply chain management:

* to test alternative courses of action
* to determine optimal policies
* to predict future events
* to communicate concepts and relationships
* to determine optimal location choices.

Testing alternative actions through the use of models is a form of »what if?« scenario. Selecting parameters for change makes it possible to explore the impact of decisions before they are made. In some cases and with specific forms of modeling, certain relationships can be optimized within the system. It may also be possible to predict when future events will occur, if not in time but under certain identifiable conditions. Models also provide a means to communicate. Because model parameters can be changed, it is possible to express concepts and relationships through the structure of the model. By expressing the outcomes in precise terms, it may also be possible to identify who will be affected and how, enabling negotiation to proceed with a greater understanding of the consequences.

In some respects, models can be better than information systems at conveying relationships among variables. They encourage experimentation to discover and learn what issues and variables are salient. Schrage (2000, p. 136) notes: »Consumers of innovation discover – rather than know – what new products and services they need.«

Reasons for Quantitative Modeling

For any researcher or manager dealing with SCM issues, it is an added advantage to understand how complex issues can be modeled quantitatively. SCM crosses the boundaries of the firm to include suppliers and customers, which makes its analyses even more challenging. Quantitative modeling enriches qualitative models by translating key elements into measurable terms. Many ERP firms, such as SAP, were created based on quantitative methods of analyzing SCM. There should be a combination of quantitative and qualitative methods in solving such complexity. Models are extremely useful in analyzing situations that are expensive or when data collection is time consuming. For instance, research on global outsourcing can be very expensive (i.e. costs incurred from traveling, translation, coordination, etc.) and it might take years to collect the data. The data might also become outdated if the researched phenomena involve products and/or services with short life cycles. Examples of SCM models include: supply chain concepts (Min & Mentzer 2004, Cohen et al. 1989), supply and demand chain management (Heikkilä 2002), product characterization model (Payne & Peters 2004), supplier involvement in product development (Clark 1989, Ragatz et al. 2002), vendor managed inventory (Waller, Johnson & Davis 1999, Kaipia, Holström & Tanskanen 2002), to name a few.

In *Modeling the Supply Chain*, Shapiro (2001) describes two types of quantitative models: descriptive and normative. Descriptive models include (Shapiro 2001: 11):

- Forecasting models
- Cost relationships
- Resource utilization relationships
- Simulation models

There are many alternatives to formulate descriptive models, such as through econometrics, mathematical modeling, computer programming, etc. Simulation models, for instance, are mathematical descriptions of operations or problems. They can be simple or developed in detail. The simulation is only a description of an operation at one particular time or for a specified time period, operating under one set of parameter estimates. They do not provide »best« answers, only one answer at a time, reflecting a particular set of numerical assumption values. It is possible by successive runs to move towards better solutions, but an optimal result cannot be guaranteed. For example, product flow has been simulated to understand the impact of supply chain disruptions on demand fulfillment and inventory over distance (Levy 1995).

While descriptive models seek to help managers understand the functional relationships between the internal and external elements of the firm, normative models (often referred to as optimization models) identify norms that the firm should strive to achieve. According to Shapiro, supply chain modeling incorporates concepts from several management disciplines, such as

- Strategy formation and the theory of the firm
- Logistics, production, and inventory management
- Management accounting
- Demand forecasting and marketing science
- Operations research

Strategy formation and the theory of the firm is closely related to Porter's value chain model (Chapter 2), transaction cost economics, network theory (Chapter 3), and resource-based view of the firm (Chapter 12). For instance, quantitative models have been devised to investigate: supplier switching costs and vertical integration (Monteverde & Teece 1982), portfolio management of supplier relationships (Olsen & Ellram 1997), product architecture strategies for SCM (Mikkola 2007, Fixson 2005, Lee & Sasser 1995), mass customization, postponement and modularity in supply chain (Squire et al. 2004, Yassine et al. 2004, Mikkola 2007, Mikkola & Skjøtt Larsen 2004, Fine, Golany & Naseraldin 2005), to name a few. These models are devised to (Shapiro 2001: 16):

- Analyze a company's resources in selecting plans to expand efficient resources while reducing inefficient resources.
- Address strategic uncertainties in demand when determining resource acquisition plans for a firm's supply chain.
- Analyze a firm's product line by simultaneously considering new product introductions, life cycle management, and product retirement.

Logistics, production, and inventory management models are related to operational strategies internal to the firm, such as purchasing, manufacturing, and production strategies. These models are often covered in the field of operations management (Slack, Chambers & Johnston 2004, Chase, Jacobs & Aquilano 2006, Heizer & Render 2006, Basu 2004).

Management accounting models in SCM are concerned with a firm's performance in relation to cost issues, as described in Chapter 11. For instance, MacDuffie, Sethuraman & Fisher (1996) provide a model of manufacturing performance. Shapiro (2001: 20) mentions that there are two essential tasks in order to create cost data for and from supply chain models:

- Development of causal cost relationships of direct and indirect costs
- Computation of transfer, product, and customer costs from an optimal solution to a supply chain model

Demand forecasting and marketing science models typically apply statistics and econometric models in order to project future demand from historical data. Forecasting can be classified into four types:

- Qualitative – use of subjective techniques.
- Time series analysis – prediction of the future based on past data
- Causal relationships – use of quantitative techniques to understand the relationship between the variables and respective relationship
- Simulation – use of computer-based techniques that allow the researcher to make assumptions about the internal variables and external environment in the model

The mostly used forecasting techniques and common models are shown in Table 13.1.

Table 13.1. Quantitative forecasting techniques and models.

Time Series	
Simple moving average	A time period containing a number of data points is averaged by dividing the sum of the point values by the number of points.
Weighted moving average	Specific points may be weighted more or less than the others, as seen fit by experience
Exponential smoothing	Recent data points are weighted more with weighting declining exponentially as data become older.
Regression analysis	Fits a straight line to past data generally relating the data value to time. The most common fitting technique is least squares.
Trend projections	Fits a mathematical trend line to the data points and projects it into the future.
Causal	
Regression analysis	Similar to least squares method in time series but may contain multiple variables. Basis is that forecast is caused by the occurrence of other events.
Econometric models	Attempts to describe some sector of the economy by a series of interdependent equations.
Input/output models	Indicates the changes in sales that a producer industry might expect because of purchasing changes by another industry.

(Chase, Jacobs & Aquilano 2006: p. 514)

Operations research (OR) is perhaps the most scientific approach to analyze SCM quantitatively, as it is mostly concerned with mathematical models that are furthermore developed into computer programs and algorithms to calculate, mostly, optimization problems. OR has been applied, to great extent, to assess most of the SCM topics mentioned in this book (cf. Tayur et al. 1999). One of the most applied optimization model is linear programming (LP). In addition to optimization models, Analytic Hierarchy Processing (AHP) method has been applied to select site location (Saaty 1980).

The overall purpose of quantitative modeling is to establish the role of strategic models in supply chain management, and fit modeling into a general management view, without becoming involved in the in-depth technical aspects of model development. In the following, few simple methods are illustrated to describe how SCM can be modeled quantitatively.

Modeling Sourcing Strategies – Statistical Approach

As companies grow from national borders into the international arena, the complexity of SCM increases as these firms seek to understand the challenges behind globalization and sourcing strategies. Before strategies can be planned, companies need to have a reasonable general understanding about the factors that are shaping global sourcing practices. One of the most used quantitative methods of this management discipline is the application of statistics and econometric methods. Trent and Monczka (2003), for instance, modeled integrated global sourcing with surveys. Their exploratory research investigated the critical success factors, benefits, results, progress, risks, methodologies, best practices and lessons learned from the development of global sourcing processes and strategies. Their methodology included the following phases:

- Phase 1 – Identification of the following critical areas for future studies (from 150 companies): global sourcing, strategic sourcing, and the use of electronic business systems
- Phase 2 – Random selection of corporate-level respondents from a database for sending surveys. A total of 1,800 surveys were sent worldwide. A total of 162 usable surveys were received, which is

equivalent to 9% response rate. A test for non-response bias between the first and last third of the sample was carried out to test that the early participants and later participants did not display statistically different means or characteristics across a number of variables.

From the survey, five sourcing levels are determined (Table 13.2):

Table 13.2. Worldwide Sourcing Levels.

	Levels		Worldwide Sourcing (Percentage of firms)	
			2003	In 3-5 years
	I	Engage in domestic purchasing only	13.4	7.8
International Purchasing	II	Engage in international purchasing as-needed	21.3	7.8
	III	international purchasing as part of sourcing strategy	31.0	14.3
Global Sourcing	IV	Integration and coordination of global sourcing strategies across worldwide locations	18.1	15.6
	V	Integration and coordination of global sourcing strategies with other functional groups	16.2	54.5

(Trent and Monczka 2003)

In addition, they identified changes due to worldwide sourcing in terms of the following performance categories and corresponding changes (Table 13.3):

Table 13.3. Performance changes due to worldwide sourcing.

Performance category	Average changes
Total purchase price	Decreased 15 %
Total cost of ownership	Improved 11 %
Supplier quality	Improved 6 %
Delivery cycle time	Lengthened 5 %
On-time delivery performance	Improved 3 %

A t-test was also performed on the average means in order to compare the overall average across 16 benefits for global sourcing firms and international purchasing firms. It was revealed that the overall average across the benefits for the global sourcing firms is 30% higher than those for firms engaged in international purchasing.

The authors predict that although most firms are expected to advance toward Levels IV or V by 2006, many are also expected to fail due to a lack of understanding concerning the complexities of integrated global sourcing. Hence, a total of 32 critical success factors (CSF) were also identified. Next, they performed another t-test to statistically compare different CSF ratings between international purchasing and global sourcing segments. The highest rated CSFs, in order of importance, include:

- Personnel with required knowledge, skills and abilities
- Availability of required information
- Awareness of potential global suppliers
- Time for personnel to develop global strategies
- Availability of suppliers with global capabilities
- Ability to identify common requirements across buying units
- Suppliers who are interested in global contracts
- Operations and manufacturing support of the global sourcing process
- Internal customer buy-in to global sourcing contracts
- Direct site visits to suppliers

Modeling the Inventory Management – EOQ Model

All manufacturing firms face the following questions about inventory volume: »How many of component X should be ordered?«, »When should they be ordered?« and »How can inventory costs be minimized?«. The economic order quantity (EOQ) model is the simplest of models that addresses inventory management. It deals with everyday's inventory management decisions, specifically with how much of any item to order and when its stock needs replenishing. A visual inventory level profile is illustrated in Figure 13.2.

Figure 13.2. EOQ model.

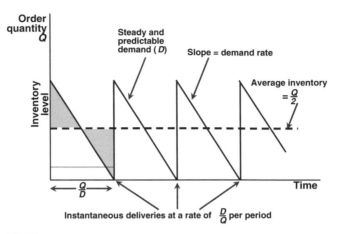

(Slack et al. 2004)

Although the assumptions of EOQ model have been considered un-realistic by many, it is a simple example that illustrates how a model is built. The assumptions of EOQ model are (Chase et al. 2006, p. 597):

- Demand for the product is constant and uniform throughout the period.
- Lead time-time from ordering to receipt is constant.
- Price per unit of product is constant.
- Inventory holding cost is based on average inventory.
- Ordering or setup costs are constant.
- All demands for the product will be satisfied.
- No back orders are allowed.

The first step of EOQ includes the development of a mathematical function that includes the variables comprising of total annual cost:

Total =	Annual +	Annual +	Annual
annual cost	purchase cost	ordering cost	holding cost

Annual purchase cost = (annual demand)*(cost per unit) = D*C

Annual ordering cost = (number of orders placed)*(cost of each order) = $(\frac{D}{Q})*S$

Annual holding cost = (average inventory)*(cost per unit for holding and storage) = $(\frac{Q}{2})*H$

$$TC = DC + \frac{D}{Q}S + \frac{Q}{2}H \quad \text{Equation 13.1}$$

where

TC = Total annual cost
D = Annual demand
C = Cost per unit
Q = Quantity to be ordered
S   = Setup cost or cost of placing an order
R = Reorder point
L   = Lead time
H = Annual holding and storage cost

Notice that average inventory is represented as Q/2. This is because the areas of the shaded areas are the same (Figure 13.2).

The next step is to find the optimal order quantity, or the order quantity at which total cost is the minimum. In simple calculus differential language, it means to take the derivative of total cost (TC) with respect to (Q) and set it to zero:

$$\frac{dTC}{dQ} = \frac{H}{2} - \frac{DS}{Q^2} = 0 \quad => \quad Q^2 = \frac{2DS}{H}$$

$$EOQ = Q_{optimal} = \sqrt{\frac{2DS}{H}} \qquad \text{Equation 13.2}$$

The reorder point (R) becomes average daily demand times $(\bar{d})$ lead time in days (L) (because the model assumes constant demand and lead time):

$$R = \bar{d}L$$

$$\text{Time between orders} = \frac{EOQ}{D}$$

$$\text{Order frequency} = \frac{D}{EOQ} \text{ per period}$$

Aligning Supply Chain – SC Performance Model

As the supply chain becomes more integrated, and business processes more complex, firms are inevitably concerned with the following questions: »How can strategic, managerial, and operational performance be aligned?«, »How can the vision of a firm be translated to other business processes, including the customers and suppliers?«. Lambert & Pohlen (2001) address these issues with a framework for developing supply chain metrics, which aligns performance at each supplier-customer link within the supply chain. The following steps are involved in developing this framework (p. 8):

- Map the supply chain in order to identify key linkages
- Analyze each link by using customer relationship management (CRM) and supplier relationship management (SRM) – Economic Value Added (EVA) analysis is applied. An example of such application with CRM is illustrated in Figure 13.3.
- Develop customer and supplier profit and loss (P&L) statements – A combined customer-supplier profitability analysis is performed
- Realign supply chain processes and activities to achieve performance objectives
- Align non-financial measures with P&Ls – By converting activities into costs through activity-based costing (ABC), identifying any revenue or asset implications, and inserting this information into an EVA or P&L analysis.
- Compare across firms and replicate.

Figure 13.3. Application of EVA on CRM.

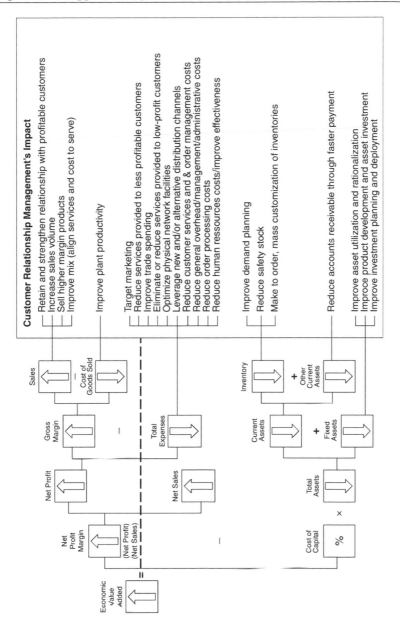

Figure 13.4. Measurement of Supply Chain Performance

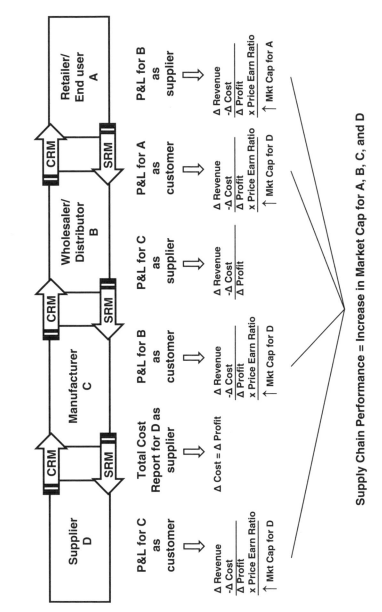

Source: Lambert & Pohlen (2001: 14).

Figure 13.4 illustrates how the resulting shareholder value and market capitalization across firms are compared, hence replicable to analyze every step at every link in the supply chain. It shows how profit and market capitalization can be measured cross four tiers of the supply chain.

Modeling the Demand Forecast – Exponential Smoothing

Why is forecasting important? Is it enough for firms to know how much inventory to order and respective costs based on historical data? Is newer demand information more relevant than older information? Exponential smoothing, for instance, forecasts the next period demand by taking into account the actual demand in the current period and the forecast which was previously made for the current period (Slack et al. 2004). In other words, the most recent occurrences are more indicative of the future than those in the most distant past. It is the most used of forecasting techniques, for the following reasons (Chase, Jacobs & Aquilano 2006: 521):

- Exponential models are surprisingly accurate
- Formulating an exponential model is relatively easy
- The user can understand how the model works
- Little computation is required to use the model
- Computer storage requirements are small because of the limited use of historical data
- Tests for accuracy as to how well the model is performing are easy to compute

The name 'exponential smoothing' is derived based on the fact that each increment in the past is decreased by $(1-\alpha)$. The smoothing constant alpha (α) determines the level of smoothing and the speed of reaction to differences between forecasts and actual occurrences. α is also referred to as the desired response rate, which is dependent upon management's reaction to how stable the demand is. A low value of α means the most recent period is weighted very lightly compared with all other past observations (Lilien & Rangaswamy 1998). For example, if α is 0.05 (assuming that the long-run demand for the product under study is relatively stable), the weighting is:

Weighting at α = 0.05
Most recent weighting = $\alpha(1-\alpha)^0$	0.0500
Data one time period older = $\alpha(1-\alpha)^1$	0.0475
Data two time periods older = $\alpha(1-\alpha)^2$	0.0451
Data three time periods older = $\alpha(1-\alpha)^3$	0.0429

The equation for a single exponential smoothing forecast is:

$$F_t = F_{t-1} + \alpha(A_{t-1} - F_{t-1}) \qquad \text{Equation 13.3}$$

where
F_t = The exponentially smoothed forecast for period t
F_{t-1} = The exponentially smoothed forecast made for the prior period
A_{t-1} = The actual demand in the prior period
α = The desired response rate, or smoothing constant.

Modeling the Resource Allocation – Linear Programming

One of the goals of production is to grow. It has been estimated that only 10% of the companies succeed at sustaining growth (Christensen & Raynor 2003). What are these companies doing right? Due to financial pressures to sustain the desired performance, firms try to optimize the utilization of their resources. How can a firm optimize its valuable assets (such as resources) with respect to trade-offs? Linear programming (LP) models this challenge. LP is a mathematical technique aimed at helping managers plan and make decisions relative to the trade-offs necessary to allocate resources (Heizer & Render 2006). The problem must be formulated in a particular mathematical structure, basically that all variables must be linear. All product movements must be considered as one commodity. Within that structure, the model provides an optimal or a close-to-optimal solution. The advantages of optimizing models are that they not only indicate a potential decision, but their optimizing behavior provides a basis for comparison. A computer run becomes a benchmark for comparison with others, where the user has changed some of the assumptions. LP has been applied in (Chase, Jacob & Aquilano 2006: 51):

- Aggregate sales and operations planning
- Service/manufacturing productivity analysis
- Product planning
- Product routing
- Vehicle/crew scheduling
- Process control
- Distribution scheduling
- Plant location studies
- Material handling

According to Heizer and Render (2006: 693) all LP problems have the following properties in common:

- LP problems seek to *maximize* or *minimize* some quantity. This property is referred to as the 'objective function' of an LP problem.
- There must be constraints that limit the degree to which the objective can be pursued.
- There must be alternative courses of action to choose from.
- The objective and constraints must be expressed in terms of linear equations or inequalities.

Although LP can be extremely complex, the following example illustrates the formulation of a simple product-mix LP problem (taken from Heizer & Render 2006):

The Shader Electronics Company produces two products: (1) Shader Walkman and (2) Shader Watch-TV. The company would like to determine how many units of each product it should produce to maximize the overall profit given its limited resources. Table 13.4 lists the number of hours required to assemble each of the products, respective profit per unit, and labor-hours available in the assembly department.

Table 13.4. Data summary of Shader Electronics products.

Department	Hours Required to Produce 1 Unit		
	Walkmans (X1)	Watch-TVs (X2)	Available hours this week
Electronic	4	3	240
Assembly	2	1	100
Profit per unit	$7	$5	

The next step is to translate the data into equations. The following notations are used:

X_1 = number of Walkmans to be produced
X_2 = number of Watch-TVs to be produced

The LP objective function in terms of X_1 and X_2 becomes:

Maximize profit = $7 X_1 + $5 X_2

Similarly, the mathematical relationships illustrating the constraints of the resource problem become:

First constraint: Electronic time used is $\leq$ Electronic time available

$4 X_1 + 3 X_2 \leq 240$ (hours of electronic time)

Second constraint: Assembly line used is $\leq$ Assembly time available

$2 X_1 + 1 X_2 \leq 100$ (hours of assembly time)

Graphically, the constraint functions are illustrated in Figure 13.5. To find the optimal profit, we need to solve the constraint equations:

$4 X_1 + 3 X_2 = 240$
$2 X_1 + 1 X_2 = 100$

This gives the following values: X_1 = 30 Walkmans and X_2 = 40 Watch-TVs.

Maximum profit = $7 X_1 + $5 X_2 = 7(30) + 5(40) = $410

Figure 13.5. Graphical Representation of Constraint Functions.

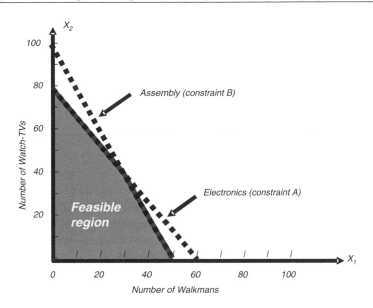

Modeling the Demand Variability in SC – Bullwhip Effect

Procter & Gamble and Hewlett-Packard have examined the order patterns of their best selling products. They realized that, while there is not much variation in their customers' demand, the inventory and back-order levels fluctuate considerably across their supply chains (Lee 1997). This 'swing' in the supply chain is referred to as the Bullwhip Effect. It describes the fluctuations in a supply chain caused by demand distortion (i.e. the variance between the actual orders downstream and upstream members of supply chain) and variance propagation (i.e. the variance of orders as they move upstream). As the demand information moves further away from the customer in a supply chain, the greater the information distortion. This also means that the perceived demand and forecast error also increase.

Since the main cause of Bullwhip Effect is related to variability in every step of the supply chain, we want to quantify or model such variability. Simchi-Levi, Kaminsky & Simchi-Levi (2003) propose the following quantitative model. It models a two-stage supply chain: (1) a retailer (who places an order) to (2) a manufacturer. The retailer reviews the inventory every period and places the order every t period of time in order to bring its inventory to the target level. The retailer faces a fixed lead time (L), which means that an order placed by the retailer at the end of period t is received at the start of period $t + L$. At this point, the order-up-to point (or reorder level) is:

Order-up-to point $=$ (avg. demand during lead time)$+$(safety stock)
$$= (L*AVG) + (z*STD*\sqrt{L})$$

L $=$ Lead time
AVG $=$ Average of daily (or weekly) of customer demand
STD $=$ Standard deviation of daily (or weekly) of customer demand
z $=$ Safety factor – a constant chosen from statistical tables to ensure that the probability of stockouts during lead time is equal to the specified level of service.

In reality, the inventory level at each order-up-to point varies during each period t, due to changes in current estimate of the average and the standard deviation. The estimation of the order-up-to point (from the observed demand) in period t becomes, y_t:

$$y_t = \mu_t L + z\sqrt{LS_t}$$

y_t $=$ Order-up-to point in period t
μ_t $=$ Estimated average of daily customer demand at time t
S_t $=$ Standard deviation of daily customer demand at time t

Let's also assume that the retailer uses the moving average forecasting technique to estimate the mean demand. This means that the retailer calculates a new mean and standard deviation based on the p most recent observation of demand, in every period. Then,

$$\mu_t = \frac{\sum_{i=t-p}^{t-1} D_i}{p}$$

$$S_t^2 = \frac{\sum_{i=t-p}^{t-1} (D_i - \mu_t)^2}{p-1}$$

D_i = Customer demand in period i

p = Previous observations of demand

The variability of orders faced by the manufacturer (placed by the retailer) $Var(Q)$ in relation to the variance of the customer demand faced by the retailer $Var(D)$, then, becomes:

$$\frac{Var(Q)}{Var(D)} \geq 1 + \frac{2L}{p} + \frac{2L^2}{p^2} \qquad \text{Equation 13.4}$$

The variability equation (Equation 13.4) tells us the relationship between L and p. For instance, when p is large and L small, the bullwhip effect due to forecasting error is negligible. In other words, the bullwhip effect increases as p decreases and L increases.

Another simulation model related to Bullwhip Effect is the Forrester Model (Figure 13.6). In this model, a small increase of 10% in retail sales passed through a series of stages: distributor, factory warehouse and factory. Each stage operated with a standard inventory reorder point discipline. Inventory would be consumed until it dropped below a pre-designated reorder point, releasing a replenishment order to the next stage where the process was repeated. Orders were the only source of information about demand available to each succeeding stage. This resulted in strong fluctuation in demand, increasing in amplitude as replenishment orders went up the chain. To meet this apparent surge in demand, the factory instituted overtime production, soon followed by lay-offs as inventory was replenished downstream. The model demonstrates the perils of using standard decision rules unsupervised by human judgment. The concept of the Industrial Dynamics model has also been used to demonstrate the dilemma of managers who must make stocking decisions without the benefit of information other than actual orders, as in the well-known »beer game« (Senge 1990).

Figure 13.6. Dynamic Behavior in the Supply Chain.

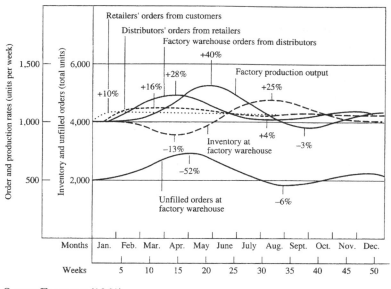

Source: Forrester (1961)

Further experimentation has focused on designing better information networks (Towill et al. 1992). These internally induced demand oscillations are reduced as information is shared across the supply chain. Fluctuation can be dampened almost completely if demand at the point of final sale is transmitted instantaneously to manufacturing and distribution. Lee et al. (1997) have provided empirical verification, calling it »the bullwhip effect«. Their discussion points out that the problem extends beyond the timing of demand data release. Distortions entering in through data errors also contribute to the problem of misreading the market.

Modeling Product Architecture Modularization for Mass Customization

It is generally known that approximately 80 percent of the manufacturing cost of a product is determined by the design of the product

(Clark & Fujimoto 1991). Some companies rely on product design and supply chain restructuring as a means to achieve mass customization and distribution activities in a supply chain (such as postponement), in such a way that the customization steps that lead to product variety occur at the most efficient point of a supply chain and at the lowest total supply chain cost (Lee 1998).

One of the motivations behind modularization is the decomposition of complex tasks into simpler portions so that the tasks can be managed independently and to achieve the desired performance as a system. For instance, the design of an automobile can be decomposed into four levels of complexity: system (automobile), subsystem (powertrain, instrument panel, etc.), module (engine, power, and rotating blocks of powertrain), and component (gear box within the rotating block of the power train). How a firm decides to decompose its product architectures and related tasks is dependent on sourcing strategies and the extent of knowledge that the firm has about the system as a whole (Mikkola 2003).

In order to capture the complexities behind product architecture design choices (a NPD task) and SCM, Mikkola (2006, 2007) introduced the *modularization function* (Equation 13.5) to model these issues.

$$M(n_{NTF}) = e^{-n_{NTF}^2/2Ns\delta}$$ Equation 13.5

$M(n_{NTF})$ – Modularization function
n_{NTF} – Number of new-to-the-firm (NTF) components
N – Total number of components
S – Substitutability factor
δ – Degree of coupling

The modularization function is interpreted as follows. A given product architecture has N components that is the sum of standard and NTF components [$N = n_{STD-C} + n_{STD-NC} + n_{NTF-C} + n_{NTF-NC}$]. The specific ways in which components are linked through interfaces create a certain degree of coupling [δ], which is approximated as the average number of interfaces per component. The impact of substitutability of NTF components in product architecture modularity is captured through the substitutability factor [s], which is estimated as the number of product families made possible by the average number of interfaces of NTF components required for functionality. The lower the number of NTF components, the higher the degree of modularization.

Hence, a perfect-modular product architecture [$M(n_{NTF})$ = 1.0] does not have any NTF components. NTF components that can be used across product families have higher substitutability factor (hence benefiting from economies of substitution, reusability, and commonality sharing) than NTF components that are dedicated to one specific product family, hence increasing the degree of modularization.

The modularization function shows that the combined effect of the variables varies exponentially with any set of NTF components. Every time the composition of NTF is altered (such as with incremental innovations) the degree of modularity also varies. In many cases, the introduction of NTF components requires changes to other parts of the product architecture as well, hence changing the values of N and δ. If we simply assessed the degree of modularity based on the number of components (be they standard or NTF) and ignored the effects of interfaces (captured in δ and s) we may overlook the impact of interfaces on product architecture modularity (Mikkola 2006).

The usefulness of the modularization function was tested with Chrysler Jeeps Windshield Wipers (case illustration in Chapter 7) and Schindler Elevators (Mikkola & Gassmann 2003). For the WIPERs, the following data was collected:

Solid-State WIPER

n_{NTF} =19 components
(n_{NTF-C}=18, n_{NTF-NC}=1)
N = 60 components
s = 0.33 components/interface
δ = 9.85 interfaces/component
b = 31.7 %
$M_{solid-state}$ = 0.40

Silent-Relay WIPER

n_{NTF} = 17 components
(n_{NTF-C}=15, n_{NTF-NC}=2)
N = 57 components
s = 1.00 components/interface
δ = 9.94 interfaces/component
b = 29.8%
$M_{silent-relay}$ = 0.77

Graphically, the modularization functions of both WIPERs are shown in Figure 13.7:

Figure 13.7. The modularization functions of WIPERS.

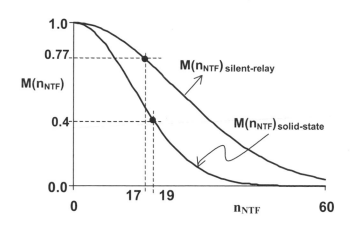

After testing the model with real cases, the *modularization function* was furthermore modified to capture the relationship between product architecture modularization and mass customization in terms of product variety realized through different components (Mikkola 2007). The modified function became:

$$MC[M(u)] = me^{-u^2/2Ns\delta}, 0.0 \leq m \leq 1.0 \quad \text{Equation 13.6}$$

Where m is an indicator of the degree of product variety present in a given product architecture, which is reflected on the number of components that are used for creating product variety (Mikkola 2007):

$$m = \frac{k_1 n_{STD-NON-CUST} + k_2 n_{STD-CUST} + k_3 u_{NON-CUST} + k_4 u_{CUST}}{N}; \quad 0,0 \leq k_1, k_2, k_3, k_4 \leq 1.0$$

$$N = n_{STD-NON-CUST} + n_{STD-CUST} + u_{NON-CUST} + u_{CUST}$$

$$k_1 = \frac{n_{STD-NON-CUST}}{\sum n_{STD-NON-CUST} \ (from \ aggregate \ MPS)} \quad k_2 = \frac{n_{STD-CUST}}{\sum n_{STD-CUST} \ (from \ aggregate \ MPS)}$$

$$k_3 = \frac{u_{NON-CUST}}{\sum u_{NON-CUST} \ (from \ aggregate \ MPS)} \quad k = \frac{u_{CUST}}{\sum u_{CUST} \ (from \ aggregate \ MPS)}$$

$n_{STD\text{-}NON\text{-}CUST}$:　number of non-customizable standard components
$n_{STD\text{-}CUST}$:　number of customizable standard components
$u_{NON\text{-}CUST}$:　number of non-customizable unique components
u_{CUST}:　number of customizable unique components

Where k_1, k_2, k_3, and k_4 are contribution percentages per component type that is used in all production lines, which can be obtained from the BOM and the master production schedule (MPS). The BOM lists the quantity of all the components used in a given product, including respective types and prices. The MPS lists the volume of components needed in production to satisfy demand, which also means that one can determine how often a particular component is shared with other products.

Limitations Related to Modeling

Models will always be with us. There appears to be no better way to understand the problems of the supply chain than by formulating a model structure and testing the variables contained within it. The ubiquity of computing resources makes potential for use very high. Supply chain managers can be more effective if they understand and use models to develop and test their decisions.

At the same time, models have limits. There are too many »soft« areas in supply chain management to rely on models alone to indicate direction. At best, they lay out choices based on their own structure and process. They may leave out important variables that cannot be quantified. They may imply organizational relationships that do not exist. In short, they must be used with caution.

Mathematical models, for instance, may not describe the reality, especially when the assumptions are incorrect. Furthermore, the complexity of the equations becomes extremely complex when additional variables are added. Although the application of statistics is the preferred methodology in SCM studies, it may not be the right approach, especially when generalization is not what the researchers want to investigate. For these reasons, both quantitative and qualitative models should be applied concurrently to assess the problem in hand.

The deeper understanding of SCM from quantitative modeling perspective is gaining increasing attention in Europe. For instance, in 2004, a European workshop was held in Germany to share perspectives on research methodologies in SCM. The contributions from the workshop were compiled into a book, *Research Methodologies in Supply Chain Management* (Kotzab et al. 2005).

The stumbling block of the past was data. The development of IT and specifically XML and ERP makes data more accessible. Geoffrion & Powers (1995) project more efficient algorithms. This, combined with the great expansion in computing power, makes models more accessible. At the least, they provide a powerful tool for communicating.

With any modeling exercise, assumptions are made in terms of variables and data collected. This is necessary in order to make accurate descriptive models, although it does not ensure the accuracy of the decisions made by managers. Hence, quantitative models and related systems are often complemented with qualitative counterparts.

14. Managing the Complexity of the Global Supply Chain

*»Organizations that can realize the full potential of
globalization will see dramatic revenue growth.
Those that can't will lose market share«.*

(Diana Farrell 2004).

Almost every supply chain is international to some degree. There
are always materials, components, or services originated in another
country that enter into the final product of the supply chain. The
global concept of the supply chain however is more than incidental.
It deliberately recognizes the necessity to supply markets in multiple
national markets, often using overseas production or contractors.
The global network is more than an extension of the domestic supply chain. It is more complex, faces a diverse set of environmental
conditions, and is inherently more difficult to understand and manage. It also deals with a global economy in transition from national
autonomy to an integrated system of producing, trading, and consuming, driven by technology, and where the vision of the ultimate
goal is also changing.

What makes the global supply chain different from the domestic
supply chain? The major differences appear to lie in higher environmental and structural complexity (Guisinger 2001). Environmental complexity encompasses a rich variety of dimensions, of
political and foreign-exchange risks, cultural and geographical differences, variations in legal systems, and differences in infrastructure. Structural complexity refers to the number of distinct businesses, functions, organizational forms, markets, and products and
their variety that the firm must manage and control.

In one way, it becomes audacious even to consider managing
systems of this degree of complexity across the world. On the other
hand, it is taking place now with increasing acceptance of the de-

mands on management to achieve immediate results in connections and product flow.

Some of the major challenges a firm faces in a globalized world, are:

- Supplying a unique value proposition to customers around the world.
- Meeting intensifying competition from around the world.
- Adapting to multiple national environments with differing cultures, political and economic systems, business practices, tax and legal systems.
- The global politics of economic and trade relationships.
- The availability and level of infrastructure in transport and telecommunications.
- The complexity of managing an extended network of suppliers, production plants, intermediaries, and customers in the supply chain.
- The impact of geography: time and distance and the location of markets.
- Responding to changes in monetary exchange rates by shifting production to lower cost sites, with the consequent changes in network configurations and routings.

The problem is illustrated in Figure 14.1. First, the most important differences relate to the customer. The global supply chain must come as close as possible to meeting specific country market requirements through products and services matched to individual customer requirements. Second, facing competition places pressures to seek out the most efficient sources of supply. This drive for efficiency often conflicts with matching customer preferences. Third, the supply chain must adapt simultaneously to multiple constraints posed by the environments in which it operates. All of these are changing rapidly along with the world economy. Fourth, the immutable constraint of distance and transit times affects the dynamic response of the supply chain as a system. The management task is immense: to coordinate a complex system when the sheer scope challenges the ability to control it.

Figure 14.1. Global Issues

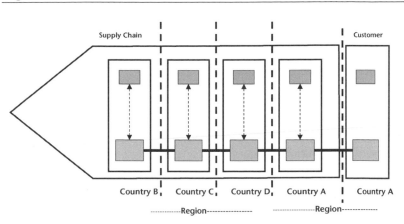

Three elements make the global supply chain possible: Changes in global economic policy and the technological revolutions in transport and telecommunication. The trend to lower tariffs and removal of non-tariff barriers plus the development of regional trading communities, such as the European Union and ASEAN, encourage international trade and investment. The development of air cargo, motor carriage and ocean container transport extend the reach of the system to new areas, and make the physical movement of goods easier and cheaper than ever before. Finally information technology and telecommunications, including ERP systems, electronic documentation, and tracking systems, make it possible to coordinate operations across the globe. Together they have changed the entire perspective on global markets and supply.

In this chapter, we first discuss the environmental complexity affecting the development of the global supply chain. The second section examines the structural complexity and its impact on the ability of the supply chain to accommodate this environmental challenge. Third, we shift to the supply chain itself. It presents issues both parallel and different from those of the international corporations it serves. The final section looks at logistics issues in international commerce. With high turbulence within the international arena, the emphasis is not on current development, except for overall understanding, but to suggest direction for a more durable framework for strategy in the supply chain.

The Environmental Complexity
of the Supply Chain

The global environment embraces a long list of possible topics. Even a shorter list affecting the supply chain must be selective in scope. This list includes political and cultural issues, information and communication technology, legal systems, and labor markets. We emphasize those with the most direct effect. There are obviously others, but the reader should look elsewhere (e.g. Dicken 2003, Lynn 2005, Plenert 2002).

Political Issues

There are several aspects to politics in global supply chains. One is protectionism, a second is trade liberalization through the World Trade Organization, a third is the development of regional trade and unification through for example: ASEAN, EU, Mercosur and NAFTA. All of these have drawn criticism because of opposition to multinational corporations. The attacks have centered on labor rights, losses of jobs, environmental issues, the free movement of capital, and the inability of any one country to control the multinational corporations. Despite avowals of commitment to free trade and the free flow of capital, local and national governments play an influential role in the development of the global economy. Emerging market economies often use protectionism through high tariff barriers and direct controls to limit internal competition and encourage locally based technology. They may also seek to attract industry through direct subsidies and special financing arrangements as Ireland did for several years to encourage specifically targeted industries and corporations to locate there. The Taiwanese government built a semiconductor industry by encouraging investment in wafer foundry facilities twenty years ago. Today, almost all semiconductor chips manufactured for global markets is done by only two firms in Taiwan, TSMC and UMC (Lynn 2005).

The W*orld Trade Organization* (WTO) is an agreement among countries to liberalize trade and investment. The WTO potentially provides a basis for eliminating discrimination and other barriers in trade, although currently has encountered difficulties in reaching consensus in specific areas. It replaced the highly successful General

Agreement on Tariffs and Trade that enabled global trade in the years following World War II. Countries that are party to the agreement must agree to pursue lower tariffs, unrestricted flow of capital, and enforcement of intellectual property rights.

In 2001, China became the fourteenth member of the WTO, and in 2007 Vietnam also joined the WTO coalition. As a result, the United States has granted them permanent most-favored-nation status in trade and tariff relations. Quotas on textiles and clothing will be phased out in accordance with the Agreement on Textiles and Clothing (ATC), other quotas will be phased out later in accordance with negotiated schedules. China and Vietnam can now resort to the WTO dispute settlement mechanism to protect their own trade interests, and participate in multilateral negotiations on trade rules and future trade liberalization. Nevertheless, to illustrate the persistence of an older pattern, the EU decided in 2006 to implement anti-dumping duties on shoes produced in China in order to protect shoe production in Southern Europe.

The underlying trend is to move from individual country barriers toward regional arrangements without barriers among countries within the agreement, and higher barriers to those outside. The intent is to build a regional self-sufficiency. Both the United States and the EU have used a tariff provision known as *generalized systems of preference* that allow less developed countries to sell products within the allowing regions without tariff barriers. This was intended to encourage less-developed countries to attract investment and further their own development.

The pressure of exchange rates forces supply chains to respond to *economic* incentives of subsidy and tariff protection. Tariffs also act as disincentives, which we discuss in more detail later. Exchange rates are of major importance because they change the cost relationships of countries and regions, and therefore change the movements of the physical products, although this normally takes place over time. Capital availability also has a strong influence on location as a partial explanation for Silicon Valley as an attractor for high-tech industry. At the same time, the high cost of labor has encouraged companies that locate there to establish production somewhere else, usually in Asia.

The EU is the strongest regional agreement, dismantling barriers to the free movement of labor, capital, goods and services with the member states that from 2007 include a total population of about

500 million people and 27 countries across Europe with a possible future enlargement to include Croatia, Macedonia, and Turkey. The result has been to establish a common market across national boundaries. The agreement abolishes tariffs and non-tariff barriers, and establishes universal technical product standards within the Union. Certain areas of the EU have become attractive because of low wages combined with educated labor forces, but all within the tariff protection of the EU.

The North American Free Trade Agreement (NAFTA) is an arrangement among Canada, Mexico, and the United States to develop free trade and industry within the combined area. NAFTA involves tariff reductions and ease of movement of goods and capital across borders. To qualify for low- or no-tariff treatment, a minimum of 60 percent of the work on the product had to be done within NAFTA. This resulted in large investments in production facilities from Japanese and European companies not only in Mexico, but also in the United States and Canada, to make sure that they would receive »national« treatment within the trade bloc (Lynn 2005). NAFTA however is not immune to pressures from low-wage countries outside of the agreement. NAFTA is also not intended to be an exact parallel to the EU. For instance, free movement of labor is not a NAFTA objective because of political issues within the United States and Canada.

Mercosur is an effort to increase trade among five countries: Argentina, Brazil, Paraguay, Uruguay, and Venezuela, with Chile and Bolivia as associate members. The South American trade group encompasses 250 million people with a GDP of US $1.1 trillion. Tariffs within Mercosur are reduced and currencies were to be coordinated. There were two apparent objectives in developing Mercosur: One is more progress towards a free market and a second is constructing better transportation infrastructure in South America. Since 1999, negotiations about an association agreement between EU and Mercosur have taken place. The association agreement should encompass three main areas: 1) Political dialogue, 2) cooperation in various sectors (research, culture, etc.), and a free trade agreement. However, failures to agree on reducing farm subsidies have until now prevented the deal to be achieved.

ASEAN includes Brunei, Cambodia, Indonesia, Laos, Malaysia, Myanmar, the Philippines, Singapore, Thailand, and Vietnam. The ASEAN region has a population of about 500 million, and a gross domestic product of almost US $ 700 billion in 2005. The aims of ASEAN are: to accelerate economic growth, social progress, and cultural development in Southeast Asia, but also to promote peace and stability in the region. ASEAN continues to develop cooperative relations with its Dialogue Partners, including China, India, the European Union, Japan, and the United States. The ASEAN Free Trade Area is now in place. It aims to promote the region's competitive advantage as a single production unit.

Social Issues

Social criticism of world trade has directly involved supply chain issues. In 1999, the former UN Secretary General Kofi Annan challenged world business leaders to »embrace and enact« the *Global Compact*, both in their individual corporate practices and by supporting appropriate public policies. The Global Compact operational phase was launched in 2000, involving three areas:

- Human rights protection and avoidance of abuses,
- Labor practices including collective bargaining, elimination of forced labor, abolition of child labor and elimination of discrimination
- Environmental support for precautionary steps, taking environmental responsibility, and supporting development and diffusion of environmentally friendly technologies.

In 2004, the Secretary-General announced a fourth area: anti-corruption, business should work against all forms of corruption, including extortion and bribery.

Phil Knight of Nike Corporation, the subject of much social activist criticism commented on the complexity of complying with these standards, »Nike and thousands of other companies have a monumental task defining what our global responsibility is, and how to act on it, in many host countries. The Global Compact provides a proper framework« (Knight 2000).

Other international organizations, including International Labor Organization (ILO), OECD, World Bank, and the EU, have developed initiatives to define ethical guidelines for multinational corporations operating in developing countries. Recently, a Global Reporting Initiative (GRI) was established as an independent, international organization, affiliated with the United Nations, with a mission to develop, promote, and disseminate globally applicable Sustainability Reporting Guidelines. Sustainability reporting encompasses a corporation's public account of its economic, environmental, and social performance in relation to its operations, products, and services.

Corporate Social Responsibility (CSR) has become common in many mission statements and annual reports from multinational corporations. The concept has many definitions and is often linked with overlapping concepts, such as corporate citizenship, triple bottom line, corporate accountability, and corporate greening. A widely accepted definition of CSR is (Marrewijk (2003:102): »...company activities – voluntary by definition – demonstrating the inclusion of social and environmental concerns in business operations and in interactions with stakeholders«. CSR relates to transparency in financial reporting, sustainability reporting, and opportunities for stakeholder dialogue. Prominent corporations implementing CSR in their global supply chains include: IKEA, LEGO Company, Johnson & Johnson, and Novo Nordisk. Thus, IKEA has within the last few years changed its supplier strategy from short-term relationships with many suppliers to long-term relationships with fewer suppliers. Whereas IKEA previously demanded a certain level of environmental and social responsibility of their suppliers, the company is now developing these issues together with their suppliers. In implementing IKEA's codes of conduct (IWAY), the company spends much time explaining to and showing suppliers how to improve their non-compliance issues. This approach signals to its suppliers that it has trust in their ability to implement IKEA's codes of conduct requirements (Pedersen & Andersen 2006).

The supply chain is influenced first by corporate strategy, shaped by products, technology and markets, and also by the moves of competing supply chains. It is further influenced by Porter's (1990) »diamond:« the governmental policies, factor markets, competition, supporting industries and demand in both home and host country markets. They define the competitive climate for the corporation. While Porter uses the diamond to explain how particular kinds of competitive advantage arise in home countries, it would appear to be useful in explaining how functions or product divisions of a multinational corporation become established in other countries as well.

Examples are electronic companies locating facilities in Silicon Valley in California, pharmaceutical companies setting up headquarters and R&D departments in Switzerland, or software companies in India. Developing nations offer both opportunity and problems. Opportunities come from potential market development and low labor costs. Interestingly they offer potential for innovative supply chain development as there is usually no legacy of past business practice. The problems however are usually a lack of infrastructure and exposure to criticism from social issues.

Infrastructure can be defined in terms of education, transport, and telecommunication. Education for the work force appears to be a crucial issue, particularly in dealing with modern technology. Parallel to capital, research and development has been a magnet for particular industries. The stimulus provided by local universities and institutes, innovation and educated labor forces create their own attraction. Some Southeast Asian countries have invested heavily in educational institutions to attract new investment beyond basic manufacturing.

Transport infrastructure consists of highways, carriers, ports and airports and access to major international routes. It can vary from primitive to highly sophisticated operations, depending on social investment and the economic level of the country. The lack of adequate transport has been a major impediment to economic development for India, China, and large parts of Africa.

Multinational corporations and their supply chains are also subject to social criticisms, including their independence from control by host governments, their ability to influence local economies, their power over local labor markets, and their disregard for the environment. They have been accused of destroying natural resources, creating pollution, and not establishing adequate safeguards in their production processes. Companies with labor-intensive products, such as clothing and textile companies, have come under fire by charges of exploiting labor markets in low-wage host countries. At the same time, they introduce and upgrade necessary skills for host countries to achieve higher levels of development and standards of living. A prominent example is India that has been able to attract IT projects from Western companies, further developing India's IT competencies and created new job opportunities for many Indian IT professionals.

The pursuit of low labor costs also creates a trade-off dilemma. Seeking the lowest costs can mean locations with long transit times to markets, leading in turn to higher costs of inventory in destination markets to compensate. Further, this may also lead to inadequate response to changing demands. The alternative is to locate at higher cost locations but closer to the market. This has led to solutions such as using Turkey and Ukraine for garment production sites close to Western European markets, or Caribbean sites for the US market. Another is to maintain plants within the United States or EU for even faster response, even at a slight cost penalty, but with substantially reduced transit times and lower inventory levels. A prominent example is the successful Spanish fashion company Zara that produces about 50 percent of its products in its own network of more than 20 factories, located in or near its headquarters in La Coruña.

Cultures

Cultures influence supply chains in several ways: institutions, organizations, data collection and interpretation, contractual practices, educational levels, attitudes towards labor, and labor practices. This last appears, not least of all in sources of innovation. Research and development has been fostered through education, as a magnet for investment by particular industries. Local universities and institutes become a basis for innovation. Ultimately, an educated labor force creates its own attraction.

Culture can be defined in many ways. A few include education, management practice, national identities, work values, and relationships. Education suggests institutions. Host countries may invest in education in hope of attracting foreign investment. A variety of management questions are associated with cultures. National identities may also be involved in attracting foreign investment, to secure new technologies, identify working interaction or to build a local industrial base. Work values reflect on organization of and motivation within the local labor force. Culture also determines the roles of organizations and contracts, and the flexibility of the supply chain to respond to change through changes in partnerships and contract terms.

Within management practice, several dimensions influence international organizational behavior: language, context, task orientation and time, power and information flow (O'Hara-Devereaux & Johansen 1994). Together they define management culture.

- *Languages* of course can be a major problem, not only between countries, but also between professional subcultures, even though English has generally been adopted as the language of business. Even so, the choice of language often determines the outcomes of meetings and negotiations.
- *Low* or *high context* becomes related to specific tasks and determines the information requirements for communication. In the case of low-context, that the explicit message carries the whole burden of communication. High context includes inclusion of relationships, history, and status.
- *Task-related time* is divisible into monochromic or polychronic time. In its simplest terms, monochromic time refers to single task management, while polychronic time is analogous to multitasking, carrying forward several activities at the same time.
- *Time orientation* influences negotiations and decision-making because it looks either to past experience or to the present and future.
- *Relative Power and equality* determine organization structures, individual roles and sensitivity to communication.
- *Information flows* describe the path and media for information within and between organizations and how decisions result in completed actions. Media describes text, graphics and means of presentation in addition to its technological context.

Social cultures lay the foundation as the primary system of thinking, feeling, behaving, and values. Above these are layers of professional and organizational cultures. Organizational cultures are the most adaptable, changeable with the group. They serve a purpose in providing application of operating behaviors and stability. Social cultures change slowly, emphasizing a need to recognize differing cultural patterns.

In general, North American and northern European social cultures tend to be low context, monocultured, forward-oriented, with low hierarchy in organizations. In contrast, Asian, Latin and southern European cultures stress relationships (high context), are polycultured, respect past experience and history and power relationships. In the supply chain, information technology follows a North American mold, low in context, and monochromic. It thus goes against the social cultures of major parts of the world. It suggests a need to build and maintain personal relationships between organizations parallel and complementary to e-mail and other electronic media.

Inter-organizational relationships become the »glue« of the global supply chain. They go beyond market buyer-seller relationships to establish personal connections. Networks of relationships precede and hold primacy over the development of electronic information systems (Yeung 1997). Yeung describes how Hong Kong-based TNCs use family and other personal connections, relying on personal assessment at governmental, external network and intra-firm levels to enable overseas expansions. However an article in the Economist points to a shift toward more reliance on professional management brought in by better access to information and contracts (Economist 2000). Personal networks may be a result of specific preconditions, and lose their value when those conditions change.

Information Technology

Information technology (IT) plays a crucial role in operational coordination. As we have noted, it has been a major driver behind the movement to globalization. IT however requires standard data and operating practices, requiring uniformity of management practice. Beyond the general problem of supply chain information systems, are specific issues related to crossing national borders. The global system includes networks, communications links, and software. The problem areas focus on governmental control, ability to access the system, the rate, and extent of adoption of technology, the nature and volume of data, and time coordination. Not all partners or even subsidiaries adopt a uniform technology at the same time, limiting the level of communication within the global system to the lowest common standard. Other communication links then become necessary.

Global networks as presently configured are often costly investments in server-client networks of computers feeding local PCs. Both hardware and software must be compatible, and changes must be consistent throughout the system. Web-based networks in prospect with resident software, coupled with thin client terminals are a smaller capital investment with reduced software changes. With widespread adoption of fiber-optic cable and high-speed lines, data transmission becomes less a problem. Advances into wireless modes such as satellite transmission make access to remote areas easier, even in emerging countries that have not invested in fixed lines. EDI is often used because it provides security. However, the Internet is already available in most areas, easier to use, and offers flexibility of use. Internet security on the Internet presents problems but will be improved with promising solutions.

Software specifically designed for global supply chain applications appears to focus on international logistics applications. New solutions involve integrated applications that route and manage shipments, link to customs tariffs and currency exchange data, interact with governmental customs, and produce documentation.

For emerging markets, the system problems emphasize delayed adoption more than technical or cultural hurdles such as the transition from paper to computer-based systems. Infrastructure is not as much of a hurdle as it was prior to the introduction of wireless and satellite networks. Computer systems and protocols have become standardized. The Internet opens up communication still further, beyond transactions to meet other communications needs.

Curiously, some companies have found it easier to install complex management software such as ERP systems in plants in emerging economies, because new systems do not have to adapt to older legacy systems, and their associated practices.

The insurmountable barrier is time, the time zone differences around the world. This however can be an advantage in programming and engineering design, when different groups around the world can work on a project and then shift the work to others in other time zones as a global product development team. This has the effect of accelerating the outsourcing of programming and other IT-related services to for example India.

The Structural Complexity of the Global Supply Chain

There is a distinction between international logistics and the global supply chain. Logistics involves movement and inventory of products. International logistics and international trade have close parallels. *International logistics* manages product movement across national or regional boundaries, including transport, inventory, customs barriers, telecommunications, and related topics. Part of logistics involves domestic processes within host countries. The other part is international. The global supply chain adds the structure and location of activities and organizations to supply and distribute products to global markets. It determines where logistics take place. Both domestic and international logistics together with the procurement, production, and distribution structure become part of the supply chain.

Globalization is a continually evolving complex of interrelated processes, rather than an end-state (Dicken 2003). Following Dicken, (p. 12) a process-oriented approach and distinguishes between two distinct processes:

- *Internationalizing processes.* These involve the simple extension of economic activities across national boundaries without major change in organization or practice.
- *Globalizing processes.* These involve not merely the geographical extension of economic activity across national boundaries, but also the functional integration of globally dispersed activities. The organization becomes transformed from a domestic unit into one that is connected to the world at large.

Options

There are many ways to become involved in the global economy: export and import trade, direct foreign investment, strategic alliances, partnerships, and other contractual relationships. *Export and import trade* may involve different modes of transport, inventory and coordinating communication. *Direct foreign investment* in production plants, joint ventures, or sales subsidiaries overseas can require both domestic and international movements. *Alliances and partnerships* bring in outside parties for production or distribution, without direct investment. *Licensing* gives the right to produce or sell products, either as independent operations, or as part of global supply and distribution networks. The global supply chain may include all of these within a single network as components of a process of supply and distribution.

International business increasingly involves corporations that span national borders. These corporations follow a shifting orientation from international, multinational, and global companies to transnational companies. Each has a particular management style and involves a specific logistics commitment. International companies serve overseas markets through exporting. The other three have some production in other countries. The reality is that companies may actually be involved in all stages simultaneously, exporting part of their product lines to supplement those produced locally, supplying local markets from local production or meeting world demand from global production networks.

International Companies

The export orientation of the *international company* from a home base implies economies of scale or specialization in production that cannot be economically duplicated outside of the home country. Products are intended to cover an entire market. It may be at risk from lower cost competitors in other countries. Other dangers are that decision-making is removed from the market, that logistics may involve long transit times, customs duties and other barriers to trade. It is also vulnerable to local pressures for production.

Multinational Companies

Traditionally, *Multinational companies (MNCs)* have responded with products and production adapted specifically to local markets. Companies such as Nestlé operated as a set of local affiliate companies. Logistics was usually domestic, although there could be some support and cross-border products from other affiliates or the parent company. Decisions were decentralized and these affiliates sought out local opportunities. From a management perspective, knowledge of markets or processes also tended to be local. However, this picture has changed dramatically during the last decade. Production has been specialized in focused plants. National distribution centers have been centralized to a few regional distribution centers, corporate functions, such as procurement, logistics, and marketing, have been concentrated in headquarters, products have become more global with less adaptation to local markets.

Global Companies

By contrast, the *global corporation* treats the world as one integrated market. Production may take place from a home base or it may be localized to local markets, but becomes identical to that of the parent company. Products are standardized. Knowledge is centralized, and the role of affiliates is to implement strategies of the parent company. The consumer electronics industry operates in this mode, essentially relying on global standards to maintain product uniformity. Logistics is also largely localized, although supplementary support from other affiliates and the parent may also create international movements to fill in product lines. Examples of global companies are: Nike, Sony, Samsung, Lenovo, LEGO, and Ikea.

Transnational Companies

The *transnational company (TNC)* combines the market flexibility of the MNC with organizational flexibility. Ultimately it becomes an integrated network embracing a variety of organizational forms with differentiated roles and responsibilities. Several writers describe the TNC as a »global-local«, or »strategic localization« solution (Mair 1997, Doz & Prahalad 1991), meaning that the corporation sets global strategy, but adapts to local conditions. The TNC is basically a knowledge-generating organization, holding a few core competencies, but varying the roles of national organizations to meet local requirements. Management decisions are decentralized. Not only production, but also product research and development and even entire product divisions can locate anywhere within the network. Supply chains can also specialize by product line and operate independently of each other, although there may be economies of scale and scope in combining. The dominant characteristics of TNCs are the dense connections of their communication and physical networks and the emphasis on joint development and sharing of knowledge. Logistics provides the physical connection as a combination of local domestic and international operations. Examples of TNCs are electronic manufacturing services, such as Flextronics and Solectron, which offer complete design, engineering, and manufacturing services to OEM customers worldwide.

The difference between global and transnational corporations stems from the need to adapt to local conditions (Storper 1997). A global corporation assumes that resources and market preferences are essentially similar, and that if labor costs become too high, the company can move its production to other countries. A TNC on the other hand recognizes differences in both resources and local markets. One country may be attractive for production because of a technology base, another because of its proximity to local market preferences.

Interpreting this difference in a supply chain context means that supply chain configurations and their resulting logistics support must be managed as unique systems even within the same corporate umbrella. This makes the task of coordinating operations more difficult than for global companies. Supply chain management also becomes localized, and corporate direction can only be one of general control over a series of separate portfolio operation.

There are also differences between developed and developing countries from the perspective of inbound investment. Most current investment in developed economies goes to the acquisition of existing firms. In developing countries, it is new plants and equipment. In both cases, it is driven by a search for economies of scale in the manufacturing process, research and development and management. There are further shifts, from large firms in traditional industries to new entrants, smaller in scale but more oriented to new technologies and from stand-alone affiliates toward incorporation in integrated production networks.

Global Production

The classification above implies production networks. Global market pressures place specific requirements on production networks to achieve lower cost, higher quality, more flexibility, rapid delivery, and faster product introductions. Dicken (2003:246) proposes four types of geographical orientation, which a company might adopt for its production units. This is shown in Figure 11.2.

One type (a) is *globally concentrated production*, where the products are exported to world markets. One example is the Danish audio-visual solutions manufacturer, Bang & Olufsen, which produces most of its products at one location in Denmark, distributing directly to retail stores or even to final customers. A second type (b) is host-market production, where each production unit produces a range of products aimed for their own national market. An example is the Danish-Swedish dairy company, Arla Foods, which produces dairy products for the national markets in the four Nordic countries A third type (c) is product specialization for a regional market. Each production unit produces only one product or product group for sale throughout a regional market. An example is the Swedish roll bearing manufacturer, SKF, that has product-focused plants specialized by type and size for roll bearings in Europe. A fourth type (d) is transnational vertical integration, where each production unit performs a separate part of a production sequence. The output of one plant is the input of the next plant including crossing borders. This type of production organization is common in the automobile, clothes, and electronic industries.

Figure 14.2. Four Types of Geographical Orientation

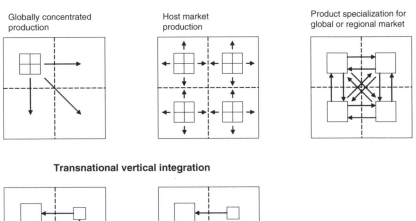

Source: Dicken (2003)

Several specific factors influence manufacturing locations. One study identified product process, product technology, competitive priorities, the need for market responsiveness and firm-specific characteristics, including the depth of international experience (Du Bois et al 1993). Products under development were produced closer to R & D facilities where coordination and control over production were easier and changes could be implemented more easily. Competitive priorities include supply cost, quality, dependability, and flexibility. Market responsiveness was particularly important in industrial markets where delivery times were important, such as JIT. Local manufacturing was necessary to penetrate some markets, even in the absence of specific tariff rules. Logistics costs related to the ratio of value-to-weight strongly influenced the decision. Low value products were produced close to markets, high value products could be produced at longer distances from the market because they can bear higher transport costs.

Ferdows (2000) proposed another view. The reasons for concentrating production in the home country are declining tariff barriers, the increasing sophistication of both production and product development, and the need for world-class suppliers. Against these are the need to establish links to markets, low-cost labor, and local research and product development. He suggests six roles for foreign factories:

- *Offshore* – oriented to low cost for export.
- *Source* – also oriented to low-cost but with more responsibility for local procurement.
- *Server* – to supply local or regional markets.
- *Contributor* – also supplying local markets, but with added responsibilities for product and process development.
- *Outpost* – a primary role is to collect information from a locally advanced environment.
- *Lead factory* – creates new technologies, products, and processes for the entire company.

Factories migrate through successive roles as they gain capabilities, moving from internal improvements to build competent supplier networks, ultimately to become centers for global products. In the process, they may gain intangible benefits such as learning to improve customer service or new technologies. Ultimately they can strengthen networks through development and exposure to the stimuli of overseas environments, although that was not a specific part of this framework.

The Global Network

The global supply chain is more than direct ownership of production and distribution. It is also a network of relationships with both internal and external partners. It requires establishing relationships with organizations operating under completely different political, economic, and physical environments. These relations require close coordination despite these differences. The networks themselves become so extended that no manager can hope to achieve close control over more than a limited part of the entire operation.

The multinational enterprises become the cornerstone of the supply chain. It is an organizational structure that internalizes markets through transfer pricing mechanisms. It may not own most of the means of production, as Dell, Nike, and Cisco demonstrate. Nevertheless, it is constrained by its environment. It is more than an economic entity engaging in foreign value-adding activities. It is also a collection of sources of comparative advantage and location-bound endowments, operating as an »eclectic paradigm« (Dunning 1998). The latter can include physical resources, factor markets (labor and capital), research and development, management and technology. The eclectic paradigm can be summarized as OLI: a firm will introduce international production if it has

- Ownership-specific advantages
- Location-specific advantages to an overseas site
- Internalizing these advantages rather than to sell products in open markets or license them to others is more profitable

Guisinger (2001) suggests two modifications of the eclectic paradigm. One is to replace the I (Internalization) in the traditional OLI framework with M (Mode of entry) to encompass the various forms of international involvement, and not only control of a subsidiary. The other is to add a fourth domain of analysis, namely the adaptation of business processes to the international business environment.

Global Management

The global corporation and its supply chains face parallel management problems. Management asserts control over other organizations that often act with varying degrees of autonomy across national borders. This autonomy also spans functional areas, such as marketing, production, procurement and research and development. Further complexity is added with multiple products marketed to multiple national markets. The paradox is that customers are local, with specific product and sales requirements, while competitors are global, competing in individual country and regional markets. Marketing also recognizes that market segments now reach across national boundaries. There is a critical balance between local orientations for operations and global orientations for strategy.

The governing concept of global management is that solutions are unique, but that organizational structure must match strategy. The term *differentiated networks* describes this mixture, where individual subsidiaries have unique relationships with headquarters, determined by the environmental complexity and their local resources (Nohria and Ghoshal 1997), shown in Figure 14.3 When complexity and unique resources are low, the corporation and the supply chain follow economic logic of economies of scale and scope for efficient production. With strong local resources, subsidiaries join federations with substantial autonomy within the MNC. With complex environments and weaker local resources, the parent dominates in a global organization. When both complexity and resources are high, management must balance the organization through integration.

Figure 14.3. Global Corporate Structure

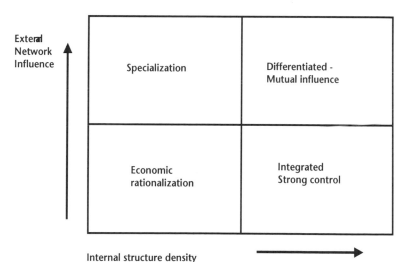

Source: Nohria and Ghoshal (1997)

Organizational Solutions

The supply chain adds complexity through its relationships beyond corporate boundaries. The structure of the supply chain itself becomes extended to a point where it becomes difficult to manage as a single entity. Markets involve traditional relationships where companies in different environments can deal with each other with differing mechanisms of contracts and trade. The supply chain however often requires integration forcing management to deal with the internal operations of affiliates and external partners in cooperation and collaboration. Even organizational units within the corporation often behave as if they are in a market relationship, negotiating over transfer prices and resources.

The global supply chain is both complex and extended in space and organization. There is little relevant guidance other than personal experience as preparation. Pressures on management tend toward fragmentation. Perceiving the full network is difficult, particularly in operating detail. The supply chain may require decisions that are counter-intuitive in the context of a single unit.

Meeting changing market demands within a fixed set of production facilities requires agility in production changeovers. Strategic options apart from the factory itself are reducing lead-time. Surviving garment manufacturers in the US use market proximity as a competitive advantage to achieve fast flexible response despite the higher costs of production. Capacity fluctuations can be met through redundant capacity within the production network.

Organizational solutions are not always clearly evident. Lateral management may be the closest solution. Strategy could be guided, at least to a point, through matrix organizations that manage headquarters-subsidiary relationships, with the addition of product dimensions. Matrix organizations build conflict into the organization as they add process on top of functional areas. Other solutions treat each product group as separate enterprises, the parent becomes a holding company controlling only financial and other overhead resources. Adding an additional product dimension takes the conflict one step further.

Leadership is particularly difficult with complexity and the span of activities. The ability to perceive problems is difficult, because of their variety, cultural divisions among partners and the sheer complexity of selecting from multiple options. Leadership begins with a global mindset (Jeannet 2000). The central vision should set direction and establish key relationships. The supply chain structure must match the global strategy of the TNC. Operating control may still be local. Some elements of control may be delegated to external partners. The management focus is on system design and coordination, with authority delegated to operating management, both inside and outside of the corporation.

Global Products

For many products, the global marketplace has arrived. Standardized products that are accepted by a global market become global products (Levitt 1986). Customers see an increasing number of products as essentially similar, used in the same ways to meet similar needs. They become commodities. The driving force behind this convergence is technology. The mantra is reliable, quality products at low prices, to gain market share, placing the focus on efficient quality production. This of course does not completely apply to all products. Some will remain completely local in orientation to meet market needs in individual countries. This appears to be particularly true for some, but not all food products. Others will be adapted to regional preferences or national legislation, such as automobiles and clothing. Japanese car producers such as Honda and Toyota have developed a regional orientation, even to establishment of research and development centers and production in both the United States and Europe. However, there will be an increasing number of products that are either standardized or adaptable for regional or global markets with minimal effort, such as electronic goods and multimedia.

Distance and time tend to influence three elements in the supply chain. First, it restricts the number of SKUs, forcing simplification of the product line. Recognizing that inventory levels reflect lead times, the cost forces attention to high turnover product lines. A second is the ability to respond rapidly to changes in market demand. This may result in dividing the production sequence by multiple locations with the stages of final production or assembly being located closer to the market. To some extent, this has taken place in garment production. For the US market, cloth production can take place in Southeast Asia, with final finishing done in Caribbean locations that are closer to the market. The third is the problem of matching capacity to changes in demand. The traditional solution has been to forecast ahead for longer periods. Nike for example will use six month forecast periods to set production schedules, recognizing that immediate response is not possible. Zara, on the other hand has been able to reduce time-to-market to about two weeks by centralizing most of its production and supplier networks in Spain.

Customization to meet local requirements has been one solution, starting with production of »raw« product in one location, to be configured in distribution centers closer to the market. Imbedded language instructions on copy machines, power supplies and automotive accessory items are candidates. Once the product is designed for modular customization, the supply chain question becomes a case of where and when to adapt to local markets (see Chapter 7).

Packaging includes two aspects. First is protection in shipping and storage under potentially poor climatic conditions. Ocean container shipping has reduced these in developed country markets, although they persist in other markets. Second, it must adapt to local markets. Package issues involve language, size and quantity. Language requirements in the US market have changed with NAFTA, packaging and instructions now come in English, French and Spanish. »Europacks« are now common in the EU, incorporating as many as six different languages. Other products, such as photographic equipment with wider geographic appeal, but smaller markets, often come with even more. Package sizes also differ and are related to materials handling requirements. They must be matched to different warehouse pallet sizes, Euro pallets versus US pallet sizes that determine case and smaller package sizes for retail display. Quantity is determined by local practice. American units are matched to dozens. Countries on metric systems use decimal sizes.

The outlines of strategy in a global market are becoming clear. Standard products around the world evolve towards commodities, subject to intense competition. Products that can be matched to individual customer preferences become the basis of competitive advantage. This results in the need to organize the supply process to make these individual adaptations. Competitive advantage however is short-lived. Pressures to reduce cost are present, but the advantage here is also short-lived. Continuous innovation is the minimum requirement to remain competitive. This in turn requires rapid product development and distribution to markets.

Information technology enables customers to follow *the law of one price* (Bryan et al 1999). Through the Internet, customers can easily search the market to find prices on comparable products. Selecting the lowest price for commodity-like products destroys profit margins. This forces supply chain managers to search continuously for the lowest cost source for the product, regardless of where it is produced. Transportation costs provide some protection although transport cost is diminishing over time as a geographic barrier to competition because of higher value products and the developing of cost-efficient global transport systems and the heavy competition within the transport industries themselves.

The alternative to global price competition is to create new value in products that meet market needs. The role of the supply chain is to provide flexibility for this innovation process, but at the same time providing advantages of economies of scale and scope in production. Distribution for many of these products must be instantaneous in all markets at the same time because of the need to beat competitors to market. These are conflicting objectives, and how they are resolved determines the success of strategy. Managing the process becomes the core of competitive advantage.

Global Sourcing

Suppliers of international scope supplant local and national suppliers. This changes the context of procurement to overcoming cultural barriers in negotiating with suppliers from remote parts of the world, managing the foreign exchange risks and in dealing with uncertainties in global logistics operations.

The increasing importance of global sourcing demands new skills. In the past, being a qualified purchasing manager required good negotiating skills, solid knowledge of the supplier market and practical insights in internal purchasing routines. Depending on the product area, it could require technical knowledge as well. Today, these requirements are still present, but must be supplemented by cross-cultural knowledge, language proficiency, knowledge of international finance, information technology, and telecommunication. Above all, procurement must establish, and manage long-term supplier relationships. To illustrate the importance of global sourcing, in 2003, Wal-Mart sourced products worth 15 billion USD from

China. No other single company purchases that much in China or accounts for as much import volume. Today, Vietnam, India and Mexico also strive to supply retailers in the US and Europe.

Concluding Comments

The supply chain is caught in a convergence between international and domestic business. The differences are real but diminishing, a result of the combined impacts of governmental policies, information technology and transportation. The three provide management with the ability to coordinate strategy and operations across geographic barriers as global systems.

The transnational corporation provides an initial perspective. Global products will dominate world markets, and competition forces a quest for efficiency. The roles of national subsidiaries in most global supply chains are shifting from the local operations of the multi-national to the globally integrated production and distribution operations of the transnational corporation. Continual change becomes the defining constant. The TNC model that stresses internalized production is not sufficient by itself to describe the new model of global organization. Geography in the sense of information transfer is not longer a technical problem. Information technology now enables one organization to coordinate with the operations of another, even around the globe. Culture still presents a hurdle, but there is a question of how much the world will need to adapt to the mold of e-mail, Internet, and graphic information transfer.

Logistics, the transfer of physical material and products, still serves as a limit to globalization. Operations are very much specific to countries, regions, and inter-regional movements. The problems of managing international supply chain operations are also specific to individual industries and regions making it hard to generalize. Each must be examined on its own merits. Choices of mode of transport, routings, and even the carrier are determined by supply chain choices, determining source and receiver. However, logistics also serves as a constraint on supply chain structure, particularly in the case of locating facilities for low cost or market proximity.

References

Abernathy, F.H., L.J.T. Dunlop, L.J.H. Hammond & D. Weil (1999): A Stitch in Time. New York: Oxford University Press.

Abrahamsson, M. (1993): Daily Direct Distribution. International Journal of Logistics Management 4(2): 75-84.

Agarwal, A., Shankar, R. and Tiwari, M.K. (2006): Modelling the metrics of lean, agile and leagile supply chain: An ANP-based approach. European Journal of Operational Research 173(1): 211-225.

Amit, R. & P.J.H. Schoemaker (1993): Strategic assets and organizational rent. Strategic Management Journal 14(1): 33-46.

ARC (2006): Supply Chain Management Worldwide Outlook. Five Year Market Analysis and Technology Forecast through 2010. www.arcweb.com/res/study.

Arlbjørn, J.S., Á. Halldórsson, M. Jahre, K. Spens, G. Stefansson (eds.) (2006): Nordic casereader in logistics and Supply Chain Management. University Press of Southern Denmark, Odense.

Bade, D.J. & J.K. Mueller (1999): New for the Millennium: 4PL. Transportation & Distribution (February): 78-80.

Bagchi, P.K. & H. Virum (1998a): Logistical Alliances: Trends and Prospects in Integrated Europe. Journal of Business Logistics 19(1): 191-213.

Bagchi, P.K. & H. Virum (1998b): European Logistics Alliances: A Management Model. International Journal of Logistics Management 7(1): 93-108.

Bagchi, P.K. & T. Skjøtt-Larsen (1995): European Logistics in Transition: Some Insights. International Journal of Logistics Management, 6 (2): 11-24.

Bagchi, P.K. & T. Skjøtt-Larsen (2003): Integration of Information Technology and Organizations in a Supply Chain. International Journal of Logistics Management 14(1): 89-108.

Bagchi, P.K. (1989): Carrier Selection: the Analytic Hierarchy Process. Logistics and Transportation Review 25(1): 63-73.

Baldwin, C.Y. & K.B. Clark (1997): Managing in an age of modularity. Harvard Business Review 75(5): 84-93.

Banfield, E. (1999): Harnessing Value in the Supply Chain: Strategic Sourcing in Action. New York: John Wiley.

Barney, J. (1999): How a Firm's Capabilities Affect Boundary Decisions. Sloan Management Review 40(3): 137-148.

Barney, J.B. & M.H. Hansen (1994): Trustworthiness as a Source of Competitive Advantage. Strategic Management Journal 15(8): 175-190.

Barratt, M & A. Oliveira (2002): Exploring the experiences of collaborative planning initiatives, International Journal of Physical Distribution & Logistics Management 31(4): 266-289.

Basu, R. (2004): Implementing Quality: A Practical Guide to Tools and Techniques. Thomson.

Beamon, B.M. (1999): Measuring supply chain performance. International Journal of Operations and Production Management 19(3): 275-292.

Bensaou, M. & E. Anderson (1999): Buyer-Supplier Relations in Industrial Markets: When Do Buyers Risk Making Idiosyncratic Investments? Organization Science 10(4): 460-481.

Bensaou, M. (1999): Portfolios of Buyer-Supplier Relationships. Sloan Management Review 40(4): 35-44.

Berglund, M., P. van Laarhoven, G. Sharman & S. Wandel (1999): Third-party Logistics: Is There a Future? International Journal of Logistics Management 10(1): 59-70.

Berman, B. & J. Evans (1998): Retail management. A strategic approach. 7th edition, Prentice Hall. Upper Saddle River.

Bettis, R.A., S.P. Bradley & G. Hamel (1992): Outsourcing and industrial decline. Academy of Management Review 6(1): 7-22.

Blackburn, Joseph D., Daniel R. Guide Jr., Gilvan C. Souza and L. Van Wassenhove (2004) Reverse Supply Chain for Commercial Returns, California Management Review 46(2): 6-22.

Blackwell, R. (1997): From Mind to Market: Reinventing the Retail Supply Chain. New York: HarperBusiness.

Boer, H. (1994): Flexible Manufacturing Systems. In J. Storey (ed.) New Wave Manufacturing Strategies. London: Chapman: 80-102.

Bowen, F.E., P.D. Cousins, R.C. Lamming & A.C. Faruk (2001): The role of supply management capabilities in green supply. Production and Operations Management 10(2): 174-189.

Bowersox, D. (1969): Physical Distribution Development, Current Status, and Potential. Journal of Marketing 33(1): 63-70.

Bowersox, D.J., Closs, D. J. & Cooper, M.B. (2002): Supply Chain Management Logistics, Boston et al.: McGraw Hill.

Brandenberger, A.M. & B.J. Nalebuff (1996): Co-opetition. Boston: Harvard Business School Press.

Brewer, P.C. & T.W. Speh (2000): Using the Balanced Scorecard to Measure Supply Chain Performance. Journal of Business Logistics 21(1): 75-93.

Brown, J.S. & P. Duguid (1998): The Social Life of Information. Boston, MA: Harvard Business School Press.

Brown, S.L. & K.M. Eisenhardt (1998): Competing on the Edge: Strategy as Structured Chaos. Harvard Business School Press: Boston, MA.

Bruce, M., L. Daly & N. Towers (2004): Lean or agile: A solution for supply chain management in the textile and clothing industry? International Journal of Operations & Production Management 24(2): 151-170.

Bryan, L., J. Frazer, J. Oppenheim & W. Rall (1999): The Race for the World. Boston: Harvard Business School Press.

Bucklin, L.P. (1960): The Economic Structure of Channels of Distribution. In M.L. Bell (ed.): Marketing, a Maturing Discipline. Chicago: American Marketing Association: 379-385.

Carr, L.P. & C.D. Ittner (1992): Measuring the Cost of Ownership. Journal of Cost Management 6:(3) 42-51.

Carbone, J. (1999): Reinventing purchasing wins the medal for Big Blue. Purchasing, September 16: 38-62.

Carbone, V. & M.A. Stone (2005): Growth, and relational strategies used by the European logistics service providers: Rationale and outcomes. Transportation Research Part E 41: 495-510.

Catia (2007): www.catia.com, accessed 27-01-2007.

Cespedes, F. (1988): Channel Management Is General Management, California Management Review 31(1): 98-120.

Chaffey, D. (2004): E-Business and E-commerce Management, 2nd edition, Edinburgh et al.:Prentice-Hall FT.

Chandrashekar, A. & P. Schary (1999): Toward the Virtual Supply Chain. International Journal of Logistics Management 10(2): 27-40.

Chase, R.B., F.R. Jacobs & N.J. Aquilano (2006): Operations Management for Competitive Advantage. 11th Edition, McGraw-Hill.

Chesbrough, H.W. & K. Kusunoki (2001): The modularity trap: Innovation, technology phase shifts and the resulting limits of virtual organizations. In I. Nonaka & D.J. Teece (Eds.), Managing Industrial Knowledge: Creation, Transfer and Utilization. London, UK, Sage: 202-230.

Christensen, C.M. & M.E. Raynor (2003): The Innovator's Solution. Boston, MA: Harvard Business School Press.

Christiansen, P.E. (2000): Vendor-managed Logistics. Logistics Solutions 2(2): 10-13.

Christopher, M. (2005): Logistics and Supply Chain Management, 3rd edition, Harlow, England: Prentice Hall Financial Times

Christopher, M., H. Peck & D. Towill (2006): A taxonomy for selecting global supply chain strategies. The International Journal of Logistics Management 17(2): 277-287.

Christopher, M., H. Peck & D. Towill (2006): A taxonomy for selecting global supply chain strategies. The International Journal of Logistics Management 17(2): 277-287.

Cicekoglu, S. (2005): The case for product life cycle management. Supply Chain Management Viewpoint. Accenture.

Clark, K.B. & T. Fujimoto (1991): Product Development Performance – Strategy, Organization, and Management in the World Auto Industry. Boston: Harvard Business School Press.

Clark, K.B. (1989): Project scope and project performance: The effect of parts strategy and supplier involvement on product development. Management Science 35(10): 1247-1263.

Clausen, U., Chmielewski, A., Schlüter, O. & Stein, F. (2006): Schnittstellenoptimierung in logistischen Anlagen, Seebauer, P. (ed.): Software in der Logistik 2006 – Marktspiegel, München: Huss-Verlag, 30-34.

Coase, R.H. (1937): The nature of the firm. Economica 4: 386-405.

Collins, J. (2004): Companies show RFID reluctance, www.rfid-journal.com

Cooper, R. & R.S. Kaplan (1999): The Promise – and Peril – of Integrated Cost Systems. Harvard Business Review 76(4): 109-119.

Cooper, R. & R. Slagmulder (1999): Supply Chain Development for the lean enterprise. Interorganizational Cost Management. Productivity, Inc.

Corbae, J. & A. Balchandani, A (2001): Consumer Direct Europe (CDE) – Erfolg durch Zusammenarbeit, in: Ahlert, D., J. Becker, P. Kenning & R. Schütte (ed.): Internet & Co. Im Handel. Strategien, Geschäftsmodelle, Erfahrungen. 2nd edition, Springer, Berlin et al., 63-78.

Coughlan, A.T., Anderson, E., Stern, L.W. & El-Ansary, A.I. (2006): Marketing Channels, 7th edition, UpperSaddle River, NJ:Prentice-Hall.

Cox, A. (1996): Relational competence and strategic procurement management. European Journal of Purchasing and Supply Management 2(1): 57-70.

Cox, K.R. (1997): Spaces of Globalization: Reasserting the Power of the Local. New York: Guilford Press: 19-44.

Coyle, D. (1997): Weightless World. Cambridge, MA: MIT Press.

Coyle, J.J., E.J. Bardi & C. John Langley Jr. (2003): The Management of Business Logistics. A Supply Chain Perspective. 7th Edition. South-Western: Thomson Learning.

Cramer, Jacqueline (2002): From financial to sustainable profit. In: Corporate Social Responsibility and Environmental Management 9(2): 99-106.

Custom Manufacturing – Nike Model Shows Web's Limitations (1999): http://www.individual.com (December 7, 1999): 2 p.

Damsgaard, J. and Hørlück, J. (2000): Designing www.LEGO.com /shop: Business Issues and Concerns, Dept. of Management, University of Aarhus.

Daum, B. & C. Horak (2001): The XML shockwave. What every CEO needs to know about the key technology for the new economy, Software AG, Lützelbach.

Day, J. (2000): They Do More than Carry the Load (January 12): via www.individual.com.

De Koster, R.B.M, M.P. de Brito & Masja A. van de Vendel (2002) Return handling: an exploratory study with nine retailer warehouses, International Journal of Retail & Distribution Management 30(8): 407-421.

De Toni, A. & G. Nassimbeni (2000): Just-in-Time Purchasing: an Empirical Study of Operational Practices. Omega: International Journal of Management Science 28(6): 631-651.

Dell, M. (1999): Direct from Dell. New York: Harper Business.

Dertouzos, M.L. (1997): What Will Be – How the New World of Information Will Change Our Lives. London: Piatkus.

Dicken, P. (2003): Global shift: Reshaping the global economic map in the 21th century, 4th edition, London: Sage Publications.

Du Bois, F.L., B. Toyne & M.D. Oliff (1993): International Manufacturing Strategies of U.S. Multinationals: a Conceptual Framework Based on a Four-Industry Study. Journal of International Business Studies (Second Quarter): 307-332.

Dunning, J.H. (1998): Multinational Enterprises and the Global Economy, 3rd edition, Harlow, England: Addison-Wesley Publishers, Ltd.

Dunphy, D., A. Griffiths, S. Benn (2003): Organizational change for corporate sustainability. Taylor & Francis Books, London.

Duray, R., P.T. Ward, G.W. Milligan & W.L. Berry (2000): Approaches to mass customization: configurations and empirical validation. Journal of Operations Management 18(6): 605-625.

Duysters, G., G. Kok & M. Vaandrager (1998): Creating win-win situations: partner selection in strategic technology alliances. Proceedings of The R&D Management Conference 1998: Technology Strategy and Strategic Alliances, Sep.30-Oct. 2, Avila, Spain, Chapter 17.

Dyer, J.H. (1997): Effective Interfirm Collaboration: How Firms Minimize Transaction Costs and Maximize Transaction Value. Strategic Management Journal 18(7): 535-556.

Dyllick, T. & Hockerts, K. (2002): Beyond the business case for corporate sustainability. Business strategy and the environment 11(2): 130-141.

Eisenhardt, K. M. & Martin, J.A. (2000): Dynamic capabilities: What are they? Strategic Management Journal 21(10-11): 1105-1121.

Eisenhardt, K.M. (2002): Has Strategy Changed? Sloan Management Review 43(2): 88-91.

Elkington, J. (1998): Cannibals with forks. The triple bottom line of 21st century business. New Society Publishers.

Ellram, L.M. & A.B. Maltz (1995): The Use of Total Cost of Ownership Concepts to Model the Outsourcing Decision. International Journal of Logistics Management 6(2): 55-66.

Ellram, L.M. & S.P. Siferd (1993): Purchasing: the Cornerstone of the Total Cost of Ownership Concept. Journal of Business Logistics 14(1): 163-184.

Ellram, L.M. & S.P. Siferd (1998): Total cost of ownership: A key concept in strategic cost management decisions. Journal of Business Logistics 19(1): 55-71.

Ellram, L.M., Tate, W.L. & C. Billington (2004): Understanding and managing services supply chain. The Journal of Supply Chain Management 40(4): 17-32.

Ellram, L.M. (1994): A Taxonomy of Total Cost of Ownership Models. Journal of Business Logistics 15(1): 171-191.

Ellram, L.M. (1995): Total Cost of Ownership. International Journal of Physical Distribution and Logistics Management 25(8): 4-23.

Emiliani, M.L. (2004): Sourcing in the global aerospace supply chain using online reverse auctions. Industrial Marketing Management 33(1): 65-72.

Emmelhainz, M. (1990): Electronic Data Interchange: A Total Management Guide. New York.

European Union (EU) (2006): Radio-Frequency IDentification tags (RFID).

Ewing, J. & M. Johnston (1999): This Smart Car's not so Dumb. Business Week September 20: 22.

Feitzinger, E. & H.L. Lee (1997): Mass Customization at Hewlett-Packard: the Power of Postponement. Harvard Business Review 75(1): 116-121.

Ferdows, K. (2000): Making the Most of Foreign Factories. In J.E. Garten (ed.) World View. Boston: Harvard Business Review Press: 143-165.

Fernie, J., F. Pfab & C. Marchant (2000): Retail grocery logistics in the UK. International Journal of Logistics Management 11(2): 83-90.

Fine, C. (1998): Clockspeed. New York, HarperCollins.

Fine, C., R. Vardan, R. Pethick & J. El-Hout (2002): Rapid-Response Capability in Value-Chain Design. Sloan Management Review 43(2): 69-75.

Fine, C.H., B. Golany & H. Naseraldin (2005): Modeling tradeoffs in three-dimensional concurrent engineering: A goal programming approach. Journal of Operations Management 23(3-4): 389-403.

Fisher, M. (1997): What is the Right Supply Chain for Your Product, Harvard Business Review 75(2): 105-116.

Fixson, S. (2005): Product architecture assessment: A tool to link product, process, and supply chain design decisions. Journal of Operations Management 23(3-4): 345-369.

Fleishmann, M., van Nunen, J.A.E.E. & Gräve, B. (2003): Integrating Closed-Loop Supply Chains and Spare-Parts Management at IBM, Interfaces 33(6) 44-56.

Fliedner, G. (2003): CPFR : an emerging supply chain tool, Industrial Management & Data Systems 103(1): 14-21.

Forrester, J. (1961): Industrial Dynamics. Boston MA: MIT Press.

Frazier, G. (1999): Organizing and Managing Channels of Distribution. Journal of the Academy of Marketing Science 27(2): 226-240.

Frost & Sullivan (2004): World Supply Chain Management. www.researchandmarkets.com

Gadde, L.-E. & H. Haakansson (2001): Supply Network Strategies. IMP Group. Chichester: John Wiley & Sons Ltd.

Gadde, L.-E. & I. Snehota (2000): Making the Most of Supplier Relationships. Industrial Marketing Management 29(4): 305-316.

Gadde, L.-E., L. Huemer & H. Haakansson (2003): Strategizing in industrial networks. Industrial Marketing Management 32(5): 357-364.

Galbraith, J.R. (1977): Organizational Design. Reading, MA: Addison-Wesley.

Garrison, R.H. & E.W. Noreen (1997): Managerial Accounting. 8th ed. Chicago: Irwin: Chapter 8.

Gartman, D. (2004): Three ages of the automobile: The cultural logics of the car. Theory, Culture & Society 21(4/5): 169-195.

Garud, R. & A. Kumaraswamy (1993): Changing competitive dynamics in network industries: An exploration of Sun Microsystem's open systems strategy. Strategic Management Journal 14: 351-369.

Garud, R. & A. Kumaraswamy (1995): Technological and organizational designs for realizing economies of substitution. Strategic Management Journal 16: 93-109.

Gelderman, C.J. & A.J. van Weele (2005): Purchasing Portfolio Models: A Critique and Update. Journal of Supply Chain Management 41(3): 19-28.

Geus, A. de (1997): The living company: growth, learning and longevity in business. London: Nicholas Brealey Publishing.

Ghoshal, S. & P. Moran (1996): Bad for Practice: a Critique of the Transaction Cost Theory. Academy of Management Review 21(1): 13-47.

Gilmore, J.H. & B.J. Pine (1997): The four faces of mass customization. Harvard Business Review 75(1): 91-101.

Global Commerce Initiative (GCI) (2006): RFID – Key technology of the 21st century. Global Commerce Initiative.

Goffin, K. (1998): Evaluating customer support during new product – An exploratory study. Journal of Product Innovation Management 15(1): 42-56.

Granovetter, M. (1973): The strength of weak ties, American Journal of Sociology, 78(6): 1360-80.

Grant, D. B., Lambert, D. M., Stock, J. R. & Ellram, L.M. (2006): Fundamentals of Logistics Management: First European Edition, Upper Saddle River, NJ: McGraw-Hill Irwin.

Grant, R.M. (1991): The Resource-Based Theory of Competitive Advantage: Implications for Strategy Formulation. California Management Review 33(3): 114-134.

Greene, A. (1999): Two Faces of Mass Customization. Manufacturing Systems 17(3): 48.

Gudehus, T. & T. Brandes (1997): Logistik: Kernkompetenz des Handels, Dynamik im Handel 1: 71-72

Gudehus, T. (2005): Logistik. Grundlagen, Strategien, Anwendungen. 3rd edition. Berlin et al.:Springer

Guide, V.D.R. Jr. & Luk N. Van Wassenhove (2003): Business Aspects of Closed-Loop Supply Chains, Carnegie Mellon University Press, Pittsburgh.

Guide, V.D.R. Jr. & Van Wassenhove, L.N. (2002): The Reverse Supply Chain. Harvard Business Review 80(2): 25-26.

Guisinger, S. (2001): From OLI to OLMA: Incorporating Higher Levels of Environmental and Structural Complexity into the

Eclectic Paradigm. International Journal of the Economics of Business 8(2): 257-272.

Gulati, R. (1998): Alliances and Networks. Strategic Management Journal 19(4): 293-317.

Gunasekaran, A. (1999a): Agile Manufacturing: Enablers and an Implementation Framework. International Journal of Production Research 36(6): 1223-1247.

Gunasekaran, A. (1999b): Agile manufacturing: A framework for research and development. International Journal of Production Economics 62(1-2): 87-105.

Gunasekaran, A. (1999c): Just-in-time Purchasing: an Investigation for Research and Applications. International Journal of Production Economics 59(1-3): 77-84.

Hald, K.S. (2006): Fra måling til målstyring af forsyningskæden. Børsens Logistikhåndbog. Copenhagen.

Hald, K.S. & P.E. Christiansen (2004): Supply Chain Performance Measurement Systems: Implications for Purchasing, 13th Annual IPSERA Conference, Cantania, Italy, April 4-7, 2004: 343-353.

Halldórsson, A. & T. Skjoett-Larsen (2004): Developing logistics competencies through third party logistics relationships. International Journal of Operations & Production Management 24(2): 192-206.

Halliburton, C. & R. Hünerberg (1993): Pan-European Marketing – Myth or Reality? Journal of International Marketing 1(3): 79-89.

Hamel, G. & C.K. Prahalad (1994): Competing for the Future. Boston, MA: Harvard School Press.

Hammer, M. & J. Champy (2001): Reengineering the Corporation. A Manifesto for Business Revolution. London: Nicholas Brealey.

Handfield, R.B. & E.L. Nichols, Jr. (2002): Supply Chain Redesign. Transforming Supply Chains into Integrated Value Systems. London: Financial Times Prentice Hall.

Hansen, H.R. & Neumann, G. (2005): Wirtschaftsinformatik I. Grundlagen und Anwendungen, 9th edition, Basel et al.: Lucius & Lucius.

Harland, C.M. (1996): Supply Chain Management: Relationships, Chains and Networks. British Journal of Management 7(March, Special Issue): 63-80.

Harrison, B. (1994): Lean and Mean. New York: Basic Books.

Heidrich, J. (2004): Implementierung von Supply Chain Management Systemen in der Stahlindustrie. Konzept zur Generierung von Schnittstellen zwischen den einzelnen Ebenen hierarchischer Planungssysteme sowie dem Legacy-System. Dissertation, TU-Berlin.

Heikkilä, J. (2002): From supply to demand chain management: Efficiency and customer satisfaction. Journal of Operations Management 20(6): 747-767.

Heizer, J. & B. Render (2006): Operations Management. 8th Edition, Prentice-Hall.

Helfat, C.E. & M.A. Peteraf (2003): The dynamic resource-based view: capability lifecycles. Strategic Management Journal 24(10): 997-1010.

Hellingrath, B. (2004): Alles über Supply Chain Management. Seebauer, P. & Roth, C. (ed.) Software in der Logistik 2004, München:Huss Verlag, 82-93.

Helper, S. (1993): An Exit-Voice Analysis of Supplier Relations: The Case of the US Automobile Industry. In Grabher, G. (ed.) The Embedded Firm on the Socioeconomics of Industrial Networks. London: Routledge.

Henderson, R.M. & K.B. Clark (1990): Architectural innovation: The reconfiguration of existing product technologies and the failure of established firms. Administrative Science Quarterly 35: 9-30.

Hertz, S. (1998): Domino Effects in International Networks. Journal of Business-to-Business Marketing 5(3): 3-31.

Hicks, M. (2001): Content Cleanup – How to avoid e-procurement pitfalls that can sap ROI, eWeek, November 5th: 51-56.

Hill, M. (1994): Computer Integrated Manufacturing: Elements and Totality. In J. Storey (ed.) New Wave Manufacturing Strategies. London: Chapman: 122–150.

Hines, P. (1994): Creating World Class Suppliers. London: Pitman Publishing.

Hines, P. (1995): Network Sourcing: a Hybrid Approach. International Journal of Purchasing and Materials Management 31(2): 18-24.

Hines, P. (1996a): Network Sourcing in Japan. International Journal of Logistics Management 7(1): 13-28.

Hines, P (1996b): Purchasing for Lean Production: the New Strategic Agenda. International Journal of Purchasing and Materials Management 32(1): 2-10.

Holmberg, S. (2000): A systems perspective on supply chain measurements. International Journal of Physical Distribution & Logistics Management 30(10): 847-868.

Holweg, M., S. Disney, J. Holmström, & J. Smaaros (2005): Supply Chain Collaboration: Making Sense of the Strategy Continuum. European Management Journal 23(2): 170-181.

Hsieh, C. & B. Lin (2004): Impact of standardization on EDI in B2B development, Industrial Management and Data Systems, 104 (1/2): 68-77.

Hsuan, J. (1999): Impacts of Supplier-Buyer Relationships on Modularization in New Product Development. European Journal of Purchasing and Supply Management 5(3-4): 197-209.

Huan, S.H., Sheoran, S.K. & G. Wang (2004): A review and analysis of supply chain operations reference (SCOR) model. Supply Chain Management: An International Journal 9(1): 23-9.

Huang, S.H., Sheoran, S.K. & Keskar (2005): Computer-assisted supply chain configuration based on supply chain operations reference (SCOR) model. Computers & Industrial Engineering 48: 377–394.

Hurkens, K., van der Valk, W. & F. Wynstra (2006): Total Cost of Ownership in the Services Sector: A Case Study. The Journal of Supply Chain Management 42(1): 27-37.

Haakansson, H. & D. Ford (2002): How companies interact in business networks? Journal of Business Research 55(2): 133-139.

Haakansson, H. & I. Snehota (ed.): (1995): Developing Relationships in Business Networks. London: Routledge.

Haakansson, H. & J. Johanson (1990): Formal and Informal Cooperation Strategies. In D. Ford (ed.) Understanding Business Markets. London: Academic Press.

ICFAI Business School, Bangalore (2006): Smart Fortwo's entry into the US. ECCHO.

Jap, S.D. (2007): The impact of online reverse auction design on buyer-supplier relationships. Journal of Marketing 71(1): 146-159.

Jeannet, J.-P. (2000): Managing with a Global Mindset. London: Financial Times.

Johnson, H.T. & R.S. Kaplan (1987): Relevance Lost. Boston: Harvard Business School Press.

Johnson, L.K. (2005): Reversing Course, Harvard Business School Publishing newsletters: Supply Chain Strategy, Harvard Business Review.

Kaipia, R., J. Holmström & K. Tanskanen (2002): VMI: What are you losing if you let your customer place orders? Production Planning and Control 13(1): 17-25.

Kanter, R.M. (2001): From spare change to real change: The social sector as beta site for business innovation. Harvard Business Review on Innovation, Boston, MA: Harvard Business School Press: 153-177.

Kaplan, R.S. & D.P. Norton (1992): The balanced scorecard – measures that drive performance. Harvard Business Review January-February: 71-79.

Kaplan, R.S. & D.P. Norton (1996): The Balanced Scorecard. Boston, MA: Harvard Business School Press.

Kidd, P.T. (1994): Agile Manufacturing: Forging New Frontiers. Wokingham, UK: Addison-Wesley.

Klaus, P. & C. Kille (2005): Die TOP 100 der Logistik, 4. Auflage. Hamburg: Deutschen Verkehrsverlag.

Knight, P. (2000): A Forum for Improving Globalisation. Financial Times (August 1): 13.

Kokkinaki, A. I., Dekker, R., van Nunen, J. & Pappis, C. (2000): An Exploratory Study on Electronic Commerce for Reverse Logistics. Supply Chain Forum – An International Journal 1(1): 10-17.

Korhonen, J. (2003): Should we measure corporate responsibility? Corporate Social Responsibility and Environmental Management 10(1): 25-39.

Kotzab, H. (1999): Improving Supply Chain Performance by Efficient Consumer Response? A Critical Comparison of Existing ECR Approaches. Journal of Business and Industrial Marketing 14(5/6): 364-377.

Kotzab, H. & P. Schnedlitz (1999): The Integration of Retailing to the General Concept of Supply Chain Management Concept. Journal für Betriebswirtschaft 49: 140-153.

Kotzab, H.(2005): Handel im Spannungsfeld von Marketing, Distribution und Kooperation. In: Holzmüller, H./Schuh, A. (ed.): Innovationen im sektoralen Marketing. Festschrift zum 60. Geburtstag von Fritz Scheuch, Physica, Heidelberg, 53-70

Kotzab, H., S. Seuring, M. Müller & G. Reiner (2005): Research Methodologies in Supply Chain Management. Germany: Physica-Verlag, A Springer Company.

Kotzab, H. (2004): Handelslogistik. In: Klaus, P. & W. Krieger (ed.): Gabler Logistik-Lexikon. Management logistischer Netzwerke und Flüsse, 3rd edition, Gabler, Wiesbaden, 180-185.

Kraljic, P. (1983): Purchasing Must Become Supply Management. Harvard Business Review 61(5): 109-117.

Krause, D.R., R.B. Handfield & T.V. Scannell (1998): An Empirical Investigation of Supplier Development: Reactive and Strategic Processes. Journal of Operations Management 17(1): 39-58.

Krause, D.R., M. Pagell, & S. Curkovic (2001): Toward a measure of competitive priorities for purchasing. Journal of Operations Management 19: 497–512.

Kuhn, A. & Helingrath, H. (2002): Supply Chain Management. Optimierte Zusammenarbeit in der Wertschöpfungskette. Berlin et al.: Springer.

Kulkarni, S. (1996): A Supply Side Strategy. Journal of Business Strategy 17(5): 17-21.

Kurt Salmon Associates (1993): Efficient Consumer Response. Enhancing Consumer Value in the Grocery Industry. Washington, DC: Kurt Salmon Associates.

Lambert, D.M. & T.L. Pohlen (2001): Supply chain metrics. The International Journal of Logistics Management 12(1): 1-18.

Lambert, D.M., Garcia-Dastugue, S.J. & Croxton, K.L. (2005): An evaluation of process-oriented supply chain management frameworks. Journal of Business Logistics 26(1): 25-51.

Lamming, R.C., P.D. Cousins & Notman, D.M. (1996): Beyond vendor assessment – Relationship assessment programmes. European Journal of Purchasing and Supply Management 2(4): 173-181.

Lamming, R. & J. Hampson (1996): The Environment as a Supply Chain Management Issue. British Journal of Management 7(Special Issue): 45-62.

Lamming, R. (1993): Beyond Partnership – Strategies for Innovation and Lean Supply. UK: Prentice Hall International Limited.

Langley, C.J. & M.C. Holcomb (1992): Creating Logistics Customer Value. Journal of Business Logistics 13(2): 1-27.

Langley, C.J. Jr., E. van Dort, A.A. & S.R. Sykes (2005): 2005 Third-Party Logistics. Results and Findings of the 10th Annual Study. Capgemini U.S.

Langlois, R.N. & P.L. Robertson (1995): Firms, Markets and Economic Change. London and New York: Routledge.

Langlois, R.N. (1992): External economies and economic progress: The case of the microcomputer industry. Business History Review Spring: 1-50.

Laseter, T.M. (1998): Balanced Sourcing – Cooperation and Competition in Supplier Relationships. San Francisco: Jossey-Bass.

Lawrence, F.B, Jennings, D.F. & Reynolds, B.E. (2005): ERP in Distribution. Eagan, Minnesota: Thomson.

Lawrence, P.R. & J.W. Lorsch (1967): Organization and Environment. Homewood, IL: Irwin.

Lee, H. (1998): Postponement for mass customization: Satisfying customer demands for tailor-made products. In Strategic Supply Chain Alignment: Best practice in supply chain management, J. Gattorna (Ed.), Gower Publishing Limited, Chapter 5: 77-91.

Lee, H.L. & C.A. Billington (1993): Material Management in Decentralized Supply Chains. Operations Research 41(September–October): 835-847.

Lee, H.L. & M.M. Sasser (1995): Product universality and design for supply chain management. Production Planning and Control 6(3): 270-277.

Lee, H.L. (2000): Creating Value Through Supply Chain Integration. Supply Chain Management Review 4(4): 30-36.

Lee, H.L. (2002): Aligning Supply Chain Strategies with Product Uncertainty. California Management Review 44(3): 105-119.

Lee, H.L., C. Billington, & B. Carey (1993): Hewlett-Packard Gains Control of Inventory and Service through Design for Localization. Interfaces 23(5): 1-11.

Lee, H.L., V. Padmanabhan & S. Whang (1997): The Bullwhip Effect in Supply Chains. Sloan Management Review 38(3): 93-102.

Levitt, T. (1986): The Globalization of Markets. In The Marketing Imagination. New York: The Free Press: 20-49.

Levy, M. & B. Weitz (2004): Retailing Management, McGraw Hill-Irwin, Boston et al.

Liebmann, H.-P. & J. Zentes (2001): Handelsmanagement, Vahlen, München.

Liekenbrock, D. (2006): Real-time logistics, Seebauer, P. (ed.): Software in der Logistik 2006 – Marktspiegel, München:Huss-Verlag,pp. 22-25.

Liker, J.K. & T.Y. Choi (2004): Building Deep Supplier Relationships. Harvard Business Review 82(12): 104-113.

Lilien, G.L. & A. Rangaswamy (1998): Marketing Engineering. Addison-Wesley.

Lindblom, C.E. (1959): The science of muddling through. Public Administration Review 19: 79-88.

Lockamy, A. III & McCormack, K. (2004): Linking SCOR planning practices to supply chain performance: an exploratory study. International Journal of Operations & Production Management 24(12): 1192-1218.

Lung, Y., M.S. Salerno, M. Zilbovicius & A.V.C. Dias (1999): Flexibility through modularity: Experimentations with fractal production in Brazil and in Europe. In Y. Lung, J.J. Chararon, T. Fujimoto & D. Raff (eds.), Coping With Variety – Flexible Productive Systems for Product Variety in the Auto Industry. Ashgate Publishing: 224-257.

Lynn, B.C. (2005): End of the Line. The Rise and Coming Fall of the Global Corporation. London: Doubleday.

Laakmann, F., Nayabi, K. & R. Hieber (2003): Market Survey 2003 – Supply Chain Management Software, Stuttgart: Fraunhofer IRB Verlag.

MacDuffie, J.P., K. Sethuraman & M.L. Fisher (1996): Product variety and manufacturing performance: Evidence from the international automotive assembly plant study. Management Science 42(3): 350-369.

Magill, P. (2000): Outsourcing Logistics. The Transition to 4th Party Partnerships in Europe. Financial Times, Retail & Consumer.

Mair, A.J. (1997): Strategic Localization: the Myth of the Postnational Enterprise. In K.J. Cox (ed.) Spaces of Globalization: Reasserting the Power of the Local. New York: Guilford: 64-88.

Maister, D.H. (1976): Centralization of Inventories and the Square Root Law. International Journal of Physical Distribution 6(3): 124-134.

Marbacher, A. (2001): Demand & Supply Chain Management Zentrale Aspekte der Gestaltung und Überwachung unternehmensübergreifender Leistungserstellungsprozesse, betrachtet aus der Perspektive eines Markenartikelherstellers der Konsumgüter-industrie 2001. Bern:Haupt Verlag.

Marrewijk, M.van (2003): Concepts and Definitions of CSR and Corporate Sustainability: Between Agency and Communion. Journal of Business Ethics 44(2/3): 95-105.

Martin, A. (1994): Infopartnering – the Ultimate Strategy for Achieving Efficient Consumer Response. Essex Junction, VT: Oliver Wright Publications.

Mas, R.F. (2005): Looking to pare costs, Ford to slash supplier base in half. American Metal Market September 30.

Mason-Jones, R., J. Naylor & D. Towil (2000): Engineering the liagile supply chain. International Journal of Agile Manufacturing Systems 2(1): 54-61.

Mazel, J. (1999): Supplier Selection and Management Report. Management Library, Newsletter, September.

McCutcheon, D.M., A.S. Raturi & J.R. Meredith (1994): The Customization-Responsiveness Squeeze. Sloan Management Review 35(2): 89-99.

McMillan, J. (1990): Managing Suppliers: Incentive Systems in Japanese and U.S. Industry. California Management Review 32(4): 38-58.

Mentzer, J.T. (2001): Supply Chain Management. London: Sage Publications.

Methé, D. (1991): Technological Competition in Global Industries. New York: Global Books.

Meyer, M.H. & A.H. Lehnerd (1997): The Power of Product Platform. The Free Press, New York.

Meyer, M.H. & J.M. Utterback (1993): The product family and the dynamics of core capability. Sloan Management Review (Spring): 29-47.

Mikkola, J.H. & O. Gassmann (2003): Managing modularity of product architectures: Toward and integrated theory. IEEE Transactions on Engineering Management 50(2): 204-218.

Mikkola, J.H. & T. Skjøtt-Larsen (2004): Supply chain integration: Implications for mass customization, modularization and post-ponement strategies. Production Planning and Control 15(4): 352-361.

Mikkola, J.H. (2001): Portfolio Management of R&D Projects: Implications for Innovation Management. Technovation 21(7): 423-435.

Mikkola, J.H. (2003): Modularity, component outsourcing, and inter-firm learning. R&D Management 33(4): 439-454.

Mikkola, J.H. (2006): Capturing the degree of modularity embedded in product architectures. Journal of Product Innovation Management 23: 128-146.

Mikkola, J.H. (2007): Management of product architecture modularity for mass customization: Modeling and theoretical considerations. IEEE Transactions on Engineering Management 54 (1):57-69.

Mill, J. (2005): RFID: A roadmap now & for the Future, ESYNC White Paper.

Min, S. & T. Mentzer (2004): Developing and measuring supply chain management concepts. Journal of Business Logistics 25(1): 63-99.

Mintzberg, H. (1994): The Rise and Fall of Strategic Planning: Reconsidering Roles for Planning, Plans, Planner. New York: The Free Press.

Mintzberg, H., B. Ahlstrand & J. Lampel (1998): Strategic Safari. New York: The Free Press.

Mollenkopf, Diane A. and David J. Closs (2005):The Hidden Value in Reverse Logistics, Supply Chain Management Review, 9(5) 34-43.

Momme, J., Moeller, M.M. & H.H. Hvolby (2000): Linking modular product architecture to the strategic sourcing process: Case studies of two Danish industrial enterprises. International Journal of Logistics: Research and Applications 3(2): 127-146.

Monden, Y. and Hamada, K. (1991): Target Costing and Kaizen Costing in Japanese Automobile Companies Journal of Management Accounting Research, Fall: 16-34.

Monteverde, K. & D.J. Teece (1982): Supplier switching costs and vertical integration in the automotive industry. Bell Journal of Economics 13 (Spring): 206-213.

Morgan, B.W. (1998): Strategy and Enterprise Value in the Relationship Economy. New York: Van Nostrand Reinhold.

Mouritsen, J., Skjøtt-Larsen, T. & H. Kotzab (2003): Exploring the contours of supply chain management. Integrated Manufacturing Systems 14(8): 686-695.

Muffatto, M. & M. Roveda (2000): Developing product platforms: Analysis of the development process. Technovation 20: 617-630.

Mulhern, F.(1997): Retail Marketing: From distribution to integration. International Journal of Research in Marketing 17(2): 103-124.

Murphy, P.R. & R.F. Poist (2000): Third-party logistics: Some user versus provider perspectives. Journal of Business Logistics 21(1): 121-133.

Møller, M.M., J. Johansen & H. Boer (2003): Managing buyer-supplier relationships and inter-organisational competence development. Integrated Manufacturing Systems 14(4): 369-379.

Narayanan, V.G. & A. Raman (2004): Aligning Incentives in Supply Chains. Harvard Business Review 82(11): 94-102.

Naylor, J.B., M.M. Naim & D. Berry (1999): Leagility: Integrating the lean and agile manufacturing paradigms in the total supply chain. International Journal of Production Economics 62: 107–118.

Neely, A, M. Gregory & K. Platts (1995): Performance measurement system design – a literature review and research agenda. International Journal of Operations & Production Management 15(4): 80-116.

Nelson, R.R. & S.G. Winter (1982): An Evolutionary Theory of Economic Change. Cambridge, MA: Belknap Harvard.

Nohria, N. & S. Ghoshal (1997): The Differentiated Network. San Francisco: Jossey-Bass.

Noorderhaven, N.G. (1995): Transaction, Interaction, Institutionalization: Toward a Dynamic Theory of Hybrid Governance. Scandinavian Journal of Management 11(1): 43-55.

Normann, R. & R. Ramirez (1994): Designing interactive strategy. From value chain to value constellation. Chichester, John Wiley & Sons.

O'Hara-Devereaux, M. & R. Johansen (1994): Global Work: Bridging Distance, Culture and Time. San Francisco: Jossey-Bass.

Olsen, R.F. & L.M. Ellram (1997): A Portfolio Approach to Supplier Relationships. Industrial Marketing Management 26(2): 101-113.

Orler, C. & D. Friedman (1998): The consumer behind consumer direct. Progressive Grocer 2: 39-42.

O'Toole, T. and B. Donaldson (2002): Relationship performance dimensions of buyer-supplier exchanges. European Journal of Purchasing & Supply Management 8(4): 197-207.

Overmeyer, L. (2006): Pre Processing Labels (PPL), Polymerelektronik & RFID – Entwicklungslinien (zukünftiger) Technologien in der Logistik. Presentation, BVL-Doktorandenworkshop, Berlin, 17.10.2006.

Paché, G.(1998): Retail logistics in France: The coming of vertical disintegration. International Journal of Logistics Management 9(1): 85-93.

Pagell, M., Z. Wu & N.N. Murthy (2007): The supply chain implications of recycling. Business Horizons 50(2): 133-143.

Pagh, J.D. & M.C. Cooper (1998): Postponement and Speculation Strategies: How to Choose the Right Strategy. Journal of Business Logistics 19(2): 13-33.

Payne, T. & M.J. Peters (2004): What is the right supply chain for your products?" The International Journal of Logistics Management 15(2): 77-91.

Pedersen, E.R. & M. Andersen (2006): Safeguarding corporate social responsibility (CSR) in global supply chains: how codes of conduct are managed in buyer-supplier relationships. Journal of Public Affairs 6(3/4): 228-240.

Penrose, E. (1959): The Theory of the Growth of the Firm. London: Billing and Sons.

Perrow, C. (1984): Normal accidents: Living with high-risk technologies. Princeton, N.J.: Princeton University Press.

Pfohl, H.C. (2000): Logistiksysteme. Betriebswirtschaftliche Grundlagen. 6th edition. Berlin et al.: Springer.

Picard, J. (1983): Physical Distribution Organization in Multinationals: the Position of Authority. International Journal of Physical Distribution and Materials Management 13(1): 20-32.

Picot, A., R. Reichwald & R. Wigand (2001): Die grenzenlose Unternehmung. Information, Organisation und Management, 4th edition, Wiesbaden, Gabler.

Pine, B.J. (1993): Mass Customization: the New Frontier in Business Competition. Boston: Harvard Business School Press.

Plenert, G.J. (2002): International Operations Management. Copenhagen: Copenhagen Business School Press.

Pohlen, T.L. & B.J. LaLonde (1994): Implementing Activity-Based Costing (ABC): in Logistics. Journal of Business Logistics 15(2): 1-24.

Porter, M.E. (1985): Competitive Advantage. New York: Free Press.

Porter, M.E. (1990): The Competitive Advantage of Nations. New York: The Free Press.

Prahalad, C.K. & G. Hamel (1990): The Core Competence of the Corporation. Harvard Business Review 68(3): 79-91.

Premkumar P.G. (2000): Interorganizational Systems and Supply Chain Management: An Information Processing Perspective. Information Systems Management, 17(3): 56-67.

Presutti, W. D. (2003): Supply management and e-procurement: creating value added in the supply chain. Industrial Marketing Management 32(3): 219-226.

Prockl G. & Pflaum, A. (2002): Consumer Direct Logistics. Germa Press, Hamburg.

Quinn, F.J. (2001): A New Agenda for the Decade. An Interview with Michael Hammer. Supply Chain Management Review 5(6): 36-40.

Quinn, J.B. & F.G. Hilmer (1994): Strategic Outsourcing. Sloan Management Review 35(Summer): 43-55.

Quinn, J.B. (1999): Strategic Outsourcing: Leveraging Knowledge Capabilities. Sloan Management Review 40(4): 9-21.

Rabs, H. & C. Bohn (2003): Bæredygtig supply chain management: et studie i muligheden for at anvende supply chain management til at gøre en virksomhed bæredygtig, M.Sc. thesis, CBS.

Ragatz, G.L., R.B. Handfield, & K.J. Petersen (2002): Benefits associated with supplier integration into new product development under conditions of technology uncertainty. Journal of Business Research 55(5): 389-400.

Roberts, S. (2003): Supply Chain Specific? Understanding the Patchy Success of Ethical Sourcing Initiatives. Journal of Business Ethics 44: 159-170.

Robertson, D. & K. Ulrich (1998): Planning for product platforms. Sloan Management Review 39(4): 19-31.

Rogers, D. and R. Tibben-Lembke (2001): An examination of Reverse Logistics Practices, Journal of Business Logistics 22(2): 129-148.

Rogers, D.S., D.M. Lambert, K.L. Croxton and S.J. García-Dastugue (2002): The Returns Management Process, International Journal of Logistics Management 13(2): 1-18.

Rosettanet (2007): www.rosettanet.org, accessed 27-01-2007:

Sako, M. (1992): Prices, Quality and Trust – Inter-firm Relations in Britain and Japan. Cambridge, UK: Cambridge University Press.

Sako, M. (1996): Supplier Relationships and Innovation. In M. Dodgson & R. Rothwell (ed.) The Handbook of Industrial Innovation. Cheltenham: Edward Elgar.

Salvador, R., C. Forza & M. Rungtusanathan (2002): Modularity, product variety, production volume, and component sourcing: Theorizing beyond generic prescriptions. Journal of Operations Management 20: 549-575.

Sanchez, R. (1999): Modular Architecture in the Marketing Process. Journal of Marketing 63(Special Issue): 92-111.

Sanders, T.I. (1998): Strategic Thinking and the New Science. New York: The Free Press.

SAP (2007): SAP PLM Software application. http://www.sap.com/solutions/business-suite/plm/index.epx.

Sarkis, J. (2003): A strategic decision framework for green supply chain management, Journal of Cleaner Production 11: 397-409.

Schary P.B. (2006): The Challenge of Systems. In D.F. Waters, Global Logistics, London: Kogan Page.

Schilling, M.A. (2000): Toward a general modular systems theory and its application to interfirm product modularity. Academy of Management Review 25(2): 312-334.

Schmitz, J. & Platts, K.W. (2004): Supplier logistics performance measurement: Indications from a study in the automotive industry. International Journal of Production Economics 89: 231-243.

Schmitz, J. & Platts, K.W. (2003): Roles of supplier performance measurement: indication from a study in the automotive industry. Management Decision 41(8): 711-721.

Schnedlitz, P. & C. Teller (1999): Aktuelle Perspektiven der Handelslogistik. In: Pfohl, H.-C. (Ed.): Logistikforschung. Entwicklungszüge und Gestaltungsansätze, Berlin, Erich-Schmidt-Verlag: 233-252.

Schrage, M. (2000): Serious Play. Boston: Harvard Business School Press.

Shapiro, J.F. (2001): Modeling the Supply Chain. Pacific Grove, CA: Duxbury.

Sharp, J.M., Z. Irani & S. Desai (1999): Working towards Agile Manufacturing in the UK Industry. International Journal of Production Economics 62: 155-169.

Siebel, L. (2000): Food Logistics: Lebensmittel via Internet, Düsseldorf.

Simchi-Levi, D., Kaminsky, P. & E. Simchi-Levi (2003): Designing & Managing the Supply Chain. 2nd Edition, McGraw-Hill.

Simon, H. (1995): Near decomposability and complexity: How a mind resides in a brain. In H. Morowitz & J. Singer (Eds.), The Mind, the Brain, and CAS. SFI Studies in the Sciences of Complexity, XXII, Addison-Wesley.

Simpson, D.F. & D.J. Power (2005): Use the supply relationship to develop lean and green suppliers. Supply Chain Management: An International Journal 10(1): 60-68.

Sink, H.L. & C.J. Langley (1997): A Managerial Framework for the Acquisition of Third-party Logistics Services. Journal of Business Logistics 18(2): 163-189.

Skjøtt-Larsen, T. (2000): Third-party Logistics – from an Interorganizational Point of View. International Journal of Physical Distribution and Logistics Management 30(2): 112-127.

Slack, N., Chambers, S. & R. Johnston (2004): Operations Management. 4th edition. Harlow: Prentice Hall.

Slack, N., Chambers, S. & R. Johnston (2007): Operations Management. 5th Edition, Prentice-Hall.

Smart A. & A. Harrison (2003): Online Reverse auctions and their role in buyer-supplier relationships. Journal of Purchasing & Supply Management 9(5-6): 257-268.

Schmitz, J. & K.W. Platts (2004): Supplier logistics performance measurement: Indications from a study in the automotive industry. International Journal of Production Economics 89: 231-243.

Schmitz, J. & K.W. Platts (2003): Roles of supplier performance measurement: indication from a study in the automotive industry. Management Decision 41(8): 711-721.

Sparks, L. (1999): The retail logistics transformation. In: Fernie, J. & L. Sparks (ed.): Logistics and Retail Management, Kogan Page, London, Boca Raton: 1-22.

Spicer, J. J. & M. R. Johnson (2004): Third-party demanufacturing as a solution for extended producer responsibility. Journal of Cleaner Production 12: 37-45.

Squire, B., Readman, J., Brown, S. & J. Bessant (2004): Mass customization: The key to customer value?" Production Planning and Control 15(4): 459-471

Stabell, C.B. & Ø.D. Fjeldstad (1998): Configuring Value for Competitive Advantage: On chains, Shops, and Networks. Strategic Management Journal 19(5): 413-437.

Stadlter, H. & C. Kilger (2004): Supply chain management and advanced planning : concepts, models, software and case studies 3rd edition, Berlin et al.: Springer.

Stadtler, H. (2004): Supply chain management and advanced planning: basics, overview and challenges. European Journal of Operational Research 163 (3): 575-588.

Stapleton, D., J.B. Hanna, S. Yagla, J. Johnson, & D. Markussen (2002): Measuring Logistics Performance Using the Strategic Profit Model. The International Journal of Logistics Management 13(1): 89-107.

Stern, L,., El-Ansary, A. & A. Coughlan (1996): Marketing Channels. 5th edition. Upper Saddle River, New Jersey.

Stewart, G. (1997), "Supply-chain operations reference model (SCOR): the first cross-industry framework for integrated supply-chain management", Logistics Information Management, Vol. 10 No. 2, pp. 62-7.

Stock, J.R. & D.M. Lambert (2001): Strategic Logistics Management. 4th edition. McGraw-Hill. Irwin.

Stock, J., T. Speh & H. Shear (2006): Managing Product Returns for Competitive Advantage. Sloan Management Review 48(1): 57-62.

Stock, J.R. (2001): The 7 deadly sins of reverse logistics. Material Handling Management (March): 5-11.

Storper, M. (1997): Territories, Flows and Hierarchies in the Global Economy. In K.J. Cox (ed.) Spaces of Globalization: Reasserting the Power of the Local. New York: Guilford: 19-44.

Supply-Chain Council (2006): Supply-Chain Operations Reference Model – Overview of SCOR Version 8.0. Pittsburgh, PA: Supply-Chain Council.

Svensson, G.(2002): A firm's driving force to implement and incorporate a business philosophy into its current business activities: the case of ECR, European Business Review 14(1): 20-29.

Saaty, T.L. (1980): Analytic Hierarchy Process: Planning, Priority Setting, Resource Allocation. New York, NY: McGraw-Hill.

Tapscott, D. (1995): The Digital Economy. New York: McGraw-Hill.

Tayur, S., R. Ganeshan & M. Magazine (1999): Quantitative Models for Supply Chain Management. Kluwer Academic Publishers.

Teece, D.J. (1986): Profiting from technological innovation: Implications for integration, collaboration, licensing and public policy. Research Policy 15(6): 285-305.

Teece, D.J., Pisano, G. and Shuen, A. (1997): Dynamic capabilities and strategic management. Strategic Management Journal 18(7): 509-533.

Tesco (2006): A Tesco Plc Annual review and summary financial statement 2005. http://www.tesco.com.

Thompson, J.D. (1967): Organizations in Action. New York: McGraw-Hill.

Toporowski, W. (1996): Logistik im Handel. Optimale Lagerstruktur und Bestellpolitik einer Filialunternehmung, Heidelberg, Physica.

Trebilcock, B. (2001): Why are returns so tough? Warehousing Management 56(11): 45-48.

Trent, R. & R. Monczka (1998): Purchasing and supply chain management: Trends and changes throughout the 1990s. International Journal of Purchasing and Materials Management 34(4): 2-11.

Trent, R.J. & R.M. Monczka (2003): Understanding integrated global sourcing. International Journal of Physical Distribution & Logistics Management 33(7): 607-629.

Ulrich, K.T. & S.D. Eppinger (2004): Product Design and Development. New York: McGraw-Hill.

Ulrich, K.T. (1995): The role of product architecture in the manufacturing firm. Research Policy 24(3): 419-440.

Van Damme, D.A., & F.L.A. van der Zon (1999): Activity Based Costing and Decision Support. International Journal of Logistics Management: 10(1): 71-82.

Van Hoek, R. (1998): Measuring the immeasurable" – measuring and improving performance in the supply chain. Supply Chain Management 3(4): 187-192.

Van Hoek, R. & A. Harrison (2003): The Smart Car and smart logistics. In R. Johnston, S. Chambers, C. Harland, A. Harrison & N. Slack (eds.), Cases in Operations Management. 3rd Edition, Prentice Hall: 316-326.

Van Hoek, R. (1998): Reconfiguring the Supply Chain to Implement Postponed Manufacturing. International Journal of Logistics Management 9(1): 95-110.

Van Hoek, R. (1999): From Reversed Logistics to Green Supply Chains. Supply Chain Management 5(3): 129-134.

Van Hoek, R., Pelen, E. & H.R. Commandeur 3rd (1999): Achieving Mass Customization through Postponement: a Study of International Changes. Journal of Market Focused Management 3(3-4): 353-368.

Van Hoek, R.I. & H.A.M. Weken (2000): Smart (Car): and Smart Logistics. Oak Brook, IL: Council for Logistics Management.

Van Hoek, R.I. (2001): The rediscovery of postponement – a literature review and directions for research. Journal of Operations Management 19(2): 161-184.

Vastag, A. & R. Kellermann (2006): Beschleunigte Entscheidungsfindung, Seebauer, P. (ed.): Software in der Logistik 2006 – Marktspiegel, München: Huss-Verlag: 78-81.

Vedpuriswar, A.V. (2004): Business Model Innovation at Dell. ICFAI Knowledge Center, Hyderabad, India. Distributed by The European Case Clearing House, England.

VICS (2002): Collaborative Planning, Forecasting and Replenishment (CPFR®), Version 2.0. As approved by the Voluntary Interindustry Commerce Standards (VICS) Association, June 2002. http://www.vics.org/committees/cpfr.

W3C (2002): XML in 10 Punkten, www.w3c.org.

Waller, M., Johnson, E. & T. Davis (1999): Vendor-Managed Inventory in the Retail supply Chain. Journal of Business Logistics 20(1): 183-203.

Wal-Mart (2007): Continued Expansion of Radio Frequency Identification (RFID), http://walmartstores.com.

Wannenwetsch, H. (2005): Vernetztes Supply Chain Management. SCM-Integration über die gesamte Wertschöpfungskette, Springer, Berlin/Heidelberg.

Wells, P. & M. Seitz (2005): Business models and closed-loop supply chains: a typology, Supply Chain Management: An International Journal 10(4): 249-251.

Wernerfelt, B. (1984): A resource-based view of the firm. Strategic Management Journal 5(2): 932-180.

Wilding, R.D. (1998): Chaos Theory: Implications for Supply Chain Management. International Journal of Logistics Management 9(1): 43-56.

Williams, J.A.S., Wongweragiat, S., Qu, X., McGlinch, J.B. Bonawi-tan, W., Choi, J.K. & J. Schiff (2007): An automotive bulk recycling planning material. European Journal of Operational Research 177: 969-981.

Williamson, O.E. (1975): Markets and Hierarchies: Analysis and Antitrust Implications. New York, NY: Free Press.

Williamson, O.E. (1985): The Economic Institutions of Capitalism: Firms, Markets, Relational Contracting. New York, NY: The Free Press.

Williamson, O.E. (1993): Calculativeness, Trust, and Economic Organization. Journal of Law and Economics 36(April): 453-486.

Williamson, O.E. (1996): The Mechanisms of Governance. Oxford: Oxford University Press.

Wolf, O., Dietze, G. & D. Daniluk (2006): WMS – heute und morgen, Seebauer, P. (ed.): Software in der Logistik 2006 – Marktspiegel, München:Huss-Verlag: 56-63.

Womack, J.P. & D.T. Jones (1996): Lean Thinking: Banish Waste and Create Wealth in your Corporation. New York: Simon & Schuster.

Womack, J.P., Jones, D.T. & D. Roos (1990): The Machine that Changed the World – The Story of Lean Production. New York: Rawson Associates.

Worthen, B. (2002): ABCs of Supply Chain Management. The ins and outs of turning components into products. http://www.cio.com/research/scm.

www.rfid-handbook.com (2004).

www.warehouse-logistics.de.

Yassine, A., Kim, K.C., Roemer, T. & M. Holweg (2004): Investigating the role of IT in customized product design. Production Planning and Control 15(4): 422-434.

Yeung, H.W. (1997): Business Networks and Transnational Operations: a Study of Hong Kong Firms in the ASEAN Region. Economic Geography 73(January): 1-25.

Yusuf, Y.Y., Sarhadi, M. & A. Gunasekaran (1999): Agile Manufacturing: the Drives, Concepts and Attributes. International Journal of Production Economics 62(1-2): 33-43.

Zajac, E. & C.P. Olsen (1993): From Transaction Cost to Transactional Value of Interorganizational Strategies. Journal of Management Studies 30(1): 131-145.

Zentes, J. (1991): Computer Integrated Merchandising - Neuorientierung der Distributionskonzepte im Handel und in der Konsumgüterindustrie. In: Zentes, J. (ed..): Moderne Distributions-konzepte in der Konsumgüterwirtschaft. Stuttgart: 1-15

Zsidisin, G.A. (2003): An Agency Theory Investigation of Supply Risk Management. Journal of Supply Chain Management 39(3): 15-27.

Aaker, D.A. & R. Jacobson (1994): The financial information content of perceived quality. Journal of Marketing Research 31(2): 191-201.

Index